UNSEA COVERS

Celebrating
30 Years of Publishing
in India

Also by the Author

Non-Fiction

*The Transformative Constitution:
A Radical Biography in Nine Acts*

Fiction

The Wall
The Horizon

UNSEALED COVERS

A Decade of the Constitution, the Courts and the State

GAUTAM BHATIA

HarperCollins *Publishers* India

First published in India by HarperCollins *Publishers* 2023
4th Floor, Tower A, Building No. 10, DLF Cyber City,
DLF Phase II, Gurugram, Haryana – 122002
www.harpercollins.co.in

2 4 6 8 10 9 7 5 3 1

Copyright © Gautam Bhatia 2023

P-ISBN: 978-93-5699-363-1
E-ISBN: 978-93-5699-362-4

The views and opinions expressed in this book are the author's own and the facts are as reported by him, and the publishers are not in any way liable for the same.

Gautam Bhatia asserts the moral right
to be identified as the author of this work.

All rights reserved. No part of this publication may be reproduced, stored in a retrieval system, or transmitted, in any form or by any means, electronic, mechanical, photocopying, recording or otherwise, without the prior permission of the publishers.

Typeset in 11.5/15.4 Adobe Caslon Pro at
Manipal Technologies Limited, Manipal

Printed and bound at
Thomson Press (India) Ltd

This book is produced from independently certified FSC® paper
to ensure responsible forest management.

For Abhinav and Utkarsh,
sanity-keepers

Contents

A Note on the Text — xiii
Preface — xv

Part One
Rights

PERSONAL LIBERTY

1. Imprisonment by Metaphor: The Safoora Zargar Bail Order — 6
2. Back to the Basics: The Delhi High Court's Bail Orders under the UAPA — 10
3. Staying with the Basics: The Bombay High Court on Bail under the UAPA — 19
4. Entrenching the Basics: The Supreme Court's UAPA Judgment — 24
5. Swimming with Your Arms Tied behind Your Back: The Supreme Court's UAPA Bail Order in Iqbal Ahmed's Case — 29
6. Forgetting the Basics: The Bail Orders in the *Jyoti Jagtap* and *Umar Khalid* Cases — 35

Privacy, Equality and Dignity

1. The Supreme Court's Right to Privacy Judgment—I: Foundations — 49
2. 'Civilization Has Been Brutal': Navtej Johar, Section 377, and the Supreme Court's Moment of Atonement — 60
3. The Sabarimala Judgment—III: Justice Chandrachud and Radical Equality — 75
4. 'Take Me as I Am—Subject to Aadhaar-Based Biometric Authentication': An Overview of the Aadhaar Judgment — 87
5. The Aadhaar Judgment: A Dissent for the Ages — 102
6. A Question of Consent: The Delhi High Court's Split Verdict on the Marital Rape Exception — 113
7. Discipline or Freedom: The Supreme Court's Split Verdict in the Hijab Case — 123

Social Justice and Reservations

1. The Supreme Court's Judgment on Jat Reservations: Problems and Prospects — 135
2. The Supreme Court Upholds Reservations in Promotions for Disabled Persons — 143
3. The Nagaraj/Creamy Layer Judgment and Its Discontents — 147
4. Reservations in Promotions and the Idea of Efficiency: *B.K. Pavitra vs Union of India* — 152
5. The Supreme Court's (New) Reservations Judgment and Its Discontents — 160
6. A Critique of the Supreme Court's Maratha Reservation Judgment—I: Equality — 166

Socio-Economic Rights

1. Delhi High Court Rules on Article 21 and Access to Medicine — 181
2. Coronavirus and the Constitution—XXXVI: The Delhi High Court's Judgment on Taxation and the Right to Health — 187
3. The Delhi High Court on Forced Evictions, Adequate Housing and a 'Right to the City' — 192
4. Responding to Illegal Home Demolitions: The Doctrine of an Unconstitutional State of Affairs — 198
5. Home Demolitions and George Orwell's Supreme Court — 203

Refugees and Non-Citizens

1. The NRC Case and the Parchment Barrier of Article 21 — 211
2. Complicity in Genocide: The Supreme Court's Interim Order in the Rohingya Deportation Case — 216
3. Breathing Life into Article 21: The Manipur High Court's Order on Refugee Rights and Non-Refoulement — 224

A Rightless Zone: Kashmir after Article 370

1. Kashmir: The 16 September Order and the Supreme Court of Convenience (or Why Separation of Powers Is like Love) — 232
2. Kashmir: Fundamental Rights and Sealed Covers — 237
3. King Menelaus at the Bar of the Indian Judiciary — 240

Part Two
Constitutional Structure

FEDERALISM

1. 'Working a Democratic Constitution': The Supreme Court's Judgment in *NCT of Delhi vs Union of India* — 250
2. The Article 370 Amendments: Key Legal Issues — 261

ANTI-DEFECTION

1. Judicial Supremacy amid the Breakdown of Constitutional Conventions: What the Karnataka Controversy Tells Us about Our Parliamentary Democracy — 267
2. Postscript: The Supreme Court's Problematic Order in the Karnataka Case — 274
3. The Supreme Court's Madhya Pradesh Government Formation Judgment—VI: Some Concluding Remarks — 277

FOURTH BRANCH INSTITUTIONS

1. The Amendments to the Right to Information Act Are Unconstitutional — 286

Part Three
The Judiciary

THE COURTS

1. 'O Brave New World': The Supreme Court's Evolving Doctrine of Constitutional Evasion — 302

2. The Land Acquisition Bench and Continuing Issues
   around the 'Master of the Roster' — 310
3. Addendum: The Concept of 'Bias' in a Polyvocal Court — 316
4. A Question of Power — 321
5. The Lawyers Collective Order and the Rise of
   Fourth-Phase PIL — 330
6. What Is a 'Review'? — 335
7. Coronavirus and the Constitution—XXXVIII:
   One Year On — 342

Judges

1. A Memory for Forgetfulness: Some Thoughts on a
   Judicial Retirement — 352
2. The Executive('s) Court: Notes on the Legacy of
   Justice A.M. Khanwilkar — 358

Chief Justices

1. ICLP Turns Four: Some Thoughts on the Office of the
   Chief Justice and Other Supreme Court Miscellany — 380
2. No Man Shall Be a Judge in His Own Cause*
   (*Conditions Apply) — 384
3. Ends without Means, Outcomes without Reasons:
   A Look Back at Dipak Misra and the Constitution — 390
4. 'A Little Brief Authority': Chief Justice Ranjan
   Gogoi and the Rise of the Executive Court — 402
5. Evasion, Hypocrisy and Duplicity: The Legacy of
   Chief Justice Bobde — 417

6. The Sound of Silence: The Legacy of Chief Justice
   N.V. Ramana   430
7. 'The Freedom of One Single Human Spirit':
   On the Legacy of Chief Justice U.U. Lalit   442

Epilogue: A Constitutionalism without a Court   449
Acknowledgements   455
Index   457

A Note on the Text

OVER THE YEARS, THE Indian Constitutional Law and Philosophy blog has featured many contributions from guest writers. For practical reasons, this collection does not include guest pieces from the blog's history; those pieces are, of course, referred to wherever necessary.

The blog's style guide limits pieces to providing hyperlinks to sources, and no footnotes. While converting the blog essays into book form, I have included footnotes to a limited degree: wherever another piece is explicitly cited or quoted. In order to retain the conversational and informal style of the blog, I have attempted to keep footnotes to a minimum. Interested readers may refer to the blog online, where all the references will be hyperlinked.

Preface

THIS BOOK BRINGS TOGETHER a set of essays published on the Indian Constitutional Law and Philosophy blog,[1] between the years 2013 and 2022. These essays focus on Indian constitutionalism and the Indian judiciary during a particularly tumultuous period. In these years, the Supreme Court's judgments on privacy, same-sex relations, the national biometric identification system, the hijab ban and reservations, among others, have made headlines in India and outside. At the same time, the court, as an institution, has come under serious scrutiny: Its refusal to hear certain high-stakes cases on time, the powers of the Chief Justice of India and the court's deferral to the executive in crucial civil rights cases have all raised critical questions around judicial independence, and the relationship between the judiciary and an assertive—and at times aggressive—executive. These essays, most of which were written in the immediate aftermath of important constitutional events, cover all of this ground, and more.

The Indian Constitutional Law and Philosophy Blog

I began the Indian Constitutional Law and Philosophy ('ICLP') blog in August 2013, with three goals in mind. The first was to *demystify*

---

1 www.indconlawphil.wordpress.com

constitutional law—that is, to break down arcane legal vocabulary in a manner that would be intelligible to non-lawyers, and to analyse, contextualize and explain court judgments in much the same way. The second was to *democratize* constitutional law—that is, to provide an open, public forum to discuss Indian constitutional law, constitutional developments and the courts. And the third was to engage in—and popularize—a mode of constitutional law writing that was distinct from the two dominant, prevailing modes: academic analysis and reportage. The blog aimed to bring together the best of both worlds: It sought to combine the immediacy of legal reportage with the rigour of academic analysis. As inspiration, I drew upon the culture of legal blogging in the United States, as well as its more nascent counterpart in India—when ICLP began, the IndiaCorpLaw, the Law and Other Things, and the SpicyIP blogs had already set an excellent standard to aspire to.

Ten years and nearly a thousand blog posts later, these core goals remain the same. My own location, however, has changed. When I set up the blog, I intended it to be a somewhat detached and dispassionate examination of constitutional issues. Many of the initial posts, thus, concerned themselves with abstract constitutional problems around free speech, equality, reservations and the nature of the State. This was to change in late 2014/early 2015, when I transitioned from a master's degree to a judicial clerkship at the Delhi High Court, and then into legal practice. Suddenly I was first a ringside watcher and then an active participant in the very subject matter that ICLP had been created to cover.

At that point, there were two options: to abandon legal blogging and limit oneself to practice, or to abandon the dream of academic detachment and write as a committed participant. I chose the latter. Thus, to borrow a phrase from Viktor Shklovsky, the essays in this book 'weren't written with the quiet consistency of academic works'.[2] Many of them were written days—and sometimes even hours—after

---

2   Alexandra Berlina, *Viktor Shklovsky: A Reader*, Bloomsbury, 2017, p. 4.

court judgments, in cases that I had been directly involved in;[3] or, if not, in cases that I had closely watched, followed and was emotionally invested in. For this reason, this book perhaps suffers from what Joseph Brodsky memorably called 'the faults of urgency'.[4] In the pages that follow, there is anger and elation, rage and relief, sadness and joy. To some, that may detract from the objectivity of the analysis, but it is, I believe, a price worth paying for the insights that come from proximity.

There is another reason I believe it is important for participants—insiders, if you will—to write about Indian constitutionalism, courts and the judiciary. This is because not every action of constitutional significance translates into a written, reasoned and publicly accessible court judgment. There is much that happens *within* the courtroom, and is deeply embedded within an internal, procedural vocabulary that is only intelligible to insiders. To take an example, in late 2019, a series of manoeuvres took place within the Supreme Court that culminated in the overturning of a long-settled interpretation of the Land Acquisition Act, 2013, which had huge ramifications for the State acquisition of land across the country (see the essay titled 'The Land Acquisition Bench and Continuing Issues around the "Master of the Roster"', in the final section of this book). None of this manoeuvring was reflected in the final judgment of a five-judge bench of the Supreme Court, of course; but to understand how it happened, one needed to know, among other things, the listing process within the Supreme Court, the administrative powers of the Chief Justice of India and the judicial proclivities as well as some of the day-to-day actions of the justices involved.[5]

---

3   These are, obviously, appropriately caveated.
4   Joseph Brodsky, 'Introduction' in Danilo Kis, *A Tomb for Boris Davidovich*, Dalkey Archive Press, 2001.
5   Indeed, it wasn't even enough being a *general* insider for this case; some of the things I came to know of only because my chamber was involved in one of the many pending land acquisition cases that were directly affected by the court's ruling.

I do not mention this by way of defence: There is no justifiable reason why wandering the Supreme Court's corridors ought to be a necessary precondition for understanding how the court works. It is, however, the reality of the moment. Indeed, as will be rather evident, very little of the last section of this book—which deals directly with the judiciary—could have been written from a position external to the institution about which I write.

The position of the insider is, of course, a fraught one. If the blog—and the book—is an attempt to translate institutional language and action for outsiders, one must remember that there is a thin line between translation and gatekeeping,[6] and that the privilege of proximity and access brings with it the temptation to take executive decisions on *how* to translate, *what* and *how much* to translate, and *when* to keep silent. There is perhaps no solution to this problem, other than to acknowledge that this book—much like the blog—will be shot through with the priorities and biases of its author, and to set out those priorities as clearly as one can (I try to do some of this in the 'Ideology and Organization' sub-section of this foreword). And it is in that spirit that I offer up the essays in this book to readers.

The Goals of This Book

As ICLP is a free and publicly available online resource, one might ask why a book is needed at all, when you can simply go and read all the blog essays online. There are two answers to this, which also inform the book's organization (see the following sub-section).

The first is that while most of the essays take the form of immediate responses to specific events (a court judgment, a judicial order or an administrative measure), *over time*, patterns emerge. These patterns— such as an evolution in constitutional jurisprudence or the development

---

[6] Or, if you are to believe Milan Kundera, between being a translator and being a traitor.

of a constitutional standard—often take months or years to become visible (for instance, a new legal doctrine may be established over several judgments, delivered over the course of a decade). In the first section of this book, for example, we see how, over time, there have evolved two opposite judicial approaches to the interpretation of the Unlawful Activities (Prevention) Act (UAPA), 1967, with serious consequences for individual liberty. And this becomes visible when we put the several blog posts—each an immediate response to a judgment—*together*, and read them together. This can only happen within the format of a book.

The second is that while the origin of this blog (mid-2013) was entirely fortuitous and unplanned from my point of view, it is significant from an external perspective. In 2014, the general election returned a majority government for the first time after many decades of coalition government. In the 2019 general election, the Bharatiya Janata Party (BJP) returned to power with an even greater majority. It is, by now, a fairly well-accepted observation that *over time*, judicial assertiveness tends to be inversely proportional to the strength and aggressiveness of the government in power. The judiciary, after all, 'controls neither the sword nor the purse', and the space in which it has to manoeuvre often depends on how much space it is *afforded* by the relative strength or weakness of the other organs of the State.

Furthermore, in our context, the ruling government has been scarcely reticent about using its power: from judicial appointments to emergency powers, from the use of governors in federal disputes to the citizenship provisions, the executive has frequently advanced its own understanding of the Constitution, which has tended to stretch text and doctrine to its absolute limits. This has, naturally, placed the courts in a spot. This book, thus, ought not to be read simply as a book of essays dealing with important judgments and with the institution of the judiciary. Rather, it should also be read as a book about how the judiciary has chosen to respond—or not—to a powerful and controlling executive (a phenomenon that is, of course, familiar across the world).

The Ideology and Organization of This Book

The essays in this book constitute less than 5 per cent of the total output of ICLP over its first decade. No criterion of selection, therefore, would be able to achieve substantial—or even partial—representation of the significant constitutional events over the past ten years, or of ICLP's coverage of them.

I have, therefore, devised my own method of selection, and it is as follows. I believe that, in essence, constitutions are 'power maps'.[7] A constitution creates, organizes, facilitates and constrains power. Furthermore, because of the ambiguity of language, a constitution is contested terrain: different visions of power are contested on the touchstone of its text and structure, with the courts being called upon to act as arbiters between those visions.

The essays in this book—and the themes under which I have organized them—reflect the many dimensions along which power has been contested on the terrain of the Indian Constitution in recent times. The issue of *contestation* is important: Constitutions are not closed or self-interpreting texts, and are best understood as being sites of ongoing struggle. Thus, wherever possible, I have sought to highlight this struggle, whether it is through duelling high court judgments on personal liberty under the UAPA, or the tension within the Supreme Court's jurisprudence on the relationship between reservations and equality. Highlighting this struggle not only illumines something important about Indian constitutionalism, but also, I believe, serves as an antidote against despair.

As many of these essays have been written from the perspective of a participant, I should also make clear that neither I—nor this book—is, or attempts to be, 'neutral' in this ongoing constitutional struggle. I approach constitutions, constitutionalism and courts from a

---

[7] Ivo D. Duchacek, *Power Maps: Comparative Politics of Constitutions* (ABC-CLIO, 1973).

perspective that is *sceptical* of structures of power, and authority, *opposed* to the concentration and homogenization of power, and *suspicious* of any form of constitutional interpretation that seeks to subordinate real, flesh-and-blood human beings to abstractions such as 'national security' or 'the larger public interest'. On the other hand, this approach *supports* the democratization and distribution of power, *celebrates* the existence of diverse and plural ways of living, and *privileges* human dignity and freedom over invocations of raison d'etat. Further, I believe that this 'anti-hierarchy' approach is characteristic of Indian constitutionalism in its best moments, moments that infuse life into that old adage about newspapers: 'To afflict the comfortable and comfort the afflicted.' It is this perspective that informs the essays in this book.

Following the understanding of constitutions as power maps, the book is organized into three broad sections.

The first section deals with rights. It considers civil rights and personal liberty through the constitutional struggles over the UAPA; gender and sexual equality through the lens of the Supreme Court's evolving anti-discrimination jurisprudence; social justice through the recent battles over reservations, socio-economic rights in the context of evictions and housing guarantees; and, finally, the judiciary's treatment of refugees. The second section deals with constitutional structure. It considers the judiciary's conflicted engagement with the division of federal power (including the events of 5 August 2019 concerning Jammu and Kashmir) and the courts' role in the increasingly frequent 'government formation and government toppling disputes'. The final section deals with the judiciary as an institution. It looks at the many dimensions of the evolving relationship between the judiciary and the executive. For instance, 'judicial evasion' (benefiting the executive by not hearing a case), the use of 'sealed covers' and the judiciary's drift towards an 'executive court' (i.e., increasing adoption of the language of the executive even in judicial proceedings). It also looks at the careers of influential judges and, in particular, at tenures of recent Chief Justices of India, whose far-reaching (but ill-understood) powers have enabled them to play crucial roles in the ongoing relationship among the judiciary, the executive, the people and the Constitution.

Before each sub-section, I have provided a brief, framing essay, which will help contextualize the issues for readers who are not intimately familiar with the constitutional battles that have shaped our contemporary legal landscape. However, these essays are brief by design: By and large, I want the essays to speak for themselves and to avoid any backward-looking analysis that would rob them of their sense of immediacy and urgency. Read together, I hope the essays would, of their own accord, yield patterns and lines of constitutional evolution, whether for better or for worse.

Conclusion

The purpose of this book is not to draw any grand conclusions about the judiciary or the state of Indian constitutionalism. Rather, the central focus of this book is to highlight the ways in which the Constitution is a contested terrain—and which have everything to do with power and powerlessness, who wields power and who is subjected to it, and the actions of those whose task it is to mitigate the impunity of power. If, at the end of this book, the reader has a clearer sense of these contestations and of the constitutional pathways towards freedom and dignity that remain open notwithstanding sustained efforts to close them, I will have succeeded in my task.

Part One

Rights

Personal Liberty

Introduction

THE UNLAWFUL ACTIVITIES (PREVENTION) Act, 1967, or UAPA, India's umbrella anti-terrorist legislation, stands out not because of its record of prosecuting and convicting terrorists, but because of how it allows—and almost *requires*—extended jail time before trial or conviction. This is achieved through Section 43(D)(5) of the UAPA, which prohibits the grant of bail 'if the Court, on a perusal of the case diary or the report made under section 173 of the [Criminal Procedure] Code is of the opinion that there are reasonable grounds for believing that the accusation against such person is *prima facie* true'. In simple language, this means that if on a bare, uncontradicted surface reading of the police's version of events, the accusations appear to be true, the court is statutorily prohibited from granting bail.

When you juxtapose this with the lengthy time that it takes to finish criminal trials in India (especially terror trials, where the number of witnesses run into the hundreds), the UAPA emerges as a powerful tool of State repression: individuals can (and have) been kept in jail for years—even decades—without trial. In recent years, the UAPA has been deployed in two particularly politically controversial cases: the Bhima Koregaon violence of 2018 and the Delhi riots of 2020. At the time of writing, a majority of the accused in these cases (including activists, writers and political dissidents) remain in jail, without the trials having commenced.

Enter the courts.

Over the past few years, the UAPA has become a bitterly contested terrain, upon which questions of State power, State impunity and human freedom have been debated at all levels of the judiciary—from the trial courts, all the way to the Supreme Court. To what extent can a judge question the police's version of events when considering bail under the UAPA? To what extent is the *defence* allowed to question it? To what degree should the police be required to establish the links between the accused and the event, especially when their case rests upon allegations of conspiracy? How broadly—or narrowly—ought the substantive clauses of the UAPA to be read? How a judge answers these questions can make the difference between freedom and years in jail.

In April 2019, in a judgment called *National Investigative Agency vs Zahoor Ahmad Shah Watali*, the Supreme Court interpreted the UAPA in a manner that skewed it further towards the State and away from the individual. It placed severe restrictions on the extent to which the courts could question the police case when considering the question of bail. The Supreme Court forbade courts from conducting a 'mini trial' at the stage of bail—a direction that seems fair enough at first glance, but becomes extremely unjust when you consider that if the *only* material that the court is allowed to consider in a UAPA bail case is material provided by the police, this effectively amounts to ordering the defence to fight with one arm tied behind its back.

After April 2019, all UAPA adjudication has been conducted in the shadow of *Watali*. It is an often-heard lament that judges cannot grant bail under the UAPA even if they want to, because they are bound by

Watali. This lament, however, ignores a central theme of this book—that law is always a terrain of contestation. Statutory texts and court judgments are always open to interpretation, and an interpretation that advances liberty and freedom over State power is, ultimately, something that a judge can *choose* for—or choose against. But in either case, it is a choice.

Thus, in the following pages, you will meet courageous and principled judges who—despite the dicta in *Watali*—have chosen to craft a UAPA jurisprudence that honours the constitutional guarantee of the right to life and personal liberty, even in the interstices of repressive laws. But you will also meet judges who have chosen to deploy the clauses of the UAPA and the observations in *Watali* as locks on prison doors. Perhaps more starkly than in any other area of Indian constitutional law, the ongoing battles over the UAPA reflect the Indian judiciary at its freedom-protecting finest, but also at its most obliging and accommodating to State power.

And as the chronicle so far shows, this is a battle that will continue to be waged for some time to come.

1

Imprisonment by Metaphor: The Safoora Zargar Bail Order

(4 June 2020)[1]

'… [W]hen you choose to play with embers, you cannot blame the wind to have carried the spark a bit too far and spread the fire.'

WHEN A COURT NEEDS to rely upon metaphor instead of law to justify keeping an individual in prison, it is perhaps time for the justice system to take a long, hard look at itself. The order[2] passed today by a district and sessions judge at Patiala House, New Delhi, denying bail to Safoora Zargar, an accused in what has colloquially come to be known as the 'Delhi riots case', is a deeply disturbing one. It is disturbing because it takes the Unlawful Activities (Prevention) Act, a law so stringent that it precludes judges from granting bail if even a 'prima facie' case is made out, and then stretches its provisions

---

1   This post was written in the aftermath of the trial court's denial of bail to Safoora Zargar, in a case arising out of the 2020 Delhi riots. Zargar was eventually granted bail by the high court on medical grounds.
2   *State vs Safoora Zargar*, Bail Application No. 1119/2020, FIR No. 59/2020 (4 June 2020).

from one side, and the facts from the other, to ensure that the prima facie case is made out. In the process, what it effectively does—as we shall see—is criminalize the exercise of one set of constitutional rights (the freedom of speech and expression) and deny the exercise of another (personal liberty).

A close reading of the bail order reveals the following:

1. Taking only the prosecution's case (as this was a bail hearing), there is evidence that there existed a 'conspiracy' to block a road in which the accused was involved (the role of the accused in this 'conspiracy'—even prima facie—is not spelt out, only some WhatsApp messages and disclosure statements are referred to).
2. That 'one cannot ignore the case of the prosecution that the accused persons have conspired to cause disruption of such an extent and such a magnitude that it would lead to disorderliness and disturbance of law and order at an unprecedented scale'. The order does not clarify what 'unprecedented scale' means. It does not clarify whether the 'unprecedented scale' refers to the same 'conspiracy' referred to in (1) or whether it refers to something else. If the latter, the order does not clarify how the participation of the accused was deduced in that *separate* 'conspiracy'; if the former, the order does not clarify the link between the 'conspiracy' to block the road and its 'unprecedented scale', in a country where blocking roads happens every second day.
3. That although there was no evidence of the accused committing any act or making any speech that instigated violence, nonetheless, as there existed a 'conspiracy', 'when you choose to play with embers, you cannot blame the wind to have carried the spark a bit too far and spread the fire'. Consequently, the 'acts and inflammatory speeches of the co-conspirators are ... admissible against the accused'. Now, it is unclear what the 'acts' are, as the order never mentions them; it is also unclear what the 'inflammatory speeches' are, as the order does not mention them either.

The lynchpin of the order, therefore, is a *prima facie* finding of a 'conspiracy', in specific terms, to 'block a road'. This conspiracy rose to an 'unprecedented level', but we are not told how. But the fact that the accused is also—prima facie—one of the conspirators (regardless of specifics, because this remains a prima facie appraisal) meant that ipso facto, the 'acts and inflammatory speeches' (we are not told which) were attributable to her. It should be immediately clear that such an approach casts the net of criminality *so wide* that just about anyone can be brought within its ambit. At the threshold level, it dispenses with the gravity requirement needed to trigger the UAPA, by failing conspicuously to specify how 'blocking a road' reaches that threshold. At the more substantive level, upon a prima facie finding of a 'conspiracy', it dispenses with the need to show any causal connection between the accused and the events in question.

This would be problematic for acts (which the accused didn't commit) as well, but when it comes to 'inflammatory speeches' (which the accused didn't give), it becomes even more problematic. This is because recognizing the stringent character of laws such as the UAPA, which makes the grant of bail effectively impossible, both the Supreme Court (in *Arup Bhuyan*[3], while examining the similarly worded TADA) and the Bombay High Court (in the *Kabir Kala Manch* cases) have *narrowly interpreted* the substantive offence, limiting it to cases involving the incitement of violence. This is, indeed, nothing new. Going back to the field of metaphors, as the Supreme Court held in *S. Rangarajan*, the proximity between speech and consequence needs to be like that of a 'spark in a powder keg' for criminality to be imposed.

---

3   In March 2023, the Supreme Court overturned its own judgment in *Arup Bhuyan*. Interested readers may refer to Abhinav Sekhri, 'Guest Post: The Arup Bhuyan Review', Indian Constitutional Law and Philosophy, 25 March 2023, https://indconlawphil.wordpress.com/2023/03/25/guest-post-the-arup-bhuyan-review/

Now, the image of a 'spark in a powder keg' suggests a relationship of immediacy and inevitability. The metaphor chosen by the sessions court, on the other hand—that of playing with 'embers' that the wind then 'carries'—is the exact opposite of a 'spark in a powder keg'. The wind can carry embers as far, and in any direction, that the State or the judge might please. What this effectively does is do away with any causal requirement between speech-act and consequence. Such a doctrine, therefore, buries the fundamental right to free speech: If there is no need for a causal requirement between speech-act and consequence, anything can be criminalized, taking us directly into the territory of thought-crimes.

A reading of the order, therefore, makes it clear that insofar as both the law and the facts stood in favour of bail, the court got around the first barrier by replacing legal doctrine with a metaphor of its own invention, and vaulted the second barrier by replacing an accounting of the facts with a set of adjectives ('unprecedented scale' and 'inflammatory speeches') that spared it the necessity of an explanation. In this way, the law was stretched from one side, and the facts from the other, and they met in the middle to make out a *prima facie* UAPA case.

This prima facie case was then used to justify keeping a pregnant woman in an overcrowded prison in the middle of a nationwide pandemic. What that says about the state of the justice system is best left to the readers' judgement.

2

Back to the Basics: The Delhi High Court's Bail Orders under the UAPA

(15 June 2021)

[**Update**:[4] At the time of writing, the Supreme Court has, in appeal, directed that the Delhi High Court's order discussed below 'not be treated as a precedent or relied on by the parties'. The effect of this is that while the grant of bail is not (yet) cancelled, the High Court's judgment itself has been suspended out of existence.

While this phrase—'not to be treated as a precedent'—has become a standard feature in Indian jurisprudence, it is worth repeating—without mincing words—that this is entirely outside the law. When a constitutional court (and the high courts are constitutional courts) delivers a reasoned judgment on an issue, the task of an appellate court

---

[4] The post was updated in July 2021, following the Supreme Court's declaration that the Delhi High Court's judgment—the subject matter of this post—was 'not to be treated as precedent' for other cases. On 2 May 2023, the Supreme Court made this interim order final. See 'A Graveyard for Civil Rights Jurisprudence: The Devangana Kalita Bail Order', Indian Constitutional Law and Philosophy, 2 May 2023, https://indconlawphil.wordpress.com/2023/05/02/a-graveyard-for-civil-rights-jurisprudence-the-devangana-kalita-bail-order/

is limited to determining whether that judgment correctly interpreted the law or did so wrongly. Until reversed, the judgment of a court has the force of law.

It is, therefore, not within the authority of the Supreme Court to act as if the judgment of another constitutional court simply does not exist, or was never delivered—and worse, to deliver an unreasoned command that all other courts also participate in this fiction. It is further important to note the impact of this order: It means that while the three individuals will not be sent back to jail (until whatever time the Supreme Court takes a final view on the correctness of the high court's judgment), what it does mean is that trial courts (and other benches of the high court) are barred by fiat from expressly citing the Delhi High Court's judgment where anyone else's civil rights are concerned. The judgment itself, meanwhile, exists like a phantom limb—not really there, but still there somewhere. This is wholly destructive of the rule of law.]

ON 15 JUNE 2021, a two-judge bench of the Delhi High Court (Mridul and Bhambani JJ) passed three orders granting bail to Asif Iqbal Tanha, Devangana Kalita and Natasha Narwal in the cases related to riots in Delhi in February 2020 ('the Delhi riots cases').[5] Along with many others, the three had been accused of participating in a conspiracy to cause violence in the wake of the anti-CAA protests, charge-sheeted under the Unlawful Activities (Prevention) Act and—at the time of writing—had spent over one year in jail without trial. Bail applications before the trial court had been rejected.

The High Court's orders are significant, as it is the first instance of regular bail—i.e., bail on merits—being granted to individuals who have been charge-sheeted under the UAPA in the Delhi riots cases. What is of even greater significance, however, is the court's reasoning. The bail orders reiterate a simple fact that has, over the years,

---

5   *Asif Iqbal Tanha vs State of NCT of Delhi*, Crl. A. 39/2021 (15 June 2021).

been repeatedly obscured—that the exceptionally stringent provisions of the UAPA (which make the granting of bail extremely difficult) are meant to apply only to *exceptional* cases and not as substitutes for ordinary penal law. This distinction between the state of exception and the state of normalcy has been blurred by laws such as the UAPA, whose broad and vaguely worded provisions allow State agencies to invoke and apply them indiscriminately, and thus keep people behind bars for years without trial. The court's orders today go some way towards restoring that essential distinction (for a background, see these two pieces by Abhinav Sekhri[6]).

As another preliminary point, in order to understand the high court's bail orders, it is important to recall the Supreme Court judgment in the *Watali* case. As we know, Section 43(D)(5) of the UAPA bars the grant of bail if, on a perusal of the case diary and in the opinion of the court, there 'are reasonable grounds for believing that the accusation against such person is prima facie true'. In essence, therefore, the UAPA limits the court to looking at the prosecution version and precludes bail if the prosecution's version— without having passed through cross-examination or challenge— appears true on the face of it. In *Watali*, the Supreme Court further held that it was not permissible for even the court to engage in a detailed analysis of the prosecution's case while considering bail under the UAPA, and to consider whether the evidence presented by the prosecution appeared sufficient. Thus, while the UAPA ties one hand of the defence behind its back (by letting only one side's version be determinative for the question of bail), the *Watali* judgment ties the other hand as well, by effectively prohibiting any

---

6   Abhinav Sekhri, 'How the UAPA Repackages Ideas as Crimes', Article 14, 21 April 2020, https://www.article-14.com/post/how-the-uapa-repackages-ideas-as-crimes; and Abhinav Sekhri, 'How the UAPA Is Perverting the Idea of Justice', Article 14, 16 July 2020, https://www.article-14.com/post/how-the-uapa-is-perverting-india-s-justice-system

substantive challenge to that version. The effect of this is to make the grant of bail *almost* impossible until the end of the trial (which could take years)—a wholly unconstitutional interpretation of the UAPA, to say the least.

Almost, however, is not *entirely*. Notwithstanding *Watali*, there remains space for courts to engage with abusive prosecution cases and (rightly) grant bail. One example of this is the pre-*Watali* Bombay High Court judgments in the *Kabir Kala Manch* cases, where the constitutional guarantees of free speech and freedom of association were invoked to read down the term 'membership' (of an unlawful organization) under the UAPA to 'active membership', i.e., to the incitement of violence.[7] In those cases, the prosecution case—taken entirely on its own terms, and as presumptively true—did not claim that the accused had been fomenting violence (at the highest, they were accused of participating in some meetings, and some literature had been recovered from them). Consequently, even on its own terms, a 'prima facie' case under the UAPA had not been made out and, consequently, Section 43(D)(5) did not apply.

Today's Delhi High Court orders belong to the same judicial line of reasoning as the *Kabir Kala Manch* cases—i.e., extending a close scrutiny to the *terms* of the UAPA, and how a responsible judiciary, committed to the protection of fundamental rights, ought to interpret them. At the heart of the lead judgment/order (*Asif Iqbal Tanha vs State of NCT of Delhi*) is the basic insight that the gravamen of offences under the UAPA is 'terrorism', and the word 'terrorism' has to be given a specific meaning—in light of the context and history of the Act— that *distinguishes* it from offences that are dealt with under ordinary law (paragraphs 28–39). This is particularly important, as the court notes—correctly—that a '*sacrosanct principle of interpretation of penal provisions is that they must be construed strictly and narrowly, to ensure that a person who was not within the legislative intendment does not get*

---

[7] This position has now been overturned by the Supreme Court, as mentioned in the previous chapter.

roped into a penal provision. Also, the more stringent a penal provision, the more strictly it must be construed [paragraph 40].' Based on these interpretive principles—and prior Supreme Court precedent—the court goes on to hold:

> … [T]he extent and reach of terrorist activity must travel beyond the effect of an ordinary crime and must not arise merely by causing disturbance of law and order or even public order; and must be such that it travels beyond the capacity of the ordinary law enforcement agencies to deal with it under the ordinary penal law [paragraph 49].

The court buttresses this by noting that the UAPA is a central legislation and therefore must fall within one of the fields of legislation that the centre is competent to legislate on, under Schedule VII. The appropriate head under List I of the Seventh Schedule—according to the court—is the 'defence of India' (as opposed to 'public order', which is a state subject) (paragraph 57). This—the court observes—also demonstrates the exceptional nature of the UAPA: '*[I]t was neither the intent nor purport of enacting UAPA that other offences of the usual and ordinary kind, however grave, egregious or heinous in their nature and extent, should also be covered by UAPA* [paragraph 57].'

Coming to the question of application, the court then notes that taking the prosecution case (as set out in its 17,000-page charge-sheet) as true, there were no *specific* accusations against the accused, other than that he handed over a SIM card to a co-accused; there was no recovery of weapons or any accusation that the accused was leading the conspirators who actually engaged in violence. In response, the State repeatedly tried to argue that the anti-CAA protest was an 'aggravated' protest that was likely to threaten the 'foundations' of the nation. The court's response to this is striking in its simplicity. It once again notes that none of this is based on any *factual* assertion, but rather '*based upon inferences drawn by the prosecuting agency*'. The anti-CAA protest itself was at no point banned or outlawed—and just as *Watali* prohibits courts from delving into the 'merits or demerits' of evidence at the state of bail, logically, so must it preclude taking into consideration 'inferences and conclusions', in the absence of *'accusations made against the appellant [that] prima facie disclose the commission of a "terrorist act" or a "conspiracy" or an "act preparatory" to the commission of a terrorist act* [paragraph 58]'.

This reasoning is extremely important: a scrutiny of the Delhi riots cases indicate that (i) the actual evidence against the accused is related to organizing protests and *chakka jam*; (ii) violence occurred, but there is no evidence linking the accused to the violence; (iii) the gap in the middle is filled by the State alleging conspiracy and the 'likelihood' of causing violence under the UAPA. It is this gap that the court correctly identifies, and notes that mere *inferences* are not sufficient to complete the chain of causation and establish a prima facie case under the UAPA, which could then be used to deny bail to the accused for years.

Having thus established that a prima facie case of terrorism under the UAPA has not been made out, the court—correctly—considers the general principles regarding bail. Applying those general principles—and in view of the fact that the charge-sheet has 740 witnesses, with no prospect of the trial beginning any time soon (here the court draws upon the Supreme Court judgment in the *K.A. Najeeb* case, which also held that S. 43[D][5] is not inflexible and does not override constitutional rights such as the right to a fair and speedy trial)—the court holds that a case for bail has been made out.

The accompanying two orders—in *Devangana Kalita* and *Natasha Narwal's* cases—are based on similar reasoning. In the *Devangana Kalita* order, the high court makes the crucial observation:

> The making of inflammatory speeches, organising chakkajams, and such like actions are not uncommon when there is widespread opposition to Governmental or Parliamentary actions. Even if we assume for the sake of argument, without expressing any

view thereon, that in the present case inflammatory speeches, chakkajams, instigation of women protesters and other actions, to which the appellant is alleged to have been party, crossed the line of peaceful protests permissible under our Constitutional guarantee, that however would yet not amount to commission of a 'terrorist act' or a 'conspiracy' or an 'act preparatory' to the commission of a terrorist act as understood under the UAPA [paragraph 47].

This is extremely important, because it goes back to the initial point of this blog post, which is the distinction between states of exception and states of normalcy. The high court notes here that there are indeed occasions where, initially, peaceful protests can spill over into the zone of illegality. In such a case, however, whatever illegalities may have been committed are to be dealt with under ordinary law, because there *still* remains a gap between illegal protests and terrorism. To make out a case of terrorism under the UAPA, 'individual, factual and particularized' allegations are needed, and that gap cannot be filled— to repeat—by inferences and insinuations.

Similarly in the *Natasha Narwal* order, the court observes:

> Allegations relating to inflammatory speeches, organising of chakka jaam, instigating women to protest and to stock-pile various articles and other similar allegations, in our view, at worst, are evidence that the appellant participated in organising protests, but we can discern no specific or particularised allegation, much less any material to bear out the allegation, that the appellant incited violence, what to talk of committing a terrorist act or a conspiracy or act preparatory to the commission of a terrorist act as understood in the UAPA [paragraph 35].

The court buttresses this point by noting—in all three judgments— that the right to peaceful protest is a fundamental right under the

Constitution. Consequently, insofar as the allegations themselves pertain to the organization of protests (regardless of the merits of the cause), they cannot be a ground for UAPA offences—including situations where protests, as indicated above, cross the line into illegality. In those situations, ordinary law may be used in response to acts of illegality, but not—in the absence of specific allegations—stringent anti-terror statutes such as the UAPA.

In sum, therefore, the following indisputable principles emerge from the high court's three orders:

1. The UAPA is a special statute, designed to deal with a state of exception, and its operation should not be blurred with ordinary legislation.
2. Criminal statutes must always be narrowly construed and their terms given due specificity.
3. A combination of (1) and (2) implies that the word 'terrorism' in the UAPA must be given specific meaning that relates to the defence of India, and is distinguishable from public-order offences.
4. In order to establish a prima facie case of terrorism under the UAPA against an accused, the allegations must be individualized, factual and particularistic. The gap between what an individual is accused of, and the actual events, cannot be filled by inferences or speculation.
5. As long as that gap exists, the prima facie case under the UAPA—and the prosecution's prima facie burden—remains undischarged, and normal principles of bail—not Section 43(D)(5)—will apply.
6. This is specifically important when the allegations pertain to organizing—and participating in—protests, which are guaranteed rights under the Constitution. The court will be especially vigilant to prevent the use of UAPA-type statutes to blur the lines between protests, illegalities committed during protests and terrorism.

These principles, it is submitted with respect, constitute an ideal template for courts to approach the issue of bail and personal liberty under special statutes such as the UAPA. If applied consistently, they can form the basis of a jurisprudence that respects civil rights, even within the restrictive confines of the UAPA.

3

Staying with the Basics: The Bombay High Court on Bail under the UAPA

(12 October 2021)

ON 13 AUGUST 2021, a two-judge bench of the Bombay High Court (speaking through Shinde and Jamadar JJ) granted bail to one Iqbal Ahmed Kabir Ahmed, who had been charged under various sections of the Unlawful Activities (Prevention) Act and several other laws.[8] What is significant about this judgment is that it is one of the relatively rare instances of an appellate court granting bail on merit to an accused in a UAPA case, notwithstanding Section 43(D)(5) of that legislation and what has been said by the Supreme Court in its infamous *Watali* judgment. I would suggest that—much like the judgment of the Delhi High Court in *Asif Iqbal Tanha* (2021), delivered a month before—the judgment of Shinde and Jamadar JJ shows how it remains possible for courts to continue developing a jurisprudence of liberty even within the interstices of Section 43(D)(5) and *Watali*, should they choose to do so.

---

8   *Iqbal Ahmed Kabir Ahmed vs The State of Maharashtra*, Criminal Appeal No. 355/2021 (13 August 2021).

As the court records, there were two main allegations against the accused—that he was part of a criminal conspiracy involving members of the (banned) ISIS terrorist group and that he had procured material to build an explosive device. The prosecution marshalled evidence to support these claims, including the recovery of an 'oath form' pledging allegiance to Abu Bakr al-Baghdadi, an electric switchboard to which the IED device was allegedly soldered and statements by witnesses about how the accused had taken part in discussions about various atrocities being inflicted upon Islam, and the need to take vengeance for said atrocities. The prosecution argued that this—taken prima facie, as required by Section 43(D)(5)—was sufficient to establish the commission of offences under the UAPA, as well as membership of a terrorist organization. The sessions judge agreed with these arguments and rejected bail.

The high court examined the standard that it would need to apply under Section 43(D)(5) of the UAPA. Relying upon the previous division bench judgment in *Dhan Singh vs Union of India*, it held that the phrase 'prima facie' did not relegate the court to the role of a passive observer, but did require it to 'cross-check' the truthfulness of the allegations on the record and ask whether they were 'improbable' or 'unbelievable' (paragraph 23). Furthermore, as the three-judge bench of the Supreme Court in *Ranjitsing Brahmajeetsing Sharma vs State of Maharashtra* (which preceded *Watali*) had observed, statutory bars to bail, as found under special laws, 'should not be pushed too far' (paragraph 26). Indeed, in that case, the court put its finger on the issue by noting that if, indeed, the statutory bar under special laws would apply only if a court was convinced that an accused had not committed an offence, then an order granting bail was tantamount to a judgment of acquittal—something that was definitely not intended by the legislature. Thus, what needed to be seen was whether, on a conspectus of the material on record, the court was of the view that '*in all probability ... [the accused] may not be convicted*' upon trial. And indeed, as the high court noted, the standard under the NDPS and MCOCA (which was what was applied in *Ranjitsing Brahmajeetsing Sharma*) was actually more stringent than that under the UAPA.

Having set out the legal standard, the court then applied it to the facts at hand. *First*, on the witness reports, the court noted that, taken at their highest, they revealed *discussion* between the accused and his friends about atrocities upon Islam and taking revenge for said atrocities. Even if the material was admitted to be true, the accused was found to have expressed support for ISIS, which—although repugnant in its own right—did not amount to conspiracy to commit an offence or incite violence. As Mihir Desai, counsel for the accused pointed out, the Supreme Court had already held in its famous *Shreya Singhal* judgment that there was a conceptual distinction between *discussion*, *advocacy* and *incitement*, with only the last being subjected to criminal sanctions consistent with the Constitution. The court agreed with this argument, noting that '*there is considerable substance in the submission of Mr. Desai that the material qua the accused, at the highest, is in the realm of discussions* [paragraph 32]'.

Secondly, on the recovery of the oath, the court found that evidence had not been adduced to show that the accused had signed it. Consequently, taken at the highest, the evidence showed that the accused had been *in possession* of an oath form. And '*mere possession of such [an] oath form*', the court held, '*without subscribing thereto, prima facie, does not appear to be an incriminating circumstance*' (paragraph 33). And *thirdly*—and most straightforwardly—while the switchboard had been recovered from the accused, there was no recovery that demonstrated—even prima facie—that this switchboard was being deployed to manufacture an explosive device.

The court then went on to note that at the time of hearing, the accused had been in custody for five years, with charges being framed only after four and a half years. Following the judgment in *K.A. Najeeb*, the court correctly noted that this was a straightforward violation of fair trial rights, and consequently—in any event—the case for bail was made out (paragraphs 36–41).

The merits analysis of the court repays close study. I would respectfully suggest that—as I had pointed out before in the analysis of the Delhi High Court's judgment in *Asif Iqbal Tanha's* case—there are a set of core principles that, if applied, constitute an appropriate balance between the stringency of Section 43(D)(5) (as it stands) and the constitutional obligation of courts to protect the fundamental rights of all citizens. While the analysis in *Tanha's* case was multifaceted, in this case, there are two primary principles. The first is that given the stringency of the UAPA and the harshness with which it operates, its definitional clauses ought to be given a strict and narrow meaning. In the present case, Shinde and Jamadar JJ deployed the *Shreya Singhal* judgment to (correctly) hold that mere discussions would not fall within the substantive clauses of the UAPA—whether the membership clause, or any other. And the second principle is that to make out a prima facie case, as mentioned earlier, the allegations must be individualized, factual and particularistic. The gap between what an individual is accused of, and the actual events, cannot be filled by inferences or speculation. This is evident in the present case from the court's refusal to *infer* a larger conspiracy simply from the recovery of an unsigned oath form or a switchboard, without further, tangible material on record.

Both these principles, I would suggest, are classic principles of criminal jurisprudence. In the context of the UAPA, they are to be deployed at the stage of determining whether the prosecution material makes out a prima facie case or not in the first place. It is only after this standard has been met that the bar under 43(D(5) kicks in. And nor are these principles in conflict with anything set out in *Watali*.

It is, therefore, submitted that the judgment of the Delhi High Court in *Asif Iqbal Tanha* (notwithstanding the Supreme Court's direction that it 'not be treated as precedent') and of the Bombay High Court in *Iqbal Ahmed Kabir Ahmed* are important in crafting a jurisprudence that ensures that individual rights are not entirely submerged under the UAPA. They are part of a longer tradition of judgments, going back to the Bombay High Court's 2013 bail orders in the *Kabir Kala Manch* cases, which remind us that even under repressive laws, courts still have a vital—and indispensable—role to play as the sentinels on the qui vive—should they choose to do so.

4

Entrenching the Basics: The Supreme Court's UAPA Judgment

(28 October 2021)

TODAY THE SUPREME COURT handed down an important judgment reading down Sections 38 and 39 of the UAPA.[9] *Thwaha Fasal vs Union of India* was an appeal from the judgment of the Kerala High Court, delivered on 4 January 2021. In that judgment, the high court had cancelled the bail granted to Thwaha Fasal by the NIA court and directed him to return to jail. I had pointed out at the time that the high court's judgment was deeply flawed.[10] On appeal, however, a two-judge bench of the Supreme Court, in a judgment authored by Oka J, set aside the high court's judgment and restored Thwaha Fasal's bail (and also dismissed the prosecution's appeal against the medical bail granted to his co-accused).

---

9   *Thwaha Faisal vs Union of India*, Criminal Appeal No. 1302/2021 (28 October 2021).
10 'The Unwholesome Servility of the Kerala High Court', Indian Constitutional Law and Philosophy, 4 January 2021, https://indconlawphil.wordpress.com/2021/01/04/the-unwholesome-servility-of-the-kerala-high-court/

To recapitulate: The accused had been booked under the UAPA for alleged association with the banned Communist Party of India (Maoist). The evidence against them consisted of: (a) possession of certain books; (b) the making of 'cloth banners'; and (c) attendance of various meetings. There was no allegation that they had themselves committed any violent act or provided material support to any terrorist organization. However, the high court seized upon the allegations to hold that the accused were 'protagonists' of the CPI (Maoist), had close links with people who, in turn, had close links with the CPI (Maoist), and that the literature in their possession had the 'seeds of promoting secessionist ideology'. As had been pointed out at the time, this was in flagrant contradiction of the well-established Supreme Court jurisprudence that limited membership of unlawful organizations under the UAPA to 'active membership', i.e., to actual incitement of violence.

The court began its analysis with a close textual reading of Sections 38 and 39 of the UAPA. The two-judge bench noted that the requirement of 'association'—the gravamen of the offence—included an intention to *further the activities* of the terrorist organization in question. This is true for both Sections 38 (which defines the concept of membership in terms of association) and 39 (which provides examples of association, such as the organizing of meetings). Thus, without material that demonstrated that the actions of the accused were committed with the intention of furthering the activities of the organization, a prima facie case under the UAPA would not be made out. Significantly, the bench of Oka and Rastogi JJ held:

> Even if an accused allegedly supports a *terrorist organization by committing acts referred in clauses (a) to (c) of subsection (1) of Section 39, he cannot be held guilty of the offence punishable under Section 39 if it is not established that the acts of support are done with intention to further the activities* of a terrorist organization [paragraph 13].

Applying this to the facts of the case, the bench of Oka and Rastogi JJ noted that on the basis of the evidence in the police charge sheet, taken at the highest, '*it can be said that the material prima facie establishes* association *of the accused with a terrorist organization CPI (Maoist) and their* support *to the organization* [paragraph 32]'. The charge sheet basically showed that the accused were in possession of various written materials related to the CPI (Maoist), were part of protests or meetings allegedly organized in connivance with the CPI (Maoist) and had made various banners/posters. Assuming all this was true, the bench held that it must nonetheless be shown that this 'association' or 'support' was given with *the intention of furthering the activities of the organization*:

> In a given case, such intention can be inferred from the overt acts or acts of active participation of the accused in the activities of a terrorist organization which are borne out from the materials forming a part of charge sheet. At formative young age, the accused nos. 1 and 2 might have been fascinated by what is propagated by CPI (Maoist). Therefore, they may be in possession of various documents/books concerning CPI (Maoist) in soft or hard form. Apart from the allegation that certain photographs showing that the accused participated in a protest/gathering organised by an organization allegedly linked with CPI (Maoist), prima facie there is no material in the charge sheet to project active participation of the accused nos. 1 and 2 in the activities of CPI (Maoist) from which even an inference can be drawn that there was an intention on their part of furthering the activities or terrorist acts of the terrorist organization. An allegation is made that they were found in the company of the accused no. 3 on 30th November, 2019. That itself may not be sufficient to infer the presence of intention. But that is not sufficient at this stage to draw an inference of

presence of intention on their part which is an ingredient of Sections 38 and 39 of the 1967 Act [paragraph 35].

These observations are extremely important. Oka J here notes that in order for Sections 38 and 39 to be attracted even prima facie, the charge sheet must demonstrate *some* overt act from which it is reasonable to infer that the accused intended to further terrorist acts or activities of the proscribed organization. In other words, vague allegations of conspiracy, based on the general behaviour of the accused or the materials that might have been recovered from them, is not enough—it is for the charge sheet to establish the prima facie existence of the requisite intention *from* specific overt acts. If that is not done, merely showing that the accused were 'associated' in some way with the organization in question is not sufficient: that association must be *active* (readers will note here the striking similarity with the distinction between active/passive membership that was developed by the Supreme Court in *Arup Bhuyan*, but which is unfortunately honoured more in the breach).

The Supreme Court's interpretive approach to the UAPA is akin to the recent judgments of the Delhi and Bombay High Courts (discussed above). This approach can be summed up as follows: Given the stringent provisions of the UAPA and the near-impossibility of getting bail, if individual liberty is not to be entirely subsumed by the imperatives of anti-terror law, then courts must follow two principles.

Principle 1: The definitional clauses of the UAPA must be given a strict and narrow construction. This was what the Delhi High Court did with respect to the meaning of 'terrorism' in *Asif Iqbal Tanha*, what the Bombay High Court did with respect to Section 20 of the UAPA in *Iqbal Ahmed Kabir Ahmed* and what the Supreme Court has now done in *Thwaha Fasal*.

Principle 2: The allegations in the charge sheet must be individualized, factual and particularistic. The gap between what an individual is accused of and the actual events cannot be filled by inferences or speculation. This, again, is exhibited excellently in the analysis in the *Thwaha Fasal* judgment.

While it may be early days yet, these three judgments—by three different courts—reveal a flicker of hope that there might finally be a glimpse of light at the end of the tunnel that the Supreme Court plunged us into with its *Watali* judgment, and that at long last, the UAPA pendulum might be beginning to swing the other way.

5

Swimming with Your Arms Tied behind Your Back: The Supreme Court's UAPA Bail Order in Iqbal Ahmed's Case

(12 February 2022)

ON 13 AUGUST 2021, a division bench of the Bombay High Court granted bail to one Iqbal Ahmed, who had been charged under various sections of the Unlawful Activities (Prevention) Act. In my analysis of the judgment on this blog, I had written that—when read alongside the Delhi High Court's judgment in *Asif Iqbal Tanha*—the bail order in *Iqbal Ahmed* was an important instance of how the Bombay and Delhi High Courts were beginning to develop a jurisprudence of liberty, even within the highly restrictive confines of the UAPA.[11]

The bail order was appealed to the Supreme Court. In a brief order passed on 11 February 2022, a two-judge bench comprising Chandrachud and Surya Kant JJ declined to interfere with the grant

---

11 Please refer to the chapter 'Staying with the Basics'.

of bail.[12] However, the two-judge bench also passed the following observation, in paragraph 2:

> In the facts and circumstances of the present case, we are not inclined to disturb the order of the High Court. However, we clarify that the observations contained in the impugned order are *confined to the disposal of the application for bail* arising out of the judgment of the Special Judge on the question of bail. Moreover, it *was unnecessary for the High Court to advert to the decision in Shreya Singhal v Union of India* and the judgment of the High Court can be sustained even independent of the said observations. *[Emphasis mine]*

There are two points I want to make with respect to this paragraph, which—in my view—highlight starkly the internal tensions that have come to characterize bail jurisprudence under the UAPA. The first is the part where the court 'clarifies' that the observations in the high court's bail order *'are confined to the disposal of the application of bail'*. Now, this would be entirely unexceptionable were this an order of bail under regular criminal law. However, where a court has granted bail on merit in a UAPA case, *this cannot be so*. The reason for this is explained at some length by Abhinav Sekhri in two articles.[13] As Sekhri points out, 'The UAPA dramatically flips the regular law of bail on its head. Here, courts are required by the statute to

---

12 *State of Maharashtra vs Iqbal Ahmed*, SLP (Crl.) 9957/2021 (11 February 2022).

13 Abhinav Sekhri, 'How the UAPA Is Perverting the Idea of Justice', Article 14, 16 July 2020, https://www.article-14.com/post/how-the-uapa-is-perverting-india-s-justice-system; and Abhinav Sekhri, 'Front-loading Criminal Justice', The India Forum, 19 August 2021, https://www.theindiaforum.in/article/front-loading-bail?utm_source=website&utm_medium=organic&utm_campaign=category&utm_content=Law

primarily focus upon the merits of the case to determine whether or not bail should be granted.' The reason for this is that Section 43(D)(5) statutorily bars the grant of bail the moment the prosecution can show that a prima facie case exists against the accused. Or, in reversal, a bail on merits under the UAPA can happen only if the court finds that *there is not even a prima facie case against the accused* on the basis of the evidence provided. For this reason, it simply does not make *logical* sense for the Supreme Court to say that the 'observations ... [in the High Court order] are confined to ... the question of bail'— the UAPA *mandated* the high court to issue findings about the case that went beyond the 'question of bail' because, without addressing those questions, it could not have granted bail on merits to start with (it's a different matter that it could still have granted bail on the separate and independent procedural ground of *delay*, as per the Supreme Court's *K.A. Najeeb* judgment).

The other reason why this observation is unjustified is simply on grounds of fairness and parity. As Sekhri has pointed out in the articles cited above, the UAPA almost entirely stacks the decks against an accused. Going into a UAPA bail hearing, the accused's counsel have to argue as if they are participating in a swimming competition with both arms tied behind their backs—they cannot deploy any part of the arsenal open to the defence team in a regular criminal trial, and they are only permitted to try and point out internal contradictions within the prosecution's case or show how, even when you assume the prosecution's case to be true, it does not meet the UAPA threshold. The Supreme Court judgment in *Watali* effectively tied a dumb-bell to the defence's legs in addition to its arms being tied behind its back, when it further restricted what materials the court could consider in a UAPA bail hearing.

This being the case, on the rare occasion when the defence *does* succeed in a bail on merits under the UAPA (in the manner indicated above), basic principles of fairness and equality of arms suggest that it ought to be entitled to the full benefits of that bail judgment—which, in this case, for the reasons advanced above, necessarily include certain judicial findings on the substantive quality of the prosecution's case. It is crucial to note that the only reason this is happening is because of how the *UAPA itself front-loads bail hearings entirely in the prosecution's favour*. In this context, the Supreme Court's observations in paragraph 2 basically amount to a situation where the swimmer with both arms tied behind their back and dumb-bells tied to their legs nevertheless wins the swimming competition, and is then told that their win doesn't count because ropes and dumb-bells are not supposed to be brought into the pool.

The second point I want to comment on is the court's observation that it was 'unnecessary' for the high court to refer to the *Shreya Singhal* judgment. This observation bears some resemblance to oral arguments before a different bench of the Supreme Court when Asif Iqbal Tanha's bail order was appealed by the State. In that case, the Supreme Court expressed surprise that the high court had spent a hundred pages discussing various judgments in a bail order. It then went on to hold that the bail order was 'not to be treated as a precedent or relied on by the parties' (something that, as many people have pointed out, was beyond the scope of its jurisdiction). The present order does not do that, but the observation in question shares the same problem. As has been pointed out before, because Section 43(D)(5) of the UAPA statutorily bars the grant of bail where there is a prima facie case against the accused, in a bail on merits application, there are two ways a court can go: (a) hold that the prosecution's case, even when taken at the highest, with all allegations presumed to be true, does not meet the *legal threshold that the offences under the UAPA require to be met*; or (b) there are gaps in the prosecution's case, and the link between the facts as alleged and the offences under the UAPA have not been filled except by surmises or inferences. Now the point is that for (a), the court must, *by the very nature of the analysis*, embark upon a detailed legal examination of what the UAPA offence actually requires.

This was what the Delhi High Court did in *Asif Iqbal Tanha*. And this was exactly why the Bombay High Court invoked the *Shreya Singhal* case in this order. As I wrote in my analysis of this order:

> While the analysis in *Tanha's* case was multifaceted, in this case, there are two primary principles: the first is that given the stringency of the UAPA, and the harshness with which it operates, its definitional clauses ought to be given a strict and narrow meaning. *In the present case, Shinde and Jamadar JJ deployed the Shreya Singhal judgment to (correctly) hold that mere discussions would not fall within the substantive clauses of the UAPA—whether the membership clause, or any other.* And the *second principle* is that to make out a prima facie case, the '*allegations must be individualized, factual and particularistic. The gap between what an individual is accused of, and the actual events, cannot be filled by inferences or speculation.*' This is evident in the present case from the court's refusal to *infer* a larger conspiracy simply from the recovery of an unsigned oath form or a switchboard, without further, tangible material on record.

It should therefore be clear that not only was it correct for the Bombay High Court to have invoked *Shreya Singhal*, but indeed, it could not have been any other way. Recall, once again, that this was a case of bail on merits under the UAPA; the Bombay High Court did not grant bail solely on the *K.A. Najeeb* ground of excessive delay in trials. It is for this reason that paragraph 2 in the Supreme Court's bail order is problematic—because both sets of observations, if taken to their *logical conclusion*, would make bail on merits under the UAPA not only very difficult (which it is now) but a *virtual impossibility*.

By way of conclusion, it is important to note that short orders of this kind—dismissing Special Leave Petitions—are invariably delivered after very brief hearings, without the bench having had the benefit of hearing proper arguments on either side. Thus, it is to be hoped that when the question of bail on merits and Section 43(D)(5) comes up before the Supreme Court again—as it inevitably will—these internal contradictions of the UAPA will be considered in greater and more substantive detail.

6

Forgetting the Basics: The Bail Orders in the *Jyoti Jagtap* and *Umar Khalid* Cases

(19 October 2022)

IN JUNE AND OCTOBER 2021, the Delhi and Bombay High Courts had passed two important judgments on bail under the UAPA. The Delhi High Court's judgment(s) granted bail to Asif Iqbal Tanha, Devangana Kalita and Natasha Narwal, who were accused of various UAPA offences arising out of the February 2020 Delhi riots. The Bombay High Court granted bail to Iqbal Ahmed Kabir Ahmed, who was accused of criminal conspiracy involving members of the banned ISIS group. The significance of these judgments—I had written at the time—lay in how they articulated a 'jurisprudence of liberty' within the stringent confines of the UAPA (see 'Back to the Basics' and 'Staying with the Basics'). The high court justices addressed themselves to the fact that Section 43(D)(5) of the UAPA—as interpreted in the Supreme Court judgment of *Watali*—effectively makes the grant of bail impossible and ensures that people are jailed without trial for years. In response, the courts formulated two principles that could guide judicial determinations of bail under the UAPA. In a post about the Supreme Court's (similar) judgment in the *Thwaha Fasal* case (see 'Entrenching the Basics'), I summarized these principles thus:

Principle 1: The definitional clauses of the UAPA must be given a strict and narrow construction. This was what the Delhi High Court did with respect to the meaning of 'terrorism' in *Asif Iqbal Tanha*, what the Bombay High Court did with respect to Section 20 of the UAPA in *Iqbal Ahmed Kabir Ahmed* and what the Supreme Court has now done in *Thwaha Fasal*.

Principle 2: The allegations in the charge sheet must be individualized, factual and particularistic. The gap between what an individual is accused of, and the actual events, cannot be filled by inferences or speculation. This, again, is exhibited excellently in the analysis in the *Thwaha Fasal* judgment.

At the time, one hoped that these judgments—especially supported by the Supreme Court ruling in *Thwaha Fasal*—marked the beginnings of a consistent judicial pushback against State and prosecutorial impunity under the UAPA. This was not to be. Two other bail judgments—again from the Bombay and Delhi High Courts—reveal that UAPA adjudication continues to be inconsistent and judge-centric, and that individual liberty is, essentially, subject to the outcome of a judicial lottery. Not only is there inconsistency within the same court, but—as we shall see—inconsistency in the pronouncements of the same *judge* within the same court. Unfortunately, the cost of this inconsistency is measured in weeks, months and years in jail.

Jyoti Jagtap and the Bombay High Court

In *Jyoti Jagtap vs National Investigative Agency and Ors*, a division bench of the Bombay High Court denied bail to Jyoti Jagtap, a member of the

Kabir Kala Manch (KKM) troupe.[14] The case arose out of the violent events around the Elgar Parishad march on 31 December 2017. The prosecution's case was that Jyoti Jagtap—and the KKM—had made various provocative speeches and performed provocative plays in the days leading up to the Elgar Parishad and on the day of the event. The prosecution argued that the KKM's actions were tied to a larger conspiracy under the aegis of the banned CPI (Maoist), with the goal of overthrowing the State. The prosecution also relied upon certain witness statements from 2011 (which, of course, had not been subjected to cross-examination at this stage of the proceedings) to the effect that Jyoti Jagtap had been seen in the forest and in meetings with Naxalites.

In its analysis, the Bombay High Court held, *first*, that the witness statements showed Jyoti Jagtap's 'active membership' of the banned CPI (Maoist) by virtue of her presence in meetings with Naxalites (paragraphs 9.1 and 9.2) and alleged involvement in arms training; receipts and documents that showed her organizational role in the Elgar Parishad event (paragraphs 9.3 to 9.7); and 'incitement of hatred and passion' on the day of the event, which showed that the KKM was seeking to 'overthrow' and 'ridicule' the government (paragraph 9.8). Evidence for this 'incitement of hatred and passion'—according to the high court—included ridiculing the phrase '*Acche Din*', referring to the Prime Minister as an 'infant' and 'atrocities on Dalits in modern India'. The high court then referred to the NIA's account of the internal structure and functioning of the CPI (Maoist), as was recorded in the previous bail order in the *Hany Babu* case, and noted that, for these reasons, Jyoti Jagtap's acts would have to be assessed in the context of the 'larger conspiracy' carried out by the CPI (Maoist). The court held (paragraph 10):

> The documents referred to herein above clearly highlights the active role of Appellant in so far as *organizing the Elgar Parishad*

---

14 *Jyoti Jagtap vs National Investigative Agency and Ors*, Criminal Appeal No. 289/2022 (17 October 2022).

event but more importantly it is *the association* of Appellant with the prominent members of CPI (M) which is a designated terrorist organization which cannot be lost sight of. *[Emphasis mine]*

Bail was accordingly denied.

Let us briefly recall the second of the two principles that I have set out before: '*The allegations in the charge sheet must be individualized, factual and particularistic. The gap between what an individual is accused of, and the actual events, cannot be filled by inferences or speculation.*' The importance of this principle has already been discussed, and we are now in a position to see how the Bombay High Court's bail order evidently violates it. The actual 'events' in question involve the violence that occurred in the aftermath of the Elgar Parishad event. Admittedly, Jyoti Jagtap was not accused of any violent act. What she *had* done—allegedly—was to play a role in the organization of the event and to perform on the day. But to link her to the violence—and deny her bail—the following inferences (none of which were demonstrably proven) had to be made:

1. That the Elgar Parishad event was a CPI (Maoist) conspiracy and that the violence was the design of the CPI (Maoist).
2. That Jyoti Jagtap's *prior* association with 'prominent members' of the CPI (M)—dating back seven years and more—demonstrated her participation in the *specific conspiracy* set out in point (1). Note that 'association' is a very broad term and, indeed, it was for this reason that the Supreme Court in the *Arup Bhuyan*[15] case had clarified that, for the purposes of the UAPA, membership meant 'active membership', i.e., incitement to violence; mere attendance of meetings, for example, wouldn't do. The high court did not engage with the *Arup Bhuyan* judgment.

---

15 As noted previously, the *Arup Bhuyan* judgment has now been overturned by the Supreme Court.

3. That the speeches and performances on the day were in furtherance of this 'conspiracy' and caused the violent events that followed.

Indeed, to fill in the gaps in the prosecution's case through inferences, the Bombay High Court resorted to increasingly strained logic, as paragraph 9.8 demonstrates: ridiculing the Prime Minister, his catchphrases and his policies, and statements on Shivaji, Tipu Sultan and on atrocities against Dalits were all construed as 'inciting passion' and in furtherance of the 'larger conspiracy'. The high court was forced to do this because the *actual* evidence against Jyoti Jagtap, as we have seen, was negligible. Thus, the only way to establish the 'prima facie' case against her and deny her bail under the UAPA was for the prosecution and the court to *create* a set of inferences that would connect her (innocuous) acts, such as playing an organizational role in the event and speaking at it, to the (actual) events—the violence—through the (unproven) vehicle of a 'larger conspiracy'.

But it is in the very nature of an accusation of 'conspiracy' that silences are damning. Absences in the prosecution's case can be explained away on the assumption that the accused is simply a good conspirator who covered her tracks. This is why judicial scrutiny—and the resistance to filling in the gaps through inferences—becomes particularly important. What is happening here can be illustratively compared to dropping a stone into still water. The stone causes a splash, and ripples emanate from the point of contact. The ripples grow in size but lessen in intensity, until the point where the calmness of the water is restored. If we think of the splash as the event in question, the legal standard articulated in the previous high court judgments was that you must at least have visible ripple that you're linking back to the splash (i.e., the link between the event and the accused actor cannot be tenuous beyond a certain degree). What we have in Jyoti Jagtap's case is someone coming along an hour after the splash and saying—without demonstrating—that a particular movement on the surface of the water is somehow traceable back to the stone. This is not a sustainable judicial standard.

Umar Khalid and the Delhi High Court

In March 2022, the sessions court denied bail to Umar Khalid in a case arising out of the 2020 Delhi riots. I had written at the time that the court's order was like being a 'stenographer for the prosecution'.[16] The prosecution's statements were not checked *even* for internal consistency, gaps were explained away through inferences (this was especially stark, as Khalid was not even in Delhi when the riots took place), vague witness statements were interpreted to the detriment of Khalid and any aspect of the case that benefited the defence was not considered on the basis that it was a 'matter for trial' (the problems with this last approach have been discussed in some detail earlier).

The Delhi High Court's judgment[17] upholding the order of the sessions judge is—by and large—a replica of that order; interested readers, therefore, can look at the 'Stenographer for the prosecution' piece for more detailed analysis. Indeed, in paragraph 49, the court notes that it is in 'full agreement with the findings of the Ld Sessions Judge' on the question of appreciation of evidence and 'does not wish to burden this judgment' through reiteration—thus exempting itself from the burden of independent analysis as well. Be that as it may, there are a few parts of the judgment that deserve to be flagged, as they demonstrate something quite similar to the Bombay High Court's judgment in *Jyoti Jagtap*—that as the gap between the event and the accused grows larger, the court needs to resort to an increasingly stretched set of inferences to fill it.

These inferences begin in paragraph 52. The high court notes that, after the passage of the Citizenship Amendment Bill, (a) a WhatsApp group called the 'Muslim Students of JNU' was formed, of which

---

16 'Stenographer for the prosecution: The Bail Order in Umar Khalid's Case', Indian Constitutional Law and Philosophy, 24 March 2022, https://indconlawphil.wordpress.com/2022/03/24/stenographer-for-the-prosecution-the-bail-order-in-umar-khalids-case/

17 *Umar Khalid vs State of NCT of Delhi*, 2022/DHC/004325.

Umar Khalid was a *member* (emphasis mine); (b) the day after, the United Against Hate group conducts an agitation against the CAA, which Umar Khalid *attends* (emphasis mine) and—allegedly—supports a call for 'chakka jam'; and (c) another WhatsApp group called 'CAB Team' is formed, of which—again—Umar Khalid is a *member* (emphasis mine). The high court concludes that, therefore, 'a collective reading of the events that unfolded on each day after 04.12.2019 cannot be shrugged aside and it cannot be said that nothing *incriminating* has been [emphasis mine]'. Thus, we can once again see the gap between fact (the membership of WhatsApp groups and participation in an agitation) and event (riots), a gap that is large enough to drive a coach-and-four through, is effectively filled by stipulation—the high court *says* that all of this is incriminating without explaining why it is so. In fact, not only does this gap not seem to bother the high court, but the court appears to positively revel in it. In paragraph 55, it notes:

> It may be reminded that under the UAPA, it is not just the intent to threaten the unity and integrity but the *likelihood* to threaten the unity and integrity; not just the intent to strike terror but the *likelihood* to strike terror; not just the use of firearms but the use of any means *of whatsoever nature*, not just causing but *likely to cause* not just death but injuries to any person or persons or loss or damage or destruction of property, that constitutes a terrorist act, within the meaning of section 15 of UAPA. Moreover, under section 18 of UAPA, not merely conspiracy to commit a terrorist act but an *attempt* to commit or *advocating* the commission or *advising* it or inciting or directing or knowingly facilitating commission of a terrorist act that is also punishable. In fact, even acts *preparatory* to commission of terrorist acts are punishable under section 18 of UAPA. Thus, the objection of the appellant that a case is not made out under UAPA is based on assessing the degree of sufficiency and credibility of evidence not the absence of

its existence but the extent of its applicability; but such objection of the appellant is outside the scope and ambit of section 43D(5) of the UAPA. *[Emphasis mine]*

Quite apart from the fact that the final sentence is borderline incoherent, the entire reason the courts exist—and why judicial review exists—is precisely to introduce an element of the rule of law oversight over State action, so that words with boundless scope—such as 'likelihood', 'likely to cause', 'of whatsoever nature', 'attempt', 'advocating' and 'preparatory'—are given a clear and precise meaning, and—most importantly—a *limit* (think of the stone-in-the-water image again). In its reproduction of these words, however, the high court does the opposite—it uses their fuzzy nature and unclear boundaries as a *justification* for the inferences that it fills the gap with. In other words, imprecision begets imprecision. In the mind of the court, the *vagueness of the legal language justifies the vagueness of the allegations*.

Indeed, the entire judgment is shot through with similar vagueness. In paragraph 57, the high court says that the fact that Umar Khalid's speech about Donald Trump was delivered despite permission for it being rejected gives 'credibility' to the prosecution's accusation that this same speech 'heralded' the Delhi riots. This is a non sequitur to end all *sine qua nons*: There is no reference to the contents of the speech (for good reason), but the mere fact that the speech was given in defiance of the administration is used by the court as a basis for buttressing the prosecution's accusation that it was meant to 'herald' the riots. In the same paragraph, the court refers to a 'flurry of phone calls' between the accused after the riots began, but the only circumstance in which a 'flurry of phone calls' *after a riot begins* becomes suspicious is if you have already decided that the accused were conspirators and their 'flurry of phone calls' was in furtherance of their conspiracy. In all other circumstances, a 'flurry of phone calls' between activists in the immediate aftermath of a riot is one of the most natural things imaginable; in fact, it would be *silence* that would be infinitely more suspicious.

We then come to paragraph 58, which is uncannily similar to paragraph 9.8 in *Jyoti Jagtap*. Having probably realized that its inferential chain stretches credulity to the extreme, the high court is now forced to look at the *actual* evidence on record and make something out of nothing. Thus, the high court seizes upon Umar Khalid's words—'*inquilabi salam* [revolutionary greetings]' and '*krantikari istiqbal* [revolutionary welcome]'—and finds incriminating material there. In a highly confusing passage that cites Maximilien Robespierre and Jawaharlal Nehru, the court says, 'Revolution by itself isn't always bloodless, which is why it is contradistinctly used with the prefix—a "bloodless" revolution. So, when we use the expression "revolution", it is not necessarily bloodless.'

What? Is the court trying to say that henceforth, whenever anyone uses the word 'revolution', they have to preface it with the word 'bloodless', otherwise they will be caught and thrown in jail under the UAPA and denied bail? The very absurdity of this paragraph should make clear that the high court is clutching at straws here. What it has before it is a set of facts (Umar Khalid's conduct) that have no conceivable relationship with what actually happened (the Delhi riots); and to establish the relationship, not only does the high court have to construct an elaborate labyrinth of assumptions and inferences, but also put some of our most common political turns of phrase into a torture rack until they crack and confess to any meaning the court wishes them to confess to.

The court concludes its analysis in paragraphs 62 and 63, where it notes the existence of a 'pre-meditated conspiracy' to do a chakka jam and incitement to violence, a 'pre-planned' attack, Umar Khalid's membership of WhatsApp groups and speeches, the 'flurry of calls' and Umar Khalid's active involvement in the protests against the CAA. As with the

Jyoti Jagtap bail order, let us identify the assumptions at work that the court uses to fill in the gaping holes in the prosecution's case:

1. That calling for a chakka jam logically entails incitement to violence and riots.
2. That membership of WhatsApp groups is indicative of participation in a conspiracy.
3. That a 'flurry of calls' after a riot has started—between activists who have been engaged with the issue in question—is indicative of a conspiracy.
4. That Umar Khalid's involvement in *protests* against the CAA is indicative of his participation in a *conspiracy to cause riots*.

The high court needs to do all this because—as the evidence showed very clearly—at no point did Umar Khalid call for violence, publicly incite violence, commit violence or participate in riots. Thus, all we have is membership of WhatsApp groups indicating a vague 'association', a 'flurry of calls' that also indicates an 'association', and involvement in protests. The high court weaves this together into a boundlessly flexible mesh of 'larger conspiracy' and tops it off with a dash of Robespierre and Nehru. Thus, an individual who has now been in jail for more than two years without a trial is condemned to a further—uncertain—spell in prison, while we still wait for the trial to begin.

Postscript: The Contradictions of Justice Siddharth Mridul

Before concluding, it is important to flag a final point. The two-judge bench of the Delhi High Court that denied bail to Umar Khalid had, as its members, justices Bhatnagar and Siddharth Mridul. The June 2021 bail judgment in the *Asif Iqbal Tanha* case had, as its members, justices Bhambani and Siddharth Mridul.

Under even the loosest standards of intellectual consistency, it is inexplicable how the same learned justice can—without further explanation—be party to two bail judgments that arose out of the same set of facts, but take *polar opposite approaches* to the issue. Let us begin with the most glaring and blatant contradiction: in paragraphs 49–58 in the *Asif Iqbal Tanha* judgment, the bench—of which Justice Siddharth Mridul was a member—gives a narrow interpretation to the word 'terrorism' under the UAPA and notes that the prosecution's argument that the anti-CAA protest was designed to threaten the foundations of the nation is based on 'inferences', and that, therefore, there is prima facie no case made out of terrorism, or conspiracy, or the commission of acts 'preparatory' to terrorism. In paragraphs 62–67 of the *Umar Khalid* judgment, the bench—of which Justice Siddharth Mridul is *again* a member—explicitly notes that the anti-CAA protest was not an 'ordinary protest', and then goes on to argue how the protests and the riots were linked, and how it all constitutes a terrorist act. *How can the same judge simultaneously appear to believe both X and not-X?* And if the same judge has changed his mind and now believes not-X where at one point he so firmly believed X that he signed a judgment to that effect, are we not owed the courtesy of an explanation? Walt Whitman might claim the luxury of contradicting himself because he contains multitudes, but it is not open for a high court judge to contain contradictory multitudes, at least not while he sits in his official capacity.

Similarly, in paragraph 35 of the *Natasha Narwal* order (which accompanied the *Asif Iqbal Tanha* order), the high court bench—of which Justice Siddharth Mridul was a member—noted that 'we can discern no specific or particularized allegation, much less any material to bear out the allegation, that the appellant incited violence, what to talk of committing a terrorist act or a conspiracy or act preparatory to the commission of a terrorist act'. In the *Umar Khalid* judgment, as we have seen, the bench—again with Justice Siddharth Mridul as a member—dispenses with the need for any 'specific or particularized' allegation at all, going, instead, with the membership of WhatsApp groups and *'inquilabi istikbal'* to justify the denial of bail. Once again, the two approaches to the issue are simply irreconcilable.

It is one thing to have a polyvocal court that speaks different tongues (although that is problematic enough), but it is quite unheard of to have a polyvocal *judge*. We can, perhaps, only shake our heads at this marvel and agree with Hamlet when he wisely said, 'There are more things in heaven and earth than are dreamt of in your philosophy.'

Conclusion

The judgments in *Jyoti Jagtap* and *Umar Khalid* show that the courts continue to be sites of contestation when it comes to the UAPA, State and prosecutorial impunity, and under-trial incarceration. These two judgments belong to the 'executive court' tradition, where the language of the court resembles—and often goes beyond—the language of the executive. In UAPA bail cases, the executive court's judgments are marked by how *judicial reasoning* fills in the gaps in the prosecution's case with inferences and assumptions, innocuous and politically legitimate forms of dissent are rendered illegal by transplanting them into a 'larger conspiracy', and how the issue of the conspiracy itself remains an assumption. As we have seen, however, this is not the only way under the UAPA. The 2021 and 2022 bail judgments—which also come from the Bombay and Delhi High Courts—show how a judiciary that is sensitive to the claims of individual liberty can act under the confines of the UAPA. Much, therefore, will depend upon which of these two approaches, over time, finally transforms into 'settled law'. In the meantime, each individual case represents an important site of the legal and constitutional struggle against the UAPA's entrenchment of State impunity.

Privacy, Equality and Dignity

Introduction

ON 24 AUGUST 2017, a nine-judge bench of the Supreme Court delivered what has come to be known as the 'right to privacy judgment' (*Justice [Retd.] K.S. Puttaswamy vs Union of India*). Arising out of a series of challenges to India's national biometric identification system (Aadhaar), the case went before nine judges because the State argued that privacy-based challenges to Aadhaar were unsustainable, as the Indian Constitution did not guarantee a fundamental right to privacy.

In the right to privacy judgment, nine justices of the Supreme Court unanimously agreed that it did. In addition to holding that the Constitution guaranteed a fundamental right to privacy, the justices took the opportunity to set out a detailed doctrine around issues of bodily integrity, decisional autonomy, dignity, the burden the State had to discharge if it wanted to infringe upon these rights, and much else. The wealth of doctrinal detail in the judgment suggested that the right to privacy judgment could be the harbinger of a significant constitutional reset when it came to the relationship between the individual and the State. It indicated the possibility of a new jurisprudential beginning, which centred on human dignity and freedom—*if* the words in the judgment were taken seriously and implemented in concrete cases that would inevitably come before the courts.

The impact of *Puttaswamy* was evident in a set of four judgments, delivered by five-judge benches of the Supreme Court, all in the month of September 2018. The Supreme Court decriminalized same-sex relations (reversing its own previous decision from 2013), decriminalized adultery and struck down a ban upon menstruating-age women from accessing the precincts of the Sabarimala temple. *Puttaswamy* was at the heart of these three judgments. But in a sign of its limits, the court also upheld most parts of the Aadhaar scheme—the case that had given rise to the right to privacy judgment in the first place.

Five years after *Puttaswamy*, its legacy remains contested. In the following pages, you will find judgments that have taken its transformative potential seriously and used it as a tool to advance social rights—especially in the domain of gender and sexuality. But you will also find judgments that have attempted to dilute or ignore it altogether. This contest is reflected particularly starkly in two judgments where the bench split down the middle: on the constitutionality of the marital rape exception (before the Delhi High Court) and the legality of a ban on the hijab in classrooms (before the Supreme Court).

At the time of writing, both cases await resolution, but it is the different opinions in the *same* cases that demonstrate the stakes at issue and how the making of constitutional meaning is a continuing struggle between the entrenchment of power and its democratization. The following pages, thus, are about adjudication in the shadow of *Puttaswamy*, and the future of privacy, equality and dignity under the Constitution.

1

The Supreme Court's Right to Privacy Judgment—I: Foundations

(27 August 2017)

ON 24 AUGUST, A nine-judge bench of the Supreme Court delivered its verdict in *Justice (Retd.) K.S. Puttaswamy vs Union of India*, unanimously affirming that the right to privacy is a fundamental right under the Indian Constitution.[18] The verdict brought to an end a constitutional battle that had begun almost exactly two years ago, on 11 August 2015, when the attorney-general for India had stood up during the challenge to the Aadhaar scheme and declared that the Constitution did not guarantee any fundamental right to privacy. The three judges hearing the case referred the constitutional question to a larger bench of five judges, which, in turn, referred it further to a nine-judge bench. The case was argued over six days in the month of July, during which the Union of India, with many supporting state governments, the Unique Identification Authority of India (UIDAI) and the Telecom Regulatory Authority of India (TRAI) repeated the

---

18   *Justice (Retd.) K.S. Puttaswamy vs Union of India*, (2017) 10 SCC 1.

attorney-general's 2015 claim—which, as we shall see, was decisively rejected by the court.

Six out of the nine judges—Chelameswar, Bobde, Nariman, Sapre, Chandrachud and Kaul JJ—delivered separate opinions (Chandrachud J wrote for himself and on behalf of Khehar CJI, Aggarwal and Nazeer JJ). Spanning 547 pages, *Puttaswamy* is undoubtedly a historic and landmark verdict of our times, and one of the most important civil rights judgments delivered by the Supreme Court in its history. Apart from affirming the existence of the fundamental right to privacy under the Indian Constitution—for which each of the nine judges must be unreservedly applauded—*Puttaswamy* will have a profound impact upon our legal and constitutional landscape for years to come. It will impact the interplay between privacy and transparency, and between privacy and free speech; it will impact State surveillance, data collection and data protection, LGBTQ rights, the legality of food bans, the legal framework for regulating artificial intelligence and many other issues that we cannot now foresee or anticipate. For this reason, the judgment(s) deserve to be studied carefully and debated rigorously in the days and weeks to come.[19]

At the outset, it is important to draw an important distinction between what is found in the *operative order* of the court and everything else that is found in the six separate opinions. The operative order is a page-long statement at the end of the verdict, signed by all the nine judges, *and it is only this order that is legally binding upon future benches of the Supreme Court and the high courts*. There are two reasons for this. The first is that it is this order that answers the two referral questions that were before the court and the reason why the nine-judge bench was established in the first place. And the second is that with six separate opinions, there is no real 'majority' judgment (Justice Chandrachud's

---

19 See the ten-part series available at 'The Supreme Court's Right to Privacy Judgment: Round-Up', Indian Constitutional Law and Philosophy, 10 September 2017, https://indconlawphil.wordpress.com/2017/09/10/the-supreme-courts-right-to-privacy-judgment-round-up/

opinion, which commands the support of four judges out of nine, is a plurality, but not a majority). There is likely to be extensive debate over whether there are certain legal propositions that command the support of five or more judges. This is an important debate, because these propositions—and how they are interpreted—will inevitably shape the way that future benches decide on concrete privacy cases brought before them.

Notwithstanding that, however, it is important to remember that ultimately, the court was answering two legal questions put to it by a smaller bench. In the course of answering these questions, it was obliged to traverse wide and extensive legal terrain. However, the very fact that this entire enquiry was conducted in the abstract should caution us against treating the discussion beyond the referral questions as laying down binding propositions of law. Rather, the 547 pages of discussion, in my opinion, are better understood as setting up signposts and guidelines that will assist lawyers, judges and academics in shaping the contours of the right to privacy under the Indian Constitution in the years to come. To take a few examples, *this* verdict does not—and could not—decide whether and to what extent the Aadhaar scheme is constitutional, whether and to what extent public figures can prevent the publication of unauthorized biographies or biopics, or the circumstances and the extent to which the State can surveil its citizens. What this verdict does do, however, is that it provides the *constitutional framework* within which these cases are to be debated and decided when they come before the courts.

Therefore, in the first essay in the series, I will begin the discussion by examining the operative order of the court: the unanimous verdict of nine judges, which is unquestionably now the law of the land. This operative order lays down four simple propositions of law.

Proposition One: The decision in *M.P. Sharma*, which holds that the right to privacy is not protected by the Constitution, stands overruled.

Recall that the reason for the initial reference was the State's contention that the judgments of the Supreme Court in *M.P. Sharma* (eight judges) and in *Kharak Singh* (six judges) had held that there was no fundamental right to privacy under the Indian Constitution, and all subsequent judgments to the contrary had been decided by smaller benches. On my blog ICLP, I have summarized the petitioners' arguments on why neither of these judgments supported the State's claim. In *Puttaswamy*, four out of the six opinions examined the issue in detail and entirely accepted the petitioners' arguments. In *M.P. Sharma*, Justices Nariman (paragraph 27), Chelameswar (paragraph 7), Bobde (paragraph 5) and Chandrachud (paragraph 26) all agreed that *M.P. Sharma* only held that the American Fourth Amendment could not be incorporated into the guarantee against self-incrimination in the Indian Constitution [Article 20(3)]. However, the Fourth Amendment, which was limited to protecting 'the right of the people to be secure in their persons, houses, papers, and effects, against unreasonable searches and seizures' was not, and had never been, exhaustive of the concept of privacy, even in the United States. Consequently, even if *M.P. Sharma* was correct in refusing to find an analogue to the Fourth Amendment in Article 20(3) of the Indian Constitution, that was no warrant for holding that there was no fundamental right to privacy—a much broader and more compendious concept. In the words of Justice Bobde:

> *M.P. Sharma* is unconvincing not only because it arrived at its conclusion without enquiry into whether a privacy right could exist in our Constitution on an independent footing or not, but because it wrongly took the United States Fourth Amendment—which in itself is no more than a limited protection against unlawful surveillance—to be a comprehensive constitutional guarantee of privacy in that jurisdiction.

Proposition Two: The decision in *Kharak Singh*, to the extent that it holds that the right to privacy is not protected by the Constitution, stands overruled.

In *Kharak Singh*, the Supreme Court had considered the constitutionality of various forms of police surveillance upon a 'history-sheeter'. It had upheld reporting requirements, travel restrictions, shadowing and so on (by arguing, in part, that there was no fundamental right to privacy), but had struck down nightly domiciliary visits as a violation of 'ordered liberty'.

The court's rejection of *Kharak Singh* was based on two prongs. First, it held that the judgment was internally contradictory, because the court *could not* have struck down domiciliary visits on any other ground but that of privacy; indeed, in doing so, the court had itself quoted American judgments affirming a right to privacy.

As Justice Nariman noted:

> If the passage in the judgment dealing with domiciliary visits at night and striking it down is contrasted with the later passage upholding the other clauses of Regulation 236 extracted above, it becomes clear that it cannot be said with any degree of clarity that the majority judgment upholds the right to privacy as being contained in the fundamental rights chapter or otherwise. As the majority judgment contradicts itself on this vital aspect, it would be correct to say that it cannot be given much value as a binding precedent [paragraph 42].

Justices Bobde (paragraph 6), Chelameswar (paragraph 9) and Chandrachud (paragraph 27) agreed that there existed a 'logical inconsistency' within *Kharak Singh*, in that the court could not have struck down one facet of police surveillance without invoking the right to privacy. Furthermore, the justices also agreed that in any event, *Kharak Singh's* finding that there was no right to privacy under Article 21 of the Constitution was based on a narrow reading of the phrase 'personal liberty', which, in turn, was a relic of the judgment in *A.K. Gopalan*. In *A.K. Gopalan*, the Supreme Court had adopted what Justice Chandrachud called the 'silos' approach to Part III of the Constitution, holding that each separate clause dealt with a separate right and that each clause was hermetically sealed from all other clauses. In this reading, 'personal liberty' under Article 21 contained only what remained after subtracting the various freedoms guaranteed in Article 19(1). The 'silos approach', however, had been comprehensively rejected by the Supreme Court in *R.C. Cooper* and, in fact, in *Maneka Gandhi*, the majority judgment in *Kharak Singh* had been held to be overruled in view of this development. Consequently, as Justice Chandrachud observed:

> The jurisprudential foundation which held the field sixty three years ago in *M.P. Sharma* and fifty five years ago in *Kharak Singh* has given way to what is now a settled position in constitutional law. Firstly, the fundamental rights emanate from basic notions of liberty and dignity and the enumeration of some facets of liberty as distinctly protected rights under Article 19 does not denude Article 21 of its expansive ambit. Secondly, the validity of a law which infringes the fundamental rights has to be tested not with reference to the object of state action but on the basis of its effect on the guarantees of freedom. Thirdly, the requirement of Article 14 that state action must not be arbitrary and must fulfil the requirement of reasonableness, imparts meaning to the constitutional guarantees in Part III [paragraph 24].

Proposition Three: The right to privacy is protected as an intrinsic part of the right to life and personal liberty under Article 21 and as part of the freedoms guaranteed by Part III of the Constitution.

The rejection of the State's claim based on *M.P. Sharma* and *Kharak Singh* was only half the story. The affirmative case for why privacy *is* a fundamental right remained to be made. At the bar, privacy was argued to be latent within liberty, autonomy and human dignity, apart from being foundational towards ensuring that the freedom of speech, expression, association and religion remained meaningful. All these arguments figure, in different ways, in each of the six opinions.

Justice Chelameswar, for example, grounded his opinion in the concept of liberty. Defining 'privacy' as comprising three aspects—

'repose', 'sanctuary' and 'intimate decision'—he held that each of these aspects was central to the idea of liberty guaranteed by both Articles 21 and 19 (paragraph 36). He then took a series of examples of privacy violations (force-feeding, abortion, telephone tapping and intimate association, to name a few) and grounded them within the broader rights to freedom of the body (Article 21) and freedom of the mind (Article 19) (paragraphs 38–40).

Justice Bobde founded his judgment on *'two values ... the innate dignity and autonomy of man'* (paragraph 12), which he located in the overarching structure of the Constitution. In addition, he held that privacy was a *'necessary and unavoidable logical entailment of rights guaranteed in the text of the constitution'* (paragraph 35). In Justice Bobde's opinion, we find the important insight that to be effectively exercised, the liberties in Article 19(1) (speech, expression, association, assembly, movement) and Article 21 (personal liberty) require, on occasion, to be exercised *in seclusion*. Privacy, therefore, was *'an enabler of guaranteed freedoms'* (paragraph 29) and *'an inarticulate major premise in Part III of the Constitution'* (paragraph 25).

Justice Nariman made an overarching argument linking the three aspects of privacy (bodily integrity, informational privacy and the privacy of choice) (paragraph 81) with the preamble of the Constitution, which guaranteed democracy, dignity and fraternity (paragraph 82). It was here that the constitutional foundations of privacy could be found. The connection was drawn by him in this manner:

> The dignity of the individual encompasses the right of the individual to develop to the full extent of his potential. And this development can only be if an individual has autonomy over fundamental personal choices and control over dissemination of personal information which may be infringed through an unauthorized use of such information [paragraph 85].

In other words, individual self-development—which lay at the heart of democracy, dignity and fraternity—was meaningless without a right to privacy that guaranteed, at the minimum, security of the body, security of personal information and security of intimate choices.

Very similar reasoning—based on dignity and individual self-determination—was employed by Justice Sapre, who noted that dignity imposes *'an obligation on the part of the Union to respect the personality of every citizen and create the conditions in which every citizen would be left free to find himself/herself and attain self-fulfilment'* (paragraph 8). It was also employed by Justice Kaul, who brought dignity and liberty together, noting that *'privacy ... is nothing but a form of dignity, which itself is a subset of liberty'* (paragraph 40) and *'key to the freedom of thought'* (paragraph 52).

These complementary strands of reasoning were brought together by Justice Chandrachud in his judgment. He grounded privacy in dignity (paragraphs 32, 107 and 113), *'inviolate personality ... the core of liberty and freedom'* (paragraph 34), autonomy (paragraphs 106 and 168), liberty (paragraph 138), bodily and mental integrity (paragraph 168) and across the spectrum of protected freedoms (paragraph 169). Therefore:

> The freedoms under Article 19 can be fulfilled where the individual is entitled to decide upon his or her preferences. Read in conjunction with Article 21, liberty enables the individual to have a choice of preferences on various facets of life including what and how one will eat, the way one will dress, the faith one will espouse and a myriad other matters on which autonomy and self-determination require a choice to be made within the privacy of the mind. The constitutional right to the freedom of religion under Article 25 has implicit within it the ability to choose a faith and the freedom to express or not express those choices to the world. These are some illustrations of the manner in which privacy facilitates freedom and is intrinsic to the exercise of liberty. The Constitution does not contain a separate article telling us that privacy has been declared to be a fundamental right. Nor have

we tagged the provisions of Part III with an alpha suffixed right of privacy: this is not an act of judicial redrafting. Dignity cannot exist without privacy. Both reside within the inalienable values of life, liberty and freedom which the Constitution has recognised. Privacy is the ultimate expression of the sanctity of the individual. It is a constitutional value which straddles across the spectrum of fundamental rights and protects for the individual a zone of choice and self-determination [paragraph 169].

There is something of tremendous significance here. Even as it agreed with the petitioners that privacy was a fundamental right, the court could have chosen to give it a narrow cast and frame. The court may have limited it to an aspect of dignity or restricted it to a derivative right under Article 21. This would have thrown up difficult initial barriers in future cases, compelling petitioners to shoehorn their claims within the shifting and largely symbolic concept of dignity (and jurisdictions such as Canada provide salutary warnings about how easy it is to constrict rights by pegging them to dignity) or the (diluted) umbrella of Article 21. The court, however, did the exact opposite. Starting with the basic idea that privacy encompassed the body (and bodily integrity), the mind (and informational self-determination) and intimate choices, all nine judges agreed that privacy was at the heart of individual self-determination, of dignity, autonomy and liberty, and *concretely* inseparable from the meaningful exercise of guaranteed freedoms such as speech, association, movement, personal liberty and freedom of conscience. Privacy, therefore, was both an overarching, foundational value of the Constitution *and* incorporated into the text of Part III's specific, enforceable rights.

This, in my view, is at the heart and soul of *Puttaswamy* and the primary reason this judgment deserves to be a landmark, not only in the annals of Indian constitutional jurisprudence, but across the world. The verdict locates privacy in the grand sweep of democracy and within the core human values of autonomy, dignity and freedom, while also placing it within the realm of the concrete, the flesh-and-blood relationship between the individual and the State. In its attention to the abstract and to the world of concepts, it does not ignore the world in which individuals struggle against coercive State power; and in its care to outline how privacy is concretely meaningful, it does not forget to include it within that constellation of ideas that frame this reality and give it meaning. This is a difficult path to travel. However, all nine judges have demonstrated the intellectual courage required to travel it, and the result is a ringing endorsement of the central place of privacy in a modern, constitutional, democratic republic.

Proposition Four: Decisions subsequent to *Kharak Singh* that have enunciated the position in (iii) above lay down the correct position in law.

As the petitioners had repeatedly argued before the court, there was no need to reinvent the wheel. After *Gobind vs State of MP*, there was an unbroken line of Supreme Court judgments, spanning forty years, that had repeatedly affirmed the status of privacy as a fundamental right (Justice Chandrachud's judgment examines all the precedent on the point). Petitioners asked the court to affirm that line of judgments. The court agreed.

The consequences of this—which we shall discuss subsequently—are that the extended discussions in the separate opinions on the scope of privacy, its operation in the public and the private spheres, and its limitations cannot be studied in isolation, but in the context of forty years of case law. The task of future benches now is to build upon this existing jurisprudence, taking into account, of course, the insights of *Puttaswamy*.

This, in conclusion, brings me to an important point. As Apar Gupta points out:

> While the privacy judgement is a cause for celebration, its full benefit will only come when it is applied to actual state actions

that undermine privacy. Adherence to constitutional principle is not an academic exercise, but requires a prompt protection of real rights and liberties. Judicial action should spring at moments when the state oversteps onto the citizen. Few would dispute that determinations on privacy would be of greater benefit when the Supreme Court protects us with foresight rather than retrospect.[20]

The nine-judge bench of the Supreme Court has given us an outstanding foundation for a progressive civil liberties jurisprudence, located in ideas of liberty, dignity, autonomy and privacy. In the times to come, citizens will look to the court to build upon that foundation and to carry through with the beginnings that it has made in *Puttaswamy*. But in future, the situations that come before the court will no longer be abstract, the questions will no longer be purely legal, and the pressures will be real, not merely academic. *Puttaswamy* only makes possible what will, in the last analysis, require judicial courage and wisdom to accomplish: meaningful protection of the rights of the individual against the creeping claims of the State. But it is that very possibility—which, if the State's arguments had been accepted, would have been snuffed out at its very inception—that gives us cause to celebrate today.

[**Disclaimer**: The writer assisted Arvind Datar, who appeared for one of the petitioners in this case.]

---

[20] Apar Gupta, 'Privacy, dignity, sexual autonomy', *The Indian Express*, 25 August 2017, https://indianexpress.com/article/opinion/columns/fundamental-rights-right-to-privacy-supreme-court-constitution-emergency-privacy-dignity-sexual-autonomy-4812162/

2

'Civilization Has Been Brutal': Navtej Johar, Section 377, and the Supreme Court's Moment of Atonement

(6 September 2018)

IN *JUSTICE K.S. PUTTASWAMY vs Union of India*, the Supreme Court did a remarkable thing. While declaring that privacy was a fundamental right under the Indian Constitution, five out of nine judges *also* noted that the court's 2013 judgment in *Suresh Kumar Koushal vs Naz Foundation* (an entirely unconnected proceeding) had been wrongly decided. In *Koushal*, the constitutionality of Section 377 of the Indian Penal Code—which criminalized 'carnal intercourse against the order of nature'—had been upheld, and the 2009 Delhi High Court judgment reading it down to exclude consenting same-sex relations had been overturned. How deeply the *Koushal* court had erred (in the view of the *Puttaswamy* bench) was evident from the fact that in his plurality opinion, Chandrachud J singled it out as one of the two 'discordant notes' in constitutional history (the other was the Emergency-era *ADM Jabalpur* judgment).

The privacy judgment made it clear that *Koushal* was living on borrowed time. That time came to an end today, when a constitution bench of the court, in *Navtej Johar vs Union of India*, formally overruled *Koushal*, effectively restored the Delhi High Court judgment in *Naz Foundation* and unambiguously held that the LGTB+ community was entitled to equal rights under Articles 14, 15, 19, 21 and the rest of the Constitution's fundamental rights chapter.[21]

Four concurring judgments were delivered in *Navtej Johar*. While concurring on the outcome of the case—that Section 377 violated Article 14 (equal protection of laws), 15(1) (non-discrimination on grounds of sex), 19(1)(a) (freedom of expression) and 21 (right to life and personal liberty)—the judges came at the issues from different angles. In this essay, I shall discuss the different strands of constitutional reasoning that we find in *Navtej Johar* and their implications for the future.

A. *The Chief Justice and the Primacy of Choice*

The Chief Justice wrote for himself and Justice Khanwilkar. His is a wide-ranging judgment, but at its heart lies the idea of *choice*. This is not as straightforward an argument as it seems at first blush. Recall that there has been a long-standing debate about whether sexual orientation is 'natural' and 'immutable', a question of choice or somewhere in between, upon a spectrum. It has always been intuitively tempting to argue that sexual orientation is simply a question of having been 'born this way'. It is tempting because if sexual orientation is 'natural' and something beyond the individual's power to alter, criminalizing it is ipso facto irrational. Our criminal law is based upon the idea of holding people to account for acts that they are *responsible* for. How then can you criminalize something that is inherent and which cannot be controlled?

---

21 *Navtej Johar vs Union of India*, AIR 2018 SC 4321.

The 'born this way' discourse, however, has been strongly criticized. As Shamus Khan's article points out, for example:

> If biology determines our expression, then there is no reason to think about making better or different worlds. It has all been decided, from the moment we became *Homo sapiens*. Yet if we recognise sexuality as constructed, we open up essential discussions about some of the most important aspects of life. Who are we sexually intimate with, and how? What do we do with the consequences of sexual intimacy (offspring and health)? Who is responsible for children's lives, development and education in a society? The arrangement of sexual relations is the key social building block of society's reproduction. Hence the importance of gay marriage. Yet we have a surprisingly limited way of engaging [in] this conversation; indeed, biological determinism helps us avoid the issue altogether. A host of social issues are pressing down upon us, and we cannot effectively address them if we deny the reality of the human condition, including sexuality, and thereby close off discussions before they begin.[22]

And, as the work of Foucault and other scholars has demonstrated, essentializing sexuality (and sexual orientation) runs the risk of trapping people in pre-constructed identities, in a manner that—in the long run—is anything but emancipatory.

To the judgment's merit, it keeps both these propositions in equilibrium and refrains from choosing one over the other. So in paragraph 9, the Chief Justice observes:

> When we talk about identity from the constitutional spectrum, it cannot be pigeon-holed singularly to one's orientation that may be associated with his/her birth and the feelings he/she

---

22 Shamus Khan, 'Not Born This Way', Aeon, 23 July 2015, https://aeon.co/essays/why-should-gay-rights-depend-on-being-born-this-way

develops when he/she grows up. Such a narrow perception may initially sound to subserve the purpose of justice but on a studied scrutiny, it is soon realized that the limited recognition keeps the individual choice at bay.

'Natural orientation' and 'choice' are discussed in a complementary manner throughout the judgment (see, for e.g., paragraphs 109 and 148). Admittedly, at various points in the judgment, the Chief Justice comes close to slipping back into the former type of vocabulary, using words such as 'inherent', 'innate', 'by birth' and so on (paragraph 143–44). A holistic reading of the judgment, however, makes it clear that the concept of choice (that he also frames as individual self-determination) is as important to the exercise of constitutional rights as the 'naturalness' of sexual orientation. Indeed, in paragraph 140, while defining the aspects of sexual orientation, the Chief Justice refers both to 'inherent orientation' and 'demonstration of choice'.

And, perhaps most importantly, it is in the language of choice that the Chief Justice rejects *Koushal's* argument (indeed, the only argument actually made in *Koushal*) that as Section 377 only criminalizes 'acts' and not 'persons', it does not violate constitutional guarantees:

> ... [I]ndividuality of a person and the acceptance of identity invite advertence to some necessary concepts which eventually recognize the constitutional status of an individual that resultantly brushes aside the act and respects the dignity and choice of the individual [paragraph 81].

Additionally, the argument for dignity is also framed in the language of choice:

> Dignity while expressive of choice is averse to creation of any dent. When biological expression, be it an orientation or optional expression of choice, is faced with impediment, albeit through any

imposition of law, the individual's natural and constitutional right is dented [paragraph 132].

This articulation of 'choice' then becomes an important basis of the Chief Justice's finding that Section 377 violates the Constitution. Because it disrespects individual choice, Section 377 is both irrational and 'manifestly arbitrary', and violates Article 14 (paragraph 240). This is, of course, in addition to the violation of expressive rights under Article 19(1)(a) and the right to privacy under Article 21—which, too, is defined in terms of 'intimacy in privacy as a matter of choice' (Conclusion X).

B. *Justice Nariman and the Presumption of Constitutionality*

Justice Nariman's opinion shares many of the interpretive commitments of the Chief Justice. He, too, holds that Section 377 violates dignity (paragraph 79) and that it is 'manifestly arbitrary' (paragraph 82). Nariman J arrives at the second conclusion from a slightly different route. He examines the Mental Healthcare Act, 2017, which expressly prohibits discrimination on grounds of sexual orientation (in the domain of mental health). Combining this with scientific evidence, he notes that the natural/unnatural distinction that is at the heart of Section 377 has no rational basis and, consequently, violates Article 14 (paragraph 82).

By far the most interesting aspect of Nariman J's opinion, however, is his holding that pre-constitutional laws do not enjoy any presumption of constitutionality. He notes:

> The presumption of constitutionality of a statute is premised on the fact that Parliament understands the needs of the people, and that, as per the separation of powers doctrine, Parliament is aware of its limitations in enacting laws—it can only enact laws which do not fall within List II of Schedule VII of the Constitution of India, and cannot transgress the fundamental rights of the citizens

and other constitutional provisions in doing so. Parliament is therefore deemed to be aware of the aforesaid constitutional limitations. Where, however, a pre-constitution law is made by either a foreign legislature or body, none of these parameters obtain. It is therefore clear that no such presumption attaches to a pre-constitutional statute like the Indian Penal Code.

While I believe this is a correct argument, it is nonetheless an incomplete argument. Nariman J does not tackle one important objection—that Parliament's failure to repeal a pre-constitutional law indicates an implicit *acceptance*. It also seems to prove too much (for example, could someone challenging the Indian Contract Act of 1872 argue that there is no presumption of constitutionality?). Consequently, I would suggest that Nariman J's argument needs to be slightly deepened: The reason pre-constitutional laws should not carry a presumption of constitutionality is that, insofar as they affect fundamental rights, they impose a *double burden* upon the individuals they impact. First, these individuals had no say in the framing of these laws (since they were passed by a non-democratic colonial regime); and secondly, now that these laws exist, it is those who suffer their effects who have to mobilize and convince Parliament to repeal them. It is this double burden that is unacceptable, and therefore mandates that the presumption of constitutionality be withheld from *those* colonial laws that affect fundamental rights (I have made this argument in greater detail elsewhere[23]).

C. *Justice Chandrachud and Indirect Discrimination*

For me, the most interesting—and complex—argument in the case was that Section 377 violates Article 15(1) (non-discrimination on grounds

---

[23] 'Is There an Interpretive Methodology for Construing Colonial-Era Statutes?', Indian Constitutional Law and Philosophy, 20 October 2013, https://indconlawphil.wordpress.com/2013/10/10/is-there-an-interpretive-methodology-for-construing-colonial-era-statutes/

of sex) and a combined reading of Articles 15 (non-discrimination) and 14 (equality before law). In Chandrachud J's opinion, this argument receives detailed treatment. As a prelude, he begins with the following, critical observation:

> Equating the content of equality with the reasonableness of a classification on which a law is based advances the cause of legal formalism. The problem with the classification test is that what constitutes a reasonable classification is reduced to a mere formula: the quest for an intelligible differentia and the rational nexus to the object sought to be achieved. In doing so, the test of classification risks elevating form over substance. The danger inherent in legal formalism lies in its inability to lay threadbare the values which guide the process of judging constitutional rights [paragraph 27].

This is an important rebuke, not just to the *Koushal* court, but also to the dominant strand of equality thinking on the Supreme Court, which—even in 2018—applied the 'classification test' to judge equality violations (i.e., a law is unconstitutional if there is either an 'unintelligible differentia' between the things that it classifies or if the classification bears no rational nexus to the State goal). Chandrachud J goes on to note:

> Article 14 has a substantive content on which, together with liberty and dignity, the edifice of the Constitution is built. Simply put, in that avatar, it reflects the quest for ensuring fair treatment of the individual in every aspect of human endeavor and in every facet of human existence.

What does this 'substantive content' of equality entail? This takes us to the heart of Chandrachud J's judgment, which his treatment of Article 15(1) claims. As he notes, Indian courts have historically interpreted the statement, 'The State shall not discriminate on grounds ... only of sex' in a highly formalistic manner and have upheld laws that—in their language—use more than one or a differently worded ground (for example, in *Koushal*, the court held that because Section 377 only criminalized 'carnal intercourse against the order of nature', there was no question of discriminating against identities). This, however, is flawed: What matters is the *effect* of law upon the exercise of fundamental rights (paragraph 34).

The effect of law must be understood by taking into account the broader social context within which law is embedded. It must therefore take into account *'the intersectional nature of sex discrimination, which cannot be said to operate in isolation of other identities, especially from the socio-political and economic context* [paragraph 36]'. Drawing from progressive gender equality judgments such as *Anuj Garg*, Chandrachud J concludes:

> A provision challenged as being ultra vires the prohibition of discrimination on the grounds only of sex under Article 15(1) is to be assessed not by the objects of the state in enacting it, but by the effect that the provision has on affected individuals and on their fundamental rights. Any ground of discrimination, direct or indirect, which is founded on a particular understanding of the role of the sex, would not be distinguishable from the discrimination which is prohibited by Article 15 on the grounds only of sex.

The words 'direct or indirect' are crucial, since this is the first time that the Supreme Court has explicitly recognized the concept of indirect discrimination (i.e., where facially neutral laws—such as Section 377—nonetheless have a disproportionate impact upon a segment of the population).

How must Section 377 be analysed within this constitutional framework? After recording the experiences of LGBTQ+ individuals subjected to the 'shadow of criminality', Chandrachud J notes,

'*Section 377 criminalizes behaviour that does not conform to the heterosexual expectations of society. In doing so it perpetuates a symbiotic relationship between anti-homosexual legislation and traditional gender roles* [paragraph 44].' How does it do so? The answer comes immediately afterwards:

> If individuals as well as society hold strong beliefs about gender roles—that men (to be characteristically reductive) are unemotional, socially dominant, breadwinners that are attracted to women, and women are emotional, socially submissive, caretakers that are attracted to men—it is unlikely that such persons or society at large will accept that the idea that two men or two women could maintain a relationship [paragraph 44].

It is in this manner that Chandrachud J draws together the indirectly discriminatory character of the facially neutral Section 377, the effects test, the prohibition of 'sex' discrimination under Article 15(1) in a case about 'sexual orientation' and the importance of social context to the enquiry. Here is how the argument goes:

1. Article 15(1) prohibits sex discrimination.
2. Discrimination on grounds of sex is premised upon stereotypes about appropriate gender roles and the binary between 'man' and 'woman'.
3. It is these stereotypes about gender roles that constitute the bases for criminalizing same-sex relations.
4. Section 377 may be neutrally worded, but its *effect* is primarily—and disproportionately—upon the LGBT community. It is therefore indirectly discriminatory on grounds of sexual orientation.
5. Since the basis of that indirect discrimination lies in stereotypes about gender roles (the background social context), Section 377 violates Article 15(1) of the Constitution.

Consequently, to sum up:

> Statutes like Section 377 give people ammunition to say 'this is what a man is' by giving them a law which says 'this is what a man is not'. Thus, laws that affect non-heterosexuals rest upon a normative stereotype: 'the bald conviction that certain behavior—for example, sex with women—is appropriate for members of one sex, but not for members of the other sex [paragraph 51].

As Terry Eagleton wrote in *Saint Oscar*, his play about Oscar Wilde:

> You hold that a man is a man and a woman is a woman. I hold that nothing is ever purely itself, and that the point where it becomes so is known as death. I therefore demand to be defended by metaphysicians rather than by lawyers, and that my jury should be composed of my peers—namely, poets, perverts, vagrants and geniuses.

I do not think it is an exaggeration to say that this represents the most advanced interpretation of Article 15(1) and non-discrimination that has come out of the Supreme Court thus far.

 Chandrachud J's judgment then goes on to examine Article 19(1)(a), focusing on how Section 377 inhibits the sexual privacy of the LGBTQ+ community, by forcing them into the closet (paragraph 61). He is careful to notice, perhaps, the only shortcoming of the Delhi High Court judgment, which was to restrict the right to 'private spaces'. Like his judgment in *Puttaswamy*, Chandrachud J once again critiques the facile public/private binary and notes, '*The right to sexual privacy, founded on the right to autonomy of a free individual, must capture the right of persons of the community to navigate public places on their own terms, free from state interference*' (paragraph 62). He goes on to discuss the rights to privacy and autonomy (paragraph 65), holds that

Article 21 also protects a right to intimacy (paragraph 67) and includes a detailed discussion on how Section 377 inhibits the right to health (including the right to mental health) (Part G). There is also an extended discussion of the limits of criminal law, which concludes with the now-familiar observation that *harm to others* is the only adequate ground for criminalization (paragraph 137).

D. *Justice Malhotra and a Truer Vision of Equality*

Justice Malhotra penned a brief, concurring judgment, which discussed Articles 14, 15, 19(1)(a) and 21 in turn. Her judgment, however, takes immutability as the basis for the 14/15 violation. In her view, Section 377 violates Article 14 because:

> [It] creates an artificial dichotomy. The natural or innate sexual orientation of a person cannot be a ground for discrimination. Where a legislation discriminates on the basis of an intrinsic and core trait of an individual, it cannot form a reasonable classification based on an intelligible differentia [paragraph 13].

In my analysis of the Chief Justice's opinion, I have noted that this view is controversial. Here, however, I want to focus on something else: the second sentence. Malhotra J argues that where a legislation discriminates on the basis of an 'intrinsic or core trait', it ipso facto fails Article 14—that is, it cannot be counted as a reasonable classification. However, there is nothing inherent about such discrimination that makes it an 'unintelligible differentia' or precludes it from having some 'rational nexus' with a possible goal. Consequently, Malhotra J actually advances a more radical reading. She argues that the very concept of equality under Article 14 *rules out certain kinds of classifications at the threshold*. In her view, legislation based on an 'intrinsic or core trait' fails that threshold inquiry. I would put it slightly differently:

Legislation based on a core trait (related to personal autonomy), a trait that has been a historical or present site of systemic discrimination, is ruled out under Article 14. This is because, for the reasons given above, I believe that the language of 'intrinsic' or 'immutable' characteristics is a dangerous road to go down. That, however, is a minor point of difference. What is crucial is that Malhotra J's reasoning—in its own way, as Chandrachud J's in his way—opens up the transformative potential of Article 14 and 15(1).

Malhotra J's argument is important for another reason. In *Dipak Sibal*, the Supreme Court held that in addition to intelligible differentia and rational nexus, Article 14 also required a 'legitimate State purpose'. However, neither *Dipak Sibal* nor any subsequent case clarified what State purposes may be illegitimate. In Malhotra J's opinion, we now have an answer: Whatever the differentia, and whatever the nexus, the State is not permitted, under Article 14, to disadvantage groups on the basis of an 'intrinsic or core' trait.

E. *Odds and Ends*

Malhotra J.'s transformative understanding of Article 14 is the best point for us to segue into some of the overarching themes of the judgment. Why is it that discriminating on the basis of an 'intrinsic or core' trait is ruled out by the constitutional vision of equality? Two themes—present in all four judgments—answer the question: constitutional morality and transformative constitutionalism. The Chief Justice notes, for example:

> Any attempt to push and shove a homogeneous, uniform, consistent and a standardised philosophy throughout the society would violate the principle of constitutional morality. Devotion and fidelity to constitutional morality must not be equated with the popular sentiment prevalent at a particular point of time [paragraph 116].

Justice Nariman observes:

> It must not be forgotten that Section 377 was the product of the Victorian era, with its attendant puritanical moral values. Victorian morality must give way to constitutional morality as has been recognized in many of our judgments. Constitutional morality is the soul of the Constitution, which is to be found in the Preamble of the Constitution, which declares its ideals and aspirations, and is also to be found in Part III of the Constitution, particularly with respect to those provisions which assure the dignity of the individual [paragraph 78].

And Chandrachud J:

> The Constitution envisaged a transformation in the order of relations not just between the state and the individual, but also between individuals: in a constitutional order characterized by the Rule of Law, the constitutional commitment to egalitarianism and an anti-discriminatory ethos permeates and infuses these relations [paragraph 52].

The wheel has turned a full circle. It was the Delhi High Court, in *Naz Foundation* (2009), which first introduced all of us to the grammar of 'constitutional morality' and linked it to the Objectives Resolution, and the qualities of inclusiveness and pluralism at the heart of the Constitution. And, nine years later, this vision of constitutional morality lies at the heart of the decriminalization of same-sex relations. The reason Malhotra J is correct when she holds that legislation discriminating on the basis of 'intrinsic or core' traits is ipso facto violative of equality is because equality—viewed through the lens of constitutional morality—is *defined* by the values of pluralism and inclusiveness: different forms of life and different ways of being are guaranteed equal treatment, equal concern and equal respect under the transformative Indian Constitution.

The Road Ahead

What lies ahead? This was, after all, a limited case: It was a constitutional challenge to Section 377 of the IPC. But as the judges themselves acknowledge, there is much work to be done ahead. As the Chief Justice notes in his judgment:

> Equality does not only imply recognition of individual dignity but also includes within its sphere ensuring of equal opportunity to advance and develop their human potential and social, economic and legal interests of every individual and the process of transformative constitutionalism is dedicated to this purpose [paragraph 104].

Chandrachud J, likewise, notes, in his conclusion, that *'members of the LGBT community are entitled, as all other citizens, to the full range of constitutional rights including the liberties protected by the Constitution'.* This clearly signals a future beyond mere decriminalization. It indicates civil rights, a guarantee against horizontal discrimination in the domains of housing, education and access to services (under Article 15(2)), a potential right to affirmative action (on the lines of the *NALSA vs Union of India*) and, of course—eventually—equal marriage, if demanded. How rocky the road will be towards full and equal moral membership, of course, remains to be seen.

What of other domains? The judgments of Chandrachud and Malhotra JJ, as I have argued above, open new windows for understanding and interpreting Articles 14 and 15(1). Will we see them play out in the future? Will Chandrachud J's observations about the limits of criminal law have an impact on litigations concerning bans upon dietary preferences? Will the salutary observations about transformative constitutionalism and the value of the individual percolate into other cases concerning State power and individual rights? In the coming months and years, these questions will be answered.

For today, it can be said: Five years ago, the Supreme Court committed a grievous error in *Koushal vs Naz Foundation*. Today—6 September 2018—the court has atoned. *'Civilization,'* observes Chandrachud J, *'can be brutal.'* That brutality was felt on 11 December 2013, and in the days and months that followed. But today is about the Constitution, and today is about emancipation and liberation.

Navtej Johar vs Union of India is a judgment worthy of our transformative Constitution.

[**Disclaimer**: The author was one of the lawyers representing Voices against 377, a coalition of organizations challenging Section 377 before the court.]

3

The Sabarimala Judgment—III: Justice Chandrachud and Radical Equality[24]

(29 September 2018)

JUSTICE INDU MALHOTRA'S DISSENTING opinion [in the *Sabarimala* case][25] sets up a crucial constitutional question: How

---

24 The excerpted post is the third in a series of four blog posts about the Supreme Court's judgment striking down the ban on menstruating-age women from accessing the Sabarimala temple in Kerala. The court split 4-1, with Chief Justice Dipak Misra (along with Khanwilkar J), Nariman J and Chandrachud J writing separate majority opinions, and Justice Indu Malhotra writing a dissenting opinion, questioning both the *locus* of the petitioners, as well as the propriety of judicial intervention in religious group practices. Because of constraints of space, I have only excerpted the analysis of Chandrachud J's concurring opinion, as his analysis broke substantive new ground. Interested readers can consult the other posts on the blog.

    At the time of writing, the legal status of the *Sabarimala* judgment was in limbo, with a nine-judge bench due to reconsider some of the issues involved. The dubious circumstances under which this came about are briefly discussed in the final part of this book.

25 'The Sabarimala Judgment – II: Justice Malhotra, Group Autonomy, and Cultural Dissent', Indian Constitutional Law and Philosophy, 29 September 2018, https://indconlawphil.wordpress.com/2018/09/29/

do you reconcile the Constitution's commitment to pluralism—which entails respect for group autonomy—with the claims of equality and non-discrimination addressed from *within* those groups? It is this question that is at the heart of Justice Chandrachud's concurring opinion.[26]

Chandrachud J sets up the issue in the introductory part of his judgment, where he observes that the Indian Constitution is transformative in two distinct ways. *First*, in setting up the governing institutions of an independent republic, transitioning from colonial rule, but *also* 'placing those who were denuded of their human rights before the advent of the Constitution—whether in the veneer of caste, patriarchy or otherwise—… in control of their own destinies by the assurance of the equal protection of law' (paragraph 2). The reference to caste and patriarchy is important, because it acknowledges that discrimination is not limited to State action, or even to hostile *individual* action, but that it also flows from *institutional design*. Caste and patriarchy are neither 'State' nor an agglomeration of individual acts, where you can attribute discriminatory agency to identifiable individuals. They are *social institutions*.

And because they are social institutions, their impact on the lives of the people that they touch is not merely a private matter. In paragraph 5, therefore, Chandrachud J observes:

> Essentially, the significance of this case lies in the issues which it poses to the adjudicatory role of this Court in defining the boundaries of religion in a dialogue about our public spaces [paragraph 5].

---

the-sabarimala-judgment-ii-justice-malhotra-group-autonomy-and-cultural-dissent/
26 *Indian Young Lawyers Association vs State of Kerala*, (2019) 11 SCC 1.

The use of the word 'public spaces' is crucial, especially when you juxtapose it with Malhotra J's dissenting opinion, which we discussed previously. Recall that for Malhotra J, there was a distinction between a 'social evil' such as *Sati*—where a court could potentially intervene—and a case such as *Sabarimala*, where the challenge was based on irrationality or immorality. It is this public/private binary—social evil (public) and bare immorality (private)—that Chandrachud J rejects, by *framing* the issue as about access to public spaces.

It is within this framework that Chandrachud J begins his substantive analysis.

Essential Religious Practices (ERP)

After surveying the body of precedent concerning the ERP test—and also noting the shift from 'essentially religious' to 'essential religious'—Chandrachud J's judgment has a section titled 'The Engagement of Essential Religious Practices with Constitutional Values'. At the threshold, Chandrachud J finds that the respondents have failed to establish that the exclusion of women from Sabarimala is either an obligatory part of religion or has been consistently practised over the years. The evidence, at best, demonstrates the celibate nature of Lord Ayappa, but this in itself does not establish that exclusion of women is part of ERP (paragraph 51).

However, apart from the traditional and straightforward analysis of whether or not a religious claim amounts to an essential religious practice, Chandrachud J also advances an important alternative argument—that 'the test of essentiality is infused with … necessary limitations' (paragraph 50), which are grounded in constitutional morality and the constitutional values of dignity and freedom. So, in paragraph 55, Chandrachud J notes:

> The Respondents submitted that the deity at Sabarimala is in the form of a Naishtika Brahmacharya: Lord Ayyappa is celibate. It

was submitted that since celibacy is the foremost requirement for all the followers, women between the ages of ten and fifty must not be allowed in Sabarimala. There is an assumption here, which cannot stand constitutional scrutiny. The assumption in such a claim is that a deviation from the celibacy and austerity observed by the followers would be caused by the presence of women. Such a claim cannot be sustained as a constitutionally sustainable argument. *Its effect is to impose the burden of a man's celibacy on a woman and construct her as a cause for deviation from celibacy.* This is then employed to deny access to spaces to which women are equally entitled. *To suggest that women cannot keep the Vratham is to stigmatize them and stereotype them as being weak and lesser human beings.* A constitutional court such as this one, must refuse to recognize such claims [paragraph 55]. [Emphasis mine]

As a piece of discrimination law reasoning, this is, of course, impeccable. But there is something more at work here, which I want to highlight. Chandrachud J's observation that the effect of the celibacy argument 'is to impose the burden of a man's celibacy on a woman' is the crucial link between the denial of the right to worship (which Malhotra J, in her dissent, regards as a private, internal matter to religion) and the *public* aspect of this case. What Chandrachud J recognizes is that the *justification* offered to exclude women is an integral part of a far broader discourse that is founded on the exclusion and subordination of women in social and community life. This becomes clear two paragraphs down, where he discusses the stigma around menstruation (another justification that was advanced by the respondents), and observes:

> The stigma around menstruation has been built up around traditional beliefs in the impurity of menstruating women. They have no place in a constitutional order. These beliefs have been

used to shackle women, to deny them equal entitlements and subject them to the dictates of a patriarchal order [paragraph 57].

The phrase 'patriarchal order' is an important one. It indicates that the exclusion of women from Sabarimala is not simply—as Malhotra J would have it—a unique and particular feature of that specific religious community and something that can be isolated from the broader world around it. Rather, the exclusion of women from Sabarimala on the grounds of celibacy and menstruation is one among countless ways in which patriarchy—as a *social institution*—works to keep women in a position of subordination.

Justice Malhotra and Justice Chandrachud, therefore, come at the issue from opposite angles. What Malhotra J sees as a claim requiring that religion be subordinated to the diktats of morality, Chandrachud J understands as a challenge to one manifestation of patriarchal subordination itself. According to Chandrachud J, you cannot divide social life into different silos and say that discrimination and subordination are fine as long as they stay within a defined silo. At least as far as religion and society are concerned, in the context of India, the silos are forever merged. As Alladi Krishnaswamy Iyer, a prominent member of the Indian constituent assembly, said in the Constitutional Drafting Committee, 'There is no religious question that is not also a social question.'

It perhaps needs to be noted that history is on Justice Chandrachud's side. In India, temple-entry movements have a long history, and have always been *framed* in the language of civil rights and access to *public spaces*. This was especially true of the great caste-based temple-entry movements of the 1920s and the 1930s (which are discussed later in the judgment). This substantiates the argument that, in India, the 'thick' character of religious life implies that you cannot simply wall it off from the rest of social life. Consequently, discrimination *within* religion is hardly an isolated event, such as—for example—the non-appointment of a woman to a clerical post in an American church, which was upheld by that Supreme Court. Rather, at the heart of Chandrachud J's judgment is the understanding that discrimination within religion both reinforces and is reinforced by discrimination in broader social life.

Untouchability

This understanding is reinforced in what is undoubtedly the boldest and most radical part of Chandrachud J's judgment. An argument was made by the intervenors that the exclusion of women from Sabarimala amounts to 'untouchability' within the meaning of Article 17. The Chief Justice and Nariman J do not address this argument, and Malhotra J rejects it on the ground that 'untouchability' under the Indian Constitution is limited to caste-based untouchability.

Chandrachud J disagrees. After a detailed survey of the Constituent Assembly Debates (which we have discussed previously on this blog), he correctly observes that there was no consensus in the constituent assembly over the precise scope and ambit of the phrase. But when you place the moment of constitutional framing within broader history, you have an answer:

> The answers lie in the struggle for social emancipation and justice which was the defining symbol of the age, together with the movement for attaining political freedom but in a radical transformation of society as well [paragraph 73].

And:

> Reading Dr Ambedkar compels us to look at the other side of the independence movement. Besides the struggle for independence from the British rule, there was another struggle going on since centuries and which still continues. That struggle has been for *social emancipation*. It has been the struggle for the replacement

of an *unequal social order*. It has been a fight for undoing historical injustices and for righting fundamental wrongs with fundamental rights. The Constitution of India is the end product of both these struggles. It is the foundational document, which in text and spirit, aims at social transformation namely, the creation and preservation of an equal social order. The Constitution represents the aspirations of those, who were denied the basic ingredients of a dignified existence [paragraph 74]. *[Emphasis mine]*

This is reminiscent of the constitutional historian Granville Austin's famous line, that the fundamental rights chapter was framed amid a history of fundamental wrongs. In these paragraphs, Justice Chandrachud argues that the meaning of fundamental rights ought to be determined by asking the following question: *What was the legacy of injustice that the Constitution sought to acknowledge and then transform?* That legacy was defined by social hierarchies and social subordination. At its most virulent form, this took the shape of caste untouchability. However, caste was not the only axis for exclusion from, and subordination within, the social order. There were others, prime among which was, of course, sex. Consequently, as Justice Chandrachud observes:

> The incorporation of Article 17 into the Constitution is symbolic of valuing the centuries-old struggle of social reformers and revolutionaries. It is a move by the Constitution makers to find catharsis in the face of historic horrors. It is an attempt to make reparations to those, whose identity was subjugated by society [paragraph 75].

It is, of course, important not to overstate the case. Not every form of discrimination or prejudice can fall within Article 17. The framers did, after all, use the specific word 'untouchability', limiting the sweep of the Article only to the most horrific kind of discrimination.

Chandrachud J is aware of this, because he then goes on to justify *why* exclusion based on menstruation falls within Article 17: 'The caste system represents a hierarchical order of purity and pollution enforced by social compulsion. Purity and pollution constitute the core of caste [paragraph 76].'

And of course, it is purity and pollution that are at the heart of excluding menstruating women—not just from temples but, as regularly happens in our country, from all forms of human contact during the menstrual period. Chandrachud J's important insight, therefore, is this: The social exclusion of a set of people (who are, in any event, historically subjugated), grounded in ideas about purity and pollution, amounts to a manifestation of the kind of 'untouchability' that the Constitution seeks to proscribe. This does not mean, of course, that it is *not* caste-based untouchability that is at the heart of Article 17. Nor does it seek to dilute the severity of that institution, or the Constitution's commitment to wipe it out. What it does acknowledge, however, is that the same logic that is at the foundation of caste-based untouchability *also* takes other forms and other manifestations. These manifestations may not be at the *core* of Article 17, but they do deserve its protection:

> Article 17 is a powerful guarantee against exclusion. As an expression of the anti-exclusion principle, it cannot be read to exclude women against whom social exclusion of the worst kind has been practiced and legitimized on notions of purity and pollution. [paragraph 75]

And therefore:

> The caste system has been powered by specific forms of subjugation of women. The notion of 'purity and pollution' stigmatizes the menstruation of women in Indian society. In the ancient religious texts and customs, menstruating women have been considered as polluting the surroundings. Irrespective of the status of a woman,

menstruation has been equated with impurity, and the idea of impurity is then used to justify their exclusion from key social activities [paragraph 81]. *[Internal footnotes omitted]*

In an important way, this links back to the previous argument about essential religious practices. It is obviously absurd to compare the exclusion of women (and mostly upper-caste women at that) from a temple with 'untouchability' as we understand it. But that is something that Chandrachud J very consciously does not do. What he *does* do is link the underlying *basis* of the exclusion in Sabarimala with something that goes far beyond and permeates every layer of society. This is why he specifies that the idea of impurity justifies exclusion from 'key social activities'. In other words, it is not about exclusion from worship, but how that exclusion both reinforces and is reinforced by an existing and overarching set of discriminatory institutions and systems.

Exit, Pursued by a Bear: Narasu Appa Mali

There is one more important thing that Chandrachud J does in his concurrence. Noting that the exclusion of women has also been justified on the basis of 'custom', he examines—and overrules—the *Narasu Appa Mali* judgment on the specific point that customs are not subject to fundamental rights.

In terms of outcomes, this is not new. In *Madhu Kishwar vs State of Bihar*, the Supreme Court has already held that customs are subject to fundamental rights. However, that case did not examine *Narasu*. Here, Chandrachud J does, and specifically finds that its reasoning is flawed.

This is very important, because *Narasu* also held that 'personal law'—that is, uncodified religious law—was outside the scope of a fundamental rights review. The reasoning for that was the same, and so, also stands discredited. As Chandrachud J points out, the reasoning given by the Bombay High Court in *Narasu*—that, for example, the existence of Article 17 shows that where the framers intended to proscribe an aspect of personal law, they specifically mentioned it in the Constitution—does not hold water. More importantly, however, is the affirmative case that Chandrachud J advances:

> Custom, usages and personal law have a significant impact on the civil status of individuals. Those activities that are *inherently connected with the civil status* of individuals cannot be granted constitutional immunity merely because they may have some associational features which have a religious nature. To immunize them from constitutional scrutiny is to deny the primacy of the Constitution [paragraph 99]. *[Emphasis mine]*

In other words, there cannot be islands of norms and prescriptions that are granted constitutional immunity. As with the ERP and the untouchability argument, the rationale is the same: The individual is the basic unit of the Constitution, and norms, practices, prescriptions, rules, commands and whatever else that have the potential to impair individual dignity or block access to basic goods in society must pass constitutional scrutiny (paragraph 100).

And indeed, Chandrachud J goes one step further with this thought, noting that the ERP test itself ought—in future—give way to a test that asks not whether a practice is 'essential' (which is, after all, a question that the believers, and not the court, should answer), but whether the impugned practice is socially exclusionary and denies individuals access to the basic goods required for living a dignified life.

[**Disclaimer**: This part of the judgment cites an article of mine, and I will readily admit to being biased in favour of the anti-exclusion argument.]

Conclusion

In her dissenting opinion in this judgment, Malhotra J raises an important question: How do we reconcile the Constitution's commitment to pluralism with judicial intervention in internal religious affairs? We have now seen how Chandrachud J has answered it: The commitment to pluralism and respect for group autonomy must be understood *within* a constitutional framework that places individual freedom and dignity at its heart. The Constitution recognizes group autonomy because, often, group life promotes individual freedom and dignity. Community, after all, is crucial to self-development. But groups can *also* restrict freedom and dignity, and it is in those circumstances that a court must step in and balance the competing claims.

In *Sabarimala*, Chandrachud J attempts to demonstrate how, in fact, the proscription in question *does* restrict freedom and dignity, and therefore, should be judicially invalidated. He does so by telescoping outwards from the singular event itself (exclusion from worship in one temple) and showing how this single event of exclusion is *nested in an entire social and institutional order that is characterized by hierarchy, subordination and exclusion*. We may call this patriarchy, or we may call this something else, but the argument is clear—it's not about worship at Sabarimala (which is what Malhotra J limits it to, and therefore classifies it as simply seeking morality or rationality), but about what exclusion from worship *means* in a broader context. To take an example, think of a whites-only signboard outside a restaurant in Apartheid South Africa. The point is not that *one* private restaurant owner has decided to exclude blacks from his private property. The point, rather, is how that signboard is an integral element of the *practice* and *institution* of apartheid. The crucial insight that Chandrachud J brings in his judgment is the recognition of the institutional character of discrimination and inequality, and how that must be constitutionally combated. As he notes towards the end:

> In the dialogue between constitutional freedoms, rights are not isolated silos. In infusing each other with substantive content, they provide a cohesion and unity which militates against practices that depart from the values that underlie the

Constitution—justice, liberty, equality and fraternity. Substantive notions of equality require the recognition of and remedies for historical discrimination which has pervaded certain identities. Such a notion focuses on not only distributive questions, but on the structures of oppression and domination which exclude these identities from participation in an equal life. An indispensable facet of an equal life, is the equal participation of women in all spheres of social activity [paragraph 117].

It is this that makes it a transformative judgment.

4

'Take Me as I Am—Subject to Aadhaar-Based Biometric Authentication': An Overview of the Aadhaar Judgment[27]

(26 September 2018)

THE THREE OPINIONS IN today's Aadhaar judgment run to a total of 1,448 pages.[28] It will require more than a single post to examine the judgment in its entirety. Over the coming days, therefore,

---

27 The constitutional challenge to Aadhaar was a six-year battle that took place between 2012 and 2018, and involved a number of detours such as the right to privacy judgment, a separate judgment on the linking of Aadhaar with PAN cards (which had to be argued *without* recourse to the right to privacy, as that was still pending at the time), and numerous ever-changing interim orders. The case was finally heard over five months between January and May 2018 (making it the second-longest case to be argued in Indian constitutional history, after *Kesavananda Bharati*). Judgment was delivered in September 2018, with a majority of the court partially upholding and partially striking down aspects of the Aadhaar scheme. Because of the complexity and sheer number of the issues, the ICLP blog analysed the judgment(s) over several posts, which interested readers can look up. For reasons of space, here I excerpt the analysis of the majority judgment and the dissent, taken as a whole.
28 *Justice K.S. Puttaswamy vs Union of India (II)*, (2019) 1 SCC 1.

I will do so in parts. In this first essay, I will provide an overview of the majority judgment (authored by Justice Sikri, with whom the Chief Justice and Khanwilkar J concurred). I will focus on the findings of the court and the reasoning that led to those findings. A critique of the reasoning (such as it is) shall be undertaken in later posts.[29]

Proportionality: The Legal Standard for Testing Infringements of Rights

The constitutional challenge to the Aadhaar programme—and to the provisions of the Aadhaar Act, 2016—was mounted primarily on the touchstone of proportionality. Previous judgments have left the contours of the standard somewhat vague, and, therefore, the issue was fiercely contested during the course of the hearings. The majority judgment attempts to provide some clarity on this point. It refers to the different shades of proportionality employed in different jurisdictions (unfortunately with hardly any reference to case law) and then adopts (without any further explanation) the articulation of proportionality that is provided by David Bilchitz, a South African constitutional law scholar. In addition to the requirement that there must exist a law (with adequate procedural safeguards), proportionality requires the following four prongs. *First*, a legitimate State aim; *secondly*, a rational nexus between the impugned measures and the aim; *thirdly*, the impugned measure as the *least restrictive* method of achieving the aim (the 'necessity' prong); and *fourthly*, a balance between the extent to which rights are infringed and the overall public benefit (the 'strict proportionality' prong). It was the third limb—necessity—which was most contested, and the majority borrows Bilchitz's formulation, restating it thus:

---

29 'The Aadhaar Judgment: A Round-Up', Indian Constitutional Law and Philosophy, 5 October 2018, https://indconlawphil.wordpress.com/2018/10/05/the-aadhaar-judgment-a-round-up/

First, a range of possible alternatives to the measure employed by the Government must be identified. Secondly, the effectiveness of these measures must be determined individually; the test here is not whether each respective measure realises the governmental objective to the same extent, but rather whether it realises it in a 'real and substantial manner'. Thirdly, the impact of the respective measures on the right at stake must be determined. Finally, an overall judgment must be made as to whether in light of the findings of the previous steps, there exists an alternative which is preferable [paragraph 124].

The majority then holds that this is consistent with the meaning of proportionality, as articulated in the *Puttaswamy* judgment, and also in the court's prior judgments dealing with the issue.

In the following posts, we will discuss the majority's failure to apply this standard to its own substantive analysis. For now, however, as a constitutional matter, it is important to note that this does, at least, bring a measure of clarity to the standard that Indian courts must apply when adjudicating rights infringements on the grounds of proportionality (or 'reasonableness', which is the word found in our Constitution). It is important, especially for future challenges in similar (but non-overlapping) contexts, such as the forthcoming DNA Profiling Bill.

'Uniqueness': The Overarching Factual Assumption

To break down the majority's analysis on the multiple issues that were up for adjudication, I suggest the following map towards navigating the judgment: Under each issue, there are a number of factual assumptions that underly the analysis. Upon these factual assumptions, the majority opinion then builds its legal argument, testing the constitutionality of the Aadhaar programme (or the statutory provision in question) against the factual background.

Underlying *all* the different legal findings is one overarching factual assumption: The majority believes that biometric authentication provides us with a *unique identification*. We see this in the opening quotation—'*It is better to be unique than the best. Because, being the best makes you the number one, but being unique makes you the only one*'—which, I have since been informed, is a WhatsApp forward. Be that as it may. In paragraph 55—under the heading 'Summing Up the Scheme'—the court observes:

> The whole architecture of Aadhaar is devised to give *unique identity* to the citizens of this country. No doubt, a person can have various documents on the basis of which that individual can establish her identify. It may be in the form of a passport, Permanent Account Number (PAN) card, ration card and so on. For the purpose of enrolment itself number of documents are prescribed, which an individual can produce on the basis of which Aadhaar card can be issued. Thus, such documents, in a way, are also proof of identity. *However, there is a fundamental difference between the Aadhaar card as a mean* [sic] *of identity and other documents through which identity can be established.* Enrolment for Aadhaar card also requires giving of demographic information as well as biometric information which is in the form of iris and fingerprints. *This process eliminates any chance of duplication …*
>
> Wherever there would be a second attempt for enrolling for Aadhaar and for this purpose same person gives his biometric information, it would immediately get matched with the same biometric information already in the system and the second request would stand rejected. It is for this reason the Aadhaar card is known as Unique Identification (UID). *Such an identity is unparalleled* [paragraph 55]. *[Emphasis mine]*

Note carefully the language here. It is not that biometric authentication is *more* accurate or simply *better* than other forms of identification.

Rather, it is perfect: It is unique, it 'eliminates' *any* chance of duplication and is 'unparalleled'. As I shall go on to show, this factual assumption—of 'unparalleled' uniqueness—is repeated several times in the judgment and forms the backbone of the majority's reasoning.

It is also important to note—without further comment—that this issue was contested (and not, as the majority makes it out to be, a given). The issue of false positives and false negatives was raised, and the existence of duplicates was demonstrated as well (as a perusal of the oral record will show).

This factual assumption of uniqueness ties in with the majority's view that Aadhaar is a document of 'empowerment'. In the next paragraph, the majority notes that the uniqueness of the ID ensures both that subsidies are delivered in a targeted manner and also that *'when an individual knows that no other person can clone her, it assumes greater significance'* (paragraph 56). This, in turn, assumes significance in the majority's assessment of the constitutional validity of Section 7, which makes Aadhaar mandatory for availing subsidies.

Surveillance

The majority begins its first substantive analysis of the constitutional challenge on Page 219 of its judgment (paragraph 129). This is on the issue of surveillance and data protection (which, for some reason, are discussed together). At the outset, it is important to draw a distinction between two kinds of arguments that could be used to uphold the Aadhaar programme against a surveillance-based challenge. The first could be to agree that there *is* surveillance, but that it is constitutionally justified in this case. The second is to uphold the programme on the grounds that there is *no* constitutionally significant surveillance. Interestingly, the majority chooses to follow the second path—that this is not a judgment that defends and upholds surveillance, but one that avoids the *legal* question by making a *factual* finding that the Aadhaar project is incapable of being turned into a surveillance engine.

Surveillance: Factual Assumptions

Indeed, the majority makes multiple factual findings on this score. First, it holds that the chain of authority that is responsible for collecting Aadhaar data is 'secure' (paragraph 151) (interestingly, the majority does not appear to address Shyam Divan's point that 49,000 such private operators were blacklisted by the UIDAI itself). Secondly, it holds that 'minimal data' is collected (only iris and fingerprints), that the UIDAI is purpose-blind and—most importantly—that 'merging of silos is prohibited' (paragraph 152) (there is no observation with respect to the demonstrated 'merging of silos' in the State Resident Data Hubs). It goes on to hold that during authentication, 'the nature of the transaction' is not known (paragraph 152) and that there can be no 'storage and replay of biometrics' (paragraph 152). The majority then notes: '[W]e are of the view that it is very difficult to create [a] profile of a person simply on the basis of biometric and demographic information stored in CIDR [paragraph 153].'

This is very important because of two reasons. The first is, of course, that this is a sweeping factual assertion and the correctness of the majority opinion stands or falls with the validity of this (and many other) factual assumptions. But equally importantly, it also lays down a *legal limit*—that is, profiling *is* surveillance and *is* constitutionally suspect. This has an impact both on future constitutional challenges involving profiling and on future cases involving the use of Aadhaar itself.

Data Protection

The majority then discusses whether the Aadhaar programme is compatible with the principles of data protection. An analysis of this section of the judgment is somewhat difficult, because the majority quotes extensively from European and American precedent, refuses to lay down any standard and then goes on to analyse the provisions of the Aadhaar Act anyway—but on *what* touchstone, it is unclear (this is a problem that plagues the majority judgment at more than one place). In any case, the majority holds that Aadhaar is compatible with 'data minimization' (by limiting itself to certain basic demographic and biometric information). This is potentially important for future challenges where the principle of data minimization is evidently not complied with.

However, the majority also finds that on five counts, the provisions are not compatible with the principles of data protection. The first is that of metadata storage. The majority holds that Regulation 26—which deals with the storage of metadata—*must be read down to include only 'process metadata'* (i.e., limited to the time of authentication, the requesting entity and the yes/no answer), and nothing further (paragraph 202) (later in the judgment, the majority refers to this as 'metabase'). Secondly, the majority also holds that the seven-year storage period is excessive, and limits it to *six months* (paragraph 205). Thirdly, the majority holds that Section 33 of the Aadhaar Act—which allows for an individual's information to be shared on the orders of a district judge—must include a right to a hearing. Fourthly, it holds that Section 33(2)—which allows for sharing of information on 'national security grounds', a decision to be made by a joint secretary—is unconstitutional (however, this is only on procedural grounds and can be rectified if a judicial member is added [paragraph 349]). And fifthly, Section 57 of the Aadhaar Act—which allows private parties to mandate Aadhaar—is unconstitutional to that extent (paragraph 219).

Privacy, Section 7 and All That

This section of the judgment is somewhat difficult to analyse, because the majority appears to conflate a number of separate and distinct arguments into one unwieldy hotchpotch: privacy, dignity, Section 7 (i.e., compulsory authentication for the availing of subsidies), Article 14-based arguments on exclusion and Article 21-based arguments on exclusion. Let us, however, make an attempt.

After setting out the parties' submissions, the majority observes that '*only those matters over which there would be a reasonable expectation of privacy are protected by Article 21*' (paragraph 260). I will pause here to note that it is a significant doctrinal error. The majority relies upon *Puttaswamy* for this proposition, but *Puttaswamy* categorically rejected the 'reasonable expectation of privacy' standard.

In any case, the majority then applies the proportionality standard to the challenge. It takes the 'legitimate State aim' as one of ensuring targeted delivery of subsidies to 'deserving beneficiaries' through accurate identification. Next, at the stage of ascertaining the rational nexus between the measure and the goal, the majority, crucially, *falls back upon its overarching factual assumption of uniqueness*:

> [G]iving unique identity of each resident of the country is a special feature of this scheme, more so, when it comes with the feature stated above, namely, no person can have more than one Aadhaar number; Aadhaar number given to a particular person cannot be reassigned again to any individual even if that is cancelled and there is hardly any possibility to have fake identity [paragraph 277].

And this uniqueness is important because:

> We have seen rampant corruption at various levels in implementation of benevolent and welfare schemes meant for different classes of persons. It has resulted in depriving the actual beneficiaries to receive those subsidies, benefits and services which get frittered away though on papers, it is shown that they are received by the persons for whom they are meant. There have been cases of duplicate and bogus ration cards, BPL cards, LPG connections etc. Some persons with multiple identities getting those benefits manifold. *Aadhaar scheme has been successful, to a great extent, in curbing the aforesaid malpractices* [paragraph 278]. *[Emphasis mine]*

This, then, forms the basis of the 'rational nexus' prong. However, there is something particularly disingenuous about the factual assumption smuggled in here. That becomes clear when you tack back a few hundred paragraphs, all the way back to paragraph 72, which is under an innocuous heading titled 'Introductory Remarks'. Here, the majority notes that the Union of India's claims of savings have been contested by the petitioners. It then makes the following observation:

> But the argument based on alleged inaccurate claims of savings by the Authority/Union of India in respect of certain programmes, like saving of USD 11 billion per annum due to the Aadhaar project, as well as savings in the implementation of the MGNREGA scheme, LPG subsidy, PDS savings need not detain us for long. Such rebuttals raised by the petitioners may have relevance insofar as working of the Act is concerned. That by itself cannot be a ground to invalidate the statute [paragraph 72].

What is important to note is this: In its overarching factual assumption about uniqueness, the majority ignores the contrary factual arguments. However, in its factual assumptions about whether Section 7 meets the proportionality standard, the majority does one better—it acknowledges that there exist contrary factual arguments, but then refuses to consider them altogether!

In fact, how much rests on this factual assumption is made clear when the majority considers the third prong of the proportionality standard—that of 'necessity'. Here, the majority says:

> Insofar as third component is concerned, most of it stands answered while in the discussion that has ensued in respect of component No. 1 and 2. The manner in which malpractices have been committed in the past leaves us to hold that apart from *the system of unique identity in Aadhaar and authentication of the real beneficiaries*, there is no alternative measure with lesser degree of

limitation which can achieve the same purpose. In fact, on repeated query by this Court, even the petitioners could not suggest any such method [paragraph 280].

What you have here, therefore, is a classic example of the assumed factual premise transforming itself into the conclusion. *Because* Aadhaar is unique (Factual Assumption No. 1) and *because* it is working to plug leakages with respect to targeting beneficiaries (Factual Assumption No. 2), *therefore* it is necessary, and the least restrictive alternative. On the first assumption, the contrary evidence is ignored, and on the second, its existence is acknowledged but is deemed irrelevant.

It should also be noted—for the record—that the court's statement that the 'petitioners could not suggest any [alternative] method' is—to put it bluntly—quite simply false. 'Alternative methods'—including smart cards—were argued in open court (a look at the oral record will confirm this) and they form part of both the written submissions as well as the rejoinder submissions of K.V. Viswanathan.

This then leads the court to the final—'balancing'—prong of proportionality. The court decides to frame this in an interesting way. On the one hand, it observes, is the individual right to privacy. On the other hand, are the rights to food, health, shelter, etc.:

> Axiomatically both the rights are founded on human dignity. At the same time, in the given context, two facets are in conflict with each other. The question here would be, when a person seeks to get the benefits of welfare schemes to which she is entitled to as a part of right to live life with dignity, whether her sacrifice to the right to privacy, is so invasive that it creates imbalance [paragraph 285]?

The court then repeats the 'reasonable expectation of privacy' standard to find that the infringement on individual privacy is 'minimal' (paragraph 295) (thus confusing 'minimal information' and 'minimal infringement') whereas, on the other hand, it says:

> As already pointed out above, the Aadhaar Act truly seeks to secure to the poor and deprived persons an opportunity to live their life and exercise their liberty. By ensuring targeted delivery through digital identification, it not only provides them a nationally recognized identity but also attempts to ensure the delivery of benefits, service and subsidies with the aid of public exchequer/Consolidated Fund of India. National Security Food Act, 2013 passed by the Parliament seeks to address the issue of food, security at the household level [paragraph 298].

It is, by now, probably tedious to point out that we have wheeled back to the two factual assumptions discussed above. Therefore:

> As against the above larger public interest, the invasion into the privacy rights of these beneficiaries is minimal. By no means it can be said that it has disproportionate effect on the right holder [paragraph 308].

I want to point out a rather important conceptual slip here. When the court first frames its 'balancing test'—see above—recall that it frames it as a clash between two rights: the right of an individual to privacy and her right to food, healthcare, etc. Towards the end, however, the court has shifted from the language of a clash of rights to that of a clash between 'rights' and 'public interest'. Why is this? The answer is very simple. If it remained a clash between two individual rights, there *would be no justification for Section 7 making Aadhaar mandatory.* The clash could just as easily be resolved by making it voluntary. The State cannot, after all, tell a person that she is being forced to give up her privacy so that she can exercise her right to food. That, conceptually, makes no sense. What does make sense is to say that the individual must give up her right to privacy in the 'larger public interest'. But when the argument ends, the court has returned to the language of clashing rights:

> Thus, even when two aspects of the fundamental rights of the same individual, which appear to be in conflict with each other ... we find that the Aadhaar Act has struck a fair balance between the right of privacy of the individual with right to life of the same individual as a beneficiary [paragraph 308].

These slips are not accidental. There is something particularly distasteful about saying openly to a person, 'Give up your right to privacy if you want food.' Even the majority in this case cannot bring itself to say this. So what it does is this sleight of hand, shifting between 'clash of rights' for rhetorical purchase and slipping in 'larger public interest', which actually does the heavy lifting of upholding Section 7.

The majority then comes to the specific argument of exclusion. Here, in paragraph 314, we find the following lines:

TO DICTATE FURTHER
Re.: Studies on exclusion
Re.: Finger prints of disabled, old persons etc. See other mode of identity[30]

I think that this should be treated with the same respect that the majority appears to have treated all of us, and will not analyse this any further. The only thing to note is that the majority takes on record the Attorney-General's submission that nobody will be denied food if authentication fails and that a circular had been

---

30 This error in the judgment was subsequently corrected, and the text filled in.

passed to this effect. That, according to the majority, *'takes care of the problem'* (paragraph 315).

It is, however, impossible not to note paragraph 317:

> In fairness to the petitioners, it is worth mentioning that they have referred to the research carried out by some individuals and even NGOs which have been relied upon to demonstrate that there are number of instances leading to the exclusion i.e. the benefits are allegedly denied on the ground of failure of authentication. The respondents have refuted such studies. *These become disputed question of facts*. It will be difficult to invalidate provisions of Parliamentary legislations on the basis of such material, more particularly, *when their credence has not been tested* [paragraph 317]. *[Emphasis mine]*

First, in 2018, after thirty years of PIL jurisprudence based on newspaper articles, this is an astonishing statement. But secondly, it is also important to note this, because in a previous part of the judgment, the majority relies extensively on a 'PowerPoint presentation' that was made in court by the chairperson of the UIDAI. It is a rather basic rule of trial that evidence submitted in court that is not on affidavit and has not been put through the rigours of cross-examination, is no evidence at all. But for the majority, 'disputed questions of fact' cannot be adjudicated upon only when they lead to inconvenient legal conclusions. This is classic constitutionalism of convenience.

One final point: The majority reads Section 7 narrowly to exclude benefits that are 'earned' such as pensions, and all initiatives that are not 'subsidies' such as school admissions (paragraph 322).

Other Provisions

The majority then examines some of the specific provisions of the Act. Section 57—as we have seen above—is struck down insofar as it allows private parties to make Aadhaar mandatory. There appears to be some confusion over the scope of this part of the ruling, with private players arguing that Parliament can authorize this through law. The judgment, however, is clear on this point: 'That portion of Section 57 of the Aadhaar Act which enables body corporate and individual to seek authentication is held to be unconstitutional.'

There is no case to be made, therefore, that Parliament can now allow this 'by law'.

On Section 47, however—which only allows the UIDAI to file an FIR for a breach of the law—we have this priceless gem:

> [W]e are of the opinion that it would be in the *fitness of things* if Section 47 is amended by allowing individual/victim whose right is violated, to file a complaint and initiate the proceedings. We hope that this aspect shall be addressed at the appropriate level and if considered fit, Section 47 would be suitably amended [paragraph 353]. *[Emphasis mine]*

Now, what on earth does this mean? Is Section 47 constitutional, or is it unconstitutional? What is 'the fitness of things'? Should a constitutional court be concerned with expressing the 'hope' that this aspect would be addressed 'if considered fit'?

Special Laws

The penultimate part of the judgment involves the analysis of making Aadhaar mandatory for bank accounts, phones, PAN cards and the payment of taxes. The analysis here follows the factual assumptions already outlined above, so I will not repeat them in detail. Suffice it to say that the court holds that Section 139AA of the Income Tax Act, 1961 is proportionate, since it helps prevent duplicate PANs and tax fraud, while bank linking and phone linking are unconstitutional, since in neither case has the State sufficiently justified what Aadhaar linking will achieve. In short, therefore, anyone who pays income tax must get Aadhaar. It is rather ironic to note, however, that the court comes down hard on the government for 'ritualistic incantation' of 'black money' in the case of banks, but that 'ritualistic incantation' of uniqueness and savings is what forms the heart of its decision to uphold Section 7.

Conclusion

The majority judgment is 568 pages long. For all that, however, as I have tried to show, its basis is a series of factual assumptions. These factual assumptions are so crucial to the judgment that—far more than any legal analysis or application of legal standards—the judgment has to stand or fall with them. But forget, for a moment, the question of whether those factual assumptions are correct. If there is one thing that characterizes this majority opinion on one of the most important constitutional questions of our generation (apart from the WhatsApp opening lines and 'TO BE DICTATED'), it is that on these foundational issues, the contrary arguments—far from being addressed adequately—have simply been ignored. That, perhaps, will be the enduring legacy of this judgment.

[**Disclaimer**: The author assisted K.V. Viswanathan, who represented one of the petitioners in this case.]

5

The Aadhaar Judgment: A Dissent for the Ages

(27 September 2018)

'Constitutional guarantees cannot be subject to the vicissitudes of technology.'
—Chandrachud J, dissenting (paragraph 269)

AS WE HAVE DISCUSSED, the majority judgment in the Aadhaar case is premised upon a series of factual assumptions, which are either unsubstantiated or lifted from a PowerPoint presentation given by the UIDAI chairperson in the court. The majority agrees, for instance, that profiling is bad and surveillance is unconstitutional—but finds, on *fact*, that the Aadhaar framework does not permit either. The majority agrees that data minimization is a constitutional principle, but finds, on *fact*, that Aadhaar does collect minimal data. And the majority agrees that the legal standard is that of proportionality, but finds that because of its 'uniqueness', biometric authentication successfully targets deserving beneficiaries and, therefore, is proportionate.

For this reason, while reading Justice Chandrachud's dissenting opinion, there is a sense that the two judgments disagree not only on legal standards (which they do), but also on something far more basic: They disagree about the very state of the world within which Aadhaar operates.

Why does this matter? It matters because judges are entitled to declare the law—and indeed bring it into being by declaring it—but facts have an independent existence. For example, one may take sides on whether the majority or Justice Chandrachud is correct in holding that Section 59 of the Aadhaar Act validates past action, while acknowledging that the majority—by virtue of being the majority—has laid down the law. However, if the majority and Justice Chandrachud disagree on the uniqueness of biometrics, or on the existence of exclusion, then, quite simply, one of them is right and the other is wrong. And if the majority is wrong on *facts*, serious questions must be asked about the sustainability of that judgment.

Overarching Assumption: The Uniqueness of Biometrics

As we saw, the factual foundation of the majority judgment is that biometrics are unique. This foundation is at the heart of the majority's decision to uphold Section 7, as well as the mandatory Aadhaar–PAN linkage. And it is with this foundational assumption that Chandrachud J takes issue. In paragraph 132, he notes that 'errors will inevitably occur' (with biometric use). In paragraph 150, he puts the point in a stronger way: 'The uniqueness of a fingerprint in forensic science remains an assumption without watertight proof.' Unlike the majority, he then goes on to substantiate this claim, citing scholarly books (paragraph 260, footnote 154) and the text of the Aadhaar Act itself, which envisages updation of biometrics. This becomes crucial in the latter part of the judgment dealing with exclusion, where (as we shall see) both authentication failures, and the existence of false positives and false negatives are key reasons for his finding of unconstitutionality.

This foundational factual disagreement between the majority and Justice Chandrachud is important—and virtually determinative—to the outcome of the case. Recall that the majority elects to pitch its case very high—not merely that a biometric database is good or efficient, but that it is *flawless*, i.e., there *cannot* be duplicates. The majority does this because it makes the rest of the case very easy. If Aadhaar is truly unique, then ipso facto it efficiently targets beneficiaries (and so Section 7 is upheld) as well as fake PAN cards (and so Section 139AA is upheld); furthermore, 'unproven' stories of exclusion cannot be taken seriously (and, in any event, are being dealt with by a circular). There is no need to engage in a messy proportionality analysis about whether biometric authentication *actually* accomplishes what the State claims it does and whether it is indeed the least restrictive way of accomplishing it. However, by stark contrast, Chandrachud J's finding that biometrics can be erroneous—as we shall see—opens his judgment up to a large number of issues. Do errors disproportionately affect the most vulnerable? Shouldn't failure be forestalled, rather than compensated? And so on.

Surveillance

Here again, Chandrachud J's disagreement with the majority starts in factual analysis. Chandrachud J notes that profiling and surveillance *are* possible under the existing Aadhaar framework. This is because, in his view, according to Regulation 17, requesting entities *can* store biometric information for a temporary period (paragraph 126), that the IP address metadata *can* be used to track location and profile (paragraph 227), that third-party vendors *have* access to the database and, most crucially, that linking of databases *can* take place:

The risks which the use of Aadhaar 'for any purpose' carries is that when it is linked with different databases (managed by the State or by private entities), the Aadhaar number becomes the central unifying feature that connects the cell phone with geo-location data, one's presence and movement with a bank account and income tax returns, food and lifestyle consumption with medical records. This starts a 'causal link' between information which was usually unconnected and was considered trivial. Thus, *linking Aadhaar with different databases* carries the potential of being profiled into a system, which could be used for commercial purposes. It also carries the capability of influencing the behavioural patterns of individuals, by affecting their privacy and liberty. Profiling individuals could be used to create co-relations between human lives, which are generally unconnected [paragraph 244]. *[Emphasis mine]*

In addition:

When Aadhaar is seeded into every database, *it becomes a bridge across discreet data silos*, which allows anyone with access to this information to re-construct a profile of an individual's life. It must be noted while Section 2(k) of the Aadhaar Act excludes storage of individual information related to race, religion, caste, tribe, ethnicity, language, income or medical history into CIDR, the mandatory linking of Aadhaar with various schemes allows the same result in effect. For instance, when an individual from a particular caste engaged in manual scavenging is rescued and in order to take benefit of rehabilitation schemes, she/he has to link the Aadhaar number with the scheme, the effect is that a profile as that of a person engaged in manual scavenging is created in the scheme database. The stigma of being a manual scavenger gets permanently fixed to her/his identity. What the Aadhaar Act seeks to exclude specifically is done in effect by the mandatory linking of Aadhaar numbers with different databases, under cover of the delivery of benefits and services [paragraph 247].

On every point, therefore, there is a *direct* factual clash between the majority and Chandrachud J. Recall that the majority categorically said that the merging of data silos *cannot* happen, that that is a fundamental reason why profiling and surveillance are impossible. Chandrachud J, on the other hand, makes it clear that the seeding of Aadhaar across databases serves to break the silos. As I have pointed out above, this is not a matter of different legal interpretation, with the majority's view being 'correct' simply because it is the majority. Here, one of them is right and the other is wrong.

Privacy

Chandrachud J's disagreement with the majority on this is legal in character. Recall that the majority undertakes the proportionality test by diminishing our privacy interest in our bodily characteristics and devaluing the importance of biometric details (fingerprints or iris scans). By contrast, Chandrachud J holds that our privacy interests in our biometric details are high, both from an informational self-determination point of view, as well as from bodily integrity and physical safety point of view (paragraph 125). In particular, Chandrachud J avoids two pitfalls that the majority falls into—that is, mixing up 'minimal information (collected)' with 'minimal interference with privacy', and applying the American 'reasonable expectation' standard. Ultimately, however, the difference is one of framing: The majority uses the fact that biometric details are given frequently and for a multiplicity of purposes, to argue that we don't have a heightened privacy interest in them. For Chandrachud J, however, that is irrelevant. What is relevant is that a 'carefully designed' biometric system may nonetheless preserve privacy (such as, for instance, ensuring anonymity) and that, therefore, *that* is the standard we must measure Aadhaar against (paragraph 127). And within this framework, he finds that the absence of consent within the Act, the extent of information disclosed, the expansive scope of the term 'biometrics', the burden placed upon the individual to update her own biometrics and the lack of access to the record cumulatively constitute a serious infringement of privacy.

Section 7 and Proportionality

Chandrachud J accepts that the Aadhaar Act—and Section 7—are designed to fulfil a 'legitimate State purpose'—that is, making the welfare delivery system better and more effective. For him, however, the programme fails on the proportionality prong. As he observes:

> The test of proportionality stipulates that the nature and extent of the State's interference with the exercise of a right (in this case, the rights to privacy, dignity, choice, and access to basic entitlements) must be proportionate to the goal it seeks to achieve (in this case, purported plugging of welfare leakage and better targeting) [paragraph 198].

This paragraph reflects three crucial differences in the way that the majority and Justice Chandrachud approach proportionality in this case. *First*—as we have seen above—the majority holds that the invasion of privacy and dignity is minimal (and it doesn't even consider the issue of choice), thus guaranteeing a very low threshold of justification to the State. *Secondly*, having made the assumption that biometric authentication is flawless, the majority cannot—and does not—admit that its use can actually impede access to basic entitlements. In the majority's approach, therefore, the question of entitlements comes on the other side of the justificatory ledger (i.e., the State *promoting* access to entitlements through Aadhaar). And *thirdly*, the factual assumption of accurate targeting and improvement of welfare delivery drive the majority into a pre-decided 'balancing' between minimal impairment of privacy and significant plugging of welfare leaks. Chandrachud J, however, remains more circumspect. He carefully notes that the plugging of welfare leakage and better targeting is only 'purported'.

The word 'purported' informs Chandrachud J's proportionality analysis. As he notes, this is not a domain where the court has to be excessively deferential to the State's assertions. This is especially true because a nationwide biometric programme is not merely one of those initiatives that applies to a one-time transaction. Rather:

> [B]y collecting identity information, the Aadhaar program treats every citizen as a potential criminal without even requiring the State to draw a reasonable belief that a citizen might be perpetrating a crime or an identity fraud. When the State is not required to have a reasonable belief and judicial determination to this effect, a program like Aadhaar, which infringes on the justifiable expectations of privacy of citizens flowing from the Constitution, *is completely disproportionate* to the objective sought to be achieved by the State [paragraph 217].

In this context, the lack of verification mechanisms by UIDAI, the lack of proper exemption handling process (if authentication fails), the lack of accountability mechanism with respect to the UIDAI (paragraph 235), the absence of an overarching regulatory framework and the vague and unbridled nature of Section 7, which allows it to be interpreted in an open-ended way without checking whether each separate use violates the proportionality standard (paragraph 248), all militate against a finding of proportionality. And the position is sealed when Chandrachud J observes that 'the state has failed to demonstrate that a less intrusive measure other than biometric authentication will not subserve its purposes'.

This time as well, the difference between the majority and the dissent is purely legal. Recall that the majority had argued that the *petitioners* had failed to demonstrate an alternative. Chandrachud J, however, reverses the legal burden: It is for the State to demonstrate that there is no *feasible* alternative, since it is the State, after all, that is infringing on one's rights. As should be obvious, in cases where there is no evidence on the other side, this finding of burden changes everything.

The Argument from Inequality

Chandrachud J's acknowledgement that biometric authentication is error-strewn (something that the majority refuses to acknowledge) leads him to study the exclusion issue carefully (which the majority dismisses in a line). Exclusion is directly linked with discrimination, because, as he notes, 'exclusion as a consequence of biometric devices has a disproportionate impact on the lives of the marginalized and poor' (paragraph 253). He deals in some detail with the work of the political scientist Professor Virginia Eubanks, who, using the concept of the 'digital poorhouse', has demonstrated that the discriminatory effects of technological solutions are inevitably visited upon the most vulnerable. Consequently, Chandrachud J holds that 'the fate of individuals cannot be left to the vulnerabilities of technological algorithms or devices' (paragraph 262).

He then substantiates this by looking at the Economic Survey of 2016–17, government reports involving pilot projects in Andhra Pradesh and the work of grassroots scholars such as Jean Dreze and Reetika Khera, to show that the exclusion percentages have been substantial (paragraphs 263–68). Now recall that the majority dealt with this issue in a line, noting that the attorney-general had made a statement that people would be allowed to use another identification and that there was also a circular providing for this. This approach, which upholds an unconstitutional statute on the basis of a promise to interpret it fairly, is somewhat bizarre. In any event, however, Chandrachud J has an answer himself, when he notes:

> Technological error would result in authentication failures. *The concerns raised by UIDAI ought to have been resolved before the implementation of the Aadhaar project.* Poor connectivity in rural India was a major concern. The majority of the Indian population lives in rural areas. Even a small percentage of error results in a population of crores being affected. Denial of subsidies and benefits to them due to the infirmities of biometric technology is a threat to good governance and social parity [paragraph 262]. *[Emphasis mine]*

This is a crucial observation. What Chandrachud J is saying is that once it is established that exclusions will occur—leading to deprivation of rights—then *the State bears the burden of first resolving these issues before rolling out the project.* Once again, the contrast with the majority could not be starker. The majority notes that Aadhaar is an ongoing project and that 'glitches' must be ironed out as they present themselves. To this, Chandrachud J replies: 'You cannot be ironing out the glitches when Articles 14 and 21 are at stake.' In other words, people—especially the most vulnerable—cannot be used as experimental subjects for improving the efficiency of technology, as that would violate every constitutional principle in the book:

> No failure rate in the provision of social welfare benefits can be regarded as acceptable. Basic entitlements in matters such as foodgrain, can brook no error. To deny food is to lead a family to destitution, malnutrition and even death [paragraph 263].

There is, of course, a bitter irony here. In the passive euthanasia judgment, it was the Chief Justice who had first articulated this principle when he asked whether the individual was to be turned into some kind of a guinea pig for an experiment. Unfortunately, it would take only a few months for him to forget, and it would be left to a dissenting opinion to remember.

A Dissent for the Ages: Individual, State, Identity

Justice Chandrachud's dissenting judgment recognizes what the Aadhaar case was *truly* about: It was the first time in its history that the court was called upon to answer serious questions about the interface between technology, the relationship between individual and State, and the Indian Constitution. The judgment is shot through with a keen awareness of this fact. Indeed, in paragraph 3, Chandrachud J notes that 'our decision must address the dialogue between *technology and power*'.

These are not careless words. The Aadhaar case was all about the relationship between the individual and the State, and how technology was altering—and even potentially inverting—that relationship. It was about how power worked itself through technology, through algorithms, becoming the arbiter of people's rights and entitlements. And it was, at its heart, a question about what our Constitution had to say about that.

This is something that the majority, in its techno-utopian celebration of greater efficiency and unique identification, misses entirely—the other side of the story, the contrapuntal notes. It is the side that comes across with particular clarity at various points in the dissenting opinion. When Chandrachud J discusses how unique data sets can lead to 'perpetuating of pre-existing inequalities' (paragraph 10), or when he refuses to play off civil rights and socio-economic rights against one another, or in his attention to how biometric systems are 'most aggressively' tried out with welfare recipients (paragraph 120). And it comes across most vividly in a brief discussion about identification and identity, an issue that plagued the hearings throughout. Consider, for example, the dissent's discussion of how the concepts of 'identity' and 'identification' are being merged with the advent of technology (and compare, once again, with the majority's celebration of a 'unique identity'):

Identity includes the right to determine the forms through which identity is expressed and the right not to be identified. That concept is now 'flipped' so that identification through identifiers becomes the only form of identity in the time of database governance. This involves a radical transformation in the position of the individual [paragraph 185].

A finding that immediately leads to the following conclusion:

The submission which has been urged on behalf of the petitioners is that an individual entitled to the protection of the freedoms and liberties guaranteed by Part III of the Constitution must have the ability to *assert a choice of the means of identification for proving identity*. Requiring an individual to prove identity on the basis of one mode alone will, it is submitted, violate the right of self-determination and free choice [paragraph 185].

In other words, in an age when *identification* has subsumed *identity*, the individual *must* be granted a choice in the means by which she elects to 'identify' herself to the State. It is a simple enough concept, but radical in its application.

They say that Minerva's Owl takes flight at dusk. And so, you may well ask: What is the point of this dissent when the Supreme Court spent six years busily allowing Aadhaar to become a *fait accompli*, and then legitimized it through a majority opinion anyway? To that, perhaps, there is only one answer: The great cases are always 4–1 in favour of the State.

Until the 1 is resurrected. And becomes the pathway for a future that is still struggling to be born.

[**Disclaimer**: The writer assisted K.V. Viswanathan, senior counsel for one of the petitioners challenging Aadhaar.]

6

A Question of Consent: The Delhi High Court's Split Verdict on the Marital Rape Exception

(11 May 2022)

TODAY, A DIVISION BENCH of the High Court handed down its judgment on the constitutional challenge to the marital rape exception (MRE).[31] Put simply, the marital rape exception states that 'sexual intercourse by a man with his own wife ... is not rape'. Petitioners, supported by *amici*, argued that the marital rape exception—which, in effect, immunizes married men from being prosecuted for rape—violated Articles 14, 15(1), 19(1)(a) and 21 of the Constitution. The two-judge bench delivered a split judgment: Justice Shakhder struck down the MRE as unconstitutional on all of the above grounds, while Justice Hari Shankar upheld its constitutionality.

Previously on this blog I have analysed the constitutional issues around the MRE in some detail.[32] In this post, I shall argue, *first*,

---

31 *RIT Foundation vs Union of India*, 2022/DHC/001825.
32 'The Marital Rape Exception: Two Constitutional Issues', Indian Constitutional Law and Philosophy, 19 January 2022, https://

that the fundamental point of difference between the two judges is on the question of consent. Justice Shakhder believes that whether in a marriage or out of it, sexual consent is paramount and inviolable. Justice Hari Shankar's judgment reflects the assumption that within a marriage, a woman's consent to sex carries less weight. *Secondly*, I shall note that under existing Indian constitutional law, Justice Shakhder is correct and Justice Hari Shankar is wrong. Consequently, when this split judgment goes for resolution before a full bench (or to the Supreme Court), Justice Shakhder's views ought to be upheld and the MRE struck down.

The Opinion of Shakhder J

The core of Justice Shakhder's argument can be found in *paragraph 135.2* of his opinion. Examining *Section 375* of the Indian Penal Code in some detail, which sets out the seven circumstances under which a sexual act counts as rape, he observes:

> A close reading of the circumstances would reveal that except for the sixth circumstance (which concerns a girl-child under 18 years of age), *willingness* (as in the first circumstance) and *consent* (as in the second to fifth and seventh circumstance) form the basis of separating acts which are lawful from those which are construed as unlawful. The circumstances are clearly agnostic to the relationship between the offender and the woman victim. *[Emphasis mine]*

As Shakhder J notes, therefore, the core of the offence of rape is *non-consensual* sexual intercourse. The MRE creates a 'firewall' that protects one class of putative perpetrators—married men—from being

indconlawphil.wordpress.com/2022/01/19/the-marital-rape-exception-case-two-constitutional-issues/

prosecuted for this offence, even though the *ingredients* of the offence are exactly the same. The question then follows: Is this distinction constitutional? Shakhder J holds that it is not, as in essence what it conveys is that 'forced sex outside marriage is "real rape" and the same act within marriage is anything else but rape' (paragraph 137.1). Thus, the MRE 'with one stroke deprives nearly one half of the population of the equal protection of laws' (paragraph 137.1). This is because:

> The immediate deleterious impact of the provisions of MRE is that while an unmarried woman who is the victim of the offence of rape stands protected and/or can take succour by taking recourse to various provisions of the IPC and/ the Code, the same regime does not kick-in if the complainant is a married woman. In this context, one may have regard to the following provisions of the IPC and the Code: Section 228A of the IPC prevents disclosure of the identity of a rape victim except in certain circumstances set out therein. Likewise, Section 26 of the Code provides that the offences concerning rape/aggravated rape shall be tried as far as practicable by a court presided by a woman. Section 53A empowers a medical practitioner to examine, a person charged with committing an offence of rape if he has reasonable grounds for believing that such examination will furnish evidence with regard to the commission of the offence [paragraph 141].

For these reasons, Shakhder J holds that the MRE fails the reasonable classification test of Article 14. He then addresses two counter-arguments: the idea of a 'conjugal expectation to sex' and the 'preservation of the institution of marriage'. On both issues, his response is grounded in the right to individual autonomy and consent. On the first, he notes that whatever the expectation might be (i.e., 'unreasonable' denial of sex counts as a ground for divorce under Indian family law), it does not extend to an 'unfettered right to sex' without consent (paragraph 146); on the second, he notes that the marital bond is *itself* based on the idea of choice and mutual respect for 'physical and mental autonomy' (paragraph 148). Once again, therefore, a legal provision predicated upon the denial of consent cannot be saved by appeals to the institution of marriage.

This focus on choice, autonomy and equality also leads Shakhder J to hold that the MRE violates Articles 21, 15(1) and 19(1)(a) of the Constitution. In paragraph 163, he holds that 'modern-day marriage is a relationship of equals. The woman by entering into matrimony does not subjugate or subordinate herself to her spouse or give irrevocable consent to sexual intercourse in all circumstances. Consensual sex is at the heart of a healthy and joyful marital relationship.' For this reason, denial to married women the right to trigger prosecution for the violation of sexual consent infringes upon Article 21; it also infringes upon Article 15(1), as it is discrimination based solely on marital status; and it infringes upon Article 19(1)(a), as 'the guarantee of freedom of expression includes a woman's right to assert her sexual agency and autonomy' (paragraph 166).

The Opinion of Hari Shankar J

How does Hari Shankar J respond to these contentions? His opinion is based on two prongs. *First*, Hari Shankar J identifies what he believes to be a fundamental flaw in the petitioners' logic—i.e., that all non-consensual sex is, by default, rape, and that the MRE is an impermissible departure from this default; and *secondly*, that when it comes to sex, the marital relationship is distinct from all other relationships, in that it carries with it a 'legitimate expectation of sex'. This—according to Hari Shankar J—provides the 'intelligible differentia' under Article 14 that justifies the legislative decision of treating non-consensual sexual intercourse within marriage as 'not rape'.

Let us examine both steps of the argument. In the first step, Hari Shankar J tries to drive his point home by drawing an analogy with the crime of murder. Just like not every instance of taking a life is deemed under criminal law to be 'murder', it follows that not every act of non-consensual sex is deemed 'rape'; rather, it is the legislature that decides *which* kind of non-consensual act is to be deemed 'rape', just as it defines when the taking of life is deemed murder (paragraph 103).

In this context, Hari Shankar J repeatedly—and rather intemperately—accuses petitioners' counsel, and the *amici*, of making arguments devoid of logic and attempting to substitute the legal definition of 'rape' for 'what they feel should be the definition of rape'. If there is anything that demonstrates a complete lack of logic, however, it is Hari Shankar J's choice of analogy. The relationship between the MRE and the offence of rape is not equivalent to the legislature defining the circumstances under which the taking of a life amounts to murder. The correct analogy—as should be immediately evident—is that of the legislature defining the offence of murder in full detail, and then adding, for example, an 'MP exception', which goes 'the killing of a human being by a member of Parliament is not murder'. This is because—and this is the point of Shakhder J's judgment that Hari Shankar J fails to deal with in any sense—Section 375 exhaustively defines the *ingredients* of the offence of rape (which, as Shakhder J correctly notes, involve non-consensual sex in various forms), and then exempts a *class* of perpetrators from prosecution *on no other ground than that they belong to that class.*

It is this simple elision that thus allows Hari Shankar J to dodge the issue of consent entirely and repeatedly insist throughout his judgment that he supports consent, and indeed—incredibly—that this case is not about consent at all. As is immediately obvious, however, this case is *all* about consent: The entire scheme of Section 375 is designed to define non-consensual sex as rape and then shield married men from the consequences of that legislative design.

Hari Shankar J then notes that there is a range of provisions in the IPC where the relationship between the parties matters (in a somewhat disturbingly violent analogy, he argues that a father slapping his child is not an offence, but a stranger slapping the same child is [paragraph 134]). This brings us to the second prong of his argument, which is the intelligible differentia. Hari Shankar J argues that the intelligible differential is founded upon the 'unique demographics' (paragraph 104). What are these unique demographics? This comes in paragraph 113:

> Equally plain, and real, is the fact that the primary distinction, which distinguishes the relationship of wife and husband, from all other relationships of woman and man, is the carrying, with the relationship, as one of its inexorable incidents, of a legitimate expectation of sex.

This idea of a 'legitimate expectation of sex' comes up repeatedly through the judgment and is the basis of Hari Shankar J's finding that the MRE is constitutional. In paragraph 116, he notes that marriage 'is the most pristine institution of mankind' and that the 'sexual aspect is but one of the many aspects' upon which the marital bond rests; in paragraph 119, he says that 'sex between a wife and a husband is, whether the petitioners seek to acknowledge it or not, sacred'. In paragraph 120, he says, '[I]ntroducing, into the marital relationship, the possibility of the husband being regarded as the wife's rapist, if he has, on one or more occasion, sex with her without her consent would, in my view, be completely antithetical to the very institution of marriage, as understood in this country, both in fact and in law.' In paragraph 127, he says that unlike in live-in relationships, 'the expectation of sex of the husband, with his wife is, therefore, a legitimate expectation, a healthy sexual relationship being integral to the marital bond'; in paragraph 130, he says that 'any assumption that a wife, who is forced to have sex with her husband on a particular occasion when she does not want to, feels the same degree of outrage as a woman raped by a stranger, in my view, is not only unjustified, but is ex facie unrealistic'. He then adds that 'it cannot even be assumed, in my view, that the perceptions of the petitioners reflect the views of the majority of Indian women'.

It is important to extract these observations in some detail, because they are characteristic of the muddled legal thinking that runs through Hari Shankar J's opinion as a whole. Even if you take all these observations and assertions to be true (and there are many who would contest them!), what they demonstrate—at their highest—is that sex within marriage is somehow qualitatively different from sex outside marriage, because it forms an integral part of a set of reciprocal rights and obligations that constitute the valuable social institution of marriage.

But even if true, this is entirely besides the point. The only evidence that Hari Shankar J can muster up as evidence in his support is that unreasonable denial of sex can serve as grounds for divorce. That is true, as Shakhder J also recognizes. But there is a chasm of difference between saying, on the one hand, that the reciprocal *social* rights and obligations in a marriage create a ground for *dissolution* of that marriage if they are not discharged by either party, and saying, on the other, that they justify immunizing the violation of sexual consent from being prosecuted as it *normally* is, outside of marriage—i.e., rape.

Indeed, when you strip away the verbiage, what Hari Shankar J is effectively saying is that marriage not only gives the husband a legitimate expectation of sex, but the further right to *violently enforce that expectation without suffering the same consequences as other people do*. This not only flouts the rule of law, but also flouts basic logic, which appears to be particularly dear to Hari Shankar J.

A quick note on paragraph 130, which I found particularly disturbing. First, there is the assertion that a married woman who is subjected to non-consensual sex (since Hari Shankar J objects to using the word 'rape') will not feel as 'outraged' as a woman who is raped by a non-married person (whether that person is a stranger, a friend or an intimate partner). This assertion has no business being in a judicial opinion. Secondly, there is the assertion that 'the majority of Indian women do not share the views of the petitioners'. Whether true or not, this is entirely irrelevant and, indeed, a return of the infamous 'minuscule minority' view that appeared in *Koushal vs Naz*; this was seemingly buried in *Navtej Johar*, but appears to have infinite lives in the halls of the court.

It is this extraordinary reasoning that allows Hari Shankar J to hold in paragraph 165:

> Plainly read, it is clear that there is nothing in the impugned Exception which obligates a wife to consent to having sex with her husband, wherever he so requests. All that it says is that sexual acts by a husband with his wife are not rape. It does not even obliquely refer to consent, or want of consent.

Once again, we see the absence of logic. It is nobody's case that the MRE *itself* 'obligates' a wife to consent to sex at all times. The case is that the MRE *devalues* a wife's consent purely by virtue of her marital status. Hari Shankar J sets up this straw man to knock it down in the second sentence—and then, in the third sentence, he comes up with a *non sequitur*, noting that not only does the MRE not force a wife into non-consensual sex, but that it has nothing to do with consent at all! Now when Section 375 says that *non-consensual sex is rape*, and the MRE says that '*except* where it is a married man', what the section, read as a whole, says is that *non-consensual sex between a married man and a wife is not rape*. Repeatedly—and belligerently—stating that all this has nothing to do with consent does not make it true.

The intellectual dodge at the heart of the judgment is finally laid bare in paragraph 169, where Hari Shankar J notes, by way of conclusion:

> [T]he legitimate conjugal expectations of the man, as the husband of the woman and the reciprocal obligations of the wife, the peculiar demographics and incidents of marriage, vis-à-vis all other relationships between man and woman, and all other legitimate considerations to which I have already referred,

and which justify extending, to sexual intercourse and sexual acts within marriage a treatment different from such acts committed outside the marital sphere.

For the reasons I have explained in some detail, the dodge is simple: It is not enough for Hari Shankar J to show that sex within a marriage is in some way 'different' from sex outside of marriage. He has to show that it is *different in such a way that justifies diluting a married woman's consent to sex*. He does not show this, because he—incorrectly—attempts to argue that the entire case is not about consent in the first place. And the only way he can show that is by ignoring the actual text of Section 375 altogether—the text that is the starting point of Shakhder J's judgment—and which makes clear that consent is baked into the very ingredients of the offence of rape.

Conclusion

Having deconstructed the fundamental flaws of law—and of logic—that constitute Hari Shankar J's opinion, it should be obvious that the opinion is unsustainable. As of 2022, Indian constitutional law *does not* support the dilution of sexual consent based on marital status. One does not need to look too far for this: The issue is considered squarely in the *Puttaswamy* judgment, where Chandrachud J's plurality opinion is explicit on this point, while many other judgments make it clear that decisional autonomy is a fundamental facet of the right to privacy, and is not lost or in any other way compromised through social institutions such as marriage. Decisional autonomy within the marriage was also the fundamental basis upon which adultery was decriminalized in *Joseph Shine*; and sexual autonomy was at the core of *Navtej Johar*. It is, thankfully, too late in the day to go back on this rather fundamental precept.

Three final points. First, I have not in this post analysed all parts of the two opinions. For example, the two judges differ on whether striking down the MRE would lead to the creation of a new offence.

I have analysed this issue in some detail in a previous post, and interested readers may refer to that.[33]

Secondly, as this post shows, I believe that Shakhder J's judgment is opinion and ought to be upheld on appeal. However, I also believe that the appellate forum needs to do more than that. I believe—and I say this with due consideration—that parts of Hari Shankar J's opinion have no place in a jurisprudence that is formally committed to the basic idea of individual autonomy, dignity, privacy, and equal concern and respect. These include, for example, the problematic statement—which occurs on more than one occasion—that a married woman who is raped will 'feel' less outraged than an unmarried woman who is raped. Examples can be multiplied; and when this judgment goes on appeal, the least that can be done is a formal expunging of these observations from the record.

And finally, this judgment shows—if anything does—the often-Janus-faced character of the courts. We have two opinions—delivered in the same case—that, like ships in the night, sail past each other without even the chance of a conversation, because their premises are so very different. One opinion sees the task of constitutionalism to be interrogating power differences and breaking down social hierarchies in order to achieve genuine substantive equality and freedom. The other opinion takes upon itself the task of defending and entrenching those hierarchies. I think we don't see the first face of the courts often enough; but when we do—as in Shakhder J's opinion—it's a powerful reminder of what constitutionalism, at its best, can be—and do.

[**Disclaimer**: The writer was involved in the initial drafting and hearing of the petitions challenging the MRE. He has not been involved in the case since 2019.]

---

33   Ibid.

7

Discipline or Freedom: The Supreme Court's Split Verdict in the Hijab Case[34]

(13 October 2022)

TODAY, A TWO-JUDGE BENCH of the Supreme Court delivered a split judgment in *Aishat Shifa vs State of Karnataka*, popularly known as the 'Hijab Case'. Petitioners appealed the judgment of the High Court of Karnataka, which had upheld a ban on the hijab in various State-run educational institutions. At the Supreme Court, Justice Hemant Gupta wrote a judgment agreeing with the high court and upholding the ban, while Justice Sudhanshu Dhulia

---

[34] The 'Hijab Case' arose out of a government order issued by the government of Karnataka that banned the wearing of the hijab in classrooms. A challenge to this order was heard by a three-judge bench of the High Court of Karnataka. The high court upheld the ban, primarily on the ground that maintaining the sanctity of the uniform was an important State purpose. The case travelled on appeal to the Supreme Court, where a two-judge bench split on the issue. This post analyses the Supreme Court judgment; readers interested in analysis of the high court judgment, as well as numerous analyses of the issue, can consult the blog: 'The Hijab Case: A Round-Up', Indian Constitutional Law and Philosophy, 25 February 2022, https://indconlawphil.wordpress.com/2022/02/25/the-hijab-case-round-up/

wrote a judgment overruling the high court and striking down the ban. The immediate upshot of this is that the Chief Justice will now have to constitute a larger bench to determine the issue. In the meanwhile, the high court judgment continues to stand and, therefore, the ban on the hijab continues to be in force as well.

The Judgment of Hemant Gupta J

Previously on this blog, I had examined the high court judgment at some length.[35] I had noted at the time that 'a close reading of the judgment reveals how the uniform haunts the court's imagination on every page'. Lurking behind the high court's judgment was the unarticulated belief that allowing the hijab would open a floodgate that would end in the destruction of the very idea of a uniform, without which education was unimaginable. It was this belief that informed the court's analysis of the constitutional rights to freedom of conscience, speech and privacy, and led it to effectively hold that these rights were either inapplicable or only weakly applicable in 'qualified public spaces' such as schools and, in any event, were subordinate to the overriding logic of the uniform.

A few months down the line, the spectre of the uniform appears to have travelled from Karnataka and now haunts the pages of Justice Gupta's judgment. A reading of the judgment reveals that Justice Gupta's response to virtually every argument advanced by the petitioners is: 'The uniform!' Article 25 and the freedom of conscience? The uniform! Article 19 and the freedom of expression? But the uniform! Article 21 and the right to privacy? Most verily, the uniform! All moral and constitutional values have come to repose in the uniform.

---

35 'Between Agency and Compulsion: On the Karnataka High Court's Hijab Judgment', Indian Constitutional Law and Philosophy, 15 March 2022, https://indconlawphil.wordpress.com/2022/03/15/between-agency-and-compulsion-on-the-karnataka-high-courts-hijab-judgment/

It is a marker of formal equality ('uniformity') under Article 14, which, in turn, justifies the restriction of the freedom of conscience under Article 25, as that article is subject to the other provisions of Part III (paragraph 87); it is the basis of permissible 'regulation' of Article 19(1)(a) (paragraph 144); and the 'homogeneity' of the uniform discourages sectarianism and encourages constitutional fraternity (paragraph 154).

Clearly, however, it is not the uniform *itself* that is doing the moral heavy lifting in the judgment. Dig a little deeper, and you find what really animates Gupta J: It is the idea of *discipline*. The word 'discipline' occurs twenty-two times in the judgment, in varying contexts, but most commonly in the precedent Gupta J elects to cite, and in his own analysis. And it occurs with particular frequency in the neighbourhood of the word 'uniform', with Gupta J stressing, on multiple occasions, how discipline (and even, once, 'discipline and control!') cannot exist without a uniform. Gupta J's depth of feeling for discipline is revealed in one particularly extraordinary passage, where he notes:

> Discipline is one of the attributes which the students learn in schools. Defiance to rules of the school would in fact be antithesis of discipline which cannot be accepted from the students who are yet to attain adulthood. Therefore, they should grow in an atmosphere of brotherhood and fraternity and not in the environment of rebel or defiance [sic] (paragraph 188).

We should, perhaps, be thankful that this grim, bleak and joyless vision of the school will always be far from reality and that wherever there will be teenagers, there will be 'rebel or defiance', notwithstanding the efforts of sergeant-teachers or of disciplinarian Supreme Court judges. But be that as it may, the real problem here is that in his enthusiasm to prescribe discipline and stamp out 'rebel or defiance' in the 'pious atmosphere of the school' (paragraph 193), Gupta J forgets to apply the law. So, while the word 'discipline' occurs twenty-two times in the judgment, the word 'proportionality'—which is the legal test to determine when the State's infringement of constitutional rights is justified—occurs a grand total of *zero* times. In a truly highlight reel moment, Gupta J holds:

> The intent and object of the Government Order is only to maintain uniformity amongst the students by adherence to the prescribed uniform. It is reasonable *as the same has the effect of regulation of the right guaranteed under Article 19(1)(a)*. Thus, the right of freedom of expression under Article 19(1)(a) and of privacy under Article 21 are complementary to each other and not mutually exclusive *and does meet* the injunction of reasonableness for the purposes of Article 21 and Article 14 [paragraph 144].

Apart from the fact that the last sentence makes no sense *at the level of the sentence*, in this single paragraph, Gupta J disposes of the Articles 19(1)(a) and 21 arguments with the familiar answer 'but the uniform!' 'But the uniform!', however, is not a constitutional test and is certainly not the constitutional test of proportionality that—in accordance with precedent—is *binding* upon Gupta J if he wishes to hold that State action meets the 'injunction of reasonableness'. Equally erroneous is his (repeated) holding that the uniform furthers the goal of Article 14 because it is about 'uniformity': The proposition that Article 14 of the Constitution requires 'uniformity' has *never* been the jurisprudential position since 1950, and at any rate, is most certainly not the jurisprudential position after the Supreme Court's landmark judgments in *Navtej Johar* and *Joseph Shine*. It is—to use a word beloved of lawyers—*trite* to say that the Indian Constitutional approach to equality, in 2022, is *contextual and substantive*. It focuses on issues around structural and institutional disadvantage, and their remedies.

Thus, once 'uniform' (not a constitutional test) and 'uniformity' (not the right constitutional test) fall away, Gupta J's judgment does not have a leg to stand on, and falls away along with them.

The Judgment of Dhulia J

In stark contrast to Gupta J, the judgment of Dhulia J commences at a different point, asks a different set of questions and, unsurprisingly, arrives at a very different answer. There are four facets of this judgment that, in particular, deserve to be highlighted.

The first is Dhulia J's treatment of the essential religious practices (ERP) test.[36] As I have argued in a previous blog post, in this case, the ERP test presented the petitioners with a fundamental dilemma. On the one hand, the case was pegged as being about constitutional values: the freedom of expression, conscience and choice of the female Muslim students who wished to wear the hijab. To put it in one word: *agency*. On the other hand, pegging the case on the ERP test would, by definition, erase agency. To show that the hijab is an 'essential religious practice', one would have to show that it is *mandated* by Islam, an injunction that leaves no room for choice or agency.

Before the high court, petitioners made extensive submissions on the ERP test, and indeed, a major prong of the high court's judgment is its finding that the hijab is *not* an ERP. Before the Supreme Court, the position was different. While some of the petitioners (now appellants) continued to nail their colours to the ERP mast, others avoided it altogether and focused, instead, on expression, choice and conscience.

Justice Dhulia's judgment deals with the ERP test in a fascinating way. He notes that the test—while indisputably a part of India's religious freedom jurisprudence—is inapplicable to the *present case*. Why? Because, on a survey of the history, Dhulia J finds that the ERP test has been historically used when the issues turn around the managements of religious property or the invocation of *group rights* against the State. In this case, however, what is at stake is an *individual right* (to wear the hijab) against the State. For Dhulia J, in such a case,

---

36   The ERP test requires a court to determine whether a particular practice is 'essential' to a religion on the basis of 'objective' parameters such as the opinions of priests, religious texts and so on.

ERP is inapplicable for the reason that in any religion, there will be *different views* on what religious doctrine truly means, and it is not the court's remit to privilege one view over another (paragraph 36).

It is impossible to overstate how *vital* a finding this is. One of the most pernicious facets of the ERP doctrine is how it completely erases the very possibility of *religious dissent* and religious pluralism. It requires the court to make a determination whether *a* particular doctrine is 'essential' to a religion or not, and in doing so, inevitably, the court relies upon the dominant viewpoints within the religion (by looking at religious books, the opinions of 'authorities' and so on). Indeed, this is starkly evident in Gupta J's judgment, where he spends reams and reams of pages reading the Quran to try and figure out if the hijab is *truly* essential or not. For Dhulia J, on the other hand, the question of ERP is simply irrelevant where an individual right is at stake. There, all that matters is the *sincerity* of belief (paragraph 34). And this is another crucial shift, because what it does is prioritize an individual's *subjective understanding and articulation of their religion* over the diktats of religious 'authorities'. In other words, in one stroke, Dhulia J rescues agency from the talons of the ERP test. If—and this is a big *if*—this finding is upheld by the larger bench, it would signal a quiet—and desperately needed—revolution in our ERP jurisprudence.

This finding then allows Justice Dhulia to move on from ERP and, instead, make the freedom of conscience, and the landmark judgment in *Bijoe Emmanuel*, the centrepiece of his analysis. This is the second important aspect of his judgment. Recall that in *Bijoe Emmanuel*, the Supreme Court had permitted three students—who were Jehovah's Witnesses—to refrain from singing the national anthem in their school assembly as long as they stood in respectful silence while it was being played. Dhulia J finds the situations to be analogous—and he, in turn, invokes *Bijoe Emmanuel* to locate the principle of 'reasonable accommodation' (which Gupta J rejects out of hand) in Indian constitutional jurisprudence. Thus, for Dhulia J, *Bijoe Emmanuel* is authority for the propositions that, *first*, the threshold to trigger Article 25(1) protection is simply a case of conscience, and that *secondly*, once that threshold has been triggered, there is a right to reasonable accommodation of difference.

What of the reasonableness in this particular case? This brings us to the third important facet of the judgment, and to Dhulia J's fundamental disagreement with Gupta J. Recall that for Gupta J, State action was reasonable because it was in the service of the uniform, and of discipline. Dhulia J's disagreement could not be starker or more unambiguous: '*[N]ot discipline at the cost of freedom, at the cost of dignity* [paragraph 52].' Freedom and dignity are *constitutional* values, and this allows Dhulia J to hold:

> Asking a pre-university schoolgirl to take off her hijab at her school gate, is an invasion on her privacy and dignity. It is clearly violative of the Fundamental Right given to her under Article 19(1)(a) and 21 of the Constitution of India. This right to her dignity and her privacy she carries in her person even inside her school gate or when she is in her classroom [paragraph 52].

Indeed, a very different picture of the classroom emerges in the judgment of Dhulia J—a space where the governing value is not discipline but freedom, and where the idea of fraternity requires us to embrace and express our differences, rather than flatten and erase them (paragraph 71).

The final important facet is perhaps the most basic of all: education. Dhulia J asks himself whether 'we are making the life of a girl child any better by denying her education, merely because she wears a hijab'. (paragraph 66). This observation comes in the context of the admitted fact that after the Karnataka High Court's judgment, many girls were unable to take their exams. Once again, the differences between Dhulia J and Gupta J are stark. For Gupta J, there is nothing to see here, as the girl students' missing exams is, essentially, their own fault for refusing to follow the uniform. Dhulia J, on the other hand, recognizes that the situation is rather more complex. It is a known fact, for example, that in many households, access to education is a contested terrain between the girl-child and her (conservative) family, with permission to go to school contingent upon the wearing of the hijab. Indeed, as Nisha Susan highlights in this article,[37] there is a range of complicated reasons why someone might wear the hijab, and it is almost never as simple as a total compulsion/unencumbered choice binary. Indeed, agency is something that is both situated and negotiated, especially when it comes to women dealing with patriarchy, both within the home and outside. Thus, for Dhulia J, what it basically comes down to is whether the effect of the court's judgment will be the denial of access to education, and if so, how best to ensure that that outcome is avoided.

Conclusion

At one level, the split within the bench turns upon different understandings of the law and its application. On a closer look, however, the difference is much more fundamental. It is a difference in worldview.

One of these worlds is governed by the iron laws of discipline and control—of inflexible rules and punitive action for those that question them; of authority that brooks no 'rebel or defiance'; of homogeneity, the denial of difference and the 'unanimity of the graveyard'; of one tune and one song; and a world in which students are like undifferentiable lumps of clay, to be moulded into what the authority considers to be 'model citizens'.

---

37 Nisha Susan, 'Every girl's hijab has a unique story, Hindutva supporters have only one reason to ban it', The News Minute, 6 February 2022, https://www.thenewsminute.com/article/every-girl-s-hijab-has-unique-story-hindutva-supporters-have-only-one-reason-ban-it-160656

The other world celebrates freedom and plurality; believes that rules should allow space to breathe instead of suffocation; values diversity—and the expression of diversity—over homogeneity; believes in the beauty of an orchestra, with many voices, rather than just one; sees the classroom as a space of liberation rather than control; and considers students to be autonomous, thinking beings, capable of making choices, even difficult, negotiated choices.

Which world would we rather live in? That question is for each of us to answer for ourselves. Which world *do* we live in? The answer to that hangs in the balance, and all eyes will now turn to the Chief Justice, and the next—and perhaps—final round in the history of this case.

Social Justice and Reservations

Introduction

RESERVATIONS IN JOBS AND in education have been one of the most contentious social justice measures implemented by the State—both in the court and out of it.

The battle over the reservations doctrine in India can be traced back to a set of fault lines arising out of a set of judgments delivered in the 1970s and the 1990s. Until 1976, the dominant understanding was that reservations (authorized under Articles 15(4) and 16(4) of the Constitution) were *exceptions* to the general rule of equality. That is, reservations were allowed only because an explicit constitutional provision said so; in the absence of that, they would be unconstitutional. This, in turn, led to a number of associated doctrines, the most prominent among which was the 50 per cent rule, i.e., that reservations, being exceptions to the general rule of equality, could not exceed 50 per cent of the total strength.

In *State of Kerala vs N.M. Thomas* (1976), a seven-judge bench of the Supreme Court radically reversed course by holding that reservations were not an exception but a *facet* of equality. In other words, the Constitution guaranteed substantive equality, which required the State to take into account material circumstances and socio-economic inequalities while deciding how to treat people. Under this vision of equality, reservations advanced that goal, rather than being a limited set of exceptions to it.

The fault lines arose in the Supreme Court's elaborate, nine-judge bench decision in *Indra Sawhney*, where the Supreme Court *both* upheld *N.M. Thomas's* vision of substantive equality, but *also* retained a number of holdovers from the pre-*Thomas* days (such as the 50 per cent rule) This created an internal tension in the Supreme Court's jurisprudence, which persists to this day. While, on the face of it, the court remains committed to the constitutional vision of substantive equality, in the application, many of the doctrines that were evolved on the assumption that reservations are *exceptions* to equality, remain.

The judgments that you will find in the succeeding pages encapsulate this tension. They relate to the following set of conflicts, among others: (a) How and when can the State expand the beneficiary groups of reservation? (b) To what extent is the State required to establish that the threshold conditions for triggering reservation—inadequacy of representation—has been met? (c) Under what circumstances can the State cross the 50 per cent 'limit' on reservations?

Each of these issues goes back to the central, normative tension in *N.M. Thomas* and *Indra Sawhney*: What vision of equality is our Constitution committed to, and how do reservations fit within this vision?

A final caveat: The Supreme Court's significant judgment on economic reservations for economically weaker sections (EWS) was delivered towards the very end of the period covered in this book. The author's close—and continuing—involvement with the case prevented him from writing publicly about the judgment. Interested readers may, therefore, consult the series of guest posts analysing the judgment, which can be found on the blog, all written in November 2022.

1

The Supreme Court's Judgment on Jat Reservations: Problems and Prospects

(18 March 2015)

YESTERDAY, IN *RAM SINGH vs Union of India*, the Supreme Court overturned a government decision to grant reservations to the Jat community in nine states (by including them in the Central List of Backward Classes [Central List]).[38] The judgment has created a significant political stir. As a legal matter, however—and subject to observations in two paragraphs, which will be discussed at the end— the case was decided on specific, narrow grounds, and breaks no new ground as far as constitutional issues are concerned. In fact, the case is probably best classified as an administrative law judgment, rather than a constitutional one.

The factual matrix of the case stretched back eighteen years. In 1997, in response to numerous petitions, the National Commission for Backward Classes (NCBC) carried out a study, at the end of which it recommended the inclusion of Jats in the Central List only for two districts of Rajasthan. Subsequently, in response to numerous

---

38 *Ram Singh vs Union of India*, (2015) 4 SCC 697.

representations to review this decision, on 19 July 2011, the NCBC decided to approach the Indian Council of Social Science Research (ICSSR), asking them to conduct a survey in six states (UP, Haryana, Madhya Pradesh, Rajasthan, Himachal Pradesh and Gujarat) to determine the socio-economic status of Jats. By a subsequent Cabinet decision, the states of Bihar, Uttarakhand and NCT of Delhi were also referred to the NCBC.

The ICSSR submitted a report (but made no specific recommendations about inclusion/exclusion in the Central List). The report was discussed by the NCBC, which also held public hearings. At the end of this process, on 26 February 2014, the NCBC submitted a report to the government, stating, '*[T]he Jat Community had not fulfilled the criteria for inclusion in the Central List of OBCs.*' But on 2 March 2014, the Cabinet rejected this report on the ground that it did not take into account '*ground realities*'. Two days later, via a notification, Jats were placed on the Central List for the nine states.

At this point, it is important to note the status of the NCBC. It is a statutory body, established under the National Commission for Backward Classes Act, 1993. Under Section 9(2), it is provided that when it comes to inclusion or exclusion from the lists, '*the advice of the Commission shall ordinarily be binding upon the Central Government*'. This closely followed the judgment of the Supreme Court in *Indra Sawhney vs Union of India*, where Justice Jeevan Reddy, commenting on the need for just such a specialized body, observed that '*its advice/ opinion should ordinarily be binding upon the Government. Where, however, the Government does not agree with its recommendation, it must record its reasons therefore.*'

Judicial review of administrative or executive action follows certain well-settled principles. Judges may not substitute their wisdom for that of the authorized decision-making body and nor may they intervene to correct what they perceive to be a mistake of policy or a mistake in interpreting existing data. *However*, if the administrative decision is made *in ignorance of* relevant material, or is based upon patently *irrelevant* material (or, for that matter, is made mala fide), the court may set it aside. What the NCBC Act does is to statutorily mandate that the report of the NCBC constitutes 'relevant material' that the government is bound to adhere to unless there are good reasons for the contrary (presumably, other relevant material). As the court correctly noted, in paragraph 26, *'[T]he advice tendered by the NCBC is ordinarily binding on the Government, meaning thereby that the same can be overruled/ignored only for strong and compelling reasons, which reasons would be expected to be available in writing.'* Consequently, all the court needed to do was verify whether the government had actually provided relevant reasons for departing from the NCBC's report.

This is exactly what it proceeded to do. First, it extracted the state-wise summary of the findings of the ICSSR. While acknowledging that elements of 'backwardness' (in terms of representation in government jobs, school dropout ratio, etc.) existed with respect to the Jat community in some of the states, the ICSSR also clarified that only limited material was available before it, and declined to make specific recommendations. On the basis of the ICSSR report, along with other reports available to it, the NCBC had decided that the evidence did not justify the Jat community's claim to 'social backwardness' for the purposes of Article 16 of the Constitution.

After a detailed examination of the NCBC's reasons, as well as its analysis of the primary material, the court noted:

> Undoubtedly, the report dated 26.02.2014 of the NCBC was made on a detailed consideration of the various reports of the State Backward Classes Commissions; other available literature on the subject and also upon consideration of the findings of the Expert Committee constituted by the ICSSR to examine the matter. The decision not to recommend the Jats for inclusion in the Central List of OBCs of the States in question cannot be said to be based on no materials or unsupported by reasons or characterized as

> decisions arrived at on consideration of matters that are, in any way, extraneous and irrelevant ... It may be possible that the NCBC upon consideration of the various materials documented before it had underplayed and/or overstressed parts of the said material. That is bound to happen in any process of consideration by any Body or Authority of voluminous information that may have been laid before it for the purpose of taking a decision. Such an approach, by itself, would not make either the decision making process or the decision taken legally infirm or unsustainable. Something more would be required in order to bypass the advice tendered by the NCBC ... An impossible or perverse view would justify exclusion of the advice tendered but that had, by no means, happened in the present case. The mere possibility of a different opinion or view would not detract from the binding nature of the advice tendered by the NCBC [paragraph 46].

Additionally, the government's contention that Jats were on the lists of eight of the nine states was rejected by the court on the ground that those lists were made more than a decade ago and that *'a decision as grave and important as involved in the present case which impacts the rights of many under Articles 14 and 16 of the Constitution must be taken on the basis of contemporaneous inputs and not outdated and antiquated data'* (paragraph 48). The court also found that the minutes of the Cabinet meeting held just before the notification reflected a focus on the *educational* 'backwardness' of the Jat community by highlighting school, college and graduate enrolment (paragraph 49). The 'backwardness' contemplated under Article 16, however, was *social* backwardness. Consequently, the court held that the Cabinet notification ignored relevant material (the NCBC report) and, in turn, based itself upon irrelevant material (educational parameters and decades-old data). Consequently, following the well-established principles of judicial review that we have discussed above, it set aside the notification.

So far, standard. However, there are three further issues, highlighted in paragraph 54 of the judgment, that call for specific comment. First, the court notes:

> Though caste may be a prominent and distinguishing factor for easy determination of backwardness of a social group, this Court has been routinely discouraging the identification of a group as backward solely on the basis of caste. Article 16(4) as also Article 15(4) lays the foundation for affirmative action by the State to reach out [to] the most deserving. Social groups who would be most deserving must necessarily be a matter of continuous evolution. New practices, methods and yardsticks have to be continuously evolved moving away from caste centric definition of backwardness.

While these lines have garnered a fair degree of attention in the press, it is important to note that this is simply a reaffirmation of the court's consistent position spanning the last fifty years. As far back as *M.R. Balaji vs State of Mysore*, in 1963, the Supreme Court held that a *purely* caste-based policy of reservations would violate the Constitution. While this blanket position was undermined in *N.M. Thomas* and *Indra Sawhney*, the position remains that while castes, which are generally '*socially and occupationally homogenous classes*' (*Indra Sawhney*, paragraph 84), can constitute a convenient *starting point* for reservations, the ultimate criterion is *class backwardness*. This means that caste groupings do not *exhaust* the scope of reservations under the constitutional scheme, and conversely, to the extent that a caste wishes to claim the benefits of the reservation scheme, it must demonstrate that *qua* class, it suffers from the social backwardness that Article 16 envisages. The failure of the Jat community to demonstrate this latter point was what prompted the court to observe, in another statement that has been widely quoted over the last twenty-four hours, that '*an affirmative action policy that keeps in mind only historical injustice would certainly result in under-protection of the most deserving backward class of citizens, which is constitutionally mandated*.

The former aspect—that castes do not exhaust the scope of reservations—leads to the second important observation in the paragraph—the court's invocation of last year's *NALSA* judgment on the rights of the transgender community. The court observes:

> New practices, methods and yardsticks have to be continuously evolved moving away from caste centric definition of backwardness. This alone can enable recognition of newly emerging groups in society which would require palliative action. The recognition of the third gender as a socially and educationally backward class of citizens entitled to affirmative action of the State under the Constitution in *National Legal Services Authority vs Union of India* is too significant a development to be ignored. In fact it is a path finder, if not a path-breaker. It is an important reminder to the State of the high degree of vigilance it must exercise to discover emerging forms of backwardness. The State, therefore, cannot blind itself to the existence of other forms and instances of backwardness.

This is a crucial point, because after the judgment in *NALSA*, the Union of India filed a clarification petition asking whether the placement of the transgender community within the lists would have to *first* go through the NCBC. Here, the court seems to clearly state that as per *NALSA*, the transgender community has been judicially recognized as a socially/educationally backward class, entitled to affirmative action. This would suggest that the NCBC *does not* need to make a separate finding on the point, since the Supreme Court has already done so. But even apart from this, in May 2014, the NCBC *did* make a finding that transgender persons ought to be provided reservations. In accordance with yesterday's judgment, the NCBC's finding will be binding upon the government, unless overriding reasons are demonstrated. Consequently, the clarification petition ought to be disposed of as soon as possible, with appropriate directions to the government to add the transgender community to the Central List.

Secondly, the Union also observed that transgender persons do not 'maintain a caste or community identity', but at the same time might belong to specific SC/ST/OBCs. Here is where the court's focus on 'new yardsticks' to measure backwardness becomes crucial, as does its acknowledgement, also in paragraph 53, that social classes might be '*internally heterogenous*' (and based on gender). In other words, both substantively and procedurally, paragraph 53 amounts to a strong endorsement of the right of the transgender community to affirmative action, and takes the promise of *NALSA vs Union of India* a significant step forward.

And lastly, in the penultimate paragraph (54), after affirming that 'backwardness' ought not to be judged relative to other groups but on absolute parameters, the court observes:

> *[The]* inclusion of the politically organized classes (such as Jats) in the list of backward classes mainly, if not solely, on the basis that on same parameters other groups who have fared better have been so included cannot be affirmed.

It is interesting that among all the adjectives that the court might have chosen to describe the Jats, it picks '*politically organized*'. This opens up a plethora of fascinating questions, the first among which is: *Is political power, or access to political power, the main criterion for determining 'social backwardness'?* Is a politically organized group, just for that reason, no longer 'socially backward'? And if not—recall that the very origins of judicial review lie in the understanding that 'discrete and insular minorities', who are likely to be sidelined or marginalized by the normal workings of the political process, need additional protection from brute majoritarianism. Is it that which is on the court's mind? Does the court mean to say that groups that have managed to gain access to political power are expected to now leverage it to lift themselves out of their social backwardness? Or is the court concerned that politically organized groups will use their clout to win reservations for themselves even when they don't need it (a fear that is also visible in some US affirmative action cases)? The court does not answer any of these questions here, but it will be interesting to see what importance, if any, it might accord to the political influence of groups claiming backward status in the future.

2

The Supreme Court Upholds Reservations in Promotions for Disabled Persons

(19 July 2016)

IN AN INTERESTING JUDGMENT handed down at the end of last month, a two-judge bench of the Supreme Court considered the question of reservations in promotions for disabled persons.[39]

The Prasar Bharati Corporation (a State employer) has four classes of posts—A, B, C and D. These posts are filled up in three ways—through direct recruitment, promotion, and partly direct recruitment and partly promotion. Now, under Section 33 of the Persons with Disability Act, 1995, the government is required to provide at least 3 per cent reservation in 'identified posts' for persons with disabilities. In pursuance of this, Prasar Bharati issued two office memoranda. Certain posts in each of the four classes were selected to be the 'identified posts'. However, while for classes C and D, the reserved-category posts could be filled up through any of the three means (promotion, recruitment and partial promotion/recruitment), under classes A and

---

39 *Rajeev Kumar Gupta vs Union of India*, (2016) 6 SCALE 417.

B, reserved posts could be filled only through recruitment. In other words, the memoranda denied reservations in promotions to disabled employees working in Class A and Class B posts.

The legality of this denial was challenged. It was argued that since a number of posts in Class A and B were filled through promotions, effectively, disabled persons were being denied equality of opportunity.

The State's response was this: In *Indra Sawhney vs Union of India*, the Supreme Court had held that reservations in promotion were impermissible under Article 16(4). Subsequently, to get around this, Parliament amended Article 16(4) by inserting 16(4A), which specifically authorized reservations in promotions for certain Scheduled Castes and Scheduled Tribes. Section 16(4A), therefore, excepted *only* SC/STs from *Indra Sawhney's* rule against reservations in promotions. That rule continued to apply to all other classes of employees, including persons with disabilities.

The basic premise of the State's argument, therefore, was that the *authority* for reservations was contained within Article 16(4) of the Constitution. If that were the case, *Indra Sawhney's* interpretation of 16(4)—that it did not allow for reservations in promotions—would hold the field and prevent the two-judge bench from reaching a different conclusion.

The court rejected the argument on the basis that Article 16(4) was *not* the authority for reservations under the Constitution. It did so by going over the history of affirmative action jurisprudence. In its earlier years, the court had held that Article 16(4) was an exception to Article 16(1)'s guarantee of equality of opportunity. In other words, the default position was a formal equality of opportunity, and Article 16(4) specifically departed from that by permitting the State to make reservations in aid of backward classes. However, starting with Justice Subba Rao's dissenting opinion in *T. Devadasan*, through *N.M. Thomas*, and finally in *Indra Sawhney*, the position changed, with the court taking the view that Article 16(4) was an instance of, or an emphatic expression of, Article 16(1). That is, Article 16(1) involved a commitment to *substantive equality* (or, in the words of Justice Mathew, *proportional equality*), and Article 16(4) illustrated one specific way in which that substantive equality could be achieved.

The corollary of this is that Article 16(1) not only permits, but actively contemplates, reservations. So far (to my knowledge), the court has been circumspect about this conclusion. In the disability judgment, however, Justice Chelameswar takes the logic to its explicit conclusion. In paragraph 21, he notes: 'Article 16(4) does not disable the State from providing differential treatment (reservations) to other classes of citizens under Article 16(1).'

He then arrives at this inescapable conclusion:

> Once a post is identified, it means that a PWD is fully capable of discharging the functions associated with the identified post. Once found to be so capable, reservation under Section 33 to an extent of not less than three per cent must follow. Once the post is identified, it must be reserved for PWD irrespective of the mode of recruitment adopted by the State for filling up of the said post.

This judgment is a good example of how the seemingly abstract shift in the court's jurisprudence from 'exception' to 'facet', starting with Justice Subba Rao's radical dissent in *Devadasan*, to Justices Mathew and Krishna Iyer's perceptive exploration in *N.M. Thomas*, and finally the culmination in *Indra Sawhney*, has a very tangible, real-life impact. The exception–facet shift changes the *locus* of reservations from 16(4) to 16(1), and allows the State to escape the straitjacket of '*backward classes*', and the accompanying judicial restrictions that have crystallized over the years. This is the practical result of the transformation of the concept of equality.

That said, there are certain parts of the judgment that are slightly confusing. In paragraph 18, Justice Chelameswar observes that '*the principle is that the State shall not discriminate (which normally includes preference) on the basis of any one of the factors mentioned in Article 16(1)*';

then, in paragraph 21: '*[H]owever, for creating such preferential treatment under law, consistent with the mandate of Article 16(1), the State cannot choose any one of the factors such as caste, religion etc. mentioned in Article 16(1) as the basis.*'

These factors, however, are not found in Article 16(1), which simply guarantees equality of opportunity in matters of employment under the State. They are found in 16(2), which states that '*no citizen shall, on grounds only of religion, race, caste, sex, descent, place of birth, residence or any of them, be ineligible for, or discriminated against in respect or, any employment or office under the State ...*' Presumably, Justice Chelameswar meant Article 16(2). However, once it is established that the equality principle animating Article 16(1)—and by extension Article 16(2)—is the principle of substantive equality, it is not clear why Article 16(2) prohibits the reservation on the basis of its stipulated markers. Surely, if reservations flow from a substantive vision of equality itself, as set out in Article 16(1), the phrase 'discriminated against' in Article 16(2) is also meant to be interpreted in that substantive manner, and therefore, reservations for subordinated religions, castes (or women, for that matter) are permitted under Articles 16(1) and 16(2)?

Be that as it may, the Supreme Court's judgment is clear, sharp and lucid on the legal issue, and demonstrates how substantive equality operates in doctrine and practice. It will be interesting to see whether and to what extent future reservation judgments follow this model.

3

The Nagaraj/Creamy Layer Judgment and Its Discontents

(30 September 2018)

ON 26 SEPTEMBER, A Constitution bench of the Supreme Court delivered judgment in *Jarnail Singh vs Lacchmi Narain Gupta*.[40] The court was essentially called upon to decide whether the correctness of the previous five-judge-bench judgment in *M. Nagaraj vs Union of India* ought to be referred to a seven-judge bench for reconsideration.

Nagaraj was a reservations case, examining a challenge to Articles 16(4A) and (4B) of the Constitution. In particular, two of its findings were under challenge. *First*, *Nagaraj* had held that as a precursor to granting reservations (including to Scheduled Castes and Scheduled Tribes), the State would have to collect 'quantifiable data' demonstrating their backwardness. And *secondly*, *Nagaraj* had held that the 'creamy layer' concept—where certain members of a group were deemed to belong to the 'creamy layer' and therefore not entitled to reservations—was also applicable to Scheduled Castes and Scheduled Tribes.

---

40 *Jarnail Singh vs Lacchmi Narain Gupta*, (2018) 10 SCC 396.

The attorney-general for India argued that both these findings were incorrect, as they were contrary to the holding of the nine-judge bench in *Indra Sawhney vs Union of India*.

Quantifiable Data

On the first issue, the Constitution bench—in a unanimous judgment authored by Justice Nariman—held that *Nagaraj* stood directly contrary to *Indra Sawhney* and was therefore incorrect:

> Insofar as the State having to show quantifiable data as far as backwardness of the class is concerned, we are afraid that we must reject Shri Shanti Bhushan's argument. The reference to—class is to the Scheduled Castes and the Scheduled Tribes, and their inadequacy of representation in public employment. It is clear, therefore, that *Nagaraj* (supra) has, in unmistakable terms, stated that the State has to collect quantifiable data showing backwardness of the Scheduled Castes and the Scheduled Tribes. We are afraid that this portion of the judgment is directly contrary to the nine-Judge Bench in Indra Sawhney (1) (supra) [paragraph 14].

While this is no doubt correct on law, and indeed on logic—the presidential list under Articles 341 and 342 containing the list of Scheduled Castes and Scheduled Tribes is *already* based on an assessment of marginalization and vulnerability—it does raise a question of judicial propriety. Can a five-judge bench hold that a coordinate bench wrongly interpreted the law and is therefore incorrect? Does not propriety require that the subsequent bench refer the case to a seven-judge bench, which can then overrule the (allegedly) incorrect judgment? Not that this is not even a case where it was argued that *Nagaraj* was *per incuriam*—rather, what was advanced was the far more modest claim that *Nagaraj* got *Indra Sawhney* wrong. But even if *Nagaraj* got *Indra Sawhney* hopelessly, irredeemably wrong, that was not for the Constitution bench in *Jarnail Singh* to decide.

Creamy Layer

Nariman J then went on to hold that even though *Indra Sawhney* had not expressly chosen to apply the creamy-layer principle to Scheduled Castes and Scheduled Tribes, it had always been clear that the principle was a facet of constitutional equality. Nariman J relied upon *N.M. Thomas* for this principle, and on some observations in Krishna Iyer J's concurring opinion, to note:

> The whole object of reservation is to see that backward classes of citizens move forward so that they may march hand in hand with other citizens of India on an equal basis. This will not be possible if only the creamy layer within that class bag all the coveted jobs in the public sector and perpetuate themselves, leaving the rest of the class as backward as they always were. This being the case, it is clear that when a Court applies the creamy layer principle to Scheduled Castes and Scheduled Tribes, it does not in any manner tinker with the Presidential List under Articles 341 or 342 of the Constitution of India. The caste or group or sub-group named in the said List continues exactly as before. It is only those persons within that group or sub-group, who have come out of untouchability or backwardness by virtue of belonging to the creamy layer, who are excluded from the benefit of reservation. Even these persons who are contained within the group or sub-group in the Presidential Lists continue to be within those Lists. It is only when it comes to the application of the reservation principle under Articles 14 and 16 that the creamy layer within that sub-group is not given the benefit of such reservation [paragraph 15].

Importantly, Nariman J went on to hold that courts could themselves 'exclude' the creamy layer from reservations (paragraph 16).

But for a conclusion of this magnitude, Nariman J's reasoning is disappointingly sketchy. There are at least two good reasons why the creamy-layer doctrine should *not* be applied to Scheduled Castes and Scheduled Tribes, neither of which are addressed or acknowledged by the judgment. *First*, the very concept of a 'creamy layer' presupposes that some members of a subordinated group have attained a level of privilege, that they no longer share the characteristics of subordination and, therefore, are no longer part of the 'group' in that limited sense. Now, when the subordination is economic or political, it makes sense to assume that it is at least *possible* for some people, or groups of people, to 'escape' that subordination, so to say. However, that is a far more dubious claim when the subordination is *social* in character, and is founded on discrimination of a certain kind, where *group identity* itself is the locus of disadvantage. We don't have to go too far afield to understand this—there are more than enough examples of Dalits who have broken free of economic marginalization or penury but continue to be subjected to the most shocking forms of social discrimination. And indeed, this has historically borne out: right from the early-twentieth century, the first lists of 'depressed classes', drawn up by British commissions, focused on *social stigma* as the basis of classification (for a detailed discussion, see Marc Galanter's *Competing Equalities*[41]). Recall Ambedkar's own words about how caste society was based on an *'ascending scale of hatred and a downward scale of contempt'*. Does the concept of a 'creamy layer' make any sense here? Well, if it does, it requires substantially more detailed justification than the court provides.

And *secondly*, even if we are to accept that 'creamy layer' makes conceptual sense in the case of SCs and STs, there nonetheless remain justifications for the existing reservation model that the court does not touch upon. It is argued, for example, that even if the benefits

---

41 Marc Galanter, *Competing Equalities: Law and the Backward Classes in India*, University of California Press, 1992.

of reservation are 'captured' by the elite within a group, even *that* constitutes positively towards greater social mobility (of the group) in the long term, apart from ancillary benefits of greater political salience. I am not saying that these arguments are correct or persuasive; however, it does behove the court to address them if it is going to introduce the creamy-layer concept into these two categories.

Conclusion

Jarnail Singh suffers from two problems. On one point, it overrules a coordinate bench without even a finding of *per incuriam*. And on the second point, it puts its seal on a significant doctrinal shift in reservations jurisprudence, but does not back it up with the depth of analysis that it demands. I suspect, however, that this is not the last that we have heard on the issue—especially from the government's side!

4

Reservations in Promotions and the Idea of Efficiency: *B.K. Pavitra vs Union of India*

(10 May 2019)

[**Editorial Note**: Justice is an indivisible concept. We cannot, therefore, discuss contemporary Supreme Court judgments without also acknowledging the court's failure—at an institutional level—to do justice in the case involving sexual harassment allegations against the Chief Justice. This editorial caveat will remain in place for all future posts on this blog dealing with the Supreme Court, until there is a material change in circumstances.]

THIS MORNING, A TWO-JUDGE bench of the Supreme Court delivered a fascinating judgment in *B.K. Pavitra vs Union of India*, concerning the relationship between reservations in promotions for Scheduled Castes and Scheduled Tribes, and the issues of seniority.[42] The facts were as follows: In 2002, the state of Karnataka enacted a law stipulating, in effect, that consequential seniority would

---

42   *B.K. Pavitra vs Union of India*, (2019) 16 SCC 129.

follow upon the promotions of SC/ST employees. To put it in simple language, if a reserved category employee (A) was promoted before a more senior colleague (B) by virtue of A belonging to the reserved category, then, in the higher level post, A would now be senior to B (when, eventually, the latter would get promoted as well).

Readers familiar with reservation will know that this issue—bitterly contested over many decades—was eventually set at rest by amendments to Article 16(4A) of the Constitution, which authorized consequential seniority in cases of reservations in promotions. In *Nagaraj*, while upholding the amendment in question, a Constitution bench of the Supreme Court also held that the government was obligated to first collect data demonstrating the 'inadequacy' of SC/ST representation in the services, their 'backwardness' and the impact on 'efficiency' before it could enact laws in accordance with Article 16(4A). In 2017, the Supreme Court found that the Karnataka law did not comply with *Nagaraj* and was therefore unconstitutional (*B.K. Pavitra—I*). In response, the Karnataka government commissioned a study (the Ratna Prabha Committee Report), and based on the results of this study, re-enacted the earlier law.

The constitutional challenge to the law raised a host of issues. It was argued that Karnataka had impermissibly 'overruled' the judgment in *Pavitra—I* by re-enacting the law that had been held to be unconstitutional—and doing it retroactively, to boot. It was argued that the Bill had been wrongly sent for presidential assent. It was argued that the study on the basis of which the law was passed was flawed, and that the law was unconstitutional because it failed to exclude the 'creamy layer'. In this essay, I will not discuss all of the above issues. (On some points, such as legislative overruling, the court essentially synthesized and restated existing law—readers interested in the subject may read the judgment for a clear and lucid exposition of the principles.) What I want to focus on, rather, are some of the novel issues that arose, as well as the novel treatment that the court accorded to older issues.

Standards of Judicial Review

As Chandrachud J correctly observed at the beginning of the judgment, this was the first time in the post-*Nagaraj* era that the court was explicitly asked to rule upon the State's data-gathering exercise, which was now a constitutional prerequisite for any law aiming to implement reservations (with consequential seniority) in promotions (paragraph 4).

The petitioners argued that the Ratna Prabha Committee Report was flawed because, inter alia, its methodology was either incorrect or insufficient (that, in many respects, such as measuring inadequacy against sanctioned posts instead of filled posts, it was not cadre-based, and so on), and because the reports on efficiency were only general in nature. The respondents contended, on the other hand, that these questions were within the 'subjective satisfaction' of the State (as had been held in *Indra Sawhney*) and that it was the State that was in the best position to 'define and measure merit'.

In response, the court noted that, as a preliminary point, it would have to set down the parameters of judicial review in a case such as this. These parameters, it held, would be based on two mutually reinforcing principles. The first was the general principle that the executive was best aware of prevailing conditions. This is nothing more than the familiar presumption of constitutionality. The second principle was more specific: In the context of reservations, questions such as adequacy of representation would be left, at the first instance, to the subjective satisfaction of the State. This was because, as Chandrachud J noted, the State was tasked with promoting substantive equality under the Constitution *through* the vehicle of reservations (paragraph 95). Applying these principles to the Ratna Prabha Committee Report, Chandrachud J observed that the report was based on sampling methods that were broadly accepted among social scientists. There was no evidence that extraneous or irrelevant material had been used. *Beyond* that assessment, it was not for the court to hold that the report was invalid because the best (or substantially better) methods were available, that had not been used. And on the basis of the report, it was open to the legislature to hold that a disparity between the population percentage of SC/STs, and their representation in the services, was the basis for determining the 'inadequacy of representation'.

A few things follow from this discussion. The first is that the court adopted a deferential attitude towards the State's collection of data and its inferences from the data it had collected. The purpose of the exercise, the court held, was for the legislature to be able to effectively advance the constitutional goal of substantive equality. In other words, the court recognized the crucial point that constitutional goals are to be advanced by *all* three wings of the State, and that in different contexts, the *primary responsibility* for that lies upon the different wings. In the specific case of reservations, that responsibility has been placed upon the legislature. For this reason, in the domain of reservations, the court would only assess the State's subjective satisfaction on the deferential threshold of rationality and non-arbitrariness. Note, also, what follows: This principle of deference will not apply to *every* situation where a law is challenged, and the State invokes data collection and analysis to justify itself. In a case where, for example, the challenge is on the basis of a violation of civil rights, the court may well elect to take on a more interventionist approach to the reliability of the data. In the specific context of reservations, though, given the constitutional text, and the clear responsibility of the State, this the court's approach has much to recommend it.

Interrogating Efficiency

Now, of course, it might be argued that the court *ought* to have been more interventionist, because the case did indeed involve a violation of rights—the Article 16(1) equality rights of non-SC/ST candidates. This point was addressed by Chandrachud J in the subsequent section, where, relying upon the judgments in *N.M. Thomas* and Subba Rao J's dissenting opinion in *Devadasan*, he correctly observed that it was the principle of substantive equality—and not formal equality—that underlay the Constitution's equality code. As Chandrachud J observed in paragraph 107:

> There is substantial evidence that the members of the Constituent Assembly recognised that (i) Indian society suffered from deep structural inequalities; and (ii) the Constitution would serve as a transformative document to overcome them. One method of overcoming these inequalities is reservations for the SCs and STs in the legislatures and state services.

Readers may consult the following paragraphs for an account of the Constituent Assembly Debates, and the place of reservations in advancing the Constitution's transformative character. This discussion, however, segued into what is perhaps the most fascinating part of the judgment. Recall that, according to *Nagaraj*, the government was also required to collect data on whether reservations in promotion would affect 'efficiency' in services (as per the requirement of Article 335). And one of the bases on which the petitioners attacked the Ratna Prabha Committee Report was precisely that it had failed to do so.

In response, Chandrachud J undertook a critique of the concept of 'efficiency' itself. In paragraph 119, he observed:

> The Constitution does not define what the framers meant by the phrase efficiency of administration. Article 335 cannot be construed on the basis of a stereotypical assumption that roster point promotees drawn from the SCs and STs are not efficient or that efficiency is reduced by appointing them. *This is stereotypical because it masks deep rooted social prejudice.* The benchmark for the efficiency of administration is not some disembodied, abstract ideal measured by the performance of a qualified open category candidate. *Efficiency of administration in the affairs of the Union or*

of a State must be defined in an inclusive sense, where diverse segments of society find representation as a true aspiration of governance by and for the people. If, as we hold, the Constitution mandates realisation of substantive equality in the engagement of the fundamental rights with the directive principles, inclusion together with the recognition of the plurality and diversity of the nation constitutes a valid constitutional basis for defining efficiency. Our benchmarks will define our outcomes. *If this benchmark of efficiency is grounded in exclusion, it will produce a pattern of governance which is skewed against the marginalised.* If this benchmark of efficiency is grounded in equal access, our outcomes will reflect the commitment of the Constitution to produce a just social order. Otherwise, our past will haunt the inability of our society to move away from being deeply unequal to one which is founded on liberty and fraternity. Hence, while interpreting Article 335, it is necessary to liberate the concept of efficiency from a one sided approach which ignores the need for and the positive effects of the inclusion of diverse segments of society on the efficiency of administration of the Union or of a State.

This needs some careful unpacking. What Chandrachud J is effectively arguing against here is an account of 'efficiency' that sees it in purely *instrumental* terms and devoid of any relationship with the socio-economic context within which such accounts are inevitably embedded. It is an account that is rooted in a deeper idea of philosophical individualism, where there exist certain mechanisms—such as standardized tests—that measure 'individual merit', independent of an individual's group affiliation. This is what efficiency is about, and it must be set off and 'balanced' against group-based affirmative action. However, this account has been challenged throughout our history (starting with Subba Rao J's dissenting opinion in *Devadasan*), and here Chandrachud J takes up the challenge. At the heart of this reasoning is the acknowledgement that assumptions about what people *are* (i.e., their 'merit' or 'efficiency') cannot be separated from what has been *done to them* (i.e., structural and social privileges, often the product of centuries of discrimination). And ultimately, constitutional values dictate that both must be taken into account. Thus, as Chandrachud J observed in paragraph 126:

> Thus, a meritorious candidate is not merely one who is talented or successful but also one whose appointment fulfils the constitutional goals of uplifting members of the SCs and STs and ensuring a diverse and representative administration.

On these bases—and on the basis of the report's finding that there had been no adverse impact even on instrumental efficiency, as the data showed—this ground of challenge was rejected as well.

Creamy Layer

A final point: It was argued that the law was unconstitutional because—after *Jarnail Singh*—it was bound to take into account the exclusion of the creamy layer among SC/STs. The court correctly observed that the question of creamy layer did not arise at the point of promotions and consequential seniority. It is worth pointing out once more, however, that *Jarnail Singh*'s finding in this respect is somewhat suspect. The reason the creamy-layer doctrine is not supposed to apply to SCs/STs is because, historically, they have been oppressed *by virtue of their group identity*. The concept of the creamy layer makes sense if we assume that it is possible to escape one's group identity (through prosperity or other ways of social advancement, for example). However, when oppression is defined by characteristics such as social stigma (as was well recognized by Ambedkar and other framers of the Constitution), the very concept of a 'creamy layer' within that group does not make sense. This aspect of *Jarnail Singh*, it is to be hoped, will be reconsidered at some point.

Conclusion

Today's judgment is a fascinating read, particularly because of the manner in which it moves between different levels of reasoning—from concrete issues of service jurisprudence to the abstract principles of substantive equality and the idea of merit—and how it weaves them together in one coherent vision of transformative constitutionalism. The court's finding on the substantive question—the constitutionality of the seniority law—is informed by its reasoning about the abstract principles that underlie the Constitution's equality code. In other words, the court believes that the Constitution ideals make a difference, and it explains precisely how it does so. And moreover, it joins an important tradition of judicial reasoning on affirmative action that does not take concepts of 'merit' and 'efficiency' as self-evident, but subjects them to critical evaluation from the perspective of the original constitutional vision, noting how they are embedded within our social realities (and inequalities). This tradition of reasoning has, so far, been underdeveloped in our constitutional history—and today's judgment marks an important milestone in its evolution.

5

The Supreme Court's (New) Reservations Judgment and Its Discontents

(9 February 2020)

THIS FRIDAY, A TWO-JUDGE bench of the Supreme Court handed down a judgment holding that Article 16(4) of the Constitution is only an enabling provision and does not confer a 'right' to reservation.[43] The context of the case was as follows: In 2012, the government of Uttarakhand decided to fill up the posts in the state's public services without providing reservation to Scheduled Castes (SCs) and Scheduled Tribes (STs) (paragraph 5). This was challenged, and after a round of litigation before the Uttarakhand High Court, the court directed 'the State Government to collect quantifiable data regarding the inadequacy of the representation of the Scheduled Castes and Scheduled Tribes in Government services which would enable the State Government to take a considered decision on providing or not providing reservation' (paragraph 7).

---

43 *Mukesh Kumar vs State of Uttarakhand*, CA No. 226/2020 (7 February 2020).

Appellants argued before the Supreme Court that the judgment of the Uttarakhand High Court was wrong, as 'there is no constitutional duty on the part of the State Government to provide reservations'. Once, therefore, the government had taken the decision (in 2012) not to provide reservation, that decision could not be challenged (paragraph 8). Appellants further argued that as the collection of 'quantifiable data' was a precursor to providing reservation, it followed ipso facto that 'there is no necessity for collection of any quantifiable data after the Government has taken a decision not to provide reservations' (paragraph 8).

The court agreed with these submissions and also agreed with its 2016 judgment in *Suresh Chand Gautam vs State of UP*, where these contentions had been accepted. In paragraph 12 of the judgment, it noted:

> It is for the State Government to decide whether reservations are required in the matter of appointment and promotions to public posts. The language in clauses (4) and (4-A) of Article 16 is clear, according to which, the inadequacy of representation is a matter within the *subjective satisfaction* of the State. The State can form its own opinion on the basis of the material it has in its possession already or it may gather such material through a Commission/Committee, person or authority. All that is required is that there must be some material on the basis of which the opinion is formed.

This, however, was limited to situations where the State made provisions for reservation. That, however, the court held, was purely discretionary. Consequently:

> As the Government is not bound to provide reservation in promotions, we are of the opinion that there is no justifiable

reason for the High Court to have declared the proceeding dated 05.09.2012 as illegal [paragraph 15].

In other words, there was no obligation upon the State to collect data in order to *deny* reservations.

There are, however, two problems with this line of reasoning that I set out below.

Article 16 and Substantive Equality

The first is the court's characterization of Article 16(4) as a purely enabling provision, and its conclusion from that, that the inadequacy of representation is a matter within 'the subjective satisfaction' of the State. This, however, is at odds with the scheme of Article 16 of the Constitution as interpreted by the Supreme Court. As readers of this blog will be aware, until the mid-1970s, the Supreme Court's position was that Article 16(4) was an *exception* to the guarantee of equality of opportunity set out in Article 16(1). In other words, 16(4) carved out a space (for inadequately represented sections) where the normal principles of equality of opportunity would not apply. It was, of course, up to the State whether or not it chose to avail of this exception and provide for reservations.

In *N.M. Thomas*, however, that position changed. It was held that Article 16(4) was not an exception to but a *facet of* Article 16(1). That changed interpretation flowed from the Supreme Court's evolving understanding that the Articles 14, 15 and 16, or the Equality Code under the Constitution, were not about bare formal equality but about *substantive equality*—i.e., equality that took into account existing social and structural disadvantages, and required the State to remedy them. This understanding of constitutional substantive equality has never seriously been questioned after *N.M. Thomas* and has recently been reaffirmed (albeit in the contexts of Articles 14 and 15) in *Navtej Johar* and *Joseph Shine*.

Consequently, if Article 16(4) is a facet of Article 16(1), it necessarily follows that what Article 16(1) guarantees is a *right* to substantive equality of opportunity (and 16[4] is—in the words of *N.M. Thomas*—an 'emphatic restatement of that right'.) Consequently, while it is correct to say that there is no right to *reservation* (as the language of 16[4] is indeed enabling), there is a right to *substantive equality*. This, in turn, means that if the status quo involves formally equal treatment of individuals in substantively unequal circumstances—when it comes to appointments or promotions in public services—Article 16(1) is breached.

The Uttarakhand High Court was well aware of this distinction (as it also was in another judgment it delivered a few days later). Consequently, it did not direct the government to provide *reservation*. What it did do was direct the government to collect data on the inadequacy of representation so that a decision could be taken on how to remedy existing substantive inequality. This—as Karan Lahiri has argued previously on the blog—is a reading of the scheme of Article 16 that places a 'power plus duty' upon the government.

As Lahiri writes:

> [A] constitutional provision conferring power/discretion on a State authority, couched in permissive language, is to be treated as a provision containing a power coupled with a duty, if the failure or conscious omission on the part of such authority to act would nullify the effect of another/other constitutional provision, or render nugatory a constitutional principle emerging from a mosaic of constitutional provisions.[44]

---

44 Karan Lahiri, 'Does Article 16 Impose a "Power Coupled with a Duty" upon the State? – I', Indian Constitutional Law and Philosophy, 13 November 2015, https://indconlawphil.wordpress.com/2015/11/13/guest-post-does-article-16-impose-a-power-coupled-with-a-duty-upon-the-state-i/

Lahiri then argues that if Article 16(4) were to be read as a purely enabling provision that conferred no duties, this would mean that while there was an obligation upon the State to collect data before it granted reservations, there would be no such obligation if it chose *not* to do so. However, this would mean:

> There is a hurdle created to pull up backward groups, but none for pulling them down, or for ignoring them entirely. This, I believe, is inconsistent with the equality code of our Constitution, and Article 16 itself contains no textual basis for such asymmetry. It is this *asymmetry problem* that can be remedied if the Supreme Court recognizes the fact that Article 16 contains within it an enabling power coupled with a positive duty.

Notice that the asymmetry problem is taken care of by *N.M. Thomas's* reading of Article 16, because that reading makes the pulling up of 'backward groups' an *obligation* upon the State. On the Supreme Court's reading, however, it is made explicit that the government must collect data if it wants to provide reservations/substantive equality ('pull up'), but is not obligated to do any such thing if it wants to deny reservations/substantive equality ('pull down/ignore'). This is obviously at variance with the constitutional scheme.

What about NALSA?

The second problem is a more straightforward one. Recall that in *NALSA vs Union of India*, the Supreme Court had taken judicial notice of the fact that the transgender community was underrepresented in government employment, and on that basis, had specifically *directed* affirmative action measures under Article 16. It follows from this that if indeed it has been found that a group falls within the scope of Article 16(4), the demands of substantive equality under Article 16(1) *require* the State to take measures to bring about real and effective parity. Thus, while admittedly there is no *free-standing right to reservation*, there is a right *contingent* upon a finding that a particular group is underrepresented.

If that is the case, however, the obligation can simply be defeated if the State chooses not to conduct the data-collection exercise at all. Consequently, it follows from *NALSA* that data collection to determine the inadequacy of representation is indeed an *obligation* upon the State, as that is the prerequisite for the further affirmative action that *NALSA* found mandatory.

Conclusion

It is submitted, therefore, that the Supreme Court's judgment is at variance with *N.M. Thomas*, with *NALSA* and, indeed, with the scheme of Article 16 and the Equality Code. Once we agree that Article 16(1) guarantees a *substantive* right to equality of opportunity, it necessarily follows, as Lahiri says, that a coherent reading of the scheme of Article 16 reveals that the discretion of the State under 16(4) is not unbounded. Article 16(4) codifies a 'power plus duty'—the State is empowered to decide upon reservations, but it has a *duty* to collect information pertinent to that decision. Any other reading would defeat the basic idea of substantive equality under Article 16(1).

6

A Critique of the Supreme Court's Maratha Reservation Judgment—I: Equality

(6 May 2021)

[**Editorial Note**: Justice is an indivisible concept. We cannot, therefore, discuss contemporary Supreme Court judgments without also acknowledging the Court's failure—at an institutional level—to do justice in the case involving sexual harassment allegations (link) against a former Chief Justice. This editorial caveat will remain in place for all future posts on this blog dealing with the Supreme Court, until there is a material change in circumstances (e.g., the introduction of structural mechanisms to ensure accountability)].

ON 5 MAY 2021, a Constitution bench of the Supreme Court struck down the Maharashtra State Reservation for Socially and Educationally Backward Classes (SEBC) Act, 2018 (the impugned Act).[45] The Act had granted reservation to the Maratha community

---

45 *Dr Jaishri Laxmanrao Patil vs The Chief Minister*, CA No. 3123/2020 (5 May 2021).

in education and public employment. As a result, the total reservation in Maharashtra had gone over 50 per cent, which was also the subject of challenge. Three substantive judgments, spanning 569 pages, were authored. The court framed six questions, which, for the sake of simplicity, can be divided into three main issues. *First*, did the 50 per cent cap on reservations (subject to 'extraordinary circumstances'), as articulated by some of the judges in the *Indra Sawhney* judgment, merit reconsideration? *Secondly*, was the impugned Act correct in granting reservation to the Maratha community? And *thirdly*, following the 102nd constitutional amendment, were the several states competent to identify socially and educationally backward classes within their jurisdictions, or did that power now lie only with the Centre? With respect to the first two issues, the five-judge bench unanimously answered 'no'. On the third issue, by a 3:2 majority (Bhat, Rao and Gupta JJ), the bench found in favour of exclusive Central competence (i.e., states can no longer identify SEBCs for the purposes of reservation).

I do not propose to address the second issue in too much detail. A perusal of the record (three separate commissions had found that the Marathas did not constitute a 'backward' community, and available data backed this up) shows that court's conclusion on this point is difficult to argue with, even though its scrutiny arguably went beyond what existing precedent permitted. Rather, in this post, I will focus on the first question (the 50 per cent cap).

On the first question, I will argue that the judgments of Bhushan J (joined by Nazeer J) and Bhat J suffer from numerous errors of law and logic. With respect, the impact of these judgments is to entrench—and perpetuate—a duplicity that has existed in Indian affirmative action jurisprudence right from the time of *Indra Sawhney*. In *rhetoric*, the court commits itself to a broad and substantive vision of equality, but in *practice*, it affirms a narrow and formal vision.

The 50 Per Cent Rule: An Overview

The '50 per cent rule' has caused significant dispute and confusion over the years. Pared down to essentials, however, the issue is straightforward, and I will set it out here before enquiring how the court dealt—or did not deal—with it. A reading of the first part of the judgment will reveal that many of the arguments I make here were placed before the court by Mukul Rohatgi, and so my task is primarily an expository one.

The '50 per cent rule' was first articulated by the Supreme Court in *M.R. Balaji vs State of Mysore*, where it was held that reservations under Article 16(4) cannot exceed 50 per cent. When *M.R. Balaji* was decided, the Indian Supreme Court believed that Articles 14, 15(1) and 16(1) embodied a *formal*, or 'caste-blind' vision of equality, where classifications based on suspected categories (caste, race, gender, etc.) were constitutionally impermissible. Article 16(4) carved out a specific *exception* to Article 16(1) by allowing reservations. Thus, formal equality of opportunity was the rule, and reservation was the exception. As the exception could not 'swallow up' the rule, reservations had to be capped at 50 per cent.

This understanding of equality was, however, overturned by a seven-judge bench of the Supreme Court in *State of Kerala vs N.M. Thomas*, where a majority held that Article 16(4) was not an exception to Article 16(1) but a facet of it (or an 'emphatic restatement' of the principle). In other words, the equality code of the Indian Constitution embodied a vision of *substantive equality*, which took into account existing structural and institutional disadvantages. Affirmative action, thus, was *part* of genuine equality of opportunity, rather than clashing with it. In *N.M. Thomas*, two judges also spelt out the logically necessary corollary—the 50 per cent cap in *Balaji* was no longer justifiable.

It was in *Indra Sawhney*, however, that waters were substantially muddied. While the plurality of opinions in the judgment makes culling out a *ratio* a difficult task (and, indeed, the ratio of *Indra Sawhney* was in dispute in the present case), it is at least plausible to argue that the judgment did two irreconcilable things: It affirmed both *N.M. Thomas* *and* the 50 per cent rule (subject to extraordinary circumstances). These two positions are irreconcilable because, as a matter of logic, the 50 per cent rule *must* stand or fall with the proposition that Article 16(4) is an exception to Article 16(1). The moment you accept that Articles 16(1) and 16(4) both embody a vision of substantive equality, the 50 per cent rule makes no sense at all. Substantive equality requires you to look at disadvantage, and if more than 50 per cent of a given population is disadvantaged (to put the point at its most abstract level), there is no reason to limit affirmative action to 50 per cent.

Indra Sawhney, thus, was an internally contradictory judgment, despite attempts by later judgments to make it make sense by holding that Article 16(4) was neither an exception to, nor a facet of, 16(1), but that both had to be 'balanced' against one another. For this reason alone, it merited reconsideration.

The Judgment of Bhushan J

Now, what reasons did the court give to decline the request for reference and reaffirm the 50 per cent rule? Let us first consider the judgment of Bhushan J. He observed, *first*, that only two judges in *N.M. Thomas* had opined on the 50 per cent rule. This is true. It is also irrelevant. As pointed out above, the 50 per cent rule and Article 16(4) being an exception to Article 16(1) are joined at the hip. If one goes, the other must necessarily go. *Secondly*, Bhushan J observed that '*Articles 15(1) and 16(1) of the Constitution are the provisions engrafted to realise substantive equality whereas Articles 15(4) and 16(4) are to realise the* [sic] *protective equality*' (paragraph 155). With respect, the learned justice provided no explanation for what he meant by 'protective equality', how it differed from 'substantive equality' and why the difference mattered (if it did). *Thirdly*, Bhushan J quoted a speech by Dr B.R. Ambedkar in the constituent assembly to argue that the intent of Article 16(4) had always been to limit reservations to a 'minority'. This use—or misuse—of Ambedkar's speech is one of the most troubling and problematic aspects of the judgment for me, and I will address it later. *Fourthly*, Bhushan J held that the judgment in *Balaji* was not premised only on the fact that Article 16(4) was an 'exception' to Article 16(1), but that it was a 'special provision'. A close reading of the actual judgment reveals, however, that this argument is pure misdirection. In *Balaji*, the Supreme Court noted:

> It is because the interests of the society at large would be served by promoting the advancement of the weaker elements in the society that *Art. 15(4)* authorises special provision to be made. But if a provision which is in the nature of an exception completely excludes the rest of the society, that clearly is outside the scope of *Art. 15(4)*.

It is, therefore, clear that the *Balaji* court used 'special provision' and 'exception' interchangeably; indeed, it could not be any other way, because the phrase 'special provision' has no independent meaning— something is 'special' in that it does not occur in the ordinary course of things. It is difficult to parse quite what Bhushan J thought he had accomplished by drawing a distinction between 'exception' and 'special provision', because the learned justice failed to explain any further and, instead, only repeated the *Balaji* dictum of 50 per cent.

Fifthly, Bhushan J noted:

> The 50% rule spoken in Balaji and affirmed in Indra Sawhney is to fulfill the objective of equality as engrafted in *Article 14* of which Articles 15 and 16 are facets. The *Indra Sawhney* [sic] itself gives answer of the question. Paragraph 807 of Indra Sawhney held that what is more reasonable than to say that reservation under clause (4) shall not exceed 50% of the appointment. 50% has been

said to be reasonable and it is to attain the objective of equality [paragraph 162].

This paragraph, unfortunately, suffers from the logical fallacy known as *begging the question*. Bhushan J observed that the '50 per cent rule' was required to fulfil the objective of 'equality' under the Constitution as held by *Indra Sawhney*, while the entire argument was that this was only true *if* equality under the Constitution was formal equality, *which* was denied by *N.M. Thomas* (and *N.M. Thomas*, of course, was affirmed by *Indra Sawhney*). Thus, on the one hand, Bhushan J strenuously argued that Articles 15 and 16 embodied a vision of substantive equality, while on the other, he equally strenuously affirmed a 50 per cent rule that *only* made sense if Articles 15 and 16 were about formal equality.

The paragraph then went on to ask, 'What is more reasonable than to say that reservation shall ... not exceed 50% of the appointment?' Unfortunately, however, this is not the mic drop that Bhushan J appeared to believe it was. The answer to the question is: Any figure that accurately reflects the extent of group disadvantage in any given context is 'more reasonable' than a flat figure of '50 per cent', assuming, of course, that the Indian Constitution is committed to substantive equality.

Mukul Rohatgi raised a number of other arguments for reconsidering the 50 per cent cap, which I will not discuss here—the significant issues, and Justice Bhushan's failure to deal with them, have already been addressed. The implications of this failure were made evident when Justice Bhushan came to consider the Gaikwad Report, which had recommended reservations for the Maratha community. The report had done so on the basis that the representation of Marathas in public employment and education was far less than their representation in Maharashtra's population. Now, as I had clarified at the beginning of this post, I will not here consider the veracity of their claims. What is important to note, however, is that Justice Bhushan held that *even if this were true*, it would not be a basis for granting reservation, as it was not an 'extraordinary circumstance' within the meaning of the *Indra Sawhney* judgment. Latching on to an observation in *Indra Sawhney* that had said that extraordinary circumstances might include 'remote and far-flung areas', where people are removed from the 'mainstream of national life', and holding that this was 'illustrative but indicative' (huh?), Bhushan J held that a finding that 80–85 per cent of the population was 'backward' (which was the reasoning given by the Gaikwad Commission) would not be a ground for increasing the reservation above 50 per cent.

It should immediately be clear that this flies in the face of any defensible understanding of 'substantive equality'. The impact of Bhushan J's observation is that *no matter* the extent of disadvantage that exists in society, no matter the caste or class composition, no matter the history or contemporary reality of oppression, *all of this is irrelevant* to determining the quantum of reservation. To put the matter in the abstract, even if one hypothetically proved to Bhushan J that in a given society, 20 per cent of the population had oppressed the other 80 per cent, and erected enduring structural and institutional barriers to their equal participation in society, he would *still hold* that 'reservation cannot exceed 50 per cent'. To say that such a blanket proposition is in any way consistent with substantive equality is to twist words and concepts out of shape. It is also particularly ironic, given that across the world, a substantial gap between representation in the total population and representation in a specific area is taken as *presumptive evidence* of indirect discrimination.

It is, therefore, submitted, with the greatest of respect, that Bhushan J's judgment is deeply flawed in every respect when it comes to the rule of 50 per cent. In all but name, it takes affirmative action back to the *Balaji* days of Article 16(4) being an exception to Article 16(1), and the Constitution of 'formal equality'. One could only wish that the learned justice had the courage of his convictions and expressly spelt this out, rather than leave us to read between the lines.

The Judgment of Bhat J

Let us now turn to the concurring opinion of Justice Bhat. This judgment is somewhat difficult to parse, as it contains a smattering of quotes from figures such as Franklin Roosevelt and Anatole France, undertakes a comparative survey of reservation jurisprudence in the USA, Canada and South Africa without explaining why those jurisdictions have been selected or what the purpose of comparative analysis is, embarks upon an entirely irrelevant excursion into various schemes and programmes for the uplift of disadvantaged sections, delivers a moral sermon on alternatives to reservation, and puts out a number of observations on the concept of merit that are entirely at odds with its conclusions.

Negotiating through the surplusage, however, one arrives at the following lines of reasoning. *First*, Justice Bhat held that a majority in *Indra Sawhney* had 'decisively' ruled in favour of the 50 per cent cap. However, as pointed out above, even if that is true, a majority in *Indra Sawhney* had *also* upheld *N.M. Thomas*, and the two propositions are contradictory. This is why the request for reconsideration of the 50 per cent rule by a larger bench was justified.

Secondly, Justice Bhat cited the principle of *stare decisis* and the need for stability in the law (paragraph 11). One might have been minded to accept this argument were it not for the fact that the learned justice's newfound respect for *stare decisis* was strangely absent a little while ago when, as part of a bench led by Arun Mishra J, he saw no problem with overruling seventeen Supreme Court judgments on Section 24 of the Land Acquisition Act, which had consistently been followed by high courts across the country. With due respect, *stare decisis* is a question of principle, not of convenience.

Thirdly, Bhat J held that *Indra Sawhney* was based on the principle of 'balance'—i.e., 'balancing' equality of opportunity and reservation. However, as I have pointed out above, a 'balance' that takes the form of a 50 per cent cap is just a subtler way of rephrasing the 'exception' paradigm. In no objective sense are you being 'balanced' if (to repeat the hypothetical) 20 per cent of a society oppresses 80 per cent, but reservation is fixed at 50 per cent. Once again, therefore, the word 'balance' simply assumes the conclusion in the premise. This was made crystal clear in paragraph 34 of Bhat J's judgment, where the learned justice noted:

> Upon examination of the issue from this perspective, the ceiling of 50% with the 'extraordinary circumstances' exception, is the just balance what is termed as the 'Goldilocks solution'—i.e. the solution containing the right balance that allows the state sufficient latitude to ensure meaningful affirmative action, to those who deserve it, and at the same time ensures that the essential content of equality, and its injunction not to discriminate on the various proscribed grounds (caste, religion, sex, place of residence) is retained.

It is impossible to reconcile this paragraph with *N.M. Thomas*. Here, Justice Bhat stated unambiguously that in his view, the 'essential content' of equality is at odds with 'affirmative action'—and not that affirmative action *fulfils* the demands of substantive equality. As with Justice Bhushan, this was a return to the *Balaji* era of the exception, only without expressly saying so.

I could not locate further substantive arguments in this concurring opinion. It is worth pointing out, however, that in a section considering the 'larger issues' around affirmative action, Bhat J noted how the concept of 'merit' is, in itself, inherently discriminatory, decontextualized and ignores situational inequalities. There is a deep irony here because the entire framework of 'balancing' equality of opportunity against reservation is *premised* on an uncritical acceptance of the concept of 'merit', which frames the understanding of formal equality of opportunity. If merit had to be understood contextually, reservation and equality of opportunity would not be at odds, and nothing would have to be 'balanced'.

(Mis)Using Ambedkar's Speech

Let me, finally, come to the issue of Dr Ambedkar's speech. There are at least four reasons why Bhushan J's use of Ambedkar's constituent assembly speech—where he stated that reservation would be confined to a 'minority'—is entirely flawed. *First*, no self-respecting theory of constitutional interpretation endorses deriving constitutional meaning from *one* speech delivered by *one* member of the constituent assembly. At the very least, the learned justice needed to do his homework on whether Ambedkar's view was the view of the assembly as a whole. He did not do so.

Secondly, even if Ambedkar's view did represent the assembly's as a whole, it was a view about how Article 16(4) ought to be *applied*, not about the meaning of 16(4) itself. As Ronald Dworkin famously argued, there is a distinction between the 'concept' of equality and competing 'conceptions' of the concept. And as long as the Constitution is framed at the level of concepts, the framers' views about what specific conceptions it might take, are to be accorded no greater deference than anyone else's view.

Thirdly, in a jurisprudential tradition that continues to uphold *Maneka Gandhi* as a crown jewel of constitutional interpretation, it is rather jarring to find a sudden love for original intent. Recall that the evidence for the fact that the constituent assembly intended Article 21 to be limited to 'procedure established by law' was far, far stronger than a single B.R. Ambedkar speech—it involved multiple debates, multiple failed amendments and a cast-iron consensus that due process was to be kept out of the Constitution. The *Maneka Gandhi* case ignored all of that. I do not here intend to get into an argument about whether that was right or wrong, but the court cannot say, 'I will use original intent when it supports my preferred conclusion and discard it when it doesn't.' That, to repeat, is a constitutionalism of convenience.

And *finally*, Ambedkar's speech—when understood in context—is not as clear-cut as it might seem. I have argued elsewhere that

Ambedkar's speech was made in the context of a debate over the introduction of the word 'backward' in Article 16, to qualify the word 'classes'.[46] Ambedkar's reconciliation of the 'competing claims' of (formal) equality of opportunity and adequacy of group representation was based on a *qualitative* addition to Article 16 (the word 'backward') and not a quantitative addition (a numerical cap, which Ambedkar discussed in his speech but consciously *refrained* from writing into Article 16[4]). I do not here claim that my reading is necessarily correct, but that it is *an alternative reading* that, at the very least, precludes easy—and lazy—conclusions about the interpretation of Article 16(4) based on Ambedkar's speech.

Conclusion

In paragraph 164 of his opinion, Justice Bhushan made this extraordinary statement:

> To change the 50% limit is to have a society which is not founded on equality but based on *caste rule*. The democracy [sic] is an essential feature of our Constitution and part of our basic structure.

What is one to make of this? All one can say is that the bogeyman of reservation leading to 'caste rule' belongs in a WhatsApp forward, not in a judgment of the Supreme Court. One should perhaps not dignify this further with serious analysis. I do think, however, that this observation is particularly revealing. In both Justice Bhushan's judgment, with its exhortations about how the country has progressed in the seventy years since Independence, and in Justice Bhat's judgment, with its lengthy detours into various government schemes for disadvantaged classes, there is a clear undercurrent of opinion:

---

46 Gautam Bhatia, 'Chapter 4', *The Transformative Constitution: A Radical Biography in Nine Acts* (New Delhi: HarperCollins India, 2019).

'*Reservations have gone on too far and too long, we really should get rid of them now.*' Justice Bhushan's statement about 'caste rule' sees those fears bubble to the surface, but, as pointed out above, the undercurrent is present throughout, and ultimately seems to play a role in the court's repeated incantation about how the '50 per cent rule' is so integral to the very idea of equality. I have previously argued that the history of reservation jurisprudence in India can be divided into three phases—the 'exception phase', the 'facet phase' and the 'balancing phase'. With recent Supreme Court judgments repeating themselves about how there is 'no right to reservation' (another overruling-of-*N.M. Thomas*-by-stealth move), coupled with today's judgment, it is possible that a fourth phase—where the Supreme Court moves to limit and rollback reservations while continuing to maintain the rhetoric of substantive equality—might have begun.

Postscript: EWS?

Does today's judgment have any impact on the constitutional challenge to EWS reservation? Justice Bhushan expressly declined to comment on the issue. However, given the insistence of both Justice Bhushan and Justice Bhat about how the 50 per cent rule is 'integral' to equality, and given the fact that equality is undisputedly a part of the basic structure, it becomes difficult to see how the Supreme Court can reach any conclusion other than striking down EWS reservation as unconstitutional. That said, we wait to be surprised![47]

---

47 We were surprised! A Constitution bench of the Supreme Court eventually upheld EWS reservation in October 2022. Because of my continuing involvement with the case as it went to review, I elected not to write about it. Interested readers can, however, consult guest posts on the blog that deal with the judgment in some detail.

Socio-Economic Rights

Introduction

THE INDIAN CONSTITUTION DOES not explicitly guarantee socio-economic rights. In theory, a number of these rights—for example, the rights to food, housing and health—have been 'read into' Article 21 of the Constitution by the judiciary. This 'reading in' has brought with it controversies around implementation, judiciary/executive relations and administration, especially when rights are articulated by the courts in abstract, programmatic language, without the infrastructure to enforce them. Indeed, it is an open question whether and to what extent the declaration of socio-economic rights by the courts has any meaning, as long as the underlying structure of the political economy—responsible for the deprivation of those rights in the first place—remains unchanged. For example, as scholars such as Amy Kapczyinski have argued, judicial dicta on access to medicine will be only partially successful—and could, at times, be counterproductive—if the system of intellectual property, which places these medicines out of reach for most, is unaltered.

Keeping this framework in mind, this section will consider the judiciary's engagement with two crucial socio-economic rights—

the right to health and the right to housing. It will look at cases where these rights were framed and articulated in concrete terms or where there existed a concrete and identifiable threat to the effective enjoyment of those rights. They will include issues around access to medicine, the role of courts in a public health crisis such as Covid-19, and the rights of individuals to shelter and against arbitrary evictions. And they will, perhaps, throw light on what courts can or cannot (and sometimes will not) do, in the context of systemic and structurally unequal economic relations.

1

Delhi High Court Rules on Article 21 and Access to Medicine

(17 April 2014)

TODAY THE DELHI HIGH Court issued an important judgment on Article 21, the right to health, intellectual property and access to medicine.[48] The issue in *Mohd Ahmed vs Union of India* is set out in the first paragraph:

> Whether a minor child born to parents belonging to economically weaker section of the society suffering from a chronic and rare disease, gaucher, is entitled to free medical treatment costing about rupees six lakhs per month especially *when the treatment is known, prognosis is good and there is every likelihood of petitioner leading a normal life. [Emphasis mine]*

The petitioner, Mohd Ahmed, was/is suffering from a rare disease called the 'Gaucher disease'. There is a known treatment—enzyme

---

48 *Mohd Ahmed (Minor) vs Union of India*, WP (C) 7279/2013 (17 April 2014).

replacement therapy—which, however, is extremely expensive, and the drugs required for it are manufactured by only three pharmaceutical companies. The reason for the high expense, as the court explains, is the rarity of the disease—it is so uncommon that pharmaceutical companies argue they can only recoup their research and development costs by pegging the price at extremely high levels. In the language of intellectual property, or IP, such drugs are known as 'orphan drugs'.

It was argued on behalf of the petitioner that failing to provide him with treatment would be a violation of his right to health (read into Article 21 via the right to life). On behalf of the Delhi government, it was argued that there were various exceptions to the right to health—in particular, exceptions based upon the resources available to the government and its own best judgment of what kind of healthcare it would prioritize. What this meant was that no individual person could make an enforceable constitutional claim upon the State for medicine—rather, it was up to the State to allocate its resources in a manner that ensured the best and widest possible healthcare to as many people as possible.

Thus, the basic issue in this case was (given that the right to health has been read into Article 21): What amount of deference ought a court to accord to the legislature's determination that the lack of resources does not allow it to provide medical treatment to a particular person? And, as a corollary, does the degree of deference change with the nature of the case, turning upon factors such as the patient's poverty, the seriousness of the disease, the availability of treatment and so on?

In its reasoning, the court found that although a number of countries had specific policies in place to address the problems of orphan drugs, no such policy existed in India (paragraphs 38–42). Because of the separation of powers, however, the court could not require the legislature to draft a law or frame a policy (paragraphs 44–45). The only question, then, was the constitutional question: *Does the government owe a constitutional duty to provide free medical treatment to the petitioner suffering from a rare and chronic disease, even though the treatment is expensive and recurring* [paragraph 46]*?*'

The court, after referring to Article 21, extensively cited the ICESCR, or the International Covenant on Economic, Social and Cultural Rights (see Article 12), and General Comment 14 to the ICESCR[49], which fleshes out in detail the *content* of the right to health. Citing the prior cases of *Parmanand Katara vs Union of India* and *Paschim Banga Khet Mazdoor Samity*, the court held that *'every person has a fundamental right to quality health care—that is affordable, accessible and compassionate'* (paragraph 59). The court conceded that availability of resources was an important factor—and that in light of competing claims such as education and defence, it could not *'direct that all inhabitants of this country be given free medical treatment at state expense'* (paragraphs 62–63).

Nonetheless, crucially—and directly echoing the ICESCR's jurisprudence, that every right has a minimum core that is not subject to resource constraints and is directly enforceable—the court held:

> By virtue of Article 21 of the Constitution, the State is under a legal obligation to ensure access to life saving drugs to patients. A reasonable and equitable access to life saving medicines is critical to promoting and protecting the right to health. This means that Government must at the bare minimum ensure that individuals have access to essential medicines even for rare diseases like enzyme replacement for Gaucher disease. Availability of a very expensive drug virtually makes it inaccessible *[paragraph 68]*.

And:

> Government cannot cite financial crunch as a reason not to fulfil its obligation to ensure access of medicines or to adopt a plan of action to treat rare diseases. In the opinion of this Court, no

---

49 'CESCR General Comment No. 14: The Right to the Highest Attainable Standard of Health (Art. 12)', Office of the High Commissioner for Human Rights, https://www.refworld.org/pdfid/4538838d0.pdf

> government can wriggle out of its core obligation of ensuring the right of access to health facilities for vulnerable and marginalized section of society *[paragraph 69]*.

And in conclusion:

> Although obligations under Article 21 are generally understood to be progressively realizable depending on maximum available resources, yet certain obligations are considered core and non-derogable irrespective of resource constraints. Providing access to essential medicines at affordable prices is one such core obligation *[paragraph 87]*.

Today's judgment does two important things. *First*, it clarifies the content of the right to health under Article 21. One of the signal problems with the court's Article 21 jurisprudence over the past twenty years has been the lack of clarity, and a cavalier, laissez-faire approach towards this constitutional provision. By more or less expressly incorporating the ICESCR—with its concomitant principles of what the scope of the right is, what the obligations of the government are (see, for example, General Comment 14), and the adjudicatory principles of progressive realization, minimum core and non-derogable implementation with respect to the most marginalized sections of society, the court brings *determinate standards* to its Article 21/right to health jurisprudence. This would be helpful in future cases involving the right to health.

Secondly, by expressly invoking the constitutional right to health in a case where the driver of inaccessibility is the regime of intellectual property (patent, in this case), the court lays the foundations of a jurisprudence that has been gaining ground in many countries: the *constitutionalization* of IP law. That is to say, although the court does not deal with IP issues in this case, it makes it clear that the Constitution is relevant. This is important because of a divide within the IP regime: IP maximalists argue that the balance between various rights and interests—the right of the inventor to profit from his work, the interest of the public in fostering more innovation and creativity by protecting inventors' rights, and the public's competing right to access medicine—are all balanced *within* the IP regime, through *inbuilt* exceptions such as compulsory licensing. However, of late, there has been a critique of this position. Scholars such as Laurence Helfer and Michael Birnhack have argued that basic human rights such as the right to free expression and the right to health ought to be invoked to *determine* the scope of the IP regime and its exceptions. So, for example, when we're dealing with the question of photocopying school/college textbooks and the question of how much copying constitutes 'fair use' under the copyright regime, these scholars argue that the right of free expression and the right to education should be invoked in determining how much use is fair use (as opposed to the traditional analysis, which focuses only on what level of exceptions would foster greatest innovation, without considering problems of individual access (that might be barred because of poverty, unaddressed by the market).

By invoking the specific, individual right to health in a case where medicines have been priced out of range because of IP, the court thus opens up the possibility of using constitutional law and constitutional rights in subsequent cases, where IP is implicated much more directly: for example, cases of compulsory licensing or the scope of Section 3(d). Invoking the right to health, for example, it could be argued that in Section 3(d) of the Patents Act, 1970, which denies patents for '*the mere discovery of a new form of a known substance which does not result in the enhancement of the known efficacy of that substance …*', and is aimed at preventing evergreening, the term 'known efficacy' should be read strictly so as to ensure that essential medicines do not remain perpetually behind exorbitant patent paywalls. Whether that step is taken by the court in future cases, of course, remains to be seen.

(Interestingly, today's decision is similar in many respects to the famous South African case, *Treatment Action Campaign vs Minister for Health*, which is well worth a read.[50])

---

50 'Minister of Health and Others vs Treatment Action Campaign and Others (No 2) (CCT8/02) [2002] ZACC 15; 2002 (5) SA 721 (CC); 2002 (10) BCLR 1033 (CC) (5 July 2002)', South African Legal Information Institute, http://www.saflii.org/za/cases/ZACC/2002/15.html

2

Coronavirus and the Constitution—XXXVI: The Delhi High Court's Judgment on Taxation and the Right to Health

(31 May 2021)

[**Update**: In an order passed on 1 June 2021, the Delhi High Court's judgment—discussed below—has been stayed by the Supreme Court. The only reason provided by the Supreme Court in its stay order is that 'arguable issues have been raised' in the appeal. Needless to say, staying a carefully reasoned high court judgment that returned a finding of unconstitutionality against State action on the ground that 'arguable issues' have been raised is problematic. This is a very low standard that keeps a high court judgment in abeyance not because there is a prima facie error of law or fact, but because, presumably, it is possible to take another view. Furthermore, the fact that the court has issued notice returnable in four weeks means that the case has effectively been decided in favour of the Union government, as, presumably, by the time the Supreme Court gets around to hearing the case, there will no longer be as pressing a need for oxygen concentrators.

One of the most frustrating parts about writing and analysing contemporary Indian constitutional law is the lack of accountability with which the Supreme Court stays high court judgments. There is no uniform or consistent principle, and in a majority of cases, the Supreme Court does not accord the high court judgment the courtesy of a proper analysis before issuing a stay order. And, as pointed out above, in most cases—especially in urgent cases—the stay effectively amounts to a decision in favour of the government, but without any judicial reasoning, as the delay between issuing notice and getting around to deciding the issue invariably renders the case infructuous.]

IN AN INTERESTING JUDGMENT handed down on 21 May (*Gurcharan Singh vs The Ministry of Finance*), the High Court of Delhi struck down the levy of Integrated Goods and Services Tax (IGST) on oxygen concentrators that had been imported into the country, as a gift or for personal use.[51] The judgment is notable because it is a relatively rare instance of a successful constitutional challenge to a tax levy, and one that succeeded on fundamental rights grounds, rather than on a demonstration that the tax was confiscatory.

The primary basis of the court's judgment was that under Notification 4/2021-Customs, imposition of IGST on oxygen concentrators was exempted as long as they were free and for the purposes of Covid relief, *and* imported by a state government or by an entity authorized by any state government. This, then, created two categories of persons who were importing oxygen concentrators for Covid relief—those who were doing it through a government-approved entity (exempted from IGST) and those who were not (IGST leviable), i.e., those who were receiving oxygen concentrators as gifts for their personal use. The court found this distinction to be arbitrary and irrational, and consequently, a violation of Article 14 (paragraph 13).

---

51 *Gurcharan Singh vs Ministry of Finance*, WP (C) 5149/2021 (21 May 2021).

What is of greater interest, however, is the court's contextualization of the issue within the Covid-19 pandemic. The bench of Shakhder and Talwant Singh JJ noted that while ordinarily, 'tax ... does not recognise equity', 'it must, however, in our view, bend to the will of equity in times of calamity which causes wholesale degradation in the human ability to contribute to the coffers of the State' (paragraph 15). In this case, therefore, the court had to examine the tax on the anvil of the right to health under Article 21 of the Constitution, keeping in mind the global pandemic (paragraph 15.1). This, in turn, required the State to demonstrate that:

> [T]he revenue, it would possibly garner, as IGST, in respect of oxygen concentrators which are imported in the circumstances, in which, the petitioner is put, would be appreciably more than the cost incurred to administer the collection of IGST on such transactions. These details need not have borne mathematical precision; a broad-brush approach would have sufficed, so that we could be persuaded to hold that denying relief to the petitioner and persons similarly circumstanced would be in public weal. The counter-affidavit filed by the State gives us no clue whatsoever concerning this vital issue *[paragraph 15. 4]*.

In the absence of any such countervailing justification, the impact of the tax on the right to health under Article 21 was evidently onerous and burdensome. It also breached the State's positive obligations under Article 21, which it could have discharged through 'delaying its collections, granting rebates, or, as in this case, permitting, import of vital medical equipment, drugs, medicines, for a defined period, till such time, normalcy is restored' (paragraph 15.7)—and which, indeed, the State had done so for other categories involving the import of oxygen concentrators.

The court's judgment in this case is undoubtedly correct, and its desire to contain the scope of its reasoning to the extraordinary situation generated by the Covid-19 pandemic is understandable, as it is difficult to displace the many decades of established wisdom that requires a judicial hands-off approach when it comes to testing tax law and policy on the touchstone of fundamental rights. However, when we think about it, the Covid-19 pandemic has only revealed particularly starkly what has always been true—tax law is one of the most potent tools in the hands of the State to shape and direct behaviour (as potent as criminal law), and for that reason, there is no reason why taxation should be given any *greater* deference by courts when it is subjected to a fundamental rights challenge. Indeed, as the Colombian Constitutional Court's judgment striking down a tampon tax, and the Canadian Supreme Court's judgment upholding business deductions, both in the context of challenges on the touchstone of gender equality, show us, issues of taxation are deeply intertwined with issues around constitutional guarantees of equality and non-discrimination. The Covid-19 pandemic (to reiterate) has only revealed this truth, rather than create it.

The Delhi High Court's judgment is nonetheless important as it breaks judicial inertia and for the first time puts these questions on the table. Admittedly, the judgment suggests that the more exacting judicial review that it applied to the IGST notification—especially on the right-to-health ground—was because of the extraordinary circumstances created by the pandemic, and that the normal policy of deference would continue to apply otherwise. That said, it is also clear that the court's analysis is not—and indeed, need not be—attached to the specific circumstances of the pandemic. Indeed, if we think of the 'tampon tax' challenge, for example, one can easily see how the issue of menstrual hygiene—as a continuing concern—is as fundamentally important to the right to health and equality as is the issue of importing oxygen concentrators to deal with Covid-19. I would say, therefore, that the high court's reasoning contains the beginnings of a more progressive—and constitutionally more just—approach to the intersection between tax and fundamental rights.

A final point on remedy: The court refrained from touching the notification itself, and instead, granted the petitioner relief by reading the term 'oxygen concentrator' into separate exemption notifications involving tax exemptions for life-saving drugs. However, I am not quite sure why this was necessary. Would not the purpose have been served equally by simply severing the words 'by a State Government or, any entity, relief agency or statutory body, authorised in this regard by any State Government' from the impugned notification? This would ipso facto have extended the benefit of the exemption, then, to goods 'imported free of cost for the purpose of Covid relief', and would have covered the case of the petitioner.

In any event, the technical quibble aside, the high court ended its judgment by noting that it was traversing over 'what was, somewhat, new and uneven terrain' (paragraph 22). The court ought to be complimented for doing so judiciously and with wisdom; it is now the task of future benches to chart a further path.

3

The Delhi High Court on Forced Evictions, Adequate Housing and a 'Right to the City'

(21 March 2019)

IN AN INTERESTING JUDGMENT handed down earlier this week, the Delhi High Court laid down some important principles concerning the rights of slum dwellers to adequate housing, and protection from forced evictions. The case itself had been filed in 2015, in response to demolitions and forced evictions (that had allegedly caused, among other things, the death of a six-year-old child) at Shakur Basti, a *jhuggi* cluster built on Indian Railways land. In its interim orders (discussed from paragraphs 3 to 48), the high court found that the Railways had failed to carry out its obligations to conduct a survey determining the eligibility of the residents for rehabilitation under law (set out in paragraph 28) before it commenced eviction. Accordingly, it passed orders on various relief measures and directed the statutory agencies involved to act in a coordinated manner to deliver them to the displaced citizens. The case proceeded in the form of a continuing mandamus, with the court monitoring the developments (including the preparation of a draft protocol that would coordinate the actions of the agencies) until December 2018, when judgment was reserved on the legal issues.

The high court was then required to consider the interaction between a complex maze of legal instruments related to the rights of slum dwellers in the context of forced evictions and rehabilitation: international law (that Muralidhar J read into the domestic legal landscape *via* the Protection of Human Rights Act, 1993) (paragraphs 56 to 68), the Indian Constitution (paragraphs 84 to 86), various statutes such as the Slum Areas (Improvement and Clearances) Act, 1956 and the Delhi Urban Shelter Improvement Board Act, 2010 (paragraphs 93 to 111) and attendant policies (paragraphs 119 to 136), and the court's own previous judgments, from the iconic *Olga Tellis* (paragraphs 87 to 92) to the more recent and specific *Sudama Singh* (paragraphs 112–118). Muralidhar J also informed his reasoning through an extensive analysis of South African constitutional jurisprudence which, of course, is based upon a categorical right to housing provided by the constitutional text, which we lack (paragraphs 69 to 79).

The court found that its previous judgment in *Sudama Singh*—which had interpreted constitutional principles in more concrete terms, providing for a right to rehabilitation and a right to a meaningful engagement before an eviction—had now been codified by the 2015 policy and by the protocol that had been worked out by the parties during the hearing, and which had received their imprimatur. Consequently, the court held that, in accordance with the law:

- Before any eviction can be commenced, there must be a survey in order to determine whether the residents are eligible for rehabilitation in accordance with the existing law and policy.
- In case the answer to the above is 'yes', the eviction cannot be commenced until provisions are made either for *in situ* rehabilitation or for alternative accommodation.

- Any eviction must be preceded by meaningful engagement with the residents on all issues, including the terms and conditions of rehabilitation (paragraphs 142–144).

Muralidhar J's judgment is important for a few reasons. At the constitutional level, it clarifies (once again) what, precisely, a 'right to housing' might mean in the Indian context. In the absence of an enforceable, textual right to housing, any court that wants to retain fidelity to the Constitution is constrained in what it can achieve. It cannot, for example, declare that every individual must be provided a house (indeed, the South African Constitution, which *does* have the right, has also baulked at going so far). However, the guaranteed rights to freedom of movement and residence, as well as the right to life, provides a basis for a more modest, but a more rigorously grounded, formulation—that the government may not *impede* access to housing (by evicting people in occupation of certain land) without complying with a substantive due process standard. This standard requires, *first*, 'meaningful engagement' with the residents before any action is taken (this is a more fleshed-out and rigorous articulation of the right to a hearing, and is drawn from South African jurisprudence), and, *secondly*, rehabilitation, where a right to rehabilitation has been established by law or policy. For readers familiar with the Forest Rights Act, 2006, it is a bit similar to the principle that no coercive action can be taken against a resident before the settlement of her rights is completed. Note that neither of the two requirements *guarantees* an individual a house in a tangible or material sense. What they do, however, is place thick procedural obligations upon the government if it wants to deprive someone of shelter—it is not enough for the government to invoke property rights, label them as 'encroachers' and drive them off.

The Delhi High Court buttressed its articulation of constitutional values by invoking two further principles. The first was the exhortation that the government is not entitled to treat slum dwellers on public land as rightless beings, with all the demeaning connotations that labels such as 'encroachers' or 'trespassers' bring. Rather, residents were at all times to be treated as rights-bearers, and the government was not entitled to derogate from its constitutional obligations while engaging with them. At the heart of this articulation is the understanding that urban poverty is a structural issue and simply targeting occupiers of public land as 'encroachers' not only mischaracterizes the problems, but also violates basic constitutional values. The Indian judiciary has not always been consistent in this understanding and, therefore, its clear articulation by Muralidhar J is very welcome.

The second was the invocation of a 'right to the city' (paragraphs 80 to 83). Drawing upon the work of famous urban space scholars such as Henri Lefebvre and David Harvey, as well as contemporary international law, Muralidhar J noted that 'the right to the city' envisaged 'stronger democratic control and wide participation in struggles to reshape the city'. In essence, therefore, the idea is *democratization*—the inhabitants of a city ought to have a voice, a stake and participation in questions such as 'how is the city to be designed?', 'who is the city for?', 'how and on what terms are spaces in the city to be accessed?' and so on. To anyone who lives in Delhi—with its gated colonies, the walled gardens of what is popularly known as the 'Lutyens Zone' and the heavily guarded entrances to gigantic malls—this will be immediately understandable. The point is this: How we access the city, which spaces are open to us and which aren't, and how we navigate those spaces, are all questions that are now dependent upon socio-economic class and status, but *ought* to be subjected to democratic control.

Now you may say that this is all well and good, and ought to be the subject of political struggle and agitation, but what does it have to do with constitutional adjudication? A court can hardly 'enforce' a right to the city by redesigning urban spaces to (for example) reverse the 'privatization of space' that gated colonies have so effectively conducted, and so on. That is a task for urban planners. In this case, however, the idea of the right to the city was what informed the court's articulation of meaningful engagement before evictions as a constitutional principle. Furthermore, its applications in other cases can be grasped. Readers will recall, for instance, a recent controversy with respect to the Delhi Gymkhana Club, when 'guests who look like maids' were denied entry.[52] Now, the debate is rather constrained as long as it is limited to a putative clash between the club's 'right' to impose a dress code and the human right to non-discrimination and dignity. However, we can think about this another way: The club occupies a vast amount of (what would otherwise have been) public space in the heart of Delhi. 'A right to the city' raises difficult—but important—questions about the nature of control over such spaces, their possible democratization, and whether and to what extent socio-economic class (of which dress is a marker) can be made the basis for exclusion. That, of course, will depend upon how future courts develop the concept.

With reference to this case, in particular, the flow of Muralidhar J's reasoning may be understood by referring to the following scheme, arranged around descending levels of abstraction:

> **Level One**: Citizens as rights-bearers and not as 'subjects', 'encroachers' and 'trespassers'/'a right to the city'.
> **Level Two**: The right to adequate housing/right against forced evictions/right to meaningful engagement/right to enforce rehabilitation schemes.
> **Level Three**: Statutory instruments and policy documents that actualize the above.
> **Level Four**: No eviction without compliance with the above.

---

52 Sangeeta Barooah Pisharoty, 'Guests Who Look Like 'Maids' Not Allowed in Delhi Gymkhana', The Wire, 19 January 2016, https://thewire.in/society/guests-who-look-like-maids-not-allowed-in-delhi-gymkhana

But at the end of the day, while this judgment demonstrates the promise of socio-economic rights adjudication, when done rigorously and emphatically, with a view to the principles of participation and engagement, it also reveals the limitations of the judicial role and the importance of other democratic actors. Here, the court was only able to do what it did because of the existence of detailed statutory instruments and policy documents that actualized the constitutional principles (to whatever limited extent)—many of which, admittedly, had only come into existence because of judicial pressure. As the court was careful to note, for example, the rights at issue would kick in if the residents had a prior right to rehabilitation *in accordance with extant law and policy* (here, for example, the relevant policy had a cut-off date of 2015). Now, what if existing law did not provide for that right? To what extent would the court be able to stipulate or decree it, given that (as everyone agrees) there is no *substantive* right to housing under the Indian Constitution? The fate of judgments such as *Olga Tellis*, for example, where much was said, but ultimately the eviction was upheld, perhaps suggests that this is not an area where the court can go it alone. The same is true for a 'right to the city'—ultimately, any substantive articulation of a 'right to the city' will butt heads against the much more entrenched legal principle of private property. The court's articulation of a 'right to the city' informs us that our present legal landscape is not the *only* way in which we might imagine the relationship between people and land; but to *change* that relationship is the onerous task of democracy.

4

Responding to Illegal Home Demolitions: The Doctrine of an Unconstitutional State of Affairs

(12 June 2022)

PREVIOUSLY ON THIS BLOG, we have discussed the recent spate of home demolitions that have been carried out at the behest of various state governments.[53] These home demolitions follow a familiar pattern. A protest takes place in a locality or a neighbourhood, which turns violent. Soon after, the police declares that a certain individual, or set of individuals, have been identified as the 'masterminds' behind the violence. Immediately after that, the municipality declares that these individuals are residing in unauthorized buildings (often, as in

---

53 Rishika Sahgal, 'The Illegality of the Jahangirpuri Demolitions', Indian Constitutional Law and Philosophy, 28 April 2022, https://indconlawphil.wordpress.com/2022/04/28/guest-post-the-illegality-of-the-jahangirpuri-demolitions/; M. Jannani, 'The Illegality of the Khargone Demolitions', Indian Constitutional Law and Philosophy, 9 May 2022, https://indconlawphil.wordpress.com/2022/05/09/guest-post-the-illegality-of-the-khargone-demolitions/

the most recent case, with backdated notices of *doubtful authenticity*[54]). The buildings (homes) are then demolished. In the normal course of things, the time period between the police declaring that it has identified the masterminds behind the violence, the municipality declaring that the buildings are illegal and the actual demolition is under twenty-four hours.

On this blog, it has been pointed out that on its own terms—that is, even assuming that the rationale for the demolitions is illegal constructions and not collective punishment—this modus operandi violates both local and municipal laws, the rule of law and the Constitution. What, then, is the remedy? As the case around demolitions at Jahangirpuri in New Delhi showed, the speed at which demolitions are undertaken ensures that even where there is judicial intervention, it is often too late to accomplish anything meaningful. Things are even worse when demolitions happen far away from Delhi, or in places—and to communities—where immediate access to courts is substantially more difficult.

This post proceeds upon the important assumption that, at present, the Supreme Court has the *will* and the *desire* to address the serious challenge of the executive flouting the rule of law through the pattern of home demolitions across the country. If that assumption is true, the question is—given the facts laid out in the above paragraph—how the constitutional violation ought to be framed and how a remedy may be crafted.

I suggest that at present, our constitutional jurisprudence may not have the precise vocabulary to address the issue. As the Jahangirpuri demolitions showed, the court was minded to treat the demolition as an *individual* State act, which it would scrutinize for compliance with the law and the Constitution. As the copycat actions across different

---

54 As pointed out by Sharjeel Usmani. See https://twitter.com/SharjeelUsmani/status/1535880160762662912?s=20&t=vzPmWwCrfCceupGpfg262g

states have shown, however, a specific instance of home demolition is not an individualized act, but is part of an *evolving pattern of collective punishment by the State*. To capture this, I suggest, new vocabulary might be needed. One place where this can be found is the Latin American doctrine of an *unconstitutional state of affairs*.

This doctrine originated in Colombia and was later adopted in Brazil. As the term suggests, an unconstitutional *state of affairs* is specifically meant for a situation where the violation of rights is not individualized but *structural*. According to a definition:

> The unconstitutional state of affairs is a legal ruling that allows the Constitutional Court to acknowledge the failure of both the Legislative and Executive branches of government to enforce public policies against widespread and systemic violation of *fundamental rights*, thus justifying a judicial intervention in order to combat the *structural causes* of the violations and to put everything back in order with the Constitution. *[Emphasis mine]*[55]

The importance of the unconstitutional state of affairs doctrine, therefore, lies in its focus on the *widespread and systematic* violation of fundamental rights. In the present situation, not only are the criteria for the application of the doctrine met, but it is the only truly effective doctrinal tool that the Supreme Court can apply to deal with the situation. There are two reasons for this. The first is that as long as the court considers individualized cases of demolitions, it needs to take at face value the entirely implausible assertion that the

---

55 Thiago Luis Santos Sombra, 'The "Unconstitutional State of Affairs" in Brazil's Prison System: The Enchantment of Legal Transplantation', ICONnect, 30 September 2015, http://www.iconnectblog.com/the-unconstitutional-state-of-affairs-in-brazils-prison-system-the-enchantment-of-legal-transplantation/

police action in 'identifying' the alleged rioters is separate from the municipality's action in demolishing the home. In true Orwellian fashion, the court has to ignore the 'evidence of its own eyes and ears'—i.e., the chronology of events that is police identification, municipality declaration and demolition, all within the space of a day. This, in turn, means that the court is forced to examine what is essentially a case of collective punishment within the framework of municipality laws.

The unconstitutional state of affairs doctrine, however, expands what the court can consider, both in time and in space. It allows the court to take into account the 'systematic nature' of this practice, both in the recent past and in its spread across the country. This is crucial, because it is only from the *pattern* of home demolitions that the court can extrapolate the fact that collective punishment has become an informal part of State *policy*. After all, it might plausibly be argued that a single occasion happens to be a coincidence; however, when the same thing—police identification, municipality declaration, demolition—repeats itself over time and space, it becomes evident that it is State policy.

Now, once an unconstitutional state of affairs has been identified (on the basis, of course, of evidence collected over time and space), what remedy follows? Here, we are back in familiar territory: the Brazilian and Colombian courts have developed the remedy of a structural injunction, or, as we know it in India, the *continuing mandamus*. The continuing mandamus allows the Supreme Court to take cognisance of the situation, issue interim orders and monitor for compliance—which, crucially, will not be limited to single cases, but will extend to the unconstitutional state of affairs *at large*. What might those interim orders look like in this situation? That, I think, would depend upon how lawyers and justices might want to craft the relief, but at a pinch, for example, mandatory judicial sanction before demolition as an interim measure is one possibility. The crucial thing to note, however, is that to be effective, the remedy must be: (a) *preventive* and (b) *extend to all cases*. Under the present circumstances, where demolition cases are being treated on an individual basis, neither is possible. The unconstitutional state of affairs doctrine, however, provides the Supreme Court with a vocabulary to do both.

5

Home Demolitions and George Orwell's Supreme Court

(13 July 2022)

THERE IS A LINE in George Orwell's *1984* that goes, '*The Party told you to reject the evidence of your eyes and ears. It was their final, most essential command.*'

Ongoing proceedings before the Supreme Court pertaining to the spate of home demolitions, which have been carried out across the country by municipal authorities, present a striking example of how judges can continuously reject the evidence of their eyes and ears. These proceedings follow a similar pattern. It is pointed out to the court (as we have discussed previously) that the home demolitions—which have now been going on in a sporadic fashion for many months—are punitive and designed to extract retribution for participation in protests. The State counsel argues that the municipal authorities are acting in accordance with the local laws. The Supreme Court bench—it tends to change—makes a rhetorical statement about how demolitions must follow the legal process, makes another rhetorical statement about how it can't pass 'omnibus' orders against the demolitions and then adjourns the case, as it did today[56] (while the demolitions continue).

In continuously refusing to take cognisance of the fact that the home demolitions are punitive and illegal, and follow the same pattern across the country, these Supreme Court judges reject the evidence of their eyes and ears. They manage to ignore the fact that, *coincidentally*, the home demolitions in question come immediately on the heels of a protest that turns violent, time after time, and are specifically targeted against people who are named by the police in FIRs about rioting; that in Uttar Pradesh, Javed Anand's home was demolished *one day after the UP Police claimed* that he was the 'mastermind' behind the 10 June riots,[57] and that in Khargone (MP), Khambhat (Gujarat), Nagaon (Assam), Jahangirpuri (Delhi) and in other places, the exact same pattern is followed (indeed, in Jahangirpuri, demolitions swiftly followed *a letter*[58] from the BJP leader to the mayor, asking for bulldozer action against 'illegal properties of the rioters').

Not only that, these Supreme Court judges reject the evidence of their eyes and ears where the punitive character is laid bare by agents of the State. A non-representative sample includes, for example, statements by the home minister of Madhya Pradesh in the wake of the Khargone riots, that the 'demolition drive *against rioters* would continue'[59]; a statement by the divisional commissioner, Indore, that 'the main idea behind the move is to instil fear of financial losses

---

56   Shruti Kakkar, 'Can Omnibus Orders Be Passed against Demolitions? Supreme Court Asks in Jamiat Pleas Challenging "Bulldozer" Actions', LiveLaw, 13 July 2022, https://www.livelaw.in/top-stories/supreme-court-asks-in-jamiat-pleas-challenging-bulldozer-actions-demolitions-203646

57   Tarique Anwar, 'Prayagraj: Questions That Beg Answers in Javed Mohammad's House Demolition', LiveLaw, 15 June 2022, https://www.newsclick.in/prayagraj-questions-beg-answers-javed-mohammads-house-demolition

58   See https://twitter.com/adeshguptabjp/status/1516454691726831616

59   Sravani Sarkar, 'Demolition Drive to Continue against Khargone Rioters: MP Govt', *The Week*, 12 April 2022, https://www.theweek.

among *the accused*'⁶⁰; the Khargone district collector telling journalists that the demolitions were done to 'send a message to rioters'⁶¹; multiple other statements by Khargone officials, collected here;⁶² a statement by the district administration in Khambhat, Gujarat, that 'the encroached properties belonging to the *accused* are being demolished'⁶³; the SDGP in Nagaon, Assam, telling journalists that 'some of the *suspects* [involved in a riot] had encroached upon land … the eviction drive was carried out after a case was registered against them'⁶⁴; and this tweet by the media adviser to the government of UP, with an image of a destroyed home, and the caption 'उपद्रवी याद रखें, हर शुक्रवार के बाद एक षनिवार ज़रूर आता है…'⁶⁵.

---

in/news/india/2022/04/12/demolition-drive-to-continue-against-khargone-rioters-mp-govt.html

60 Vijaita Singh, '45 Properties of Suspected Rioters Demolished in Madhya Pradesh', *The Hindu*, 11 April 2022, https://www.thehindu.com/news/national/properties-of-suspected-rioters-demolished-in-madhya-pradesh/article65311707.ece?homepage=true

61 Bismee Taksin, '"Message to Rioters" or "Anti-encroachment Drive"—What Exactly Happened in Khargone after Riot', The Print, 16 April 2022, https://theprint.in/india/message-to-rioters-or-anti-encroachment-drive-what-exactly-happened-in-khargone-after-riot/917939/

62 'Ram Navami Clashes: MP Govt Runs Demolition Drive, Does the Law Allow It?', The Quint, 11 April 2022, https://www.thequint.com/news/india/khargone-unrest-police-undertakes-demolition-drive-following-ram-navami-clashes#read-more

63 As quoted by the ANI. See: https://twitter.com/ANI/status/1514916254636597254?ref_src=twsrc%5Etfw%7Ctwcamp%5Etweetembed%7Ctwterm%5E1514916254636597254%7Ctwgr%5E%7Ctwcon%5Es1_&ref_url=https%3A%2F%2Fthewire.in%2Fgovernment%2Fgujarat-bulldozer-ram-navami-accused-clash-raze

64 'Houses of Suspects in Assam Violence Razed', *The Hindu*, 23 May 2022, https://www.thehindu.com/news/national/other-states/houses-of-people-accused-of-setting-assam-police-station-ablaze-demolished/article65446516.ece

65 See https://twitter.com/MrityunjayUP/status/1535507915414548481?ref_src=twsrc%5Etfw%7Ctwcamp%5Etweetembed%7Ctwterm%5E1535507915414548481%7Ctwgr%5E%7Ctwcon%5Es1_&r

Examples could be multiplied, but what is abundantly clear is the two-faced character of the State. To maintain the veneer of legality, in its formal orders, the State claims that the demolitions are following due process and that the action has nothing to do with retribution. These are the arguments that the State's counsel then makes in court. Quite apart from the fact that these arguments fail on their own terms, the basic point is this: The only way that you can accept the State's arguments—*pace* Orwell—is if you choose to reject the evidence of your eyes and ears—not once, not twice, but every single time that State agents engage in targeted demolitions after protests, publicly brag about 'teaching the rioters a lesson' and then send their lawyers to argue in court that the demolitions have nothing to do with the protests.

Finally, it is important to note that the court is *not* precluded from taking the evidence of its eyes and ears into account and crafting appropriate relief. After all, this is a court that has, over the past four decades, prided itself on turning postcards into PILs, basing interim orders on (credible) newspaper reports and wielding Article 142 as a sword of complete justice. Nor is it helpless when it comes to framing remedies. We have discussed the doctrine of an 'unconstitutional state of affairs', which can allow the court to take cognisance of a systemic pattern of home demolitions across the country. But even without that, existing doctrines such as that of continuing mandamus can serve to address the situation.

However, having taken on this power to do substantive justice, the court's refusal to use it in a case where the violation of the rule of law is clear and unambiguous is a choice from which it cannot escape responsibility. The court's bland, oral observations about 'omnibus orders' and 'following the law', and its continued kicking of the can down the road while the demolitions continue, allow this two-faced

---

ef_url=https%3A%2F%2Fwww.abc.net.au%2Fnews%2F2022-06-16%2Findia-bulldozer-politics-justice-muslim-protesters-bjp%2F101147882

State action to continue with impunity. And its continued refusal to even acknowledge the evidence of its eyes and ears—the evidence of all our eyes and ears—makes us wonder whether the Supreme Court is on the way to becoming George Orwell's court.

Refugees and Non-Citizens

Introduction

UPENDRA BAXI ONCE FAMOUSLY called the Supreme Court of India 'the last refuge of the oppressed and the bewildered'. There is perhaps no better occasion to test that claim than by looking at how the Supreme Court—and the judiciary in general—responds when cases involving refugees (and other non-citizens) are brought before it. Refugees—especially refugees fleeing murderous regimes—are the most vulnerable and marginalized group one can imagine. By definition, they have no political power (as they do not have the vote), and as both history and the present have shown, it is the easiest thing in the world for governments to whip up contempt and loathing of refugees. It is precisely these groups of people—whose entrenched political powerlessness makes them ripe targets of abuse—that independent judiciaries exist to protect.

In the following pages, you will read about the judiciary's response to cases involving Rohingya refugees fleeing genocide in Myanmar, its engagement with the global principle of *non-refoulement* (i.e., a State cannot send back a persecuted people to the country that is persecuting them) and proceedings around foreigners' tribunals and the National Register of Citizens (NRC) in Assam. The essays speak for themselves and do not need any further contextualization.

1

The NRC Case and the Parchment Barrier of Article 21

(26 April 2019)

THERE HAVE BEEN MULTIPLE procedural irregularities that have characterized the Supreme Court's NRC (National Register of Citizens) case—the use of sealed covers, consequential decisions being taken in closed-door hearings and the bench's disturbing disregard for due process rights.[66] In the course of this years-long proceeding, the court has far exceeded its brief as the apex judicial organ of the country, with its repeated stress on deportations making it appear more executive-minded even than the executive—more the 'Supreme Deportation Authority' than the sentinel on the qui vive. But yesterday's hearing in *Harsh Mander vs Union of India* marks a low point even within this ongoing story.

According to accounts of the oral proceedings, the government of Assam brought forward a plan to secure the monitored release of foreigners who had been in detention centres for more than five

---

66 Gautam Bhatia, 'In the Court of Last Resort', *The Hindu*, 3 October 2018, https://www.thehindu.com/opinion/lead/in-the-court-of-last-resort/article25105456.ece

years. The plan entailed the detainees paying a hefty deposit amount of Rs 5 lakh, having their biometric details taken and then set free from the detention centres. The Chief Justice-led bench reacted to this with great anger, questioning the government repeatedly about its failure to deport individuals who had been held to be foreigners (this has been a common theme of every hearing). The Chief Justice claimed that the government was asking the bench to be '*part of an illegal order where a foreigner who has no right to stay in the country will remain and sign a bond and so on*'. He further lectured the government about what it *should* have been arguing, noting that '*the stand of the government of India and the state of Assam should be that the foreigners detenues should be deported as soon as possible. But we do not see that stand, Mr Chief Secretary.*' When the amicus curae made the rather basic point that technically, deportation could hardly be carried out without the cooperation of the host country, the Chief Justice's only response was that '*we can say that the government has failed to do its job*'. The Chief Secretary then promised to come up with '*better measures*'.

Separation of Powers and International Law

There are a few things worth noting here. To start with, *Harsh Mander vs Union of India* is a PIL about inhumane conditions in detention centres. How it has become a case about deportations is anyone's guess. And there is a particularly cruel irony in the fact that a case filed to draw attention to inhumane conditions in detention centres has now brought us to a pass where the court nixes the government attempts to release a small class of detainees from those centres.

But leave that aside for the moment. The Chief Justice's repeated enquiries about deportation suggest not only an ignorance of the basic international law principles of *non-refoulement* and against statelessness, but also either ignorance—or contempt—of the principle of separation of powers. Section 3 of the Foreigners Act, 1946, is pellucidly clear: the entry, departure or presence of foreigners in India is a matter for the Central government. It is not for the court to browbeat the government into taking a stand on whether or not to deport (notwithstanding some observations in *Sarbananda Sonowal*, which are not only obiter, but completely unsupported by any legal principle of authority). Matters are worse confounded by the fact that when a foreigners' tribunal makes a decision on the status of an individual, its decision is limited to deciding whether or not the said individual is an Indian national. The tribunal does not—and cannot—return a finding on whether that individual is a national of a named other country. The Chief Justice's reaction—'why don't you deport?'—therefore flies in the face of reality as well, because there will be—and there are—many situations where a foreigners' tribunal declares an individual as a foreigner, but *there is no country to deport that individual to, because no country is claiming them as their national*.

In sum, therefore, the law on deportation is that it is a decision for the government to make—a decision that is constrained by principles of customary international law. What the court is doing in these proceedings is taking a bludgeon to this legal structure by ignoring both these core legal elements. This is damaging in many respects, but it is particularly damaging because the task of checking whether the government is exercising its discretion to deport in consonance with principles of customary international law is a judicial task. However, when the court *itself* is acting in this fashion, to which forum are people supposed to appeal if they think that the government is acting illegally? This is why the separation of powers exists—for courts to *review* the actions of the government and ensure that the government acts legally. And this is why the blurring of the line between the court and the political executive—of which the entire NRC case is exemplary—is so profoundly dangerous.

Article 21

But let us come to an even more serious issue. As indicated above, the government set out a plan where detainees who had spent more than five years in detention centres were to be conditionally released.

The conditions of release are so onerous that in my view, they rise to the level of being unconstitutional—but let us ignore that for the moment. The court refused to accept this proposal as, in the opinion of the CJI, it amounted to sanctioning an 'illegality'. Why? Because the government should have been deporting them.

It is at this stage that it becomes necessary to revisit the text of Article 21 of the Constitution—a provision that has come to mean everything to everyone in recent years, but which seems to mean nothing when it actually matters. Article 21 of the Indian Constitution states, 'No person shall be deprived of his life or personal liberty, except according to procedure established by law.'

There is no—*no*—law that authorizes indefinite detention of an individual, whether citizen or foreigner. And if there was a law that did so, it would almost certainly be struck down as unconstitutional. On what basis, therefore, does the court say that releasing detainees who have spent more than five years in detention would be endorsing an illegality? The boot of illegality, rather, is on the other foot: By refusing release, it is the court that is sanctioning a flagrant and continuing violation of Article 21, the provision that is supposed to be the heart and soul of the Constitution. And one can hardly ignore (once again) the almost brutal irony at the heart of this: It is the *government* that wants to release detainees from detention centres, and the *court* that wants to stop it. Which is the political executive and which is the sentinel on the qui vive? Who is the protector of rights and who the encroacher? It is impossible to tell any more.

Conclusion

Like every other legal culture, we, too, have our 'never again' moment. For us, that 'never again' moment is the notorious judgment in *ADM Jabalpur*, the *Habeas Corpus* case. The Supreme Court's judgment in that case, which sanctioned Emergency-era excesses—most of which were visited upon detainees—is what we hold up as the marker of that 'valley of shadow' into which we've been, and into which we must not go again.

But when the Supreme Court prevents the government from (conditionally) releasing detainees who have been in detention centres (which, by all account, are inhumane places) for more than five years, thus condemning them to a continuing, lawless deprivation of personal liberty, it is perhaps time to ask whether all we can do is keep saying 'never again', even as it happens all over again.

2

Complicity in Genocide: The Supreme Court's Interim Order in the Rohingya Deportation Case[67]

(8 April 2021)

WHEN AN ORDER OF the Supreme Court of India is likely to have the direct effect of sending a group of persecuted refugees back into the hands of a genocidal military State, quibbling over legalities is perhaps a fool's errand. However, the six-page interim order of the court allowing the deportation of Rohingya refugees back to Myanmar—authored by Chief Justice Sharad Arvind Bobde, and Justices Bopanna and Ramasubramanian—stands out not only for its inhumanity, but also for its failure to comply with the most basic principles of legal reasoning.[68] It, therefore, becomes important to continue to hold the Supreme Court to account upon the touchstone of the rule of law, even when the court itself has abandoned it—both to

---

67 This case involved an urgent, interim application to prevent the deportation of certain Rohingya refugees back to Myanmar, where they faced an ongoing genocide. The Supreme Court rejected the application.
68 *Mohammad Salimullah vs Union of India*, (2021) I.A. No. 38048/2021 in WP (C) No. 793/2017.

maintain a record, and in the (perhaps forlorn) hope that a day will come when orders such as these will be remembered in the same way as the turning away of the Jewish refugees on board the *MS St. Louis*, back into the Nazi death camps.

The Issues

The legal and constitutional issues arising out of the Rohingya deportation case were set out by Suhrith Parthasarathy in a guest post.[69] In short, Suhrith pointed out that *even if* it were to be accepted that the international law principle of *non-refoulement* (that refugees cannot be sent back to their home country if they face a well-founded fear of persecution) was not a principle of *jus cogens*—and therefore not directly binding upon India—there are other reasons in the Indian Constitution for why it is impermissible for the State to deport the Rohingya back into an ongoing genocide. These are:

- At least two high court judgments have held that the principle of *non-refoulement* is part of Article 21's guarantee of the right to life and personal liberty, available to all persons.
- Even though India has not ratified the Refugee Convention, it is signatory to a number of international treaties that incorporate the principle of *non-refoulement* (and other applicable principles, such as the prohibition against racial discrimination).
- Even though India has not ratified the Refugee Convention, there is nothing in Indian domestic law that requires the Indian government to *contravene* the principle of *non-refoulement*.

---

69 Suhrith Parthasarathy, 'Article 21 in a Time of Genocide: The Rohingya Case before the Supreme Court', Indian Constitutional Law and Philosophy, 28 March 2021, https://indconlawphil.wordpress.com/2021/03/28/article-21-in-a-time-of-genocide-the-rohingya-case-before-the-supreme-court-guest-post/

Consequently, following the principles outlined in the *Vishaka* judgment (among others), *non-refoulement* and other treaty principles are part of the Indian legal landscape.

The Reasoning

Unsurprisingly, the six-page interim order of the Supreme Court fails to address a single one of these contentions. The reasoning of the court, such as it is, is to be found in three paragraphs—paragraphs 12–14—of the order, which I extract here:

> We have carefully considered the rival contentions. There is no denial of the fact that India is not a signatory to the Refugee Convention. Therefore, serious objections are raised, whether Article 51(c) of the Constitution can be pressed into service, unless India is a party to or ratified a convention. But there is no doubt that the National Courts can draw inspiration from International Conventions/Treaties, so long as they are not in conflict with the municipal law. Regarding the contention raised on behalf of the petitioners about the present state of affairs in Myanmar, we have to state that we cannot comment upon something happening in another country.
>
> It is also true that the rights guaranteed under Articles 14 and 21 are available to all persons who may or may not be citizens. But the right not to be deported, is ancillary or concomitant to the right to reside or settle in any part of the territory of India guaranteed under Article 19(1)(e).
>
> Two serious allegations have been made in reply of the Union of India. They relate to (i) the threat to internal security of the country; and (ii) the agents and touts providing a safe passage into India for illegal immigrants, due to the porous nature of the landed borders. Moreover, this court has already dismissed

I.A.No. 142725 of 2018 filed for similar relief, in respect of those detained in Assam.

It would be hard to cram in more non-sequiturs, sleights of hand and untenable legal propositions in the space of three short paragraphs. After noting that India has not ratified the Refugee Convention (which is correct), the court observes that *'National Courts can draw inspiration from International Conventions/Treaties, so long as they are not in conflict with the municipal law'*. Having observed this, the court then goes on to say ... nothing at all. Recall that the entire argument of the petitioners was that there *do* exist international treaties, which are *not* in conflict with municipal law, and compliance with which would require that the Rohingyas not be deported. However, the court makes no mention of that argument, thus leaving the legal proposition hanging.

Instead, the court makes an utterly senseless statement: 'Regarding ... the present state of affairs in Myanmar, we ... cannot comment upon something happening in another country.' This is senseless, because there exists a whole range of situations in which courts *have* to comment on 'something happening in another country' (think of extradition disputes, for example, or even common-or-garden conflict-of-laws cases). Indeed, in *this* case the situation in Myanmar is relevant to the adjudication, precisely because the petitioners' argument was centred on *non-refoulement*, which, in turn, is premised upon the *fact* that in that 'other country', there is a genocide in progress. Thus, the court's glib 'we ... cannot comment upon something happening in another country' is not only senseless as a judicial statement in a judicial order, but amounts to active abdication of the court's role under the Constitution and allows the court to completely evade the core of the petitioners' argument. The moment an argument of *non-refoulement* is made, the court cannot but comment on 'what is happening in another country'.

So much for the first paragraph. In the second, the court advances a regressive and disturbing legal proposition, based upon an unsubtle sleight of hand. After noting that the rights under Articles 21 and 14 are available to non-citizens (a record of the hearings indicates that the court was unaware of this during oral argument until it was specifically pointed out), the court then holds that 'the right not to be deported' does not fall within Articles 21 or 14, but 19(1)(e) (freedom to reside or settle in any part of India), which is available only to citizens. The sleight of hand, of course, lies in the fact that the petitioners were not claiming a free-standing right against deportation—they were claiming a right against *deportation to a country where they were in active danger from an ongoing genocide*. This is where the right to Article 21 comes in, which perhaps needs to be restated as the court appears to have forgotten it: 'No person shall be *deprived of his life or personal liberty*, except according to a procedure established by law. *[Emphasis mine]*'

It perhaps needs to be spelt out for the benefit of the court that deporting people back into an ongoing genocide might violate an individual's right to life and personal liberty. That said, the court's attempts to confine the issue to Article 19(1)(e) appears a lot like an approach to Part III of the Constitution that walls off individual fundamental rights into separate silos, with no overlap between Articles 14, 19 and 21. In popular imagination, there is a case that did that. It was called *A.K. Gopalan vs State of Madras*. It was, we are told, overruled by *Maneka Gandhi vs Union India*, and that Articles 14, 19 and 21 now formed a 'golden triangle', but perhaps that is also only in popular imagination. That apart, the court's order drives home yet again a tragic irony that this blog has frequently pointed out. In 2021, Article 21 and 'the right to life' includes everything under the sun, but the *one* thing it does not include is an individual's right to *life*.

We now come to the third paragraph, which is quite extraordinary. In courtroom lingo, there is a term that counsel often use to describe their rival's arguments—that he or she is 'only creating prejudice'.

A lawyer says this when their rival is not making a legal argument, but attempting to manipulate the emotions of the judge to influence the outcome of the case (for example, through character assassination of one of the parties in a divorce case). In the past few months, we have regularly seen government counsel attempt to create prejudice by playing the national security card, especially in the litigation around the restriction of internet access in Kashmir. In this third paragraph, however, it is the *court* that engages in creating prejudice. It does so by reiterating the 'serious allegations' of the Union of India (which have already been set out in its summary of arguments of parties)—of a 'threat to internal security' and the misuse of 'porous borders by touts'. Notice that the court makes *zero* effort to engage with either of these 'serious allegations'. There is no question of evidence, of burden of proof, of sifting arguments, of legal standards—the things that you expect from a 'court of law'—there are only these 'serious allegations', simply hanging there, without anything more. What business the court has inserting 'serious allegations' into the operative part of its judgment if it has no intentions of engaging with them is left to the imagination of its readers.

We can, therefore, see that in what passes for 'reasoning' in this judgment, not only does the court fail to address any of the arguments of the petitioners, but the 'arguments' it does provide come from judgments that it keeps telling us belong to the bad old *Gopalan* days, long consigned to infamy. Indeed, if there is one judgment that the final paragraph is eerily reminiscent of, it is (unsurprisingly) *ADM Jabalpur* (a frequent occurrence these days). The court says that the Rohingyas 'shall not be deported unless the procedure prescribed for such deportation is followed'. Just like in *ADM Jabalpur*, where the court said that a policeman could shoot someone on sight with impunity as long as the right official had signed the authorizing order, here the court is saying that the refugees can be deported back into an ongoing genocide as long as the right officials (presumably) have signed the deportation papers.

One final point. In paragraph 3 of the judgment, the court says:

> Sh. Chandra [sic] Uday Singh, learned senior counsel representing the Special Rapporteur appointed by the United Nations Human Rights Council also attempted to make submissions, but serious objections were raised to his intervention.

Much like in the third paragraph discussed above, the court simply says 'serious objections were raised' and leaves the rest to the imagination. What were these objections? What made them serious? How did Shri Chander Uday Singh respond to them? On what basis did the court refuse to allow him to place his submissions? None of this is explained. That apart, to anyone remotely familiar with the workings of the Supreme Court, the hypocrisy here is simply staggering. Recall that this is a court that has built its entire reputation over the past four decades on loosening the rules of standing and easing access, in the 'larger interests of justice'.

There is little doubt that where the issue concerns the legal rights of refugees under international law, the UNHRC Special Rapporteur has excellent grounds for intervention—or, at the very least, far better grounds than the interventions the Supreme Court allows on a daily basis, from persons who have *no* connection to a case at hand.

Conclusion

By way of conclusion, there is one thing about the order—taken as a whole—that is perhaps the most disturbing. Historically, when courts pass morally unconscionable orders, they do so shamefacedly. Judges write about how *if* they had a choice, they would not pass such an order—but that they are bound by the law, which leaves them no choice. *ADM Jabalpur* is, of course, a famous example of this, where the judges repeatedly emphasized how their moral senses were outraged at the State's arguments, but that the law compelled them to take a course they had no option to deviate from.

The Rohingya order reflects none of that. There is not even a smidgen of unease that the result of the order might be to deliver refugees into the hands of a genocidal military. In fact, the only thing the judges have to say on the issue is: '*We cannot comment on another country.*'

Perhaps what is the most disturbing, then, is not the absence of legal sense in the court's order, but the death of its moral sense.

3

Breathing Life into Article 21: The Manipur High Court's Order on Refugee Rights and Non-Refoulement

(13 May 2021)

[**Update**: To no one's surprise, the Supreme Court has stayed this judgment at the time of writing. (April 2023)]

PREVIOUSLY WE HAVE DISCUSSED various issues arising out of the government's attempts to deport Rohingya refugees back to Myanmar, as well as the Supreme Court's refusal to engage with the legal and humanitarian questions at stake. What the Supreme Court refused to do in the *Salimullah* case, however, the Manipur High Court did, today, in *Nandita Haksar vs State of Manipur*. In its final judgment and order, the high court—through Chief Justice Sanjay Kumar and Lanusungkum Jamir J—held that the principle of non-refoulement was part of Article 21 of the Indian Constitution and that in light of that fact, seven Myanmarese refugees were to be allowed to travel to Delhi and claim refugee status before the United Nations High Commission for Refugees (UNHCR).[70]

Before discussing the high court's brief and illuminating thirteen-page order, it is worth noting the speed with which this case was decided. A notice to the Union secretary was issued on 17 April 2021; on 20 April 2021, while adjourning the case so that counsel could seek instructions, the high court issued an interim order granting protection from deportation to the refugees, pending completion of the case. Arguments were concluded on 29 April 2021, and the high court handed down a judgment on merits on 3 May 2021. This is exactly how it should be. Compare this, however, with the very similar writ petition pending before the Supreme Court concerning the deportation of Rohingya refugees, which was filed in 2017 and has not been decided in four years. Consider, further, the fact that during the pendency of that petition, the two benches of the Supreme Court—headed by Chief Justices Gogoi and Bobde, respectively—passed interim orders *allowing* deportation to go ahead, even though the question regarding the constitutional rights of refugees was still open, and deportation would have rendered it infructuous for good. The Manipur High Court's judicial conduct—both in its interim order and in its swift disposal of the case—thus stands in stark contrast to that of the Supreme Court.

There are five salient features underlying the high court's judgment. *First*, the high court restated the basic principle that the protection of Articles 14 (equality before law) and 21 (right to life and personal liberty) is not limited to citizens, but extends to *all* individuals (paragraph 8).

Leading on from this, *secondly*, the high court held—as had numerous other high courts before it—that the principle of non-refoulement ('the right to freedom from expulsion from a territory in which [a refugee] seeks refuge or from forcible return to a country or

---

70 *Nandita Haksar vs State of Manipur*, WP Crl. No. 6/2021 (3 May 2021).

a territory where he or she faces a threat to life or freedom because of race, religion, nationality, membership in a social group, or political opinion [paragraph 9]') is part of Article 21 of the Constitution. This is particularly important. In a previous blog post, I asked what the purpose of an expanded interpretation of Article 21—the crown jewel of the fundamental rights chapter—was, if it couldn't be invoked to protect even *bare* life. As the Manipur High Court correctly noted, '*The far-reaching and myriad protections afforded by Article 21 of our Constitution, as interpreted and adumbrated by our Supreme Court time and again, would indubitably encompass the right of non-refoulement …* [paragraph 9].' Indeed, responding to the additional solicitor-general's argument that the Foreigners Act and the Foreigners Order of 1948 mandated that 'illegal entrants suffer for their consequences', the high court observed that '*these arguments proceed on a rather* narrow and parochial *consideration of the larger issues that arise in this case*' (paragraph 12)'. In particular, the refugees:

> [F]led the country of their origin under imminent threat to their lives and liberty. They aspire for relief under International Conventions that were put in place to offer protection and rehabilitation to refugees/asylum seekers. In such a situation, insisting that they first answer for admitted violations of our domestic laws, as a condition precedent for seeking 'refugee' status, would be palpably inhuman *[paragraph 12]*.

Thirdly, the high court gave short shrift to two arguments that had, apparently, found favour to the Supreme Court. Responding to the argument that Article 19(1)(d) of the Constitution, which guaranteed the freedom to move and reside in any part of India, was available only to citizens, the high court correctly observed that the issues at stake flowed from Article 21, and not Article 19 (paragraph 13). And furthermore, responding to the government counsel's argument that these refugees represented a 'threat to the security of the country', the high court simply noted that '*no material is produced in support of the same*'. Indeed, a few of the refugees had already been granted UNHCR certification on an earlier occasion, and one of them had previously been granted an Indian visa. Consequently, allegations of a security threat were '*therefore purely speculative, born of a fertile imagination*' (paragraph 14). Once again, this is in stark contrast to the Supreme Court order in the *Salimullah* case, where the CJI Bobde-led bench not only appeared to believe that refugees were trying to claim Article 19(1)(d) rights (they were not), but also placed on record—without any scrutiny or investigation whatsoever—the government counsel's 'serious' contention that there was a security threat. As we have discussed on many occasions before, in questions involving individual rights when the State attempts to cloak itself by invoking 'national security', almost always a court will not need to 'supplant' executive wisdom with judicial fiat. Often, simply *asking* the State to justify its stand will reveal that there is little more than a set of bald statements being made before the court, with no further evidence.

Fourthly, the high court anchored its decision to precedent, noting both decisions of the Supreme Court concerning dignified treatment (under Article 21) to foreign nationals, as well as numerous Supreme Court and high court decisions where refugees were allowed to travel to Delhi and apply to the UNHCR for refugee status, instead of being deported, or where deportation had been stayed pending determination of refugee status (paragraph 16). Thus, not only did the high court root its decision in constitutional principle, but it also made its reasoning watertight by grounding it entirely within the scope of existing precedent.

And *finally*, when the governments' counsel attempted to cite the order in the *Salimullah* case to make the high court stay its hand, the court correctly noted that not only was that an interim order that laid down no binding *ratio*, but also that concerns about 'security threats', which were among the putative bases in that order, did not apply to the present case (paragraph 18). The high court, therefore, neither ignored the Supreme Court's order and nor did it slavishly follow it, but carefully distinguished it on the basis of established constitutional principles. Finally, the court held:

> On the above analysis, this court finds it just and proper to extend protection under Article 21 of the Constitution to these seven Myanmarese persons and grant them safe passage to New Delhi to enable them to avail suitable protection from the UNHCR. Some of them seem to be in possession of their passports but in any event, their details and particulars have been noted by the Immigration authorities of our country. There shall accordingly be a direction to the FRRO at Imphal airport to immediately provide them with temporary identification cards to enable them to travel to New Delhi by air, if such identity proofs are necessary. The State and Central Governments shall facilitate their travel to New Delhi and shall not cause any obstruction *[paragraph 19]*.

For the reasons discussed above, the high court's judgment is entirely correct, both from the perspective of law and from the perspective of humanity, and goes somewhat towards expressing the promise of Article 21 in all its richness. There is, perhaps, one point of critique: The high court's sharp distinction between 'refugees' (who flee military or other kinds of persecution) and 'migrants' (who leave for 'economic' reasons) was not strictly necessary to its adjudication of the case, and is problematic. The refugee-migrant distinction has been extensively criticized, and there is, by now, an understanding of how economic violence is no less a form of violence than religious, political or ethnic persecution. That said, the distinction appears to be part of the contentions raised in the case, and is dealt with in a paragraph. One hopes, therefore, that when a court has an occasion to address these issues in greater detail, a more nuanced approach will be taken.

While in the ordinary course of things the Manipur High Court's judgment would be seen as a reaffirmation of basic principles, the Supreme Court's two interim orders have necessarily compelled many of us to re-examine what we considered to be 'basic', especially with respect to Article 21 of the Indian Constitution. It is from that perspective that the Manipur High Court's judgment is remarkable and stands out as an example of judicial courage.

A Rightless Zone: Kashmir after Article 370

Introduction

ONE OF LORD ATKIN'S most memorable lines from the bench is 'amidst the clash of arms, the laws are not silent'. The response of the judiciary to the sweeping internet shutdowns and mass detentions in Jammu and Kashmir after the effective abrogation of Article 370 on 5 August 2019 suggests that Lord Atkin might have been too optimistic. In the following pages, readers will find out just how silent the courts can be 'amidst the clash of arms'.

1

Kashmir: The 16 September Order and the Supreme Court of Convenience (or Why Separation of Powers Is like Love)[71]

(18 September 2019)

UNTIL 16 SEPTEMBER 2019, we believed that there were some fundamental principles that underlay our constitutional system. These principles were as fundamental as breath, and as natural. We took them for granted. For example:

1. Fundamental rights cannot be infringed upon in the absence of a law (*Kharak Singh vs State of UP*).
2. If there exists a law, that law must be promulgated publicly, so that citizens may know what it says, and know the basis on which fundamental rights are being restricted. Secret laws are an

---

71 This blog post is one of many that covered the widespread violations of civil rights in Jammu and Kashmir after the events of 5 August 2019, and the Supreme Court's (in)action in response. Interested readers may consult the blog for the full chronology.

anathema to the very concept of the rule of law (*Harla vs State of Rajasthan*).

3. If that law is challenged in a court of law, it is that court's constitutional duty to decide whether (a) fundamental rights have been infringed, and (b) whether that infringement is justifiable under the Constitution *(do I really need to give you a citation here?)*.

4. After the petitioner has discharged her initial burden of showing a prima facie infringement of her rights, the burden shifts to the State to justify that infringement (see point 3).

5. When assessing the infringement of rights under Articles 19 and 21, the court is not expected to vacate the field and enable executive supremacy, as the Emergency-era judgment in *ADM Jabalpur vs Shivkant Shukla* has been buried 'ten fathom deep with no chance of resurrection' (*Puttaswamy [I] vs Union of India*).

6. Instead, when examining the infringement of rights under Article 19 (freedom of speech, association, etc.) or 21 (life and personal liberty), the court will apply the proportionality standards. The proportionality standard requires a showing that the infringing measures were *necessary* (i.e., there were no reasonable available alternatives) (*Puttaswamy [II] vs Union of India*).

7. The right to freedom of expression under Article 19(1)(a) can be restricted only on the eight sub-grounds mentioned under Article 19(2). The court cannot add additional grounds through judicial fiat (*Sakal Papers vs Union of India*).

8. The court must give reasons for its judgment (see point 3).

In its order dated 16 September 2019, in the *Anuradha Bhasin* case, the three-judge bench of the Supreme Court, led by the Chief Justice, has taken each of these principles to the shredder.[72] In doing so, it has fashioned new constitutional 'law' that resembles a directive from the home ministry more than it does a reasoned judgment

---

72 *Anuradha Bhasin vs Union of India*, I.A. No. 124176/2019 in WP (C) 1031/2019 (16 September 2019).

from a constitutional court. The petition involved a challenge to the communications lockdown that has been imposed in the state of Jammu and Kashmir since 5 August (the extent of the lockdown is disputed). According to the eight principles stated above, the task of the court was simple. It had to (a) examine the order under which the lockdown was imposed (did it flow from Section 144 of the CrPC, for example, or from the telecommunication suspension rules of 2017?); (b) examine the grounds of the lockdown and assess whether a state-wide suspension of communications infrastructure met the test of proportionality; and (c) provide a reasoned judgment.

In other words, the court had to hear the case and decide it.

What did the court do? After footballing the hearing from one date to another—thus enabling a continuing violation of fundamental rights without a decision on its legality—on 16 September, it passed a two-paragraph order. After stating that the matter will next be listed on 30 September, the relevant portion of the order reads:

> The State of Jammu & Kashmir, keeping in mind the *national interest and internal security*, shall make *all endeavours* to ensure that normal life is restored in Kashmir; people have access to healthcare facilities and schools, colleges and other educational institutions and public transport functions and operates normally. All forms of communication, subject to *overriding consideration of national security*, shall be normalized, if required on a selective basis, particularly for healthcare facilities. *[Emphasis mine]*

Let us examine this paragraph. The first thing to note is that the order authorizing the communications shutdown has still not been made public, after more than forty days. It stands to reason that if the government (either the Central government or the state government) has passed this order without publicly promulgating it, the responsibility lies upon the government to produce it before the court so that adjudication may take place. In exempting the government from these most basic principles of the rule of law and natural justice, the court's order violates principles (1) and (2) mentioned above.

Next, the court has returned no finding on the constitutional validity of the communications shutdown. It has therefore violated principle (3). It has not recorded any justification from the government in the order or examined its validity. It has therefore violated principle (4). And by choosing to include an exhortation to the government to restore normalcy by making 'all endeavours' keeping in mind the 'national interest and internal security', an exhortation without any binding force, and subject to what the *government* believes are the requirements of 'national interest' and 'internal security', the court has taken us straight back to 1976 and *ADM Jabalpur*, violating principle (5). Ten fathoms deep, apparently, is not deep enough, because nothing of *ADM Jabalpur* doth fade—it only suffers a sea change, into something rich and strange (ding dong bell!).

Further, the court has engaged in no proportionality analysis. It has not examined whether a communications lockdown of an entire state is a proportionate response to what the external affairs minister referred to as the goal of stopping terrorists from communicating with each other. It has not even asked the State to show that other alternatives were contemplated and found wanting (if the court was concerned about national security implications, it could even have asked for the evidence in its favourite manner, i.e., in a sealed cover). So perhaps the judgments that have actually been buried ten fathoms deep—to resurrect whenever convenient—are *Puttaswamy I* and *II*.

'National interest' and 'internal security' are not grounds under Article 19(2). By inventing new grounds to justify the restriction of the fundamental right to freedom of speech and expression, the court has violated principle (6). Words matter, especially when they are being used to justify a clampdown on rights.

And lastly, no reasons have been provided in this order. This is why I observed, at the beginning of this post, that this 'order' resembles more a directive from the home ministry than a reasoned opinion from a constitutional court. Not only does it provide no reasons, but it is so vague and broadly worded that is has practically no impact. What does 'all endeavours' mean? The government will decide. What does 'national interest' require? The government will decide. To what extent does 'internal security' require a clampdown on rights? The government will decide.

In *ADM Jabalpur*, the Supreme Court had the minimum courtesy of telling citizens that during the Emergency, fundamental rights stood suspended—and it provided some reasons for that conclusion. Here, by framing an order for 'restoring normalcy' subject to whatever the government thinks is fit, the court has effectively done exactly the same thing without extending that courtesy.

The order of 16 September 2019, therefore, is not recognizable under any theory of constitutional adjudication, and the bench delivering is not recognizable as what we commonly understand as a 'constitutional court'. What it resembles more is a branch of the executive, enabling and facilitating the executive, instead of checking and balancing it, and reviewing its actions for compliance with fundamental rights.

And this has been a long time coming. Throughout the 1980s and the 1990s, in the PIL litigation, the court emphasized that it was not adversarial litigation, that normal standards of evidence and fact-finding were dispensable and that it was effectively acting in partnership with the government to achieve national goals. It may have been possible to predict that if the court began to fashion itself as a partner of the government, its role as an oversight body would be severely compromised. But legal academics of the time did not mind; indeed, some of them referred to concepts such as the separation of powers as 'Anglo-Saxon' and outmoded, and indicated that they ought to be jettisoned, as the court became the 'last refuge of the oppressed and the bewildered'.

But perhaps, all along, Anglo-Saxon or not, separation of powers has been like love—you only realize what you had when it is lost.

Beyond any chance of 'resurrection'.

2

Kashmir: Fundamental Rights and Sealed Covers

(17 October 2019)

IN A PREVIOUS POST, we discussed one of the peculiar features of the litigation regarding the communications shutdown and other restrictions in Kashmir. One of these features is the absence—in court—of the government's orders that constitute the basis of the restrictions (whether under the telecom suspension rules or Section 144 of the CrPC). As we discussed, one of the basic requirements for a restriction upon fundamental rights is the existence of a law, and its *publication* (i.e., the law being made available to the citizens whose freedoms it seeks to restrict). There can be no restriction of fundamental rights in the absence of law, or on the basis of secret laws.

In the hearing of 16 October, this question was (finally) put to the State by the Supreme Court justices. It is reported that Solicitor-General Tushar Mehta stated that he had no objection to showing the orders to the court, but considerations of national security may require him to withhold them from the petitioners—and that the petitioners had no 'right' to claim access to the orders. Accordingly, the court's order records that if the solicitor-general wants to claim 'privilege' over the orders, the court 'requests him to file an affidavit indicating the reasons for claiming such privilege'.

While we wait for the government's affidavit, it is important to note that what is at stake here is a creeping expansion of the 'sealed cover', which we have seen so often in recent times. It is also important to note that it is entirely unjustifiable. Executive orders—passed under cover of law—restricting the rights of citizens *are not* and *cannot* be subject to legal privilege or submitted to the court in a sealed cover.

On one level, it is questionable whether a legal order revealed only to the court and hidden from citizens counts as 'publication' in the relevant sense. But there is a more basic reason this is unconstitutional. If I, as a citizen, do not have access to the legal order that purports to restrict my rights, I have no effective way of challenging it in court and demonstrating it to be unconstitutional. I cannot show that it is disproportionate and fails the reasonableness standard under Article 19(2). What this means, in turn, is that effectively, I have no *remedy* to enforce my fundamental rights. And a right without a remedy is, of course, meaningless.

Effectively, therefore, denying the order on the basis of which rights are infringed amounts to a suspension of the rights. As explained in a previous post, this can *only* be done—and that, too, partially—through a formal declaration of emergency. In other words, the government's arguments are entirely based upon the logic of an emergency, without the courtesy of a formal declaration of emergency.

It is important to remember the last time the contrary argument was made. The last time it was made, unsurprisingly, was in *ADM Jabalpur*. There, the argument made on behalf of the detenues was that the *suspension* of the right to *move the court* to enforce habeas corpus amounted to the denudation of Article 21 itself. To this, the court said that the mere fact that you could not move the court did not mean that the *rights* ceased to exist—it just meant that you had no way of enforcing them. But if *ADM Jabalpur* has been buried 'ten fathoms deep' by *Puttaswamy*, surely there is no remaining scope for the government, in 2019, to make this argument.

Consequently, therefore, no 'affidavit' can justify keeping the communications suspension and Section 144 orders secret, and there is no justification for handing them over to the court in a 'sealed cover'. They must be disclosed—and not only to the petitioners, but also to the *general public*, so that affected parties are in a position to seek remedies before the courts of law. Any other outcome would only amount to a justification of the logic of emergency.

3

King Menelaus at the Bar of the Indian Judiciary

(8 February 2020)

MIAN ABDUL QAYOOM IS the seventy-six-year-old president of the Jammu and Kashmir High Court Bar Association. Since 5 August—the day the constitutional status of Jammu and Kashmir was altered—Qayoom has been undergoing 'preventive' detention under the Jammu and Kashmir Public Safety Act, 1978, which authorizes detention for up to two years without trial. The ostensible basis of the detention has been that he would *'motivate people to agitate against abrogation of Article 370'*. Despite ill health (diabetes and a single kidney), Qayoom's detention was extended last week. And on Friday (7 February), the Jammu and Kashmir and Ladakh High Court dismissed a legal challenge to his detention.[73]

Among other things, in its judgment, the high court took the view that the *'subjective satisfaction* of the detaining authority to detain a person or not is not open to objective assessment by a court. A court is not a *proper forum* to scrutinize the merits of administrative decision

---

73 *Mian Abdul Qayoom vs State of J&K*, WP (Crl) No. 251/2019.

to detain a person.' This, of course, essentially gives absolute impunity to the State on the issue of detention. If 'subjective satisfaction' is the standard and the court is not the 'proper forum' to challenge detention, effectively, the right to personal liberty exists at the absolute discretion and mercy of the government. That, needless to say, makes the right meaningless.

Now what does one say about this? One could say that this line of 'reasoning' parrots the executive supremacy logic that was at the basis of the *ADM Jabalpur* case, which was allegedly buried 'ten fathoms deep with no chance of resurrection' by the Supreme Court in 2017, except that ten fathoms are evidently not deep enough (in fact, the high court judgment quotes a number of cases—both before and after *ADM Jabalpur*—that foreshadowed and echoed its most notorious lines, including that of preventive detention being a 'jurisdiction of suspicion'). After all, when the memo on overruling *ADM Jabalpur* hasn't even reached some of the judges of the Supreme Court, how could it be expected to reach the still-locked-down Kashmir, where it is anyway too cold for people to exercise their Article 19(1)(d) rights (according to a former Chief Justice of India)? One could say that far from being buried ten fathoms deep, or any fathom deep, it has by now become abundantly clear that *ADM Jabalpur* is the dominant logic that governs judicial action in India today, and that the high court was at least refreshingly honest in giving that to us straight.

One could say all that, but there probably comes a point at which repetition grows tedious and is necessary only to complete the record, rather than present any new or interesting insight about the workings of the judiciary today. But thankfully, the high court has also given us something more to think about. It quoted the Greek 'thinker' Sophocles, noting that 'law can never be enforced unless fear supports them'.

No quote exists, of course, without context. And a closer look at the context of the Sophocles' quote that the high court chose is perhaps more revealing than the actual order. A preliminary point, of course, is that the society that gave us the 'Melian Dialogue' might not be the most reliable contemporary guide to ideas of law, justice and morality; indeed, one would hope that the concept of law would have progressed somewhat in the 2,500 years since the time of the classical Greeks.

More than that, however, is the specific background of the quote. These words—that the high court paraphrases—are found in Sophocles' play *Ajax*. And Sophocles puts them into the mouth of Menelaus— the (semi-mythical) Greek king other contemporary playwrights denounced for his arrogance and cruelty, and who initiated a destructive and pointless ten-year war because his wife left him for another man. Not, perhaps, the model statesman you want expounding on the idea of law. And if the high court had paid attention to Menelaus' speech where the quoted words occur, a few lines above it would have found the following words: *'Tis a sign of wickedness, when a subject/deigns not to obey those placed in power above him.'* This is unsurprising—equating law with fear is the hallmark of societies where power flows from hierarchy and is kept by force.

Notably, in both cases, Menelaus is referring to the conduct of (the now-dead) Ajax and is refusing permission to bury his body. Ajax had killed himself after going on a killing spree, triggered by his rage at being adjudged the second-best Greek warrior when it came to massacring soldiers during the just-concluded Trojan War. After a lengthy dispute between Menelaus and another character, Teucer, the body of Ajax was indeed buried.

The literary, dramatic and artistic merits of *Ajax* notwithstanding, here, in essence, is what the play is about. It is the aftermath of a destructive and unjustifiable war of aggression, where a soldier from the army of conquest massacres innocent civilians because he feels that he has not been credited enough for his role in the war, then kills himself, leading to higher officials having an argument—*not* about the massacre—but about whether his body should be given a burial. The higher official is angry, not because innocent civilians have been killed, but because his 'subject' has disobeyed someone 'placed in power above him'. But he is finally persuaded to overlook the indiscretion, and impunity survives untouched. And it is within this context, this society and this cast of characters that we find the words the Jammu and Kashmir and Ladakh High Court thought fit to apply to preventive detention in a twenty-first-century constitutional democracy: 'Laws can never be enforced unless fear supports them.'

Perhaps the high court *did*, after all, intend to make exactly this point—that we do live in the world of Ajax and Menelaus, and the world of the 'Melian Dialogue'. Perhaps, then, we should applaud—once again—the refreshing honesty, topped off with a dash of literary flourish.

Or perhaps the high court would have been better served by remembering that the Greek army camps outside a ruined Troy were not the best models for a constitutional democracy, and looked elsewhere in Sophocles' oeuvre—perhaps the legendary play *Antigone*, where a guard told another king: ''Tis sad, truly, that he who judges should misjudge.'

Mian Abdul Qayoom, meanwhile, remains in jail without trial.

[**Update**: He was released in August 2020.]

Part Two

Constitutional Structure

Federalism

Introduction

FEDERALISM UNDER THE INDIAN Constitution has always been a significant arena of contestation. The Constitution formally declares India to be a 'union of states', with legislative and executive power divided between the 'union' (centre) and the 'states' (after the 73rd and the 74th Amendments, there is also a third tier of government—the local government). However, the Constitution also skews power significantly in favour of the Union. Parliament can alter and modify the boundaries of states, and even extinguish them; residuary legislative power belongs to the Union; in a clash between Union law and state law, Union law prevails (except in certain specific circumstances); during declared emergencies, the Union can dissolve state governments and effectively take over the governance of states; fiscal and financial provisions significantly empower the Union at the cost of the states; and so on.

There are historical reasons for the Constitution's centralizing skew, which we shall not go into here. The past seven decades have seen significant litigation within the interstices of the constitutional text, with states asserting their powers as equal partners within the federal scheme, while the Union has attempted to further entrench its own overriding powers.

Over the past few years, this contest has played out in multiple domains. Two of the more well known of these are the conflict between the government of Delhi and the Union of India, and the constitutional alterations to the status of Jammu and Kashmir.

NCT of Delhi vs Union of India is, at the time of writing, a seven-year-running legal dispute, which began almost as soon as the Aam Aadmi Party (AAP) won power in Delhi (the government at the Centre was—and is—of the Bharatiya Janata Party, or the BJP). The dispute stems from the unique constitutional status of the national capital territory (NCT) of Delhi, set out in Article 239AA of the Constitution. Delhi is something less than a 'full state', but something more than an ordinary, Centre-controlled union territory. It has its own legislature and cabinet, whose existence is guaranteed by the Constitution, but at the same time, it grants overriding powers to the Union government-appointed lieutenant-general, in *certain circumstances*. The tussle, thus, is over who controls the governance of Delhi—and to what extent. The elected Delhi government or the Union-appointed lieutenant governor (LG)? At the time of writing, the litigation had resulted in three judgments (one by the Delhi High Court and two by the Supreme Court), with a fourth round on.[74]

On 5 August 2019, the President of India issued two orders that effectively abrogated the 'special status' of the state of Jammu and Kashmir, which had hitherto been guaranteed by Article 370 of the Constitution. Simultaneously, the Parliament passed a law

---

74 In May 2023, just before this book was to go into print, the Supreme Court delivered judgment in the fourth round. See 'At the Third Time of Asking: Federalism, the Centralising Drift, and the Supreme Court's Judgment in NCT of Delhi vs Union of India (2023)', Indian Constitutional Law and Philosophy, 11 May 2023, https://indconlawphil.wordpress.com/2023/05/11/at-the-third-time-of-asking-federalism-the-centralising-drift-and-the-supreme-courts-judgment-in-nct-of-delhi-vs-union-of-india-2023/

downgrading Jammu and Kashmir from a state to a Centrally controlled union territory. These constitutional moves raised many issues, including federal issues. In particular, given the fact that Jammu and Kashmir had no elected government at the time and was already under (temporary) Central rule, to what extent could the Union make fundamental and permanent changes to the character of a state, acting under temporary emergency powers?

In the following essays, you will find analyses of both these significant constitutional events, from the perspective of the federal structure and the division of power between the levels of government.

1

'Working a Democratic Constitution': The Supreme Court's Judgment in *NCT of Delhi vs Union of India*[75]

(4 July 2018)

TODAY, A CONSTITUTION BENCH of the Supreme Court delivered its judgment in *NCT of Delhi vs Union of India*. Previously, I have written about the political consequences of the court's delay in hearing this case,[76] and Vasudev Devadasan wrote a

---

75 This post covers the 2018 judgment of the five-judge bench of the Supreme Court in *NCT of Delhi vs Union of India*. Readers interested in a critical account of the full history of the conflict—and the role of the court—can consult Gautam Bhatia, 'Judicial Evasion, Judicial Vagueness, and Judicial Revisionism: A Study of the *NCT of Delhi vs Union of India* Judgment(s)', SSRN, 27 June 2020, https://papers.ssrn.com/sol3/papers.cfm?abstract_id=3637009. The paper, however, does not consider the May 2023 Supreme Court judgment, which potentially brings the dispute to an end at last.

76 'Judicial Evasion and the Referral in Delhi vs Union of India', Indian Constitutional Law and Philosophy, 22 February 2017, https://indconlawphil.wordpress.com/2017/02/22/judicial-evasion-and-the-referral-in-delhi-vs-union-of-india/

three-part series on the main substantive issues (Part I,[77] Part II,[78] Part III[79]). Readers will recall that the dispute turned upon the 'special status' of the National Capital Territory of Delhi. Not a 'full state' and neither just a Union Territory, Delhi has an entire article dedicated to it—239AA—which, read with the Government of the National Capital Territory of India Act, 1991, and the Transaction of Business of the Government of National Capital Territory of Delhi Rules, 1993, sets up a complicated legal structure defining how governance is to be carried out in Delhi.

Put simply, this legal structure envisages two constitutional authorities—the elected chief minister of Delhi (at the head of the Council of Ministers) and the LG, the appointee of the Central government. When Delhi began life in the colonial era as the Chief Commissioner's Province, it was ruled by an administrator who, in effect, ruled as an autocrat. The spread of representative government through British India passed Delhi by, and it was only after Independence that, through incremental amendments to the Constitution (culminating in Article 239AA), representative institutions came to Delhi. During this time, the position of the administrator was transformed into the LG, and he became a representative of the Central government in Delhi. This, ultimately, is what led to the constitutional ambiguity. In Indian

---

[77] Vasudev Devadasan, 'Government of Delhi vs Union of India', Indian Constitutional Law and Philosophy, *31 October 2017,* https://indconlawphil.wordpress.com/2017/10/31/guest-post-government-of-delhi-vs-union-of-india/

[78] Vasudev Devadasan, 'Government of Delhi vs Union of India – II: the Legislative Relationship', Indian Constitutional Law and Philosophy, *7 November 2017,* https://indconlawphil.wordpress.com/2017/11/07/guest-post-government-of-delhi-vs-union-of-india-ii-the-legislative-relationship/

[79] Vasudev Devadasan, 'Government of Delhi vs Union of India – III: the Executive Relationship', Indian Constitutional Law and Philosophy, 15 November 2017, https://indconlawphil.wordpress.com/2017/11/15/guest-post-government-of-delhi-vs-union-of-india-iii-the-executive-relationship/

states, the equivalent of the LG—the governor—was little more than a titular head, bound to act upon the 'aid and advice' of the elected government, with only a narrowly circumscribed sphere of discretion. However, as Delhi moved from an autocracy to a representative government, its status as the national capital prompted Parliament to refrain from granting it *full* statehood. It is this that led to the unique situation where you had *both* an elected government *and* an LG, who retained something of the old powers. And it was the precise demarcation of powers that brought the case to the Supreme Court.

At the heart of the dispute lay two articles: Article 239AA(3)(a) and Article 239AA(4). These articles state:

(3)(a): Subject to the provisions of the Constitution, the [Delhi] Legislative Assembly shall have the power to make laws for the whole or any part of the National Capital Territory with respect to any of the matters enumerated in the State of List or in the Concurrent List in so far as any such matter is applicable to Union territories except matters with respect to Entries 1, 2, and 18 of the State List and Entries 44, 65 and 66 of that List in so far as they relate to the said Entries 1, 2, and 18 …

(4) There shall be a Council of Ministers consisting of not more than ten per cent, of the total number of members in the Legislative Assembly, with the chief minister at the head *to aid and advise* the lieutenant governor in the exercise of his functions in relation to matters with respect to which the Legislative Assembly has power to make laws, except in so far as he is, by or under any law, required to act in his discretion.

Provided that in the case of difference of opinion between the lieutenant governor and his ministers *on any matter*, the lieutenant governor shall refer it to the President for decision and act according to the decision given thereon by the President and pending such decision it shall be competent for the lieutenant governor in any case where the matter, in his opinion, is so urgent that it is necessary for him to take immediate action, to take such action or to give such direction in the matter as he deems necessary.

To put matters very simply, there were two broad issues that arose. The first was the meaning of the phrase 'aid and advise'. It was settled law—and also written into the Constitution through amendment—that in the case of the Central government and the state governments, the words 'aid and advise', which are used in reference to the President and the governors, mean 'aid and advice that is binding'. In other words, the President and the governors *must* act in accordance with the 'aid and advice' tendered to them by the Council of Ministers. However, Delhi's status as not-quite-a-state and the absence of any explicit recognition that the LG had to act upon the aid and advice, allowed the Union government to argue—and the Delhi High Court to hold—that in this regard, the LG's position was not equivalent to the President and the governors, and that he was not bound by the aid and advice of Delhi's elected Council of Ministers. Let us call this 'Phase One: The Demarcation of Executive Power'.

The second issue was about the meaning of the phrase 'on any matter'. *If* the constitutional position was that the executive power of Delhi lay with the elected Council of Ministers, the next question arose whether in *all* cases, the LG was authorized to have a 'difference of opinion' and escalate the matter to the President. In other words, did the phrase 'any matter' mean 'every matter'? Let us call this 'Phase Two: The Scope of the LG's Power to Refer a Difference of Opinion to the President'.

Phase One

I do not propose to go into the detailed arguments advanced in the three separate opinions, which together clock in at 535 pages. Broadly, this was the line of argument that all five judges agreed upon.

1. Representative democracy, exercised through parliamentary institutions, characterized by principles of collective responsibility and accountability (the Westminster system), is at the heart of the Constitution.
2. Parliamentary democracy under the Indian Constitution envisages an elected, law-making body (legislature) and a council of ministers (executive). The scope of operation of the legislature is defined under the Seventh Schedule of the Constitution, which lists out the fields under which the Central and the state legislatures can pass laws. The power of the executive is *co-extensive* with that of the legislature—the executive can act in the same fields in which it is open to the legislature to pass laws. The head of the executive (President/governor) acts in accordance with the 'aid and advice' of the council of ministers.
3. Article 239AA, which explicitly creates an elected legislature for Delhi, clearly envisages that, at a broad level, Delhi is to be governed in accordance with the two principles set out above. To the extent that the text of Article 239AA is open to more than one interpretation, the interpretation that furthers the Constitution's commitment to representative democracy must be preferred (see Chandrachud J's concurring opinion for a particularly clear articulation of this interpretive principle).
4. Therefore, the Council of Ministers for Delhi has the executive power to take action in all the fields in which the Delhi Legislative Assembly can pass laws (as per Article 239AA[3], this includes the state list [barring land, police, and law and order] and the Concurrent List of the Seventh Schedule). In this context, the aid and advice of the Council of Ministers is binding upon the LG. Under the Allocation of Business Rules, the Council of Ministers must at all times keep the LG informed, but do not need to seek his concurrence. The purpose of information is so that the LG can decide whether to exercise the power vested in

him under the proviso to Article 239AA(4) (which is what we shall discuss next).

Consequently, the judgment of the Delhi High Court, which held that the LG was the *actual* head of the executive in Delhi, was incorrect.

Phase Two

In Phase One—the demarcation of executive power—the court held that, *subject* to the express constitutional limitations, which took land, police, and law and order out of the remit of the Delhi assembly and government (and placed other procedural limitations such as overriding federal legislative power and presidential assent), Delhi had the character of a state. Its assembly had legislative power and its Council of Ministers had co-extensive executive power. The role of the LG, to this extent, was that of a titular head: He had a right to be informed, but he was also bound by the decision of the Council of Ministers.

This, then, led to the second issue: The proviso to Article 239AA(4) gave the LG a unique power that state governors do not possess. If the LG had a difference of opinion with the Council of Ministers, then—subject to some conciliation measures provided for in the Government of National Capital Territory of Delhi (GNCTD) Act, 1991 and the Allocation of Business Rules—he could escalate the matter to the President. However, all five judges were in agreement that, contrary to the submission of the Union of India, the words 'any matter' could not mean 'every matter'. As Chandrachud J correctly observed, if such an interpretation were to be placed on the proviso, the rest of the scheme of Article 239AA would come crumbling down. All three judgments are replete with statements to the effect that, under the guise of referring to a difference of opinion, the LG cannot bring governance to a standstill.

However, the question that followed logically was: If 'any' did not mean 'every', what *did* it mean? The government of Delhi suggested that the word 'any' be restricted to the three entries of List II that were excluded from Delhi's legislative competence under the state list—land, police, and law and order. On every other issue, the LG would remain bound by the 'aid and advice' of the Council of Ministers. However, the court rejected this interpretation on the basis that if Delhi's power was altogether denuded in respect of these three subjects, the question of a 'difference of opinion' would never arise.

The majority opinion, authored by the Chief Justice, did not enumerate a list of subjects upon which the LG could 'differ' and escalate the matter to the President. Instead, the majority held that a reference could be made only in 'exceptional' circumstances, but did not elaborate, even illustratively, on what the word 'exceptional' meant. A similar issue plagued Justice Bhushan's opinion. He observed that the LG could not interfere in 'routine' matters. But what does 'routine' mean? In fact, Justice Bhushan's 123-page opinion, in which he substantively agreed with everything that the other four judges held, was undone by some very loose language in Conclusion VIII, where he noted that the LG's power is 'not to be exercised in a routine manner … [but] when it becomes *necessary to safeguard the interest* of the Union Territory'. 'Safeguard the interest' is so broad that it practically converts 'any matter' to 'every matter', which is exactly what all five judges held was *not* the way to read the proviso.

It was left to Chandrachud J, in his concurring opinion, to provide concrete shape to the 'exceptional' circumstances that might trigger the proviso. The basis of Chandrachud J's reasoning was that there was a reason why Delhi did not have full statehood. It was the national capital, and therefore, by its very nature, the Union government *would* have a stake in it. Article 239AA recognized the Union government's stake in the national capital in two distinct ways. *First*, it did so in the legislative sphere—by taking land, police, and law and order out of the ambit of Delhi's legislative powers, and giving Parliament the option to exercise law-making power even in the state list; and *secondly*, it did so in the executive sphere—by giving the LG the power to refer a difference of opinion to the President. It logically followed that the *scope* of this power would have to be defined on the same basis—the LG could only make a reference when the issue concerned *national interests*, and not the interests of the NCT. According to Chandrachud J:

> [I]t would be appropriate to construe the proviso as a protector of *national concerns* in regard to governance of the NCT. The Lieutenant Governor is a watchdog to protect them. The Lieutenant Governor may, for instance, be justified in seeking recourse to the proviso where the executive act of the government of the NCT *is likely to impede or prejudice the exercise of the executive power of the Union government*. The Lieutenant Governor may similarly consider it necessary to invoke the proviso to *ensure compliance with the provisions of the Constitution or a law enacted by Parliament*. There may well be significant issues of policy which have a bearing on the position of the National Capital Territory *as a national capital*. Financial concerns *of the Union government* may be implicated in such a manner that it becomes necessary for the Lieutenant Governor to invoke the proviso where a difference of opinion remains unresolved *[paragraph 142]*.

Although Chandrachud J declined to set out an 'exhaustive', subject-wise list under the proviso, the illustrative list provided in the paragraph above—within the broader rubric of 'national concerns'—makes it clear *how* the proviso is to be understood. It is submitted that the judgment is best interpreted by taking Chandrachud J's concurring opinion as *clarifying* the meaning of the phrase 'exceptional situations' in the majority's opinion. In other words, the proviso kicks in if there is an 'exceptional situation', and an exceptional situation is where some executive action of the Delhi government clearly impinges upon a legitimate interest of the Union government *qua* Union government *physically based in Delhi.* To take a tangible example, the opening of *mohalla clinics* has nothing to do with national concerns and, therefore, does not fall within the scope of the proviso.

Two further points: If the LG differs with the Delhi government, must she record her reasons in writing? And is there a specific time limit within which the 'difference of opinion' must be forwarded by the LG to the President? On the first issue, the judgments are silent. However, given that all the judgments stress that the difference of opinion must be *reasoned* and not a 'contrived difference', it follows virtually as a necessary implication that the LG must reduce the reasons for differing into writing. On the second issue as well, the judgments are silent—and, I submit, regrettably so. Only in his concurrence, Justice Bhushan suggested that the difference in opinion must be referred within a 'reasonable time' of the LG having 'seen' it, but declined to define with any further specificity what 'reasonable time' meant.

No doubt the judges intended that such issues be resolved through 'constitutional statesmanship'—a phrase that, along with its variants, recurs throughout the judgments. However, given that this case only came to court because of a breakdown in 'constitutional statesmanship', it might have been better had these loopholes been firmly closed. This would have been in tune with the Supreme Court's closing of various other loopholes that the framers, in their mistakenly optimistic view of human nature, had left to the mercy of constitutional conventions (the most recent example being the ordering of 'floor tests' within 48–72 hours of election results, in case where there is more than one claimant to chief ministership).

Services and the ACB

There were two specific issues that were litigated before the court—who had control over Delhi's civil service and who had control over the Anti-Corruption Bureau (ACB). The former, as everyone knows, has acquired specific salience in recent days. The court did not return a specific ruling on either issue, and, presumably, it will be settled by smaller benches.[80]

On the first issue, my reading of the judgment is that the Delhi government clearly has control over the services. This follows from a combined reading of the majority judgment and Chandrachud J's concurrence. The majority clearly held that *barring* the three excluded subjects—land, police, and law and order—GNCTD had co-extensive legislative and executive powers over all other fields in Lists II and III. 'Services' features under Entry 41 of List II, which states *'State public services; State Public Service Commission'*.

The Union of India argued that Entry 41 specifically used the word 'state'. Delhi was not a 'state'. Consequently, services were excluded from its ambit. This argument, however, was specifically addressed by Chandrachud J in paragraphs 128–130 of his judgment, where he noted that the use of the word 'state' throughout the Constitution was not dispositive; where appropriate according to context, 'state' would include 'union territories'. When you read this back into the majority's clear statement that the executive power extends to every entry apart from the three specifically excluded, the conclusion that services lie within the executive power of the Delhi government becomes irresistible.

The ACB issue, however, remains unresolved. Before the court, the dispute was whether the ACB came within the definition of 'police'. The court expressed no opinion on this, and so this, now, must be argued afresh before a smaller bench.

Conclusion

The Supreme Court's judgment (I take 'judgment' here to refer to all three opinions) in *National Capital Territory of Delhi vs Union of India* correctly identifies representative democracy as a fundamental feature

---

80 In its May 2023 judgment, the court authoritatively held that services were under the control of the Delhi government.

of the Indian Constitution, and correctly interprets Article 239AA in a manner that, within the textual boundaries of the provision, strengthens representative democracy. Its analysis of the constitutional history of Delhi and the application of constitutional principles to the interpretation of Article 239AA repays close study. On the subject of the proviso to Article 239AA(4), however, it suffers from a lack of specificity, a defect that, I submit, can be remedied by treating Justice Chandrachud's concurrence as clarifying the majority.

One last point: the length. Again. 535 pages. How unnecessary it is, once again, is conceded by the judges themselves. In paragraphs 117 and 118, respectively, Justice Bhushan notes:

> I have perused the elaborate opinion of My Lord, the Chief Justice with which I *substantially agree*, but looking to *the importance of the issues*, I have penned my own views giving reasons for my conclusions.
>
> I have also gone through the well researched and well considered opinion of Brother Justice D.Y. Chandrachud. The view expressed by Justice Chandrachud *are substantially the same* as have been expressed by me in this judgment.

That this occurs on page 531 of 535 tells its own story. If there is 'substantial agreement', the 'importance of the issues' simply does not justify penning a full-fledged separate opinion, which multiplies pages, multiplies the effort involved in reading and also multiplies the possibilities of future confusion when lawyers use semantic distinctions between separate opinions to re-litigate issues that everyone thought were settled.

2

The Article 370 Amendments: Key Legal Issues[81]

(5 August 2019)

IN THIS POST, I will attempt to break down the constitutional changes to Article 370 and highlight some key legal issues surrounding them. In essence, to understand what has happened today, there are three important documents. At the heart of everything is Presidential Order C.O. 272, which constitutes the basis for everything that follows. The second is a Statutory Resolution introduced in the Rajya Sabha, which, *invoking the authority that flows from the effects of Presidential Order C.O. 272*, recommends that the President abrogate (much of) Article 370. The third is the Reorganization Bill, which breaks up the state of Jammu and Kashmir into the Union Territories of Ladakh (without a legislature) and Jammu and Kashmir (with a legislature).

To understand the legal issues, we need to begin with the language of unamended Article 370. As is well known, Article 370 limited the

---

81 Subsequent to the writing of this post, the author was engaged in one of the constitutional challenges to the events of 5 August 2019. At the time of writing, the Supreme Court was yet to decide the issue.

application of the provisions of the Indian Constitution to the state of Jammu and Kashmir. Under Article 370(1)(d), constitutional provisions could be applied to the state from time to time, as modified by the President through a Presidential Order and upon the concurrence of the state government (this was the basis for the controversial Article 35A, for example). Perhaps the most important part of 370, however, was the proviso to clause 3. Clause 3 itself authorized the President to pass an order removing or modifying parts of Article 370.

The proviso stated, 'Provided that the recommendation of the *Constituent Assembly of the State* referred to in clause (2) shall be necessary before the President issues such a notification.'

In other words, for Article 370 *itself* to be amended, the recommendation of the Constituent Assembly of J&K was required. Now, the Constituent Assembly of J&K ceased functioning in 1957. This has led to a long-standing debate about whether Article 370 has effectively become *permanent* (because there is no Constituent Assembly to give consent to its amendment), whether it would require a revival of a J&K Constituent Assembly to amend it or whether it can be amended through the normal amending procedure under the Constitution.

C.O. 272, however, takes an entirely different path. It uses the power of the President under Article 370(1) (see above), to *indirectly* amend Article 370(3) via a third constitutional provision—Article 367, which provides various guidelines about how the Constitution may be interpreted. Now, C.O. 272 *adds* to Article 367 an additional clause, which has four sub-clauses. Sub-clause 4 stipulates that 'in proviso to clause (3) of Article 370 of this Constitution, the expression "Constituent Assembly of the State referred to in clause (2)" shall read "Legislative Assembly of the State"'.

In other words, this is what has happened. Article 370(1) allows the President—with the concurrence of the government of J&K (more on that in a moment)—to amend or modify various provisions of the Constitution in relation to J&K. The Article 370(3) proviso states that

Article 370 *itself* is to be amended by the concurrence of the Constituent Assembly. C.O. 272, therefore, uses the power under 370(1) to amend a provision of the Constitution (Article 367), *which*, in turn, amends Article 370(3), and *takes out* the Constituent Assembly's concurrence for any further amendments to Article 370. And this, in turn, becomes the trigger for the *statutory resolution*, which recommends to the President the removal of (most of) Article 370 (as the Constituent Assembly's concurrence is no longer required).

This is very clever. Is it legal? One serious objection is Article 370(1)(c), which (unamended) stated that 'notwithstanding anything contained in this Constitution, the provisions of Article 1 and *this Article shall apply in relation to that State*'. This is absolutely crucial, because it makes clear that the power of the President to amend provisions of the Constitution in relation to J&K does not extend to Article 1 and 'this Article', i.e., Article 370 itself. Article 370(1)(d) makes it even clearer where it refers to the 'other provisions' of the Constitution that may be altered by Presidential Order (and this is how the present Presidential Order is different from previous ones, such as those that introduced Article 35A). Article 370 itself, therefore, cannot be amended by a Presidential Order such as C.O. 272 (the one exception was a clarificatory amendment, which is not analogous to this one).

Now, it may be immediately objected that C.O. 272 does not amend Article 370—it amends Article 367. The point, however, is that the *content* of those amendments does amend Article 370, and as the Supreme Court has held on multiple occasions, you cannot do indirectly what you cannot do directly. I would therefore submit that the legality of C.O. 272—insofar as it amends Article 370— is questionable. As that is at the root of everything, it throws into question the entire exercise.

There is a second important point to be noted here. C.O. 272 says, as it must, that the concurrence of the government of the state of Jammu and Kashmir has been taken. However, Jammu and Kashmir has been under President's Rule for many months now. Consequently, *actually*, the consent is that of the governor. However, there are two serious problems with basing C.O. 272 upon the consent of the governor. The first is that the governor is a representative of the Central government, like the President. In effect, therefore, Presidential Order 272 amounts to the Central government taking its own consent to amend the Constitution.

There is, however, a more important issue. President's Rule is temporary. It is only meant to happen when constitutional machinery breaks down in a state and an elected government is impossible. President's Rule is meant to be a stand-in *until* the elected government is restored. Consequently, decisions of a *permanent* character—such as changing the entire status of a state—taken *without* the elected Legislative Assembly but by the governor are inherently problematic. *Formally*, they may be within the bounds of legality; however, as the Supreme Court held in *D.C. Wadhwa*, on the question of re-promulgation of ordinances, formal legality can nonetheless amount to fraud on the Constitution. Using the governor to sign off on a Presidential Order that fundamentally alters the constitutional character of a federal unit appears to me to be straying dangerously close to the constitutional fraud line.

Therefore, for these two reasons—*first*, on the indirect amendment of Article 370(3) proviso via 370(1), and *secondly*, on the use of the governor as a substitute for the elected assembly in a matter of *this* kind—I would submit that there are serious legal and constitutional problems with Presidential Order C.O. 272, which, of course, forms the basis of both the statutory resolution and the Reorganization Bill.

Anti-Defection

Introduction

THE PAST FEW YEARS have seen a spate of what have come to be known as 'government formation and toppling disputes', memorialized in public imagination by the repeated images of political parties taking their legislators to five-star hotels in order to prevent—or facilitate—'poaching' by their opponents. These disputes can be grouped into two types. *First*, when an election throws up a fractured or close mandate, leading to the break-up or switching of pre-poll alliances, and/or switching of allegiances by soon-to-be legislators; and *secondly*, 'defections' from a ruling party or ruling coalition, which causes it to lose its majority, triggering a floor test and the eventual downfall of the government.

These disputes have engaged a range of constitutional functionaries, who are *meant* to be impartial but whose conduct has been anything but. These include governors—Central government appointees in the states—who, in cases of fractured mandates, have the discretion to decide the order in which they will call upon parties or alliances to stake a claim to government. Often, this has a non-trivial impact on the allegiances of would-be legislators (including independents), and can play a pivotal role in determining who *does* form the government. Governors also have the power to summon the assembly (among other things, for the purposes of calling for a floor test), a power that has often been used to tilt a delicate political situation one way or another.

Government-toppling situations have brought to the forefront the role of the Speaker of the Assembly. This is because, in theory, toppling governments through defections is supposed to be addressed by the Tenth Schedule of the Indian Constitution, popularly known as the anti-defection law. The anti-defection law provides for the disqualification of any legislator who votes against the party whip. To get around the Tenth Schedule, legislators have resorted to increasingly creative methods, such as 'resigning' instead of 'defecting', refusing to attend party meetings and so on. The Tenth Schedule makes the Speaker the adjudicating authority in such cases, thus marking out a political—and partisan—role for the chairperson of the Assembly.

Unsurprisingly, the actions of governors and Speakers have repeatedly been challenged before the courts, with a spate of government-formation and government-toppling disputes being brought to the Supreme Court. Arunachal Pradesh, Uttarakhand, Maharashtra (twice), Rajasthan, Karnataka (twice) and Madhya Pradesh are just a few of the examples from the time period covered in this book.

The essays in this section analyse how the courts have dealt with such disputes. The number of times that functioning governments *have* been toppled through defections or disguised defections suggests that the Supreme Court, in particular, has failed in its primary task of ensuring that the *ground rules* of democracy are respected: Maharashtra, Karnataka and Madhya Pradesh are three recent examples where a mid-term government has been 'toppled' (and replaced by the Opposition, which also happens to be the ruling party at the Centre) due to legislators 'switching sides'. The following essays indicate how and why this has happened—and what could be done about it.

1

Judicial Supremacy amid the Breakdown of Constitutional Conventions: What the Karnataka Controversy Tells Us about Our Parliamentary Democracy

(16 July 2019)

IT HAS LONG BEEN observed that the smooth functioning of parliamentary democracy depends upon constitutional conventions. Put simply, a constitutional convention refers to a set of uncodified norms that are sanctified by a long tradition of unbroken practice. Political functionaries tend to adhere to these norms either out of a sense of public duty or out of fear of paying a political cost by breaking them.

A written Constitution can reduce the extent to which governance relies upon conventions. It cannot, however, eliminate them. The range of human behaviour can never completely be captured in text. In a written Constitution with judicial review, an extra wrinkle is added to the situation. It creates situations where courts may be asked to rule upon the scope and the content of these conventions, and, in exceptional circumstances, even be asked to guarantee their enforcement. This will require the court to enter the 'political thicket' (see this recent article by Mukund Unny[82]), along with all its attendant dangers.

All this is difficult enough. In India today, however, there is an even further layer of complexity. Constitutional conventions and judicial review depend upon one basic premise—that constitutional functionaries tasked with implementing constitutional conventions act in good faith. For example, parliamentary democracy vests substantial power in the office of the Speaker of the House. The Speaker of the House conventionally comes from the ruling party, but once they occupy the Chair, they are expected to shed their partisan affiliation and impartially administer the rules of the House (including its conventions). The presumption of the Speaker's impartiality is the underlying basis for another very important constitutional convention—that courts shall not be called upon to adjudicate disputes related to what goes on in Parliament. The Parliament has its own adjudicating authority—the Speaker—and the doctrine of the separation of powers requires courts to defer absolutely to how the Speaker manages the affairs of the House.

However, once it becomes clear, as it arguably has in India, that Speakers repeatedly and blatantly act according to partisan motives (the conduct of the last Lok Sabha Speaker in certifying money Bills and refusing to hold votes of confidence is a case in point), a judicialization of the Speaker's conduct becomes inevitable. If Opposition parties have good reason to believe that the game in the House is rigged, they have little choice but to go to court. And the court is then faced with an impossible situation: Constitutional conventions require it to stay out of Parliament, but at the same time, staying out would result in

---

82 Mukund P. Unny, 'Doctrine of Political Thicket - Throwback to Baker v. Carr', LiveLaw, 14 July 2019, https://www.livelaw.in/columns/doctrine-of-political-thicket-throwback-to-baker-v-carr-146355

another set of conventions being violated with impunity. There is no clean—or good—answer in such a situation.

What is happening in Karnataka represents a classic example of the breakdown of constitutional conventions and its knock-on effect on the judiciary. Recall that the ruling Congress–JDS combine in Karnataka has a thin majority. Recently, a number of MLAs of the ruling combine offered their resignations to the Speaker. The result of this would be to deprive the ruling combine of its majority and offer the chance to the Opposition—the BJP—to stake a claim to form the government. The MLAs have argued that they are resigning of their own free will, while the Congress–JDS argues that they have been bribed and threatened by the BJP to do so.

At this point, Article 190 of the Constitution comes into play. Article 190 provides that MLA resignations are to be offered to the Speaker. It also allows the Speaker the discretion to reject the resignations if, in her view, they are not 'voluntary or genuine'. Article 190, therefore, presumes that legislators act in good faith when resigning, and makes the Speaker the judge of that. What Article 190 does not do—indeed, what it *cannot* do—is guarantee that the Speaker herself will act in good faith (that presumption is a constitutional convention).

Before the Supreme Court, the legislators have argued that the Speaker was deliberately delaying deciding on the resignation letters, and therefore violating his duty to act in good faith. They asked the court to direct the Speaker to decide upon the resignations in a 'time-bound manner' (notice that the idea of a judicial authority 'directing' the Speaker of the House to do anything would be unheard of in most parliamentary democracies in the general course of things, and indeed, that is what the Speaker himself effectively said after the Supreme Court passed an interim order). The legislators have also argued that the Speaker is acting out of partisan motives—basically, he is waiting until the ruling coalition issues a three-line whip to its party members, at which point, the anti-defection Tenth Schedule will kick in. The moment the rebel legislators vote against the whip, their *resignations* will become infructuous, because *disqualification* will kick in.

As mentioned above, this puts the court in an impossible situation. The existence of partisan Speakers is an indisputable fact (indeed, there is already a pending petition before a Constitution bench on the issue of Speakers deliberately sitting on disqualification decisions to allow ruling parties to maintain their majority). But the existence of horse-trading and defections to secure ministerial berths or for other similar reasons is equally indisputable. But while both these facts are indisputable, for obvious reasons, and to avoid a complete breakdown of governance, neither of these can be acknowledged *in the open*, and in court. The court, thus, has to pretend that constitutional functionaries act in good faith, while, in specific cases, carve out remedies that are meant to operate in a world in which they do not.

What is the court to do in a case like this? One (tempting) solution that it must avoid is full-scale intervention. That will swiftly drag the court into the political weeds and make accusations of partisanship inevitable. Already the court has been placed in a situation where whatever it does will have the *direct effect* of favouring one set of political parties over the other. That is a very dangerous position for a constitutional court to find itself in.

The contours of a solution, however, might be visible from the court's own precedent: In particular, what it did in Karnataka last year, when the controversy was about government formation.[83] In that case, the tables were somewhat reversed: The issue concerned the actions of the governor in allowing the BJP to form the government despite the Congress–JDS's claims of having a majority, and then allowing the chief

---

83 Gautam Bhatia, 'Why the Supreme Court's Verdict after Karnataka Polls Is Critical for India', *Hindustan Times*, 29 May 2018, https://www.hindustantimes.com/analysis/why-the-supreme-court-s-verdict-after-karnataka-polls-is-critical-for-india/story-TLYgpIUgmMmen6GZPsxkML.html

minister fourteen days to prove his majority (it was alleged that this inordinately long time was given to enable the BJP to use its superior financial power to buy out opposition MLAs). The court refused a full-scale intervention (i.e., setting aside the governor's decision), but did reduce the time given to the chief minister to forty-eight hours by ordering a videographed floor test. The BJP was unable to prove its majority and, ultimately, the Congress–JDS combine came to power.

The Supreme Court thus accomplished two things. *First*, it made it more difficult for the parties involved to act in bad faith by reducing the time period to forty-eight hours; and *secondly*, its solution was not judicial (setting aside or upholding the governor's actions as valid), but *parliamentary*—a floor test. The blueprint, therefore, seems to be this—the task of the court in cases such as these is to fashion a remedy where the solution to the crisis is found through the existing democratic processes, but where it becomes far more difficult for constitutional functionaries to subvert the process and break conventions by acting in bad faith. In the present controversy, that *might* be accomplished by the following solution: The court asks the Speaker to decide upon the resignations within a reasonable time (but enough time for the Speaker to make an enquiry as envisaged by Article 190), but makes it clear that the Speaker's decision will be subject to judicial review under the *Bommai* standard (relevance/existence of material and an absence of mala fides). If it is later found that the Speaker acted wrongly, his decision on the resignations will be set aside, and—as happened in the Arunachal Pradesh case—the status quo ante as of today will be restored, with the resignations being treated as valid. In the meantime, the other democratic processes (the trust vote, the operation of the anti-defection law, etc.) can go on as per their own logic.

This solution, it is submitted, would respect the constitutional authority given to the office of the Speaker while also subjecting him to judicial oversight in case he decides to act in bad faith. At the same time, it would allow the Speaker to form an assessment of whether the rebel legislators are acting in good faith or not, *with the knowledge* that his decision can—and will—be challenged. And the court is saved from wading into murky political disputes (for now) in a way that will open it up to accusations of partisan bias.

This is, of course, an imperfect solution, and there may be other potential solutions that may strike the balance better. (Should the court insist that the decision on resignations precede the trust vote/three-line whip? Would that involve a direction to delay the state budget?) But I want to make one final point: The very fact that we are here today discussing the range of alternatives open to the court demonstrates a disturbing development. The repeated bad faith actions and breaches of constitutional conventions by political functionaries have created a gaping, open space that is being filled by judicial supremacy. This has been going on for a while now. Speakers' partisan decisions on certifying money Bills have made court challenges inevitable; governors' partisanship and horse-trading has made judicial interventions into government formation inevitable; and so on. The beginning of all this, of course, was the repeated and unprincipled imposition of President's Rule, which first dragged the court into such questions.

But dragging the court into this domain presents a deep threat to judicial independence. A court whose decisions will regularly have such huge political ramifications presents a ripe and tempting target for capture, to unscrupulous political parties. It is for this reason that, in every case of this sort, the court must be profoundly careful about what it is doing and what the consequences of that are—because, ironic as it may sound, judicial supremacy in the political process is the shortest road to a compromised judiciary.

Postscript

An additional point—and an additional way in which the Supreme Court, in particular, can avoid being tainted by a partisan brush—is the importance of sticking to procedural rules in cases such as this. It is unclear how an Article 32 petition is maintainable in the present case—

and even more unclear why the Supreme Court did not ask the parties to approach the Karnataka High Court as the jurisdictional forum (recall that a similar case from Tamil Nadu, involving the AIADMK [All India Anna Dravidian Progressive Federation], was argued before the Madras High Court). This becomes particularly pertinent because the present court has indeed sent constitutional cases back to the high courts recently (the challenge to the Aadhaar ordinance being a good example). Ensuring that such cases come to it through proper channels will help the Supreme Court—as an institution—avoid one particular Article 32-shaped pitfall. Of course, that issue is infructuous in the present case.[84]

---

84 I am grateful to Suhrith Parthasarathy for having pointed this out to me.

2

Postscript: The Supreme Court's Problematic Order in the Karnataka Case

(17 July 2019)

YESTERDAY, I WROTE THAT the ongoing Karnataka controversy represents a breakdown of constitutional conventions. This breakdown creates a space for inevitable judicial intervention—but a space that is fraught with risk for the court. In fashioning a remedy, the court ought to make it *as difficult as possible* for the warring political functionaries to subvert constitutional conventions, while leaving the final solution to the existing democratic processes.

This morning, the court passed an order in the case. Noting that it had to maintain a 'constitutional balance between the competing and conflicting rights', it refrained from issuing any directions to the Speaker to decide upon the resignation and disqualification petitions. However, the court also held that *'until further orders the 15 Members of the Assembly, ought not to be compelled to participate in the proceedings of the ongoing session of the House and an option should be given to them that they can take part in the said proceedings or to opt to remain out of the same'*.

In an article on LiveLaw, Manu Sebastian has written that this second part of the order conflicts with the Tenth Schedule as it effectively authorizes the rebel MLAs to disregard the party whip.[85] That point aside, does the order meet the two-part test set out above—of allowing the democratic process to decide the issue while making its subversion more difficult? On the first count, it certainly does, a point made particularly evident by the court's own observation that there is a trust vote scheduled for tomorrow.

On the second point, however, I would argue that the order comes up notably short. The court's attempted 'balance' is to give both parties freedom to act. The Speaker has the freedom to decide on the petitions, while the rebel MLAs have the freedom not to attend the proceedings of the House. However, on closer scrutiny, this balance is not a balance at all, *as the second part of the order—on the issue of attending the proceedings of the House—effectively and presumptively holds the resignations to be valid until and unless the Speaker decides otherwise.* This is because it is only if the resignations were valid would the party whip—and thereby the Tenth Schedule—cease to apply. In all other circumstances, the rebel MLAs' defiance of the whip would be *subject to* disqualification under the Tenth Schedule.

The matter grows murkier when we consider the fact that the court expressly notes in its order that its 'balance' is occasioned by the fact that there is a trust vote tomorrow. This being the case, the court's apparent granting of freedom to the Speaker becomes effectively chimerical—because the whole point is that the ruling combine is likely to lose its majority *in the circumstances that the rebel MLAs are able to defy the party whip without being disqualified,* which is precisely what the court's order allows. In effect, therefore, the order—while purporting to grant the Speaker unlimited time—effectively grants the Speaker time until

---

[85] Manu Sebastian, 'Why SC Order in Karnataka MLAs Case Goes against the Spirit of Anti-Defection Laws?', LiveLaw, 17 July 2019, https://www.livelaw.in/columns/why-sc-order-karnataka-mlas-case-anti-defection-laws-146465

the trust vote to decide, after which any decision the Speaker makes will, for all practical purposes, be infructuous.

As I had mentioned in my previous post, the two subversions of constitutional conventions at stake here are the Speaker abusing his powers on the one hand and large-scale horse-trading on the other. The Supreme Court's order, unfortunately, is framed in a way that makes the former far more difficult (in a similar manner to how the Supreme Court fettered the governor's ability to abuse his powers the last time around), but *at the same time, actively allows for the facilitation of the latter*, by judicially noting that the rebel MLAs 'ought not' to be subjected to the party whip.

This, it should be obvious, is no balance at all.

3

The Supreme Court's Madhya Pradesh Government Formation Judgment—VI: Some Concluding Remarks

(31 May 2020)

[**Editorial Note:** Justice is an indivisible concept. We cannot, therefore, discuss contemporary Supreme Court judgments without also acknowledging the court's failure—at an institutional level—to do justice in the case involving sexual-harassment allegations against a former Chief Justice. This editorial caveat will remain in place for all future posts on this blog dealing with the Supreme Court, until there is a material change in circumstances (e.g., the introduction of structural mechanisms to ensure accountability)].

LATE LAST MONTH, THIS blog hosted an extensive debate on the Supreme Court's judgment in the Madhya Pradesh government-formation case[86] (see Rishav Ambastha's initial post on

---

86 *Shivraj Singh Chouhan vs Speaker, Madhya Pradesh Legislative Assembly and Ors*, WP (C) 439/2020.

jurisdiction;[87] Anmol Jain's post questioning the correctness of the judgment;[88] Amlan Mishra and Nivedhitha K.'s posts responding to Anmol;[89] and Anmol's rejoinder[90]). The judgment is a particularly important one, because it is the first *reasoned* verdict by the Supreme Court, after many years of interim orders that were passed every time a government-formation crisis arose.

In this post, I want to offer a few brief concluding remarks, drawing from the debate. Recall once again that the key question before the Supreme Court was whether the governor of a state had the power to direct a convening of the Legislative Assembly for the purposes of

---

[87] Rishav Ambastha, 'The Supreme Court's Madhya Pradesh Government Formation Judgment – I: A Question of Jurisdiction', Indian Constitutional Law and Philosophy, 24 *April 2020*, https://indconlawphil.wordpress.com/2020/04/24/the-supreme-courts-madhya-pradesh-government-formation-judgment-i-a-question-of-jurisdiction-guest-post/

[88] Anmol Jain, 'The Supreme Court's Madhya Pradesh Government Formation Judgment – II: On the Powers of the Governor', Indian Constitutional Law and Philosophy, 25 April 2020, https://indconlawphil.wordpress.com/2020/04/25/the-supreme-courts-madhya-pradesh-government-formation-judgment-ii-on-the-powers-of-the-governor-guest-post/

[89] Amlan Mishra, 'The Supreme Court's Madhya Pradesh Government Formation Judgment – III: A Response to Anmol Jain', Indian Constitutional Law and Philosophy, 27 April 2020, https://indconlawphil.wordpress.com/2020/04/27/the-supreme-courts-madhya-pradesh-government-formation-judgment-iii-a-response-to-anmol-jain-guest-post/; Nivedhitha K, 'The Supreme Court's Madhya Pradesh Government Formation Judgment – IV: A Response to Anmol Jain (2)', Indian Constitutional Law and Philosophy, 29 April 2020, https://indconlawphil.wordpress.com/2020/04/29/the-supreme-courts-madhya-pradesh-government-formation-judgment-iv-a-response-to-anmol-jain-2-guest-post/

[90] Anmol Jain, 'The Supreme Court's Madhya Pradesh Government Formation Judgment – V: A Rejoinder', Indian Constitutional Law and Philosophy, 3 May 2020, https://indconlawphil.wordpress.com/2020/05/03/the-supreme-courts-madhya-pradesh-government-formation-judgment-v-a-rejoinder-guest-post/

holding a floor test. The Supreme Court held that the governor did indeed have that power. The key constitutional question was whether this power fell under the 'discretion' of the governor—i.e., whether it was an exception to the general principle that the governor could only act upon the 'aid and advice' of the Council of Ministers. The Supreme Court held that it did.

As the debate between Anmol, Amlan and Nivedhitha on this blog demonstrates, a close reading of the Constituent Assembly Debates does not yield a definitive answer to this question. This is why the answer lies in a structural and purposive reading of the Constitution. Which interpretation better *fits* with the Constitution's overall structure and guiding principles? According to the court, the argument goes something like this: In the ordinary course of things, when you have an existing government and a functioning house, the accepted way of challenging that government's legitimacy is through a no-confidence motion, which then culminates in a floor test ordered by the Speaker. However, there may arise situations where a government that has lost the confidence of the legislature impedes or prevents the holding of a floor test and continues in office de facto. This would be a violation of the principle of collective responsibility and undermine the executive–legislature relationship within a parliamentary structure. It is, therefore, *justified* for the governor to step in and direct a floor test, for the limited purpose of determining whether or not the government continues to enjoy the confidence of the House. The power of the governor is thus *derived* from a structural reading of the Constitution and the principles of parliamentary democracy.

The problem with the argument, however, is this: The protection of one principle of parliamentary democracy (executive accountability to the legislature) comes *at the cost of* another—the sovereignty of the legislature to determine the proceedings within the House, and the supremacy of the Speaker. This, indeed, is the key distinction between a government-formation dispute *after elections but before the formation of the government* (which is what happened, for example, in the first Karnataka case in 2018), and a government-formation dispute when the composition of a *functioning House* is altered because of the resignation of sitting MLAs. This distinction was drawn by senior counsel Dr Abhishek Manu Singhvi during oral arguments, but was rejected by the court. The distinction, however, is crucial, for the reasons pointed out above.

Now, the argument made by the court—and in Amlan's piece—is that vesting the discretion with the governor is required because the standard method of bringing down a government that has lost the confidence of the House—i.e., a no-confidence motion—can be circumvented either by an adjournment of legislative proceedings or by the Speaker simply sitting on the no-confidence motion (indeed, readers will recall that during the previous NDA government at the Centre, the Speaker, quite literally, did not allow a no-confidence motion tabled by the Opposition to be voted upon). *However*—and this came out in Anmol's rejoinder piece—both these attempts have a straightforward solution: judicial review. The UK Supreme Court has recently taught us exactly how and when a court may declare a prorogation unlawful—when it is clear that the effect of that prorogation is to defeat the constitutional principle of executive accountability to the legislature. And our own Supreme Court, last November, while considering the issue of the judicial review of the Speaker's certification of money bills, provided strong and persuasive reasons when the discretion of the Speaker can be challenged in court. If mala fide certification of Bills as money Bills attracts judicial review, there is no reason why mala fide refusal to hold a no-confidence vote cannot.

The question, therefore, boils down to this: Structurally, which is the better option to ensure executive accountability—the governor or the court? It is, to my mind, obvious that it is the latter, for the very straightforward reason that the governor is a Central government appointee, and judges are not. Given a choice, further accretion to the powers of the governor infringes the federal structure in a way that expanded judicial power does not.

I think this issue is particularly important because, in deciding these cases, the court must necessarily navigate three sets of facts that it cannot turn a blind eye to (and, indeed, all three are flagged in the judgment). First: Governors should be neutral, but they are not. They effectively act as agents of the Central government. Second: Speakers should be neutral, but they are not. They effectively act as agents of their parties. And third: Horse-trading happens. Legislators are paid staggering amounts of money to switch sides and bring down the government, and the technique of resignations is used to circumvent the rigours of the anti-defection law. A judgment that proceeds on the assumption that any one of these three things does not exist essentially operates in a parallel reality, where constitutional principles have come entirely unmoored from the factual situation that they are meant to apply to.

Now given these facts, how should the court decide? In an earlier post I argued that the judicial doctrine should evolve in a manner that the court does not determine substantive outcomes (such as installing or replacing a government);[91] but also that the court needs to ensure that the impact of the three issues highlighted above, upon the democratic process, is minimized. So, for example, in cases involving government formation immediately after a closely run election, the court cannot stop horse-trading from happening, but it can—by ordering an immediate floor test—minimize the time open to parties to engage in horse-trading and curtail gubernatorial abuse (as happened in the Karnataka case). Once again, if in the case of a sitting government, a host of MLAs resign in a coordinated fashion to alter the composition of the House, this is not something the court can stop. What it can do, however, is prevent the emergence of collusive situations involving the governor and the political party that appointed the governor by eliminating him from the power equations at play. In addition, the court's approach should be informed by the fact that coordinated resignations *suggest*

---

91 'Judicial Supremacy', supra.

that horse-trading is going on. Thus, just as there is an overriding need in post-election government formation cases to *prevent* horse-trading through an immediate floor test, when the horse-trading *has already happened* (through resignations), an immediate floor test that does not allow the Speaker at least a reasonable amount of time to decide upon the resignations (the extent of the Speaker's discretion here is a debate for another day) will have the effect of *entrenching* horse-trading.

Some of these factors, I suggest, were bracketed by the court, as it did not believe it could go into such issues. That, however, is a mistake. The court is *already* making (correct) assumptions about the lack of neutrality of the Speaker, when it gives the governor the power to direct a floor test. What is sauce for the goose is sauce for the gander: In an ideal world, Speakers and governors are neutral, and horse-trading does not happen. But we cannot recognize *one* departure from the ideal—the politicization of the office of the Speaker—without recognizing the other—bringing down governments through horse-trading. A holistic recognition of the structural problems involved, I would submit, would lead one to Anmol's answer as the preferable one—the no-confidence motion remains the sole means of testing the continued legitimacy of an elected and functioning government, with the possibility of judicial review in case of an impediment is thrown up.

A final, somewhat unrelated point: As I have noted above, the court acknowledges, towards the end of its judgment, that horse-trading is a feature of the polity. But here's the thing—horse-trading is enabled and facilitated by vast amounts of money sloshing through politics, and for the past two years, the sloshing of unimaginable sums has been enabled by the mechanism of electoral bonds, which allow opaque and limitless corporate donations to political parties. Constitutional challenges to the electoral bond schemes have been pending in the Supreme Court for more than two years, and successive Chief Justices have dodged, ducked and evaded hearing the case. For this reason, one can only read judicial lamentations about horse-trading with a wry smile. The institution that actually has the power to do something about it (even if a little bit) is the institution that is refusing to act. Of course, the decision to hear the case lies with the Chief Justice. Therefore, it is not that the two judges who authored this judgment are responsible for the delay. But that, unfortunately, is becoming an enduring issue with the poly-vocal character of the Supreme Court. The same institution, speaking through different judges, criticizes horse-trading while refraining from hearing a case that would have a non-trivial impact on that same horse-trading. If the Supreme Court is to retain its character as a *constitutional court*, this problem desperately requires a solution.

Fourth Branch Institutions

Introduction

THE LONE ESSAY IN this section considers an important 'Fourth Branch Institution'—the information commissions—and asks whether, in the absence of constitutional entrenchment, it is possible to protect the independence and autonomy of bodies such as this.

1

The Amendments to the Right to Information Act Are Unconstitutional

(25 July 2019)

YESTERDAY, THE RAJYA SABHA passed a set of amendments to the Right to Information (RTI) Act of 2005, clearing the way for their enactment into law (after presidential assent). These amendments, as I have summarized here, effectively undermine the independence of the information commissioners by bringing their salaries and terms of appointment under the control of the Central government.

In this essay, I will argue that these amendments are unconstitutional. The argument is a complex one, and so I will set out the fundamental premises at the beginning, before developing each in turn. These are:

A. The right to information is a fundamental right. It is an aspect of Article 19(1)(a) of the Constitution (the freedom of speech and expression).
B. The Constitution's guarantee of fundamental rights includes a guarantee of those incidental and ancillary aspects that are necessary to ensure that the right is effective and not merely illusory.

C. Fundamental rights under the Indian Constitution have a negative and positive dimension. In their negative dimension, they protect the individual against State interference. In their positive dimension, the State is required to take affirmative action to respect, protect, promote and fulfil these rights.
D. The court cannot direct Parliament to legislate in order to discharge its positive obligations under Part III of the Constitution. However, what the court *can* do—and has done—is (1) in case of a legislative vacuum, pass guidelines that have statutory force until a law is enacted and (2) if a law exists, test whether it fulfils the State's positive obligations under Part III.
E. In the case of (2), if the court finds that the legislation comes up short, it *can*—and *has*—interpreted or struck down parts of the statute with a view to bringing it in compliance with constitutional requirements.
F. It follows logically from (E) that if an existing statute that meets the positive obligations of the State under Part III is *downgraded* (via amendment) to a level where it no longer does so, the court *can*—and *should*—strike down the amendments and restore status quo.

Conclusion

On a combination of (D2) and (F), the RTI amendments are unconstitutional. The RTI is a classic example of a 'constitutional statute'—a statute enacted in pursuance of the State's positive obligation to fulfil a constitutional right. Judicial review extends to testing whether it does so, and to fashioning an appropriate remedy if—and depending on the manner in which—it fails to do so. In this case, that remedy is striking down the amendments and restoring the pre-amended RTI. This remedy does not amount to directing the State to legislate and does not amount to judicial overreach.

A. *The right to information is a fundamental right under Article 19(1)(a) of the Constitution.*

As recently as 2013, the Supreme Court held, in a judgment dealing with the Right to Information Act, that '*the right to information is a facet of freedom of speech and expression contained in Article 19(1)(a) of the Constitution of India ... [The] right to information thus indisputably is a fundamental right, so held in several judgments of this Court.*' This Supreme Court has consistently maintained this position—over decades—and there is little need to set out the plethora of judgments affirming this proposition.

Apart from being firmly entrenched in judicial precedent, the reading in of the right to information into the freedom of speech and expression makes eminent sense as a matter of first principles. For more than a century now, one of the three core underlying justifications for the freedom of speech and expression has been its importance to democracy. Only through the free flow of ideas and information, it is rightly argued, will citizens be in a position to effectively exercise their democratic right of choosing their representatives. It is trite to point out that if information held *by* State authorities is choked off from the public domain, the bridge between freedom of speech and democracy crumbles entirely. The right to information, therefore, is, by necessary implication, entailed within a substantive account of the freedom of speech and expression, without which the latter would be illusory (much like how the right to privacy underlies numerous other civil rights—such as speech, association, movement, etc.—and is necessary to make them effective).

B. *The Constitution's guarantee of fundamental rights includes a guarantee of those incidental and ancillary aspects that are necessary to ensure that the right is effective and not merely illusory.*

This, again, is a venerable and incontestable proposition. It has been upheld in a number of cases. One classic example is *PUCL vs Union of*

India, where the Supreme Court directed the Election Commission of India to provide a 'None of the Above' (NOTA) option to voters using Electronic Voting Machines (EVMs). This direction was justified on the basis that NOTA was essential to maintaining the secrecy of the ballot as well as the fairness of elections—both of which, in turn, were linked to the freedom to vote under Article 19(1)(a). Note that the court *specifically* held that by failing to provide the NOTA option, the Conduct of Election Rules, 1961, were not only ultra vires the parent statute, *but also violated Article 19(1)(a) of the Constitution*.

Again, it is unnecessary to multiply examples for the proposition. Its application to the present case should be evident as well. Insofar as the independence of the information commissioners—who stand between the individual and the State, and are tasked with the implementation of the RTI—is integral to the right to information remaining an *effective* right; undermining of the same is ipso facto a violation of that right.

C. Fundamental rights under the Indian Constitution have a negative and positive dimension. In their negative dimension, they protect the individual against State interference. In their positive dimension, the State is required to take affirmative action to respect, protect, promote and fulfil these rights.

This proposition has been affirmed by different judgments in different contexts. For example, in *Prithipal Singh vs State of Punjab*—a case about police atrocities—the Supreme Court held that Article 21 'includes both so-called negative and positive obligations for the State. The negative obligation means the overall prohibition on arbitrary deprivation of life … [while] positive obligation requires that State has an overriding obligation to protect the right to life of every person within its territorial jurisdiction. The obligation *requires the State to take administrative and all other measures* in order to protect life and investigate all suspicious deaths.' In *Amita vs Union of India*—a discrimination case—the Supreme Court held that 'Article 14 of the

Constitution of India is both [a] negative and positive right. Negative in the sense that no one can be discriminated against anybody and everyone should be treated as equals. *The latter* is the core and essence of right to equality and *[the] state has obligation to take necessary steps* so that every individual is given equal respect and concern, which he is entitled to as a human being.' The Supreme Court's much-discussed highway liquor ban judgment, in fact, was based on the argument that the State had failed to discharge its positive obligation to protect life under Article 21, by failing to ban liquor vends next to highways in order to prevent accidents. Examples may be multiplied.

Of course, the most recent—and famous—example of this proposition is the *Right to Privacy* judgment (and, as we shall shortly see, both the privacy judgment and the subsequent *Aadhaar* judgment are crucial to this argument). In *Puttaswamy* (Privacy), Chandrachud J, writing for the plurality, correctly observed that 'the Constitutional right is placed at a pedestal which embodies both a negative and a positive freedom. The negative freedom protects the individual from unwanted intrusion. As a positive freedom, it obliges the State to adopt *suitable measures for protecting individual privacy.*' As is obvious from the rest of his judgment—noting, in particular, the work of the Srikrishna Committee—suitable measures includes suitable *legislative* measures.

Let us briefly take stock. It has been established so far that the right to information is a fundamental right under Article 19(1)(a) of the Constitution. The right to information includes incidental and ancillary aspects that ensure it is an *effective*—and not *illusory*—right, one of which is the independence of the individuals charged with implementing the right (particularly against the State). And the right to information requires the State to 'adopt suitable measures' guaranteeing its adequate fulfilment. It follows—necessarily—that these 'suitable measures' provide for the effective independence of the aforementioned individuals (because, naturally, measures providing for an illusory right to information are hardly 'suitable' under any meaning of the word and hardly effectuate the positive content of the right).

D. *The Court cannot direct Parliament to legislate in order to discharge its positive obligations under Part III of the Constitution. However, what the Court can do—and has done—is (1) in case of a legislative vacuum, pass guidelines that have statutory force until a law is enacted, and (2) if a law exists, test whether it fulfils the State's positive obligations under Part III.*

Let me begin this section by quickly getting a red herring out of the way. It is nobody's case that what follows from (A), (B) and (C) is that the court can issue a mandamus directing Parliament to legislate a Right to Information Act providing for suitable independence of the information commissioners. Such a move would be a blatant violation of the separation of powers, and the court has not resorted to it—and should not.

At the same time, however, the Supreme Court has devised a set of more conservative remedies to deal with situations where the State refuses to discharge its positive obligations, or discharges them in an illusory fashion. A legendary example of the first kind of case, of course, is the *Vishaka* judgment. It is important to note that the *Vishaka* judgment consisted of two parts. In the first part, the court returned an affirmative finding that sexual harassment at the workplace was hit by Articles 14 and 15 of the Constitution. In the *second* part, it found that the State had failed to discharge its obligations by ... doing nothing at all. Obviously, the obligation that the court was referring to was the positive obligation to enact an appropriate law (this much was mentioned, although the court, admittedly, did not use the word 'positive').

Now, what did the court do? It stated that it would discharge its duty of enforcing fundamental rights under Article 32 of the

Constitution by laying down guidelines; these guidelines would be treated as law under Article 141 *until* replaced by a statute (something that happened many years later, in 2013). Thus, the court responded to the State's failure to discharge its positive obligations by temporarily standing in for it, *until* Parliament got its act together and *legislated* to do so.

I want to make one basic point here. If *Vishaka* is still good law—and nobody argues that it is not—the argument I make in this essay falls well within the scope of existing judicial precedent. Because if the court is entitled to *making* a law to discharge positive obligations under Part III, where the State has failed to act (1), surely it is entitled to *striking down* a law that *changes* an existing legislative framework, bringing it into non-compliance with Part III (2). From the scope of the separation of powers and judicial overreach, the latter is far, far more restrained than the former (although, I submit, it is defensible on its own terms).

E. In case of (2), if the court finds that the legislation comes up short, it can—and has—interpreted or struck down parts of the statute with a view to bringing it in compliance with constitutional requirements.

But we don't even need to rely upon *Vishaka* and reason through analogies. There is an excellent recent example of a case where the Supreme Court found an existing statute to fall below the standards required by positive obligations under Part III, and amended and struck down parts of it to bring it into compliance. This is, of course, the *Aadhaar* judgment (*Puttaswamy II*). Recall that in *Aadhaar*, the Supreme Court found that several aspects of the Aadhaar Act *were insufficiently protective of individual data*. For our purposes here, these included (a) a five-year storage period for metadata and (b) authorization to a joint secretary-level officer to disclose Aadhaar data.

What did the court do? It did two things. First, it held that any period beyond six months was excessive, and consequently, the relevant regulations had to be *amended* to limit collection to six months (the court also read down the meaning of 'metadata'). Second—and this is the most important to us—the court held that 'there has to be a higher ranking officer along with, preferably, a judicial officer. The provisions contained in Section 33(2) *of the Act to the extent it gives power to* the joint secretary is, therefore, *struck down giving liberty to the respondents to suitably enact a provision on the aforesaid lines,* which would adequately protect the interest of individuals.'

In both cases, therefore, the Supreme Court required the protection level to be *scaled up*, because on its terms, the *legislative framework* of the Aadhaar Act fell short of adequately protecting privacy and the right to personal data. In the first case—after finding that the constitutional limit on data retention was six months—it was directed that subordinate legislation be amended to comply; and in the second, the inadequately protective provision was struck down; it was spelt out what adequate protection entailed; and it was left up to the State to 'suitably' legislate. Note that it is irrelevant in the first case that subordinate legislation was directed to be amended, because it is not being argued here that the court can *direct* Parliament to amend the RTI (or indeed, to legislate the RTI, were it to be repealed). What is relevant here is the court's finding that the level of protection afforded by an existing legislative framework was insufficient, its declaration of what *was* the adequate level (six months and a higher-level officer along with a judicial officer) and its fashioning of a remedy (amending subordinate legislation and striking down law to prevent disclosure altogether until suitable protection was offered). And that, it will be noted, is *exactly* the form of the argument being made here.

F. It follows logically from (E) that if an existing statute that meets the positive obligations of the State under Part III is downgraded (via

amendment) to a level where it no longer does so, the court can—and should—strike down the amendments and restore the status quo.

We are now in a position to understand the corollary that flows from the above arguments. There are numerous ways in which the State can fail to fulfil its positive obligations under Part III. It can refuse to enact any legislation. Or it can enact legislation that clearly and self-evidently fails to discharge the obligations in question. In both sets of cases, the court has fashioned remedies *that stop short of a mandamus directing the State to legislate*. In the first set of cases, the court has passed guidelines that hold the field until Parliament steps in. In the second set of cases, it has spelt out how the legislative framework falls short, what manner of framework is *minimally* necessary for the burden to be discharged, and then, accordingly, fashioned the remedy of changing subordinate legislation or striking down primary law in a way that the pre-existing position (which was more rights-protective) is restored.

But if all this is par for the course, the argument in the RTI case is positively conservative by comparison. Here, there was no vacuum, and therefore, no requirement for the court to (effectively) legislate. Nor was there a finding that an originally enacted statutory framework fell short of effectively discharging positive obligations. What was there was an existing framework that *did* discharge the positive obligation, which was then consciously *downgraded* to a level that was *below* effective—or, to put it more bluntly, to a level that made the positive aspect of the right illusory. Now, if the court (and you, the reader) agrees with the *substantive* argument that the RTI amendments undermine the independence of the commissioners and, by bringing them under governmental control, *do* make the right illusory, there can be no doubt that the court does have the power to strike down the amendments and restore the status quo ante. In other words, while there may be a disagreement on the merits of the amendments, if the merits argument is conceded, there can be no disagreement—based on separation of powers or any other procedural grounds—about the fact that the court *must* strike down the amendments as unconstitutional.

Conclusion

On a combination of (D2) and (F), the RTI amendments are unconstitutional. The RTI is a classic example of a 'constitutional statute'—a statute enacted in pursuance of the State's positive obligation to fulfil a constitutional right. Judicial review extends to testing whether it does so, and to fashioning an appropriate remedy if—and depending on the manner in which—it fails to do so. In this case, that remedy is striking down the amendments and restoring the pre-amended RTI. This remedy does not amount to directing the State to legislate, and does not amount to judicial overreach.

It remains to clear up a few brief points. One of the government's justifications for the amendment was that under the old Act, information commissioners had been placed on a par with Supreme Court judges and election commissioners, which was impermissible, as the latter are constitutional posts. Now, first of all, note that this argument is entirely irrelevant to the core point at issue, which is whether governmental control compromises independence in a manner that makes the right illusory (and indeed, the Supreme Court's own *NJAC* judgment has eloquent passages on why the answer to that is a clear 'yes').

There is, however, a more important point to be made here. Yes, *formally*, information commissioners are statutory officers and do not occupy constitutional posts, but the matter is not one of pure form. At the beginning of this essay, I had referred to the RTI as a 'constitutional statute', in the sense that it implemented a core fundamental right under the Constitution. Note that this terminology is not new. In the United States, for example, there is the concept of 'super-statutes', which have achieved a 'quasi-constitutional significance' beyond ordinary statutes. The phrase 'constitutional statutes' itself was used by the famous scholar Charles Beard, who noted that 'if we regard as constitutional all that body of law relative to the fundamental organization of the three branches of the federal government–legislative, executive and judicial—then by far the greater part of our constitutional law is to be found in the statutes'. The term has also been used in recent British scholarship.

What I am trying to argue, therefore, is this: We miss the woods for the trees if we draw a facile distinction between the fact that information commissioners owe their position to a statute, while judges and election commissioners occupy constitutional posts. The whole *point* of drawing a statutory equivalence between the former and the latter was precisely because the RTI is a constitutional statute, implementing a fundamental right. In substance, therefore (although not in form), the information commission is what Tarunabh Khaitan has called a 'fourth branch institution', performing a function that is as valuable (although not formally equivalent) as that performed by the Election Commission or the judiciary. And it follows from this that an attack upon the independence of the information commissioners needs to be taken as seriously as an attack upon the independence of other, formally constitutional posts.

One final point: Subjecting the RTI amendments to a rigorous standard of review is not only well within the judicial domain, but would actually be part of the classic function of the court acting as a counter-majoritarian institution. By its very nature, the RTI is something that the government is instinctively hostile to, as it *compels* transparency in governance. With the vanishing difference now in India between the executive and Parliament, the role of the court in preserving and protecting legislation such as the RTI has only grown in importance.

Consequently, and in sum, the RTI amendments compromise the independence of the information commissioners by bringing them under substantive governmental control. The information commissioners are tasked with implementing the RTI and stand between the individual and the State, when the former makes fundamental rights claims upon the latter. *Under the existing statutory framework,** therefore, the right to information is illusory without the independence of the information commissioners. Consequently, the amendments violate Article 19(1)(a) of the Constitution and deserve to be struck down, with the status quo ante being restored.

---

*   To repeat a point made earlier, the existing statutory framework is crucial to the argument, because that is what the amendments depart from, and that is what will be restored if they were to be struck down. To the question of what the court would do if Parliament repealed RTI altogether, the answer is: 'That brings us into *Vishaka* territory.' But the fact that Parliament *could* repeal the RTI has no bearing on what the court should do when the challenge is to an amendment to the existing framework (and which must, therefore, be measured *against* that framework)—and not to a legislative vacuum.

Part Three

The Judiciary

The Courts

Introduction

THE FOLLOWING SET OF essays speaks to a range of institutional issues that have arisen over the past few years. These issues do not feature directly in court judgments, but are nonetheless extremely important, as they relate to the courts' relationship with the executive, the courts' relationship with their own precedent (which has a direct bearing upon the rule of law), the internal organization of the judiciary (which has a non-trivial impact on the outcomes of cases) and so on.

In the following pages, you will read about the persistent problem of *judicial evasion*, where the courts' refusal to hear and list important cases creates a fait accompli in favour of the executive; the role of the Chief Justice in the allocation and listing of cases, and the controversies that this has created; the Supreme Court's institutional failure in adequately addressing a complaint of sexual harassment against a former Chief Justice; and, finally, a survey of the courts' institutional response to the Covid-19 pandemic.

1

'O Brave New World': The Supreme Court's Evolving Doctrine of Constitutional Evasion

(6 January 2017)

THE GOVERNMENT INITIATES A programme on a national scale, which has far-reaching effects on the lives of citizens. It stakes its credibility and prestige upon the programme, and defends its transformative potential for the country. Critics disagree. Among other things, they argue that the programme is illegal without the sanction of law and infringes constitutionally guaranteed fundamental rights. The critics move the court and request an early hearing, since the government's programme is changing facts on the ground on a daily basis. The court hears the case. Perhaps it agrees with the critics, and invalidates the programme. The government then has to go back to the drawing board, iron out the illegalities and come back with another programme (if it considers it to be worth the effort). Or the court agrees with the government and holds the programme to be legally and constitutionally valid, and the government carries on. In both situations, the court pronounces upon the scope and limitations of the fundamental rights at issue.

That is an example of a well-working system of checks and balances. However, over the past few months, there have been indications that this system is not working in quite the manner that it should. This is a cause for significant concern.

The Aadhaar Hearing

The first substantive hearing in the constitutional challenge to the government's Aadhaar programme took place on 23 September 2013. On that day, a two-judge bench of the Supreme Court admitted the petition for hearing and passed the following order: '[N]o person should suffer for not getting the Aadhaar card in spite of the fact that some authority had issued a circular making it mandatory.'

On 8 October 2013, the case was listed for a 'final hearing' on 22 October 2013. On 26 November 2013, the court passed directions for the impleadment of all states and union territories. The case then proceeded to a three-judge bench. Through January to April 2014, the three-judge bench heard arguments by Shyam Divan, senior counsel for the petitioner, on a number of dates. At the end of April, the case was listed for July, but only came up for hearing next more than a year later, on 21 July 2015. Through the last week of July and the first week of August, the three-judge bench heard arguments from both Divan and Gopal Subramaniam.

At this point, the attorney-general argued that there was no fundamental right to privacy under the Indian Constitution and cases that had consistently held to the contrary since *Gobind vs State of MP* in 1975 were wrongly decided, since they had ignored binding eight- and six-judge-bench decisions. He asked for a reference to a larger bench. The court agreed. On 11 August 2015, it passed a detailed reference order. In the order, it noted:

> We are of the opinion that the cases on hand raise far reaching questions of importance involving interpretation of the Constitution. What is at stake is the amplitude of the fundamental rights including that precious and inalienable right under Article 21. If the observations made in *M.P. Sharma* (supra) and *Kharak Singh* (supra) are to be read literally and accepted as the law of this country, the fundamental rights guaranteed under the Constitution of India and more particularly right to liberty under Article 21 would be denuded of vigour and vitality.

The court also stated, 'Having regard to importance of the matter, it is desirable that the matter be heard at the earliest.'

Until the time that the case could be heard by a larger bench, the court also issued the following directions:

> The production of an Aadhaar card will not be condition for obtaining any benefits otherwise due to a citizen … [and] the Unique Identification Number or the Aadhaar card will not be used by the respondents for any purpose other than the PDS Scheme and in particular for the purpose of distribution of foodgrains, etc., and cooking fuel, such as kerosene. The Aadhaar card may also be used for the purpose of the LPG Distribution Scheme.

There was one more substantive hearing on 15 October 2015. A five-judge bench of the court added some more schemes to the ones listed out in the 11 August order, for which the Aadhaar card could be used. The court reiterated:

> We will also make it clear that the Aadhaar card scheme is purely voluntary and it cannot be made mandatory till the matter is finally decided by this Court one way or the other.

And:

> Since there is some urgency in the matter, we request the learned Chief Justice of India to constitute a Bench for final hearing of these matters at the earliest.

A five-judge bench is constituted by the Chief Justice at his discretion. After the hearing of 15 October, the case has not been heard. In the meantime, the government's conduct is well known. The Aadhaar Act was passed to give statutory sanction to the programme (questions have been raised about the constitutionality of the Act as well, especially regarding excessive delegation and the fundamental right to privacy). Despite numerous Supreme Court directions that Aadhaar could not be made mandatory, there have been reports on an almost weekly basis that an Aadhaar card is effectively a requirement for some or the other benefit (the most recent one being today for MGNREGA). Contempt petitions have been filed before the court, which remain pending.

In light of the government's conduct over the past year and a half, the court's refusal to hear the case goes beyond ordinary situations of matters being stuck in the courts for long periods because of judicial backlog and pendency. *Aadhaar* is a classic case where the more the court delays, the greater the government's ability to eventually present it with a fait accompli—the fait accompli being that Aadhaar coverage becomes so deep, pervasive and intertwined with citizens' lives that even if the court were to hold it unconstitutional, it would be, virtually, a technical or physical *impossibility* to undo it—or, if not an impossibility, the cost of disruption would be so prohibitively high that no government could reasonably implement it, even if it wanted to.

For these reasons, when the new Chief Justice assumed office this week, the case was mentioned before him for an urgent hearing. The request was declined (with observations that are deeply concerning, if they reflect the court's institutional position on fundamental rights).

Presumably, it will not be heard any time soon—despite two judicial observations from the middle of 2015 highlighting the urgency of the case and the need for a quick hearing.

Demonetization

On 8 November 2016, the Prime Minister announced that Rs 500 and Rs 1000 notes would cease to be legal tender from midnight. In the coming weeks, this announcement was followed by a slew of notifications from the Reserve Bank of India that placed various restrictions on what citizens could or could not do with their money—how much they could withdraw from ATMs, how much they could withdraw from banks, etc. At the time, the Prime Minister made the prediction—which now appears to be a little optimistic—that normalcy would return within fifty days—that is, by the end of the year.

As Namita Wahi argues, there are substantive legal arguments for the proposition that the demonetization policy violated both law and the Constitution.[92] On the first, arguably, the policy was ultra vires the Reserve Bank of India Act, 1934, and, consequently, required the sanction of either a law or an ordinance (there is an ordinance now). And secondly, that the policy violated the right to property (Article 300A), as well as the fundamental rights to trade and life.

These arguments were raised by various petitioners challenging various aspects of the policy, who moved the court soon after 8 November. A number of abortive hearings took place over the course of the last week of November and the first half of December. Finally, the

---

92 Namita Wahi, 'Why Demonetisation Notification Is Illegal and Violates the Constitution', *The Economic Times*, 11 December 2016, https://economictimes.indiatimes.com/news/economy/policy/why-demonetisation-notification-is-illegal-and-violates-the-constitution/articleshow/55916594.cms

court referred the case to a five-judge bench and formulated a number of questions about the legality and constitutionality of demonetization.

It is now almost two months after the initial announcement. The Prime Minister's self-imposed time limit of 31 December has expired. Many deaths have been reported. Much of the cash that was supposed to have been taken out of circulation is—reportedly—back in banks. Whether or not that is true, surely, if not now, then soon enough, demonetization will begin to wind itself down. In the meantime, there is no sign of the Constitution bench.[93]

Judgment by Evasion

Rarely, if ever, are contesting parties before a court on equal terms. Before the Supreme Court, one party will always have the judgment of the lower court in its favour, and consequently (absent a stay) will benefit from the case getting held up in the court. In that sense, *Aadhaar* and *Demonetization* are simply incidents of a broader problem of delay and backlog, where failure to hear and decide cases expeditiously does not cause equal harm to both sides but benefits one at the cost of the other.

However, there is something more here. First of all, *Aadhaar* and *Demonetization* are not ordinary cases—they are classically about the exercise of immense coercive State power against citizens. Adjudicating the legal validity of such State action is at the heart of why we have an *independent* judiciary. It is the reason why there is a system of checks and balances: because when power on such a scale is unrestrained by

---

93 A Constitution bench was finally set up by Chief Justice U.U. Lalit in late 2022, which delivered its judgment upholding demonetization in January 2023, six years after the policy. See '"Every Noble Clause Claims Its Martyr": The Supreme Court's Demonetisation Judgment', Indian Constitutional Law and Philosophy, 3 January 2023, https://indconlawphil.wordpress.com/2023/01/03/every-noble-cause-claims-its-martyr-the-supreme-courts-demonetisation-judgment/

the rule of law and by constitutional norms, history has told us more than enough times what follows.

Secondly, as discussed above, this is not a case involving disputed property, where, ten years later, the court can decide the case and order the person in possession of the property to hand it over to the victorious litigant. *Aadhaar* and *Demonetization* are cases where, if the court does not decide the issue within a certain period of time, any future decision will be an exercise in futility. It makes no sense to decide *Demonetization* the next year, after the policy has run its course—whatever rights were violated (if, that is, rights *are* being violated) cannot then be redressed. Similarly, it makes no sense to decide the constitutionality of *Aadhaar* after the programme has begun to be used to avail virtually all (public and some private) social services and can no longer feasibly be disentangled from the daily lives of citizens.

Consequently, by refusing to decide, the Supreme Court effectively *does* decide—in favour of the government. In effect, it upholds the validity of Aadhaar without hearing arguments on the constitutional questions and without passing a reasoned judgment on Aadhaar and the right to privacy. In effect, it upholds the government's demonetization policy without deciding whether it is open to the State to place onerous restrictions on what citizens are allowed to do with their own money. In effect, it takes the side of State power, against the citizen.

It is open to the Supreme Court to do so. But if that is what it is doing, it ought to have the moral courage to defend its position in a reasoned judgment. It ought to explain—publicly—to citizens the scope of their fundamental right to privacy and the manner in which Aadhaar is consistent with it. Once the Supreme Court decides, its judgment can be engaged with, defended, criticized, its reasoning scrutinized closely and its positions critiqued. That is how it ought to be. But by simply refusing to hear and decide the case, where the consequences of non-decision are both terribly high and absolutely decisive, the court only ends up abdicating its role as the organ of the

State that is meant to stand between citizen and government power, and to keep the latter within its constitutionally defined spheres.

The fact that this is how two of the most important constitutional issues in recent times have fared in the Supreme Court suggests that scholars of the court can no longer make do simply with studying what the court has held, and the jurisprudence that it has created through its judgments. Scholars must now also study this evolving jurisprudence of constitutional evasion, which is defined by refusal and by silence.

2

The Land Acquisition Bench and Continuing Issues around the 'Master of the Roster'

(14 October 2019)

[**Editorial Note:** Justice is an indivisible concept. We cannot, therefore, discuss contemporary Supreme Court judgments without also acknowledging the court's failure—at an institutional level—to do justice in the case involving sexual-harassment allegations against the Chief Justice. This editorial caveat will remain in place for all future posts on this blog dealing with the Supreme Court, until there is a material change in circumstances.]

ON 12 OCTOBER, IT was reported that a five-judge bench of the Supreme Court would start hearing a set of cases about the interpretation of Section 24 of the Land Acquisition Act (2013). The bench would be led by Arun Mishra J, and would commence hearings on 15 October. The composition of the bench, however, immediately raised eyebrows. To understand why, it is important to set out a brief history of the dispute.

The legal controversy itself, which involves the fate of huge tracts of land across the country, has been ably summarized by Suhrith Parthasarathy[94] and Namita Wahi.[95] For our purposes, the point is this: In 2014, a three-judge bench of the Supreme Court interpreted Section 24 of the Land Acquisition Act in one way (*Pune Municipal Corporation*). The Supreme Court's interpretation (as is normal) was followed by high courts across the country, and by multiple two-judge benches of the Supreme Court itself, for the next four years. However, in December 2017, a two-judge bench of the Supreme Court took a contrary view and asked for a larger bench to consider the matter.[96] In accordance with convention, the Chief Justice constituted a three-judge bench to look into the issue. Very swiftly after that (in February 2018, within two months of the December 2017 judgment) that three-judge bench (*Indore Development Authority*) also took the opposite view on Section 24 from *Pune Municipal Corporation*.

Now, in the normal course of things, the judgment of a three-judge bench is binding on all coordinate benches; consequently, if a three-judge bench disagrees with another three-judge bench, the correct thing to do is to refer the issue to the Chief Justice, so that a higher bench can lay down the position of law authoritatively.[97] However, instead

---

94 Suhrith Parthasarathy, 'United by a Common Purpose', *The Hindu*, 1 March 2018, https://www.thehindu.com/opinion/lead/united-by-a-common-purpose/article22882621.ece
95 'Conflict of Benches', LiveLaw, 5 March 2018, https://www.livelaw.in/conflict-benches-scs-february-8-judgment-indore-development-authority-not-supported-text-intent-act-says-namita-wahi-expert-land-acquisition/
96 *Indore Development Authority vs Shailendra*, CA No. 20982/2017 (7 December 2017).
97 In this case, it is also interesting to note that until 2018, a very large number of Supreme Court judgments had followed *Pune Municipal Corporation without demurral about its correctness;* the controversy actually began with the Indore Development Authority judgment, where a bench suddenly realized—after four years—that multiple Supreme Court judgments had all got it wrong.

of doing this, a majority of the three-judge bench—over a dissent by Justice Shantanagoudar—held that *Pune Municipal Corporation* was per incuriam (a judgment delivered without the authority of law), and therefore not binding. In one stroke, therefore, the bench in *Indore Development Authority* exempted itself from being bound by *Pune Municipal Corporation*, overruled all the two-judge-bench decisions that had followed it and declared that its reading of Section 24 was now the law. Soon after that, pending land acquisition matters in the Supreme Court began to be disposed of in accordance with the new understanding.

As Suhrith Parthasarathy pointed out at the time, in a legal system that rests upon the principle of stare decisis (consistency and uniformity of interpretation), coordinate benches overruling each other—especially to upset a settled interpretation of law—is improper.[98] To this it may be added that calling another judgment per incuriam is not something that is done in the normal course of things. Per incuriam does not simply mean that the prior judgment is wrong, but that it is *so* wrong (it missed a binding statute or ignored a binding judgment) that it has no legal force at all. *Indore Development Authority*'s understanding of per incuriam, therefore, is itself open to doubt; but what is not open to doubt is the problematic manner in which the *Indore Development Authority* bench acted.

Unsurprisingly, this led to immediate chaos in the Supreme Court. The issue was brought to the notice of another three-judge bench of the Supreme Court, headed by Lokur J, who had been one of the parties to the original *Pune Municipal Corporation* decision (full disclosure: the author was, at the relevant time, working in the chambers of one of the senior counsel involved in the petitions). Lokur J passed an order noting that the question of whether a three-judge bench could hold the decision of another three-judge bench to be per incuriam needed to be considered. Until this question—and the question of whether

---

98 'United by a Common Purpose', supra.

there needed to be a reference to a larger bench to decide the issue—was decided, he also requested other Supreme Court benches not to continue disposing of pending land acquisition matters. The very next day, however, two two-judge benches of the Supreme Court—which were hearing the land acquisition cases—referred the matter directly to the Chief Justice. That was how the matter ended up with the Chief Justice (at the time Dipak Misra CJI) and how the present Constitution bench came to be set up.

I discuss this history because it reveals that there existed two clear—and *very* entrenched—views in the Supreme Court about the interpretation of Section 24 of the Land Acquisition Act. These views were entrenched enough for coordinate benches to declare judgments per incuriam, to overrule a long line of settled precedents on one side and to request benches within the same Supreme Court to temporarily suspend hearing land acquisition cases on the other (for the avoidance of doubt, this does not imply, of course, an equivalence).

That a five-judge bench is needed to resolve this controversy and lay down the law on the meaning of Section 24 may, ultimately, have been inevitable. However, here is the problem: The December 2017 two-judge bench order doubting the correctness of *Pune Municipal Corporation* was authored by Arun Mishra J. The February 2018 three-judge-bench decision in *Indore Development Authority*, holding *Pune Municipal Corporation* to be per incuriam, was authored by Arun Mishra J. The 22 February order referring the question to the Chief Justice—in the teeth of Lokur J's order—was *also* authored by Arun Mishra J. And the five-judge bench that has been set up now to resolve the 'conflict' is headed by Arun Mishra J. In other words, the same judge, sitting in a two-judge bench, doubted the correctness of a three-judge bench; then, sitting in a three-judge bench, overruled that decision (over a dissent) in favour of his interpretation of the law; when this was questioned by another three-judge bench, referred the case to the Chief Justice; and is now heading the five-judge bench to decide who was correct.

On any conceivable understanding of natural justice and the rule of law, this is simply unsustainable, especially in a Supreme Court that has thirty-four judges. And this brings us to the root of the problem, which is not really about personalities, but is *institutional*—the institution of the 'master of the roster'. Recall that the Chief Justice's position as the 'master of the roster' (as entrenched in a series of judgments early last year) vests in her *absolute discretion* to constitute benches and allocate matters in the Supreme Court. When the controversy was at its height last year, I had written that the principle of the 'master of the roster'— which originated out of administrative needs and the requirement of needing someone to administer the court—was very problematic in the context of the modern Supreme Court.[99] The court's strength (at that time, twenty-six judges), combined with the gradual weakening of the gravitational force of precedent effectively means that the office of the Chief Justice's administrative power of selecting benches can *at least potentially, in some cases*, translate into the power to *affect* outcomes (if not to determine them).

The composition of the Land Acquisition bench gives us a textbook example of this. Because of the absolute discretion of the master of the roster in constituting benches, there is no questioning *why* the bench is the way it is. However, the effect is self-evident—the bench, which has been set up to resolve an interpretive controversy within the Supreme Court, is led by a judge who has been a *protagonist* on one side of the controversy, expressing his views not once but on several occasions—and not in extra-judicial forums but through *judgments* of the court. What would a detached and objective observer conclude upon seeing this? They would conclude that in this five-judge bench, at least one vote—the vote of the senior-most judge—is *more or less*

---

99 'No Man Shall Be a Judge in His Own Cause* (*Conditions Apply)', Indian Constitutional Law and Philosophy, 13 November 2017, https://indconlawphil.wordpress.com/2017/11/13/no-man-shall-be-a-judge-in-his-own-cause-conditions-apply/

decided (and it is unsurprising that the All India Farmer Association has already written to the Chief Justice making exactly this point).

And the solution, it bears repeating, has to be institutional. As long as absolute power remains concentrated in a single individual—who happens to be occupying the office of the Chief Justice—issues of this kind will continue to arise, especially when the stakes are as high as they are in this case. The master of the roster has created a single point of failure, something that, as is well known by now, is the surest death knell for institutional integrity. And the damage is long-lasting. In this case, for example, even if the bench is now to be reconstituted, questions will linger over why it was constituted this way in the first place, and the continuing trustworthiness of a process that has been vitiated so badly in the first instance.

There are possible solutions—the establishing of Constitution benches by a random draw of lots, or having a permanent Constitution bench with the five senior-most judges (at any given time) occupying it, and so on. But what is clear is that the concept of the 'master of the roster' has become—and will continue to be—a huge albatross around the neck of the Supreme Court. And in a polyvocal court of thirty-four judges, the present controversy has shown just how unsustainable it is.

3

Addendum: The Concept of 'Bias' in a Polyvocal Court

(15 October 2019)

[**Editorial Note:** Justice is an indivisible concept. We cannot, therefore, discuss contemporary Supreme Court judgments without also acknowledging the court's failure—at an institutional level—to do justice in the case involving sexual-harassment allegations against the Chief Justice. This editorial caveat will remain in place for all future posts on this blog dealing with the Supreme Court, until there is a material change in circumstances.]

IT IS IMPORTANT TO begin this post with a clarification. Yesterday, I wrote a blog post pointing out that the composition of the Constitution bench scheduled to hear the case concerning the interpretation of Section 24 of the Land Acquisition Act raised some important issues, specifically concerning the powers of the Chief Justice as the 'master of the roster'. The post was one of many public interventions that raised similar questions about the bench. During the hearings of the case today, it is reported that Justice Mishra observed that 'there are attempts in the media and social media to "malign" the institution by raising questions about the bench and CJI's decision'. The solicitor-general agreed, and stated that 'there is a pattern here, where a few days before a major case is heard, things are written on social media or web magazines raising certain objections, that are intended to influence the proceedings'. Another judge on the bench, Justice Vineet Saran, also agreed.

As two justices of the Supreme Court, and the government's second-highest-ranking law officer have seen fit to hold forth from the bully pulpit against nameless 'critics', a few points need to be made in response. The first is that the composition of the bench was made public this Saturday (three days back). The hearing was scheduled for today. Unless the solicitor-general believes that critics of the court had divined the composition of the bench in advance and were only keeping their powder dry until it was formally announced, the only time these objections *could possibly* have been raised was between Saturday and Tuesday, i.e., 'a few days before the hearing'. Secondly, the Supreme Court is a public institution in a democratic republic that is committed to the principle of open justice. That the court's conduct will be subjected to rigorous public scrutiny is exactly how it should be. Critics of the court put their names to what they write, take responsibility for their writing and set out their arguments (along with the grounds on which they are based) openly and in the public domain, which is exactly how it is supposed to happen in a democracy. The critics are, in fact, considerably *more* transparent than the subject of discussion, which is the allocation of benches by the Chief Justice—a process that is entirely opaque and discretionary.

And thirdly, the only pattern that is visible here is Supreme Court judges' reaction to public scrutiny by shielding themselves in a cloak of defensiveness and self-righteousness, where we go straight from criticism to a 'maligning' of the institution (and, by extension, an equation of individual judges with 'the institution'). Readers will recall that this was exactly the reaction at the time of the sexual-harassment allegations against the Chief Justice—a reaction that, again, was supported by the highest law officers of the government.

With these preliminary points out of the way, I want to focus on one specific issue that was raised during oral arguments today—the issue of deciding bias. The issue arose out of the petitioners' request that Justice Arun Mishra recuse himself from hearing the case. Much of the questioning on this point was led by Justice S. Ravindra Bhat. In particular drawing on precedent from common law countries, Justice Bhat made a distinction between 'pecuniary bias', 'personal bias' and 'intellectual bias', and questioned whether 'intellectual bias' alone was sufficient ground for a recusal; he also observed that in *Indore Development Authority*, Justice Mishra had only expressed a 'view' and could, in theory, be persuaded to change his mind. Senior Counsel Shyam Divan's response to these questions can be read here[100], but in this post, I want to make a separate point: Questions of bias and recusal cannot be adjudicated without paying close attention to the unique nature of the Indian Supreme Court as an *apex court*—that is, its polyvocal character. To directly copy standards of bias that have been evolved in common law jurisdictions—as Justice Bhat's line of questioning suggests—without paying attention to the Indian Supreme Court's institutional character, is to essentially be making a category mistake.

Almost uniquely among the major English-speaking apex courts of the world, there exists in the Indian Supreme Court a massive numerical difference between the strength of the court (thirty-four judges) and the strength of benches hearing day-to-day cases (two or three judges). The US Supreme Court, for example, sits en banc (as a full court) of nine justices. The South African Constitutional Court sits en banc for the most part as well. The UK Supreme Court has twelve judges, who often sit in panels of five (but can also sit en banc or close to it for important cases, such as the recent prorogation judgment). Similar situations exist for the apex courts of Kenya, Canada, New Zealand and Australia. What this means is that these apex courts possess an

---

100 https://twitter.com/VakashaS/status/1183975065886457856

institutional coherence—judgments can be fairly said to express a 'view of the court' (as an institution). And if you want a judgment of the apex court to be set aside, you have to, effectively, convince the same body to go back on its earlier view.

In India, however, we have a situation where *within the highest judicial body*, the existence of a multiplicity of judicial panels undermines institutional coherence and creates a situation where the apex court is effectively *disagreeing with itself*. This is what has happened in the present case. Abstracting for a moment from the thicker context, what has happened is that two three-judge benches of the Supreme Court have taken diametrically opposite views on the same issue. Now the existence of thirty-four judges on the Supreme Court means that there is a ready solution at hand—send the issue to a bench that has a higher number of judges to 'resolve' the conflict.

Shorn of the legalese, what this *effectively* means is that within the highest judicial body, there is an *internal appellate mechanism* to deal with the problem of institutional incoherence, flowing from the court's unique structure. I use the word 'appellate' in its ordinary sense; it is, obviously, not an 'appeal' as that word is defined in Indian law, but is basically a sui generis response to a situation where even within the apex court, there are situations when conflicting views require a resolution in the interests of institutional coherence.

Once we understand this, however, it becomes clear that if the same judge is going to be present at *both* stages of the process, this form of resolution becomes pointless. This is why it is important to understand Shyam Divan's argument that what this *effectively* amounts to is a judge adjudicating upon the correctness of his own judgment in 'collateral' proceedings; it is not *formally* an appeal, but in every significant respect, these latter proceedings are *doing the work of an appeal*. The source of the confusion is that—for understandable reasons—we continue to think of the Supreme Court as a unified body that speaks in one institutional voice, while the reality has moved very far away from this. A more accurate analogy would be with the European Court of Human Rights (ECHR), where the same court is divided into a 'chamber' and a 'grand chamber'. Chamber judges and grand chamber judges are drawn from the same overall *pool* of ECHR judges: 'The Grand Chamber is made up of the Court's President and Vice-Presidents, the Section Presidents and the national judge, together with other judges selected by drawing of lots.'[101] But: *'When it hears a case on referral, it does not include any judges who previously sat in the Chamber which first examined the case.*[102] [Emphasis added]'

The issue, therefore, is not—as Justice Bhat's line of questioning suggests—about how we are to understand 'bias' from common law precedent. The issue is an institutional one. If what we now have is a situation where the Supreme Court has thirty-four judges, hears cases in panels of two or three that end up disagreeing with each other, and the resolution to that disagreement is by a panel of larger strength, it is clear that the only way this system can work is if the latter panel has fresh judges. The alternative—that the same judge (or judges) sit on the larger bench—borrows from two incompatible worlds. The problem is caused because of our polyvocal court with its thirty-four judges, but the solution comes from a world in which there is still one institution that automatically speaks with one voice.

And, of course, it is here that the role of the Chief Justice—as the 'master of the roster'—is a crucial one; it is here that the need for standards that guide that discretion in the establishment of benches becomes so crucial. The establishment of these standards, it bears repeating, is not because people are out to 'malign' the Chief Justice, but to ensure that the uncanalized discretion that *opens up* the Chief Justice to malignant accusations is subjected to public and democratic norms.

[**Disclaimer**: The author clerked with Justice Bhat (as he then was) at the Delhi High Court in 2014.]

---

101 European Court of Human Rights, 'The ECHR in 50 Questions', https://www.echr.coe.int/Documents/50Questions_ENG.pdf
102 Ibid.

4

A Question of Power[103]

(1 May 2019)

ON TUESDAY, 30 APRIL, the complainant in the sexual harassment case against the Chief Justice of India decided against participating further in the proceedings of the in-house inquiry being conducted by three sitting judges of the Supreme Court. In a press release, the complainant set out reasons for her decision: that she was not allowed to have her lawyer accompanying her, that there were no video or audio recordings of the committee proceedings, that she had not been given copies of her depositions, and that she had not been informed of the procedure that the committee was following.

At this point, it is unclear what will happen. Technically, having heard the complainant, the in-house committee *could* now proceed without her, examine any witnesses it deems fit and come to its conclusions ex parte. At the same time, the legitimacy of these proceedings—which have been of an informal and ad hoc character so far (more on that

---

[103] This blog post is one of many that covered sexual harassment allegations against the Chief Justice of India, which were finally dismissed ex parte by an 'ad-hoc' in-house committee of three Supreme Court justices. The report is still to be made public. Interested readers can consult the blog for a more detailed discussion.

anon)—cannot but be significantly damaged by the public exit of the complainant herself.

While we wait to see how events unfold, it is perhaps an apt moment to recall how it is that we got here. But before that, a few points need to be made.

Structures and Institutions

Sexual harassment is bound up with questions of power. Power operates along multiple axes in ways that it structures our lives and relationships, and in ways that it distorts them. It is of little surprise, then, that cases of sexual harassment (of varying degrees of severity) so often flow out of situations where differences in power are at their starkest and the possibilities of abuse are rife—between teachers and students, employers and employees, the rich and the poor, army men and occupied populations, and so on. And structuring all these relationships is the institution of patriarchy, which, in its own way, distorts relationships even in the absence of these more obvious markers of power. For example, the sense of impunity that society often attaches to male conduct ('boys will be boys'), accompanied by the corresponding sense of stigma attached to those at the receiving end of sexual harassment, skews power dynamics right from the outset.

Why is this important? It is important because the way in which power dynamics frame and characterize sexual harassment cannot but spill over into the structures of accountability that are set up to address them. If those structures of accountability do not take into account this fact, and do not seek to proactively mitigate its effects, accountability itself will remain a mirage. To put it in simple terms, when two deeply unequal parties are brought before a tribunal, where the powerful stands as the accused and the powerless as the accuser, 'neutral' rules that treat them as formally equal will invariably perpetuate the initial injustice.

Progressive anti-sexual-harassment laws recognize this. For example, the famous *Vishaka* judgment recommended that complaint committees involve third parties (either an NGO or someone else familiar with issues of sexual harassment) *precisely* to 'prevent the possibility of any undue pressure or influence from senior levels [of the organization]'. The POSH Act, 2013 requires that an internal complaints committee be headed by a senior woman *employee*. Among other things, it allows for a complainant to ask for a transfer to another workplace while the enquiry is pending. These are all provisions (and there are others) that specifically recognize the inequalities of power that seep into accountability processes, and the need to design structures that can adequately address them.

The Background

Keeping this framework at the back of our minds, let us now look at what has transpired in this case. The facts are well known and have been discussed threadbare in the public domain. On the (Saturday) morning that the allegations broke, the Chief Justice convened a bench of himself and two other judges (Arun Mishra and Sanjiv Khanna JJ). The government's top law officers (the attorney-general and the solicitor-general) were present in court. From the bench, the Chief Justice proclaimed his innocence, declared that the allegations were part of a conspiracy to destabilize the judiciary and pointed to the criminal antecedents of the complainant and her family; in this, he was supported by both the law officers.[104]

There has been extensive criticism—including by the Supreme Court Bar Association (SCBA) and the Supreme Court Advocates-on-Record Association (SCAORA)—on the procedural improprieties of this hearing. However, there is something even more important here. The deeply unequal power relations that structured the relationship between the accuser (a former employee) and the

---

104 Note, however, that the order of the court does not bear the Chief Justice's signature, even though he was physically present on the bench.

accused (the Chief Justice of India) were distorted even further when the latter decided to ascend the judicial pulpit to exonerate himself, *with the support* of two other judges of the Supreme Court, *as well as* the government's top two law officers. A blanket denial of allegations, an attack upon the character of the complainant and references to a larger conspiracy are all common responses in cases such as this; not everyone accused of sexual harassment, however, has the chance to proclaim his innocence in Courtroom No. 1 of the Supreme Court, with the attorney-general and the solicitor-general to call upon. In effect, the complainant was damned by five of the most powerful men in the country before being heard.

This situation was compounded by the hearing on 24 April. The bench now comprised Mishra, Nariman and Gupta JJ. This bench decided to look into an affidavit filed by Utsav Bains, claiming that he had been offered a bribe to frame the Chief Justice. Once again, I will not discuss the controversy that has erupted around Utsav Bains and his affidavit(s). There is a different point: In the morning hearing, the bench expressed its desire to combat the 'larger conspiracy' ostensibly at play and summoned the chiefs of the Delhi Police, the Intelligence Bureau and the Central Bureau of Investigation, for a closed-door meeting. When an apprehension was expressed about how this would affect the sexual-harassment allegations, Nariman J emphasized that the two issues were entirely separate.

Unfortunately, Nariman J's protestations ring hollow. When the special bench in question was following up the hearing that the Chief Justice had convened on Saturday, and when the claims about a larger conspiracy against the Chief Justice and the judiciary were themselves now linked to Utsav Bains's accusation that he had been bribed *to* fix the Chief Justice in a sexual-harassment case, nobody could possibly maintain with a straight face that the two issues are separate. But, most damningly of all, in that very morning hearing, Mishra J specifically observed that 'CJI Gogoi was trying to clean up the system'—hinting, thus, that it was for his independence that he was being targeted.

How could anyone *possibly* argue that the judicial discourse around the 'larger conspiracy' had nothing to do with the allegations of sexual harassment?

It is at this point that the question of power once again comes to the fore. Without having (yet) heard the complainant, the entire focus of the three-judge bench was on a possible conspiracy against the judiciary, a conspiracy that could have legs—and let's be blunt here—*only if the complainant was a liar*. And every act taken by the bench—from Mishra J's statements in the morning hearing to the decision to summon law-enforcement agencies for a closed-door meeting, to the decision to have the matter probed by (Retd) Justice A.K. Patnaik was, once again, a distortion of the power relationship against the complainant. Here was a bench of three Supreme Court judges saying that there were strong enough indications that the complainant *was* indeed a liar, very publicly summoning high-level law-enforcement agencies to their chambers (indeed, one of those agencies—the police—was precisely the entity that the complainant accused of having victimized her) and finally ordering a probe by a retired Supreme Court judge. And all this—and this cannot be stressed enough—without the complainant having been heard. Even once.

Meanwhile, Bobde J—the second senior-most judge of the Supreme Court—had set up an in-house committee, consisting of himself, Indira Banerjee J and N.V. Ramana J, to look into the sexual-harassment allegations. At this point, it took a public intervention by the complainant for Ramana J to (correctly) recuse himself from the panel—for the very simple and straightforward reason that on the day that the allegations broke, he had *already* dismissed them (effectively) as having been motivated.

It is one of the most basic principles of procedural justice, that if you have already commented upon the merits of the case in a way that shows a clear view one way or another, you should not be on the enquiry committee probing that case. So why did it need the complainant to point this out before appropriate action was taken?

Why wasn't this evident at the time the in-house committee was being constituted? What does it do to the power relations in this case, already distorted beyond recognition after the Saturday-morning hearing and the 24 April hearing, for the Supreme Court to constitute an in-house committee seemingly either oblivious or indifferent to the fact that one of its members had conflicted themselves out by very publicly taking the side of the Chief Justice?

The Committee

It is in this *institutional* context that the complainant's final act—to withdraw from the proceedings—now needs to be understood. When the in-house committee was constituted, the Women in Criminal Law Association published a letter asking that best practices in cases of enquiries into sexual harassment, as set out under the POSH Act, be followed. What the court elected to do instead was set up what was effectively an ad-hoc process, with the constitution of the in-house committee (where, after Justice Ramana's recusal, Indu Malhotra J came in). Among other things, one crucial departure from the Vishaka Guidelines was the absence of an external member on the committee, rendered even more critical by the fact that the complaint was against the (administrative) head of the institution himself.

That being the case—and given everything that had already happened before, as discussed above—the onus upon the committee was particularly strong to ensure that the unequal power relations that characterized this case were mitigated by a set of structures and procedures that were designed to level the playing field in substantive ways. In particular, the in-house committee had to deal with how best to restore the balance after two separate benches, one judge and two government law officers had already suggested that the allegations were fabricated; how to deal with a situation where some of the witnesses testifying would be effectively testifying against their employer; how to deal with the fact that it was three *sitting* judges who were hearing allegations against their *sitting* colleague, the CJI; and, above all else, how to correct the sheer imbalance of power that exists between an ex-employee and the Chief Justice of India.

The complainant's press release suggests that the committee comprehensively failed to address any of these issues. Each of the four points raised by the complainant speaks to issues of power:

- The refusal to allow the complainant a lawyer/support person while she was facing a committee of three judges handling a complaint against one of their own colleagues, and the (administrative) head of their own institution, in a context when multiple other judges had publicly come out against the complainant, distorts the power relationship;
- The refusal to record the proceedings and the refusal to provide the complainant with a copy of her deposition (a procedural right that is guaranteed under the POSH Act) deprives the complainant of any kind of effective oversight over the process, and distorts the power relationship;
- But perhaps most of all, the refusal to disclose the procedures—in a case where procedures matter *vitally*, because they are critical to addressing the power imbalance—distorts the power relationship into something that is beyond hideous.

And underlying all this is one simple fact: In any other situation, the complainant could have taken her dissatisfaction with the procedure to an appellate authority, and eventually, yes, to the court. But here, there is no appeal from what the in-house committee does. That makes sensitivity to every single aspect of the process doubly, triply important. But once again, the facts reveal that the court is either oblivious or indifferent to these issues.

Conclusion

It hardly needs to be said that this is not an essay about innocence or guilt, but rather, about the preconditions necessary to ensure that questions of innocence or guilt can be answered adequately. And for that, this is the point: At the time of writing, the sexual-harassment complaint against the Chief Justice has been handled by no fewer than nine judges of the Supreme Court. As the above analysis demonstrates, *each one of them* has acted in ways that perpetuate the existing power imbalance. In the Saturday hearing, three of them either made statements against the complainant or were complicit in the making of those statements by their silence. In the hearing of 24 April, two others did much the same. One judge agreed to sit in the in-house committee despite being conflicted out on the most basic application of standards of conflict. And three judges who did finally conduct the in-house enquiry did not follow processes that were sensitive to the power imbalances in this case—rather, it appears, quite the opposite.

In 1997, following the murder of Stephen Lawrence, the United Kingdom government commissioned what would come to be known as the MacPherson Report. Among other things, the MacPherson Report set out the definition of 'institutional racism':

> The collective failure of an organization to provide an appropriate and professional service to people because of their colour, culture, or ethnic origin. It can be seen or detected in processes, attitudes and behaviour which amount to discrimination through *unwitting prejudice, ignorance, thoughtlessness and racist stereotyping* which disadvantage minority ethnic people. *[Emphasis mine]*[105]

The crucial point about the MacPherson definition was that for an organization to be institutionally racist, it did not need to have people who *intended* to be racist, and to act upon those intentions. Rather, institutional racism stems from 'unwitting prejudice', 'ignorance' or

---

[105] Sir William MacPherson, 'The Stephen Lawrence Enquiry' (February 1999), paragraph 6.34, https://assets.publishing.service.gov.uk/government/uploads/system/uploads/attachment_data/file/277111/4262.pdf

'thoughtlessness'—almost internalized conditions, acted upon without any conscious desire or motivation to oppress or disadvantage anyone.

It is in a similar way that the above events demonstrate that there exists an *institutional* problem at the Supreme Court when it comes to dealing with allegations of sexual harassment, a problem that has been laid bare over the past two weeks. No doubt unwittingly, judges of the Supreme Court who have been tasked with handling the case have shown themselves unequipped to address, or even acknowledge, the bleeding heart of the problem—that this is a question of power, and without addressing that, you address nothing.

5

The Lawyers Collective Order and the Rise of Fourth-Phase PIL

(8 May 2019)

Earlier today, a two-judge bench of the Supreme Court—consisting of the Chief Justice and Deepak Gupta J—issued notice in a PIL filed by an organization that styled itself 'Lawyers Voice'. The petition asked the court to constitute a special investigating team that would investigate (under court supervision) 'the apparent illegality and non-action of the government in registering IPC, PC Act, PMLA, Income Tax Act and other offences [sic]' against Indira Jaising, Anand Grover and the Lawyers Collective. While providing no specific details, the petition alleged that 'various malpractices' had been committed by the respondents (the Ford Foundation and its CIA connections also features in the petition). In a press release released shortly afterwards, Indira Jaising pointed out various irregularities in the manner in which the PIL was listed and heard before the court today, and stated that these proceedings were initiated to harass her because of her support for the complainant in the case involving allegations of sexual harassment against the CJI.

That apart, the decision of today's bench to issue notice in the case raises a few crucial questions:

A. Maintainability: After three-and-a-half decades of PIL, one basic legal point remains clear: Because it is filed under Article 32 of the Constitution, a PIL is maintainable *only* if there is a violation of one or more of the fundamental rights guaranteed under Part III of the Constitution. No matter how much the requirements of *locus* are loosened and how expansively Article 142 is interpreted, this threshold bar continues to exist and cannot be wished away by the court. With that in mind, what fundamental right of the petitioner NGO—or of anyone else, for that matter—has been violated by the government's alleged inaction in prosecuting Indira Jaising, Anand Grover or the Lawyers Collective? The petition is silent on this point, and for good reason—there is none. But if the PIL is non-maintainable, why has the Supreme Court issued notice on it?

B. Threshold for an SIT Investigation: In the *Judge Loya* case, the threshold for ordering a court-monitored investigation was made very clear, and a high bar was set—a point that I made recently, in the context of the Supreme Court not following that very precedent in the *Utsav Bains* case. Recall that in *Loya*, notice was not issued and the petition was dismissed on the basis of pleadings and oral arguments. Clearly, therefore, precedent dictates that the notice threshold in cases such as these is a high one as well (a position that makes eminent sense under classic separation of powers theory, where the job of carrying on investigations is not that of the court). Why, then, has the court refused to follow *Loya* twice in two weeks?

C. The Statutory Scheme: Leading on from the previous point, there is a specific procedure to be followed in case a crime has been committed, and it appears that the police is not registering an FIR—and that is to approach the magistrate under Section 156(3) of the Code of

Criminal Procedure. Admittedly, in 'special cases', the Supreme Court has ordered investigations in PILs before, without this requirement being fulfilled (see Abhinav Sekhri's critique here[106]). In this case, however, given points A and B above, there surely ought to have been something showing that the PIL petitioner had tried the 156(3) route and failed—*and if not, reasons why this was a special case, where the normal procedure needed to be bypassed.* However, the petition does not contain even a whisper about any of this.

D. Why Not the High Court? As the PIL itself points out, there are ongoing proceedings before the High Court of Bombay pertaining to the cancellation of Lawyers Collective's FCRA licence by the government. That being the case, why was this petition not filed before the Bombay High Court? More particularly, a few weeks ago, when the Aadhaar Ordinance was challenged before the Supreme Court, the Chief Justice dismissed it and asked the petitioners to approach a high court (this was a constitutional challenge, no less). Here, on the other hand, notice is issued in a PIL where at least a part of the bundle of facts upon which it (purports to be) based is *already* in litigation before the Bombay High Court. Is there no obligation of basic intellectual consistency?

At a deeper level, today's PIL—and the court's decision to issue notice—marks the high point of what I propose to call 'fourth-phase PIL'. I use the term 'fourth-phase PIL' in response to classic PIL theory, which divides the evolution of the jurisdiction into three phases. The first phase (1980s), where PIL was a tool to vindicate the rights of the vulnerable and the marginalized; the second phase (1990s), when it was primarily used by the court to tackle environmental (and other related issues); and the third phase (2000s), when the court used PILs to intervene in issues of corruption and secure good governance.

---

106 Abhinav Sekhri, 'The Sahara-Birla Diaries Controversy', The Proof of Guilt, 15 January 2017, https://theproofofguilt.blogspot.com/2017/01/the-sahara-birla-diaries-controversy.html

I define fourth-phase PIL as follows: The use of the court as a vehicle, through public interest litigation and the procedural and substantive flexibilities that it allows, to restrict or curtail individual rights guaranteed under Part III of the Constitution, and/or to achieve political goals that are blocked by normal political routes, and/or to stymie existing legal proceedings or bypass statutory process.

While fourth-phase PILs are *often* filed by political parties or their proxies (a prominent contemporary PIL filer, for example, is also the spokesperson of a national party), this need not always be the case. Recent examples of fourth-phase PILs include the national anthem proceedings, the NRC proceedings and the attempts to have Aadhaar linked to SIM cards and to voter ID cards through judicial fiat; readers who have followed the Supreme Court over the past couple of years will doubtless be able to add many more.

Fourth-phase PIL takes to the extreme the various procedural and substantive innovations that were evolved—in very different contexts—in the first three phases. From the first phase, it takes the loosening of locus standi (which was done so that people who were not able to access the court could be represented) and turns it into an absence of locus standi. Now, it seems, anyone can file a PIL about anything, without having to demonstrate that there exists an affected party unable to approach the court. From the second phase, it takes the elongation of Part III provisions and transforms them into irrelevance. Now, a PIL petitioner need not even mention in their petition how a Part III right has been violated. And from the third phase, it takes the expansion of Article 142 and transforms it into a power vaster than empires. There is now no question about separation of powers, institutional capacity or judicial encroachment. In fact, if fourth-phase PIL were to be given a moniker, it should be titled 'Article 142 litigation'. It is as if the only article in the Constitution is Article 142. There is no Article 32, no Part III (not even Article 21) and no basic structure separation of powers once fourth-phase PIL is engaged.

Today's proceedings exemplify the place that fourth-phase PIL has taken us to. An NGO approaches the Supreme Court, asking it to order the government to take criminal action against another NGO (and two lawyers). It does not show locus, it does not show how the petition is maintainable, it does not explain why the Supreme Court should take it up while the Bombay High Court considers an overlapping petition, it provides no justification for shredding the existing statutory scheme and it provides no documentary evidence. In any other court in the world, this petition would have been dismissed with punitive costs. The Chief Justice of India, on the other hand, issues notice.

But perhaps that's why fourth-phase PIL/Article 142 litigation is a unique phenomenon in global constitutionalism.

6

What Is a 'Review'?[107]

(14 November 2019)

[**Editorial Note:** Justice is an indivisible concept. We cannot, therefore, discuss contemporary Supreme Court judgments without also acknowledging the court's failure—at an institutional level—to do justice in the case involving sexual-harassment allegations against the Chief Justice. This editorial caveat will remain in place for all future posts on this blog dealing with the Supreme Court, until there is a material change in circumstances.]

ARTICLE 137 OF THE Constitution of India allows the Supreme Court to 'review' any judgment passed by it. According to the jurisprudence of the court, a review is to be granted in exceedingly rare circumstances. In *Union of India vs Sandur Manganese and Iron Ores Ltd*, for example, the Supreme Court restated the position of law

---

107 This post considers the developments after the judgment in the *Sabarimala* case, where, in review proceedings, a slightly different bench (Chief Justice Dipak Misra had been retired and replaced by Chief Justice Ranjan Gogoi) referred the case to a larger bench. The circumstances in which this happened are highly dubious and cast serious doubt about the sanctity of precedent in the Supreme Court.

as follows: A review can only be allowed in cases of *'discovery of new and important ... evidence'*, an *'error on the face of the record'* or another *'sufficient reason'* that had to be analogous to the first two.

In this context, today's order in *Kantaru Rajeevaru vs Indian Young Lawyers' Association* concerning the Supreme Court's 2018 judgment in the *Sabarimala* case is a curious one.[108] The Chief Justice begins his order by observing:

> Ordinarily, review petitions ought to proceed on the principle predicated in Order XLVII in Part IV of the Supreme Court Rules, 2013. *However, along with review petitions several fresh writ petitions have been filed as a fall out of the judgment under review.* All these petitions were heard together in the open Court [paragraph 1]. *[Emphasis mine]*

This is bewildering. Let us say that there are two sets of petitions before the court. One set of petition seeks 'review' of the impugned judgment on the grounds set out at the beginning of this post. The other set comprises fresh writ petitions that assail the correctness of the same judgment. 'Hearing them together in open court' makes no sense, because not only is the scope of arguments entirely different, *the forum within which these cases have to be heard is different too!* A review is heard by the same judges who delivered the original judgment (apart from those who may have retired). In this case, as the *Sabarimala* judgment was heard by a bench of five judges, the review would also be heard by five judges (in this case, four of them—apart from the Chief Justice—were parties to the original judgment). A fresh writ petition, on the other hand, would have to go through an entirely different process. It would first come up before a division bench (two or three judges) of the Supreme Court, where the petitioner would have to make out an initial case for even having the petition admitted,

---

108 *Kantaru Rajeevaru vs Indian Young Lawyers' Association,* Review Petition No. 3358/2018 (14 November 2019).

given the existence of binding precedent to the contrary, on the same issue. If that was successful, the petitioner would then have to convince the division bench that there was a prima facie mistake in the earlier judgment, which was required to be reconsidered by a larger bench (another substantial hurdle). The division bench would, if convinced, refer the matter to a five-judge bench, where the same process would be repeated, and *then*, if the petitioner was successful in each of these stages, would the matter go before a seven-judge bench to reconsider.

These processes are of fundamental importance. They are important because they preserve one of the crucial pillars of the justice system—the sanctity and finality of judgments (especially those of the Supreme Court). One may agree or disagree with a judgment, but in the interests of legal certainty and stability, the judgment (for better or for worse) is law, and remains law, unless there are powerful reasons to depart from it. Of course, no judgment is set in stone. That is why review jurisdiction exists and that is why referrals exist. And both processes, as we have just seen, cast an onerous burden upon those who would have the court revisit judgments that have attained finality.

The first problem with today's order, then, is that it mixes up two things that are fundamentally different in character. Indeed, in no sense is this a 'review' at all. The court does not even attempt to point out 'an error on the face of the record' in the original *Sabarimala* judgment that was ostensibly under review. But if this is actually a judgment about *referral*, how did the writ petitioners short-circuit the entire process that exists for these cases and land up directly before a five-judge bench in proceedings that *everyone* understood at the time to be proceedings in review?

That said, let us consider the substance of the order itself. In paragraph 3, the court notes that issues surrounding the entry of women into religious spaces arise in respect of some pending cases before the court, involving mosques and Parsi fire temples—and that there is also a pending case on the legality of female genital mutilation (FGM). In paragraph 4, the court then observes:

> [I]t is time that this Court should evolve a judicial policy befitting to its plenary powers to do substantial and complete justice and for an authoritative enunciation of the constitutional principles by a larger bench of not less than seven judges ... It is essential to adhere to judicial discipline and propriety when more than one petition is pending on the same, similar or overlapping issues in the same court for which all cases must proceed together.

With respect, this is bizarre. What this appears to be is something wholly new, which we can perhaps define as an 'anticipatory referral'. The Supreme Court is due to hear some cases that have overlapping issues. So *before* it hears those cases, a larger bench should decide those issues! But unless these different cases are all heard *simultaneously*, by different five-judge panels of the court—which then throw up contradictory rulings—this has absolutely nothing to do with 'judicial discipline and propriety' (in fact, some of the cases the court mentions have not even been referred to larger benches!). Let us take a tangible example. *Sabarimala* was decided last year. Let's say the next case to be heard is the Parsi fire temple case. To the extent that legal questions arise in the latter that have already been resolved in the former, the bench hearing the fire temple case *will be bound to follow them, unless it decides to refer the matter* to a larger bench for resolution. That is how it has always worked. And there has never been a reason to depart from that practice—certainly not by ostensibly citing 'judicial discipline and propriety'!

This is made clear by the fact that the court goes on to note that the issues arising in these pending cases '*may be overlapping and covered by the judgment under review*'. Yes, exactly—and unless the 'judgment under review' is *set aside in review* for having an error apparent on the face of the record, these pending cases will be bound by it! Which brings us back to what the court was actually asked to rule on in this case, and which it simply did not do—decide the review.

The judgment then frames some issues that it says 'could arise' in these pending cases, pertaining to the interplay between various constitutional articles. It also points to an apparent conflict between *Shirur Mutt* and *Dawoodi Bohra*, on the issue of 'essential religious practices' (the conflict is more apparent than real, but that is a debate for another day), which needs to be resolved by a larger bench.

Notice, however, so far, that what has been referred to a larger bench are certain suggested constitutional questions that may have an *impact* on the *Sabarimala* judgment, but are not *about* that case. But it is now that we come to yet another bizarre part of this judgment. In the penultimate paragraph, the court notes that *'while deciding the questions delineated above, the larger bench may also consider it appropriate to decide all issues, including the question as to whether the Kerala Hindu Places of Public Worship (Authorization of Entry) Rules, 1965 govern the temple in question at all. Whether the aforesaid consideration will require grant of a fresh opportunity to all interested parties may also have to be considered.'*

But where on earth has this sprung from? It would be appropriate for this 'larger bench' to consider *this* question, which was settled in *Sabarimala*, only if it was sufficiently proven to another bench, either in review or in referral proceedings, that a mistake had been made that warranted reconsideration. But, as already indicated above, the court does not even attempt to show that a mistake has been made, or *may* have been made. It simply *decrees* that the larger bench 'may' consider it appropriate to decide 'all' issues. How and why? It does not say. This is not how a court is supposed to reason.

The court then ends by noting that the review petition and writ petitions shall be kept pending until these 'questions' are answered. So, once again, we are back to the same point—it is not the judgment in *Sabarimala* that has been referred for reconsideration, but certain 'questions' that are common to *Sabarimala* and other pending cases, without any judicial finding that *Sabarimala* got them wrong! What on earth is happening here?[109]

---

109 Incidentally, a corollary of this is that, for obvious reasons, the majority has not stayed the *Sabarimala judgment itself.* Until the seven-judge bench is constituted, therefore, the judgment remains good law, and binding and enforceable on all parties, including the State.

The incoherence of this judgment is highlighted in the dissenting opinion authored by Nariman J, on behalf of himself and Chandrachud J. In paragraph 2, Nariman J sets out the exact point that this blog post has been making:

> What a future constitution bench or larger bench, if constituted by the learned Chief Justice of India, may or may not do when considering the other issues pending before this Court is, strictly speaking, not before this Court at all. The only thing that is before this Court is the review petitions and the writ petitions that have now been filed in relation to the judgment in *Indian Young Lawyers Association and Ors. vs State of Kerala*, dated 28 September 2018. As and when the other matters are heard, the bench hearing those matters may well refer to our judgment in *Indian Young Lawyers Association and Ors. vs State of Kerala*, dated 28 September 2018, and may either apply such judgment, distinguish such judgment, or refer an issue/issues which arise from the said judgment for determination by a larger bench. All this is for future Constitution benches or larger benches to do. Consequently, if and when the issues that have been set out in the learned Chief Justice's judgment arise in future, they can appropriately be dealt with by the bench/benches which hear the petitions concerning Muslims, Parsis and Dawoodi Bohras. What is before us is only the narrow question as to whether grounds for review and grounds for filing of the writ petitions have been made out qua the judgment in *Indian Young Lawyers Association and Ors. vs State of Kerala*.

And indeed, it is difficult to understand how it could be any other way. Nariman J then actually goes on to write a judgment *applying* the standards required in a review, and finds that no grounds for review are made out (and that, at the same time, writ petitions directly attacking the judgment are not maintainable). A debate on this could have been had if the majority judgment had actually engaged with any of the points that Nariman J makes. But, of course, as we have seen, they do not. And finally, Nariman J goes on to point out that arguments around the protests that followed the original *Sabarimala* judgment cannot possibly constitute a ground for the court to retrace its steps in a country governed by the rule of law.

It should, therefore, be clear that what the majority judgment does in this case is indefensible under any standard. One may agree or disagree with the original judgment in the *Sabarimala* case. But what a three-judge majority has done here—exhibit a cavalier disregard for a reasoned judgment of a Constitution bench and invent a whole new method for people to *collaterally* challenge judgments they don't like—cannot but have profound and dangerous consequences for the rule of law. In a court of thirty-four judges—as I have pointed out before—these issues become particularly important. The more the gravitational force of precedent is weakened—either by declaring coordinate benches per incuriam or by judicial pyrotechnics, as in this case—the more we head towards a factionalized and divided court, where judicial interpretation becomes less about principle and more about power play. *Sabarimala* will be a small casualty in that conflagration.

7

Coronavirus and the Constitution—XXXVIII: One Year On[110]

(24 March 2021)

THE FIRST INDIAN NATIONAL lockdown in the wake of Covid-19 was announced on 24 March 2020. The management of the pandemic by the Central and state governments is a matter for the history books. Over the course of the past year, however, these governments' far-reaching actions—aimed at containing the pandemic, but with numerous spill-over effects—raised numerous constitutional issues. These involved, for example, civil rights, access to

---

110 The Covid-19 pandemic saw a range of legal measures and judicial interventions, from the invocation of the DMA, the use of apps such as Aarogya Setu, issues around federalism (including finances), the availability of medical equipment and of vaccines to the plight of migrant labour, labour laws and so on. This post was written on the first anniversary of the 2020 nationwide lockdown and summarizes the judicial response to Covid-19. Interested readers may consult the blog for the thirty-eight individual posts dealing with specific cases that arose out of the pandemic, which can be collectively found here: 'Coronavirus and the Constitution: Round-Up', Indian Constitutional Law and Philosophy, 25 March 2021, https://indconlawphil.wordpress.com/2021/03/25/coronavirus-and-the-constitution-round-up/

healthcare, the rights of migrants and so on. On this blog, there have been thirty-seven posts examining the interface between Covid-19, State action, the Constitution and the courts. On the first anniversary of the lockdown, it is a good time to take stock.

Pandemic Management by Decree

The greatest concern remains how Covid-19 turned into a cover for executive aggrandisement, both at the Central and the state level. At the Centre, this involved the invocation of the Disaster Management Act (DMA) of 2005, and a somewhat extended interpretation of its provisions, to arm the Central government with wide-ranging powers over everyday life. At the state level, several state governments invoked the colonial Epidemic Diseases Act, 1897 to exercise similar powers over their territories (including the arguably ultra vires 'sealing off' of certain districts from time to time). This, in turn, was supplemented by the liberal use of Section 144 of the Code of Criminal Procedure to restrict movement in specific areas.

At all levels, therefore, Covid-19 was managed by an interlocking set of executive decrees, passed under broadly worded laws, leaving no scope for the representative bodies—parliament of the state legislatures—to debate or question these moves. It is, of course, trite to say that the legislature in India has become effectively moribund, and even a functioning Parliament and state assemblies would have scarcely made a difference to the handling of Covid-19. That is true enough, but the formal exclusion of deliberative representative bodies from the management of a crisis by invoking broadly worded laws remains a matter of concern, whatever the state of those bodies. As Abhinav Sekhri put it, it took us into a space of 'permanent crisis governance'.[111]

---

111 Abhinav Sekhri, 'Coronavirus and the Constitution – XXVII: On (Permanent) Crisis Governance', Indian Constitutional Law and Philosophy, 17 May 2020, https://indconlawphil.wordpress.

Civil Rights and Proportionality

That Covid-19 was, and remains, a public health crisis that would require governments to take far-reaching measures—many of which would have a severe impact on everyday life and on civil rights—is unquestionable. But what is equally unquestionable is that Covid-19 does not accord governments a carte blanche to suspend Part III of the Constitution altogether. State action violating rights would still need to conform to the principles of proportionality, albeit with the rider that the importance of the State goal (preventing the spread of a global pandemic) would necessarily allow the government a wide degree of leeway in fashioning measures to deal with the problem.

That said, throughout the pandemic, especially in its early stages, there was a range of dubious State action that arguably fell foul of the proportionality standard. These included, for example, curfews, public disclosure of the private details of quarantined individuals, restrictions on individual movement, compelling quarantined people to upload 'selfies' to a government portal, the notorious Aarogya Setu app (with its Aadhaar-esque mandatory-voluntary nature) and bans on vehicular movement. Unfortunately, most of these measures escaped judicial scrutiny. The exception was Odisha's vehicle ban, which was modified by the Odisha High Court in a measured and well-reasoned judgment. It is a good example of the application of the proportionality standard in a public health emergency.

Equality and Non-Discrimination

Pandemics do not discriminate between the rich and the poor, but the State certainly does. A lockdown, for example, has a severely disproportionate impact, depending on the socio-economic status of a

---

com/2020/05/17/coronavirus-and-the-constitution-xvii-on-permanent-crisis-governance-guest-post/

person. 'Work from home' jobs statistically track along socio-economic lines (the higher paid your job, the more likely it's a job that can be done from home) and the forced closure of all establishments has a direct impact on the right to life and livelihood of migrant workers, living on daily payments, in particular. The decision to impose a hard national lockdown, therefore, raised important constitutional concerns around equality and non-discrimination. Note that this does not mean that the lockdown should not have been imposed (scientific evidence shows that lockdowns are essential to breaking the chain of transmission of the virus). What it does mean, however, is that once the lockdown *was* imposed, the State had an affirmative obligation to deal with its discriminatory impact—and that its failure to do so merited constitutional scrutiny.

Unfortunately, however, the unequal and discriminatory impacts of the lockdown were given short shrift. For example, the Supreme Court passed a cursory judgment failing to properly engage with the multiple equality concerns with the University Grants Commission's circular on the conduct of examinations. Secondly, a PIL requiring the State to guarantee the payment of minimum wages to workers affected by the lockdown was not taken seriously by the Supreme Court, with the court, unfortunately, indicating that it viewed the issue as a matter of 'policy' (the rights to equality and to livelihood are not matters of policy).

Eventually, it was the government that took action, with a regulation under the DMA requiring payment of wages to workers for a certain period of the lockdown. In one of the most unfortunate orders to have been passed during the pandemic, the Supreme Court effectively stayed this provision (ironically, the *only* provision the court stayed under the DMA was the one provision that sought to protect workers' rights), and then buried the case by adjourning it while asking the employers and employees to 'negotiate' (as the old saying goes, a mediation between the sword and the neck). Thus, the regulation requiring the payment of wages to those who had suffered from job loss because of the lockdown was *judicially* nullified.

By contrast, the Supreme Court's decision in the *Gujarat Mazdoor Sabha* case—where the state of Gujarat's attempts to cut back on labour protections by citing Covid-19 as an excuse were turned back by a thoughtful and closely reasoned judgment—stands out precisely because, for once, the court refused to accept Covid-19 as a carte blanche for the curtailment of rights, especially on the basis of vague invocations of 'public emergency'. One wishes that this judgment had been the exception, and not the norm, as we shall see below.

The Supreme Court's Deference

The Supreme Court's excessive and undue deference to the executive was starkly visible in multiple separate instances. First, despite legitimate constitutional and legal concerns, PILs challenging the PM CARES fund were dismissed as frivolous and ill-founded. It is telling that to this day, we do not know the breakdown of spending under the PM CARES fund, something that should be anathema to any jurisdiction styling itself a constitutional democracy.

Secondly—and in what will undoubtedly go down as a moment of great infamy—when the Supreme Court was petitioned about the severe difficulties faced by migrants due to the sudden and unplanned lockdown, first accepted the solicitor-general's statement that there were no migrants on the road and then passed an extraordinary order blaming migration on 'fake news' and praising the government for its efforts in tackling Covid-19.

Thirdly, acting on a petition before it, a bench of the Supreme Court in April 2020 ordered that Covid testing be made free of cost. While the order had gaps, in my view—as I argued at the time—given the nature of the Covid-19 pandemic, it was legitimate (but sparked an extensive debate upon the blog). However, upon various private bodies moving the court, and at the instance of the State, it did a complete, and wholly unreasoned, volte-face, changed its own order and, while appearing to introduce a means-testing requirement, effectively killed it. Now, there is a debate to be had over whether the court's initial order was right or wrong. What is troubling, however, is that in a matter as important as this, involving the right to equality and the right to health during a global pandemic, the court provided no reason for its flip-flops. Indeed, it accorded no judicial scrutiny to the most basic of factual claims—for example, that Rs 4,500 as the price for a test had been determined after consulting experts (reports showed that no experts had been consulted), or of a causal link between making testing free (or cheaper) and the availability of tests.

Thus, both in the migrants' case and in the free-testing case, the issue was not that the court interfered—or declined to interfere—with questions of policy. It was that the court failed to hold the government to account in following *its own policies*. This does not require judicial activism, but classic, old-school judicial scrutiny—scrutiny that was made all the more necessary because of the bypassing of Parliament, leaving the courts as the only checking bodies left. The court's failure to do so effectively created a situation of Caesarism—rule by acclamation, not under democratic checks and balances. But the larger issue it revealed is perhaps even more important: At present, under our Constitution, there is no consistent standard for the recognition and enforcement of socio-economic rights. While this has always been known, it was the (often failed) attempts to actually enforce these rights during Covid-19 that brought the point home.

The High Courts' Vigilance

There was, however, a marked difference in how the several high courts approached their responsibilities during the pandemic—demonstrating, perhaps, that in public health emergencies that are managed at a more localized level, high courts might be in a better position to adjudicate a range of issues involved. For example, the Delhi High Court passed an important order regarding the implementation of the right to food and keeping open PDS shops during the pandemic. The

Madras High Court passed a good order on the right to movement of migrant workers.

Most importantly, in a series of excellent orders, the Karnataka and the Gujarat high courts held the state governments to account on issues involving the rights of migrants, medical care, food, shelter and other grave lapses in pandemic management. The actions of the Karnataka and Gujarat high courts stand out as models of judicial engagement with State action during the pandemic—both courts engaged in dialogic judicial review, i.e., not substituting judicial wisdom for State policy, but by *holding the governments to account for their failure to protect constitutional rights* during the pandemic (unfortunately, in the Gujarat High Court, one of the judges hearing the case was swiftly replaced and the hearings died a quiet death). Both courts, for example, asked the state governments to file affidavits, and it was quickly found, on a reading of those affidavits, that the governments were failing on their own terms. The courts' orders were then premised on a rectification of those failures and, indeed, directing the government to act to mitigate those failures. It is in this way that the high courts engaged in dialogic judicial review and ensured executive accountability under the Constitution on a continuing basis.

The Bombay High Court also engaged in dialogic judicial review when considering the issue of price-capping N-95 masks, closely engaging with information provided by the government, on its own terms. There were also thorough and detailed orders passed on access to food, migrant rights and the right to a decent burial.

Conclusion

Whenever we face an emergency of any kind, it becomes particularly easy to argue that rights are a luxury that cannot be afforded in times of existential threat and that the State must be given complete leeway to tackle the emergency as long as it lasts. It is also tempting to turn the truism that the courts should not get into the day-to-day management of the pandemic, into an excuse for judicial abdication. Tempting as it is to make these arguments, history has also *repeatedly* shown us that it is wrong-headed. Not only is it more than possible to handle emergencies while being protective of basic rights, but it is also the case that executive aggrandisement of power during an emergency inevitably becomes permanent, with emergency and normalcy eventually bleeding into each other.

There is little purpose in knowing history if we do not intend to learn from it. In this context, the invocation of the DMA and the Epidemic Diseases Act to manage the pandemic *via* executive decree is the repetition of an old story, which recurs every time there is an emergency. One can only hope that when the pandemic is over, we will be vigilant about the expansion of such executive rule into daily life.

Secondly, the pandemic has revealed the hollowness, in a sense, of India's Article 21 jurisprudence. Ultimately, when it came to the crunch, the grand rights to livelihood, food and health meant very little in practice, especially at the Supreme Court. The migrant and free-testing cases are testament to how, in the enforcement, these rights are paper tigers.

Thirdly, however, there are reasons for optimism as well. The Supreme Court's judgment in *Gujarat Mazdoor Sabha* was a classic example of the role a vigilant judiciary *can* play in stopping a government that tries to use the pandemic as a cover to cut back on workers' rights. And the orders of the Karnataka and Gujarat high courts provide models of dialogic judicial review and the walking of the delicate tightrope between judicial abdication on the one hand and the judiciary (wrongly) trying to 'manage the pandemic' on the other. As we eventually emerge from the pandemic, there is a lot to reflect on—and learn—from the legacy of this past year, and about the role of courts and of rights in a crisis.

Judges

Introduction

THE FOLLOWING TWO ESSAYS address two judicial tenures—of Justice R.F. Nariman and Justice A.M. Khanwilkar, for different reasons. The assessment of Justice R.F. Nariman asks questions about judicial legacy in the context of far-reaching and consequential judgments, such as that of the NRC. The assessment of Justice A.M. Khanwilkar uses his judicial tenure to cast light on a wider institutional issue around the judiciary's will—and ability—to stand as a bulwark between the individual and the State.

1

A Memory for Forgetfulness: Some Thoughts on a Judicial Retirement

(13 August 2021)

THE RETIREMENT OF A Supreme Court judge is marked by a few time-worn traditions—a farewell ceremony on the Supreme Court lawns, brief addresses by high constitutional functionaries, a rendition of the judge's qualities (some evident through the course of their judgeship, others not so much), and *curtain*. It is over in an afternoon—harmless enough, as these things go.

The 12 August retirement of R.F. Nariman J has been characterized by something a little more. On Twitter, a senior counsel tells us that his was 'an exemplary career in the law—as a jurist, a counsel and a judge'.[112] On Moneylife, another senior counsel calls him 'the perfect judge', a 'model professional with a high EQ', and says that his legacy is 'unmatched'.[113] On BQ Prime, a third senior counsel quotes

---

112 https://twitter.com/MenakaGuruswamy/status/1425742041917497349
113 Anand Grover, 'Looking Back at the Legacy of Justice Rohinton Fali Nariman', Moneylife, 13 August 2021, https://www.moneylife.in/article/looking-back-at-the-legacy-of-justice-rohinton-fali-nariman/64852.

Marc Antony and asks, 'Whence comes such another?'[114] Other encomiums of this kind can be found on the internet.

As a preliminary point, I want to say that, even accounting for the demands of the profession, such breathless hyperbole does our legal culture no favours. It is worth remembering, yet again, that judges of the Supreme Court (one of the three wings of the State) wield tremendous power, and the exercise of said power requires respectful, but critical, scrutiny and not reams of purple prose. That apart, however, I believe that these encomiums are particularly inapposite in the case of *this* particular judicial retirement, as they seek to obscure a set of events—in which the judge in question was an active participant—that reflect the Supreme Court, as an institution, in particularly poor light. As we shall see, these pieces—and others[115]—either ignore, or acknowledge but attempt to minimize, Nariman J's role in those events.

Any honest reckoning of Nariman J's legacy must, I believe, place at least two of these events at its centre. Why is this important? It is important because what we choose to tolerate, justify or explain away now is very revealing of what we will continue to tolerate, justify and explain away in the future. I thus offer up this critique not as a personal attack, but in the spirit of Hagai El-Ad's anti-hagiographic assessment of the legacy of Aharon Barak[116]—that in the struggle of memory against forgetting, there are some things that are vital to remember.

---

html?__cf_chl_jschl_tk__=pmd_4a6447d4865c01f7724afa83fa07fb2bb66c3178-1628841352-0-gqNtZGzNAjijcnBszQiO

114 Sanjay Hegde, 'Justice Rohinton Nariman's Legacy: "Whence Comes Such Another"', BQ Prime, 11 August 2021, https://www.bqprime.com/opinion/justice-rohinton-narimans-legacy-whence-comes-such-another

115 Indira Jaising, 'How Justice Rohinton F. Nariman Will Be Remembered', The Leaflet, 12 August 2021, https://theleaflet.in/how-justice-rohinton-f-nariman-will-be-remembered/

116 Hagai El-Ad, 'The Man Who Helped Build Israel's Legal Infrastructure of Oppression', +972 Magazine, 4 July 2019, https://www.972mag.com/aharon-barak-israeli-democracy-occupation/

The NRC

It is by now tedious, yet important, to reiterate the Supreme Court's role in ramming through the Assam National Register of Citizens. The process started with the 2014 judgment in *Assam Sanmilita Mahasangha vs Union of India*. This judgment—authored by R.F. Nariman J— 'referred' a number of constitutional questions regarding amendments to the Citizenship Act, 1955 to a Constitution bench (one of them being whether immigration constitutes 'external aggression' against the country), and, in the same breath, directed the immediate preparation of the NRC (even as the question of its constitutionality had been referred to a larger bench in the *same* judgment). What followed is a matter of historical record: The Supreme Court repeatedly drove the State to complete the citizenship list as soon as possible, set hard deadlines, threw due process to the winds, took information in sealed covers, elevated the State coordinator to some kind of privileged high priest mediating between God (the court) and the citizens in secret conclaves, and essentially violated every basic principle underpinning the judicial function.

In history, there are innumerable instances of governments setting in place spirals of exclusion, violence, detention camps and death through the making of 'citizenship lists'. To my knowledge, the series of orders passed between 2014 and 2019 is the only case where a *constitutional court* did so, and to an obsessive degree. And the results were indeed violent—more than fifty people took their own lives in fear of the consequences of being off the NRC list; Genocide Watch issued two warnings; and we continue to pay the cost in human suffering.

What do senior counsel have to say about this? One says, astonishingly, that the 'bench passed crucial orders which led to the publication of the final NRC in July 2018'—a bit like saying that Winston Churchill took 'crucial decisions' regarding food distribution in West Bengal in 1942. In the Marc Antony piece, we are told that, admittedly, *Assam Sanmilita Mahasangha* was the 'one blot' in an otherwise magnificent judicial career, but that R.F. Nariman J was likely 'influenced' by his companion on the bench, CJI Gogoi. At this stage, Nariman J seems to have turned into 'Schrodinger's judge'—both fiercely independent-minded and subject to 'influence' by his companion judges, both unyielding and malleable, all at the same time. This will not do. The Marc Antony piece then goes on to note that '*as these issues are still at large before the Constitution Bench of the Supreme Court and are still being debated politically, it may be best to say no more on the subject*'. But this is an utter cop-out. Every order passed by the Supreme Court between 2014 and 2019 was a continuation of the 2014 judgment, and every order had a real-world impact. When assessing a judge's legacy, you cannot cherry-pick the things that make him look good and lightly pass over the rest, as if it were the shadow of a dream. These things happened.

But it seems that, reading the encomiums, they happened elsewhere, at another time, to someone else. *The past is a foreign country*. And it is this distance, this detachment, which we seem to achieve so easily, that I find of concern. Just as there was very little critique of the court when these orders were passed, there appears to be an equal unwillingness to acknowledge them as part of the judge's record and legacy. That indicates that if it happens again, we will only too easily look away again.

Re: *Matter of Great Public Importance Concerning the Independence of the Judiciary*

Once again, reams have been written about the events that took place in May 2019, when allegations of sexual harassment were levelled against the Chief Justice. It is now almost universally accepted that the treatment of the complainant was unjustified at every level and that a grave injustice was done. But injustice does not happen by an invisible hand—injustice is *done*, people do it. And in this case, at various points over the course of that week or so, no fewer than eight Supreme Court justices were involved in that injustice.

Nariman J's role was in the second hearing, on the Monday following the Saturday. This was the hearing at which a lawyer showed up out of nowhere and claimed he had evidence that the Supreme Court Registry was being manipulated, ostensibly to 'fix' the Chief Justice. The insinuation was that the accusations against the Chief Justice were politically motivated, a weapon of blackmail. It is a story that has repeated itself across time and place.

The Supreme Court hearing in which Nariman J was an active participant gave credence to exactly this story. It completely derailed the actual accusations, turned the case from a sexual-harassment one to an 'independence of the judiciary case', and by asking for an affidavit in a 'sealed cover' and directing an investigation under a former Supreme Court judge, reinforced and entrenched exactly the kind of victim-blaming narrative that—it is well documented by now—makes justice and accountability for sexual harassment an impossibility. And this is what is genuinely astonishing—that two days after an accusation of sexual harassment, someone shows up muttering darkly about conspiracies and threats to the nation, is so wild a plotline that fiction editors would reject it out of hand as too contrived. But instead of throwing it out and keeping the focus on the allegations themselves, the Supreme Court bench bought—or chose to buy—into it hook, line and sinker. The Moneylife and the Marc Antony pieces, unfortunately, equally chose to ignore it.

Two and a Half: Santosh Gupta

I found it a little surprising that none of the assessments of Nariman J's legacy dealt with the judgment in *Santosh Gupta*, where Nariman J held that to the extent of repugnancy, the provisions of the Securitization and Reconstruction of Financial Assets and Enforcement of Security Interest (SARFAESI) Act, 2002 overrode Section 140 of the Jammu and Kashmir Transfer of Property Act, 1920 (as it then was), which had specific protections regarding certain kinds of property transfers. Opinion may vary about the correctness of *Santosh Gupta*, but there is little doubt that it had a huge impact with respect to issues of federalism and freedoms; its omission from legacy assessments is, I think, a little telling about how, even after 2019, Kashmir continues to occupy a collective black hole in our constitutional imaginations (something I have been frequently guilty of as well).

Conclusion

It is impossible not to be deeply moved on reading Marc Antony's funeral speech for Julius Caesar. In his speech, Antony was inventing a legacy on the spot, transmuting Caesar's dictatorial tendencies into humility and abnegation, and explaining away inconvenient facts. Antony knew what he was doing: After successfully exhorting the Plebs to violence and riot, he ends the scene by quietly saying to himself, '*Now let it work. Mischief, thou art afoot.*'

Let us, therefore, take the encomiums to R.F. Nariman J, framed through the lens of Marc Antony's funeral speech, on their own terms. Soon after that funeral speech, the Roman Republic fell and Caesar's dictatorial tendencies were solidified into an empire. Perhaps the lesson there is that we should all take funeral—and farewell—speeches with an appropriate amount of salt.

2

The Executive('s) Court: Notes on the Legacy of Justice A.M. Khanwilkar

(29 July 2022)

THIS BLOG HAS A long-standing tradition of assessing the judicial legacies of Chief Justices of India upon their retirement. This tradition has hitherto been limited to Chief Justices, because of the sway they exercise upon the Supreme Court as 'master(s) of the roster' and because, during their tenures, they tend to hear significant constitutional cases themselves.

Last year, an exception was made upon the retirement of Justice R.F. Nariman, for reasons that were explained. Today, the retirement of Justice A.M. Khanwilkar requires, I believe, a second exception. One reason for this is that during the course of his career (as we shall see in this post), Justice Khanwilkar has written some of the most consequential judgments concerning State power and the rights of the individual. But secondly, and more importantly, when you study these judgments together, you glimpse a certain *judicial philosophy*—such as it is—at work. This judicial philosophy—subject to a few important exceptions—is, I believe, largely representative of the Supreme Court today (which also perhaps explains why, across Chief Justices, such cases have been regularly assigned to Justice Khanwilkar, one of its most forceful proponents).

What is this philosophy? In my earlier analysis of Justice Khanwilkar's judgment in the *Foreign Contribution (Regulation) Act (FCRA)* case (also discussed below) I had compared it to the Peruvian President Óscar R. Benavides's famous line, '*For my friends, anything; for my enemies, the law.*' In a similar vein, the common thread running through Justice Khanwilkar's constitutional law judgments is: '*For the State, anything; for the individual, the law.*' It is the philosophy not just of the executive court, but of the executive('s) court.

Before we begin, a final point, by way of caveat. It is almost trite to say that I do not agree with the outcomes of the cases that I discuss below. I have criticized some of these judgments when they were delivered, and in the *Central Vista* case (that I flag, but do not discuss), I was one of (many) arguing counsel on the losing side. My analysis below, however, is not founded simply upon the fact of disagreement with the outcome, or of dislike of these judgments. Regardless of my predilections, I believe that these judgments reveal something important, both about Justice Khanwilkar's judicial career and about the contemporary Supreme Court, which is important to articulate and discuss. This post should be read in that spirit.

Watali: Taking a Sledgehammer to Personal Liberty

Any discussion of Justice Khanwilkar's legacy must begin with the 2019 judgment in *National Investigation Agency vs Zahoor Ahmad Shah Watali*.[117] The case involved the interpretation of Section 43(D)(5) of the Unlawful Activities (Prevention) Act (UAPA), 1967, India's umbrella anti-terrorism statute. Section 43(D)(5) prohibits a court from granting bail to an accused if, '*on a perusal of the case diary or*

---

117 *National Investigation Agency vs Zahoor Ahmad Shah Watali*, (2019) 5 SCC 1.

the report made under Section 173 of the [Criminal Procedure] Code, [the court] is of the opinion that there are reasonable grounds for believing that the accusation against such person is prima facie true'*. In layperson's language, Section 43(D)(5) bars the grant of bail if it appears that the police version (through the case diary or the charge sheet) against the accused is, on the face of it, true.

Watali was an appeal by the National Investigation Agency (NIA) against an order of the Delhi High Court. In that order, the Delhi HC had granted bail to Watali (the accused), under Section 43(D)(5) of the UAPA. The high court took into account the (uncontroversial) legal proposition that 'as far as the statutes concerning serious offences inviting grave consequences are invoked, the trial Court will scrutinize the material with extra care'. The court's job was not to proceed simply on the basis of the statements made by the investigative agency, nor to act as a 'post-office' for the State. On this basis, the high court subjected the police version—according to which Watali was involved in terror funding—to rigorous scrutiny. It found that many of the witness statements were inadmissible under the law of evidence, that the documents purporting to originate from the accused were neither signed by him and nor on his letterhead, and that other documents were entirely innocuous and consistent with his position as a prominent Kashmiri businessman. On this basis, the court found that at that point, the police version was speculative and there was no ground for denying bail to the accused.

When the case came up in appeal, the Supreme Court, in a judgment authored by Justice Khanwilkar, overturned the high court's order and put Watali back in jail (he stayed in jail, awaiting trial, for three more years, until, in February 2022, he was moved to house arrest because of a terminal disease). Crucially, Khanwilkar J's problem with the high court was not that it had incorrectly appreciated the facts of the case. Rather, it was that the high court had applied the wrong legal standard altogether and that the true role of the court under Section 43(D)(5) of the UAPA *was*, effectively, to act like a post office. He noted that while examining the question of bail, 'elaborate examination or dissection of the evidence is not required to be done' and that, furthermore, to reject inadmissible statements at the stage of bail was akin to entering into the 'merits and demerits of the case'. Instead, the court was to form a view based on the 'broad probabilities' flowing from all the materials supplied by the police.

The judgment in *Watali* was criticized at the time as being incorrect (see, for example, Abhinav Sekhri's blog post[118]), and I do not intend to traverse covered ground once again. It is worthwhile, however, to recall once again just what it *did*. As is well known, at the time of bail, the defence cannot present its own arguments, put forward its own witnesses or cross-examine the prosecution's witnesses. It has no real way to effectively contest the State's case. All that is for the stage of trial. At the time of bail, all the court can look at—and all that the defence can point to—is the State's version of events. Thus, when Section 43(D)(5) prohibits the court from granting bail if 'there are reasonable grounds for believing ... that the accusation is prima facie true', *everything* turns upon how closely and deeply the court is authorized to examine the State's version on its own terms—for internal consistency, for plausibility, for whether the State is relying on materials that would even be admissible at trial (such as hearsay statements)—to come to its prima facie conclusion. And when, in *Watali*, Khanwilkar J barred all courts from 'examining' or 'dissecting' the evidence, he effectively made the grant of bail in UAPA cases borderline impossible. As Sekhri wrote at the time, he 'actively chose a legal position that makes lengthy undertrial detention more likely'.[119]

The asymmetry in power is glaring. UAPA trials in India take years—decades—to complete. If the grant of bail is made borderline impossible, all the police are required to do is slap the UAPA on to a charge sheet and an individual will be condemned to years—or decades—in jail without trial. The charge sheet and the materials need

---

118 Abhinav Sekhri, 'Bail in Terror Cases: Zahoor Watali, and the Fault Lines in the UAPA', Proof of Guilt, 11 April 2019, https://theproofofguilt.blogspot.com/2019/04/bail-in-terror-cases-zahoor-watali-and.html
119 Ibid.

not be persuasive, need not be internally coherent and, in addition to all this, may even rely on plainly inadmissible material (as in Umar Khalid's case[120]). All that ceased to matter once, in *Watali*, Khanwilkar J turned all courts into stenographers for the prosecution, while attaching dumb-bells to the feet of the defence and throwing it into the river to swim or sink. In this sense, Sekhri's 2019 warning has turned out to be prescient: 'It is hard to conceive of outcomes which are anything but fearsome. The decision could make the UAPA an even more attractive tool to law enforcement agencies now that getting bail is harder...' We now know that this is exactly what has happened: The UAPA is the foremost tool of political repression in India, and *Watali* has become the chant that almost all courts (barring a few) invoke to justify keeping people in jail for years without trial.

PMLA: Taking Another Sledgehammer to Personal Liberty

If the UAPA is the executive's weapon of choice to keep inconvenient individuals in jail for years without trial, the Prevention of Money Laundering Act (PMLA), 2002, is its political weapon. By now, every Indian knows about the Enforcement Directorate, or the ED. The eyeball impression that the ED is used to overwhelmingly jail political opponents without trial has been confirmed in this detailed analysis[121]; that the purpose *is* jail without trial is borne out by the fact that while the number of PMLA cases filed by the ED has risen by eight times over the past eight years, the conviction rate under the law

---

120 'Stenographer for the prosecution: The Bail Order in Umar Khalid's Case', Indian Constitutional Law and Philosophy, 24 March 2022, https://indconlawphil.wordpress.com/2022/03/24/stenographer-for-the-prosecution-the-bail-order-in-umar-khalids-case/
121 Supriya Sharma and Arunabh Saikia, 'How the Modi Government Has Weaponised the ED to Go after India's Opposition', Scroll, 5 July 2022, https://scroll.in/article/1027571/how-the-modi-government-has-weaponised-the-ed-to-go-after-indias-opposition

is under 1 per cent[122]—a statistic that should send alarm bells ringing for everyone (other than, it seems, the Supreme Court).

Amendments to the PMLA, passed in 2019, which made the legal regime more draconian, were challenged before the Supreme Court. On 27 July—two days before his retirement—a three-judge bench led by Khanwilkar J delivered judgment, upholding all the provisions under challenge[123] (see here,[124] here,[125] and here[126]).

A similarly exhaustive analysis of the judgment is not the subject of this post. However, its underlying philosophy is simple enough. While in every sense the officials of the ED act like the police—as coercive appendages of the State, and in the power that they hold over citizens—the court liberated them from following the minimal procedural constraints under the Code of Criminal Procedure that *do* apply to the police. For instance, the court exempted the ED from sharing the equivalent of the police's First Information Report—the Enforcement Case Information Report (ECIR)—with the accused, noting that communicating the 'grounds' was enough; the court held that as an ED summons was not an 'arrest' (even though

---

122 'Only 23 Convicted in 5,422 Cases under PMLA Till Date: Govt to Lok Sabha', *Hindustan Times*, 26 July 2022, https://www.hindustantimes.com/india-news/only-23-convicted-in-5-422-cases-under-pmla-till-date-govt-to-lok-sabha-101658774947795.html

123 *Vijay Madanlal Choudhary vs Union of India*, SLP (Crl) No. 4364/2014 (27 July 2022).

124 Umang Poddar, 'How the Supreme Court Has Handed a Free Pass to the Enforcement Directorate', Scroll, 28 July 2022, https://scroll.in/article/1029187/explainer-how-the-supreme-court-gave-a-free-pass-to-the-enforcement-directorate

125 Abhinav Sekhri, 'Of Old Wine in New Bottles – The Judgment in Vijay Madanlal Choudhary (Part One)', The Proof of Guilt, 28 July 2022, https://theproofofguilt.blogspot.com/2022/07/of-old-wine-in-new-bottles-judgment-in.html

126 Abhinav Sekhri, 'Of Old Wine in New Bottles – The Judgment in Vijay Madanlal Choudhary (Part Two)', The Proof of Guilt, 29 July 2022, https://theproofofguilt.blogspot.com/2022/07/old-wine-in-new-bottles-judgment-in.html

functionally indistinguishable from it), the constitutional right against self-incrimination doesn't apply to statements made under ED questioning; that because ED officials weren't 'police officers' (even though functionally indistinguishable from them), confessions made to them were admissible in evidence (even though the whole purpose of making confessions to the police inadmissible was the fear of coercion); and that because the ED wasn't a police force (even though functionally indistinguishable from one), the procedures that it followed (the ED manual) wasn't required to be made public but could remain an 'internal document'. If all of this sounds somewhat reminiscent of the Stasi, it is because it is *rather* reminiscent of the Stasi (or, in Pratap Bhanu Mehta's words, 'Kafka's Law'[127]).

The effect of the judgment is clear—it is the sanctioning of a State-controlled, coercive militia, exempt from the basic principles of due process and the rule of law. To this heady cocktail, the court added further dangerous mixes. It upheld a bail requirement even harsher than Section 43(D)(5) of the UAPA and which the Supreme Court had *itself struck down* four years earlier (Khanwilkar J overruled precedent, which ensured that bail would become almost impossible under the PMLA) and upheld the 'reverse burden' clause—that, under the PMLA, the burden was on the individual to prove their innocence and not on the State to prove guilt.

And, finally, to expand the scope of the PMLA, Khanwilkar J went further. Section 3 of the Act stipulates that '*whosoever directly or indirectly attempts to indulge or knowingly assists or knowingly is a party or is actually involved in any process or activity connected with the proceeds of crime including its concealment, possession, acquisition or use and projecting or claiming it as untainted property shall be guilty of offence of money-laundering*'. In other words, for the PMLA to be attracted, two conditions had to be satisfied: involvement (whether intentional or

---

127 Pratap Bhanu Mehta, 'By Upholding PMLA, SC Puts Its Stamp on Kafka's Law', *The Indian Express*, 29 July 2022, https://indianexpress.com/article/opinion/columns/pratap-bhanu-mehta-by-upholding-pmla-sc-puts-its-stamp-on-kafkas-law-8057249/

unintentional) in connection with the proceeds of crime, *and* the (definitely) intentional 'projecting' or 'claiming' of it as untainted property. Khanwilkar J held, however, that *actually*, the word 'and' meant 'or' (just like 'day' means 'night'), and that, therefore, simply being in possession of 'tainted' property was enough for guilt under the PMLA.

When you now combine this with the reverse burden clause (that under the PMLA, the individual is guilty until proven innocent) and Khanwilkar J's finding that *any* criminal offence could be brought under the PMLA (thus effectively making the CrPC wholly redundant), the effects of this judicial rewriting exercise are terrifying. They also exacerbate and worsen the already wide definition of tainted property under the PMLA, which effectively covers just about everything (and makes just about everything subject to attachment orders [see here[128]], financially crippling someone under PMLA scrutiny; note that Khanwilkar J *also* held that property can be attached right from the beginning of PMLA proceedings).

But there are three things of importance here. The first is that the reworded section makes no grammatical sense (try reading it aloud and see for yourself). The second is that this interpretation turns basic criminal law principles on its head: because criminal legal statutes are coercive and impose jail time on people, there is a time-honoured, well-worn principle in criminal law that they are to be read *strictly* and *narrowly*. In Khanwilkar J's judicial philosophy of 'for the State, everything; for individuals, the law', however, every canon of interpretation is upside down and nobody is safe from arbitrary State action. And finally, of course, to accomplish this task, he had to rewrite the section, taking the word that existed and replacing it with its opposite. This is what I like to call the 'Humpty Dumpty jurisprudence', where the court—like Humpty Dumpty in *Alice through the Looking*

---

[128] Abhinav Sekhri, 'Attachment of Property, Freezing Orders, and PMLA Investigations: The Need for Reasonable Exclusions', Proof of Guilt, 27 May 2020, https://theproofofguilt.blogspot.com/2020/05/attachment-of-property-freezing-orders.html

Glass—decides that words mean what it decides them to mean, just because it can:

> 'When I use a word,' Humpty Dumpty said, in rather a scornful tone, 'it means just what I choose it to mean—neither more nor less.'
>
> 'The question is,' said Alice, 'whether you can make words mean so many different things.'
>
> 'The question is,' said Humpty Dumpty, 'which is to be master—that's all.'

In his analysis of the judgment, Abhinav Sekhri points out that there was material on record to show that while drafting Section 3, the legislature had made a genuine error and used the word 'and' while it meant to use the word 'or'.[129] However, when it comes to criminal law, it is most certainly not the court's job to save the legislature from the consequences of its own incompetence (especially when the same leniency is hardly accorded to the individual!). The whole point of the doctrine of reading criminal statutes, literally, narrowly and strictly, is that, given the differences in power between the State and the individual, the reach of criminal law is not to be expanded any further than what the words can bear. It is that principle that Khanwilkar J entirely forsook in rewriting Section 3.

Let us take a step back and sum up. When we look at the judgment in a broader context, it is important to keep in mind Sekhri's observation[130] that not all of this is entirely new. In many respects, the PMLA judgment is a continuation of the Indian Supreme Court's long-standing tradition of expanding the State's coercive powers and erasing the procedural safeguards that the law extends to individuals. In the PMLA context, however, the statute's provisions magnify that substantially: The statute 'weaves together all

---

129 'Of Old Wine (Part One)', supra.
130 Ibid.

the restrictive, rights-effacing clauses from this illustrious past in one fine blanket, and it then goes further.'[131]

And the PMLA judgment, in turn, is perhaps unique in that it brings all of those rights-effacing judicial predilections together in one case—what Sekhri calls a 'greatest hits' video, and to which we can add: The band is the Supreme Court and the 'hits' are direct hits to our constitutional rights. In sum, Khanwilkar J rewrote a criminal statute to substantially widen its ambit; authorized the State to bring any offence within that ambit; upheld the reverse burden of proof within that widened ambit; deprived individuals of their procedural and constitutional rights within that widened ambit; made the grant of bail almost impossible within that widened ambit; and exempted the State authorities from any effective constraints once they began to operate within that widened ambit. When you put all of these together, what emerges is the classic definition of a lawless law, blessed by the executive's court.

Noel Harper: Taking a Hatchet to the Freedom of Association

In April 2022, Khanwilkar J wrote a judgment upholding various amendments to the FCRA, 2022.[132] Elsewhere, I have analysed this judgment at some length and pointed out how the court accorded its imprimatur to a set of provisions that had turned India's NGO regulation law into a Russian-style legislation that effectively made the work of most NGOs either impossible, or prohibitively difficult.[133] A few salient points stand out from this judgment.

---

131 Ibid.
132 *Noel Harper vs Union of India*, WP No. 566/2021 (8 April 2022).
133 'Comforting the Comfortable and Afflicting the Afflicted: The Supreme Court's FCRA Judgment', Indian Constitutional Law and Philosophy, 12 April 2022, https://indconlawphil.wordpress.com/2022/04/12/comforting-the-comfortable-and-afflicting-the-afflicted-the-supreme-courts-fcra-judgment/

First, at the time of hearing *Noel Harper*, there were challenges to the FCRA pending in high courts. *Noel Harper* itself was a limited challenge to one set of restrictions. Now, ordinarily, the Supreme Court is quick to talk about how the high courts should not be bypassed; however, it seems that all that rhetoric ceases to matter when legislation that the political executive really cares about is at stake. Here, the Khanwilkar J-led bench could not wait to bypass those same high courts, and hear and decide all questions about the constitutional validity of the FCRA, thus effectively depriving the high courts of hearing the cases before them.

Secondly, the judgment in *Noel Harper* applied different standards to the State and to the petitioners, where the State's factual claims (contrary to the prevailing legal standard of proportionality) were taken as true without any scrutiny, whereas the petitioners' claims—and bona fides—were taken with the highest level of mistrust. In my post analysing the judgment, I wrote:

> The Court begins by framing the issue in a way that is most favourable for the State, and least favourable for the citizen. Having framed the question thus, it then goes on to accept the State's factual claims at face value, but does not extend the same courtesy to the citizen. Having done that, it then applies those parts of existing legal doctrine that favour the State, and ignores—or misrepresents—those parts that protect the rights of citizens. Having framed the question in favour of the State, accepted the State's version of reality, and applied the doctrine in favour of the State—*voila!*—the conclusion is that the challenged State action emerges validated from the tender caresses of judicial review.

Indeed, this is a thread that runs throughout Khanwilkar J's judgments, and for a more elaborate articulation in *this* case, interested readers may consult the relevant blog post as a whole.

However, the most glaring aspect of Khanwilkar J's judgment (other than its impact on the freedom of association) is that he explicitly and unashamedly framed its arguments in *ideological* terms, and this ideology was evidently the ideology of the political executive. Lines from the judgment include: *'The question to be asked is: "In normal times", why developing or developed countries would need foreign contribution to cater to their own needs and aspirations?'*; *'Indisputably, the aspirations of any country cannot be fulfilled on the hope (basis) of foreign donation, but by firm and resolute approach of its own citizens'*; and *'There is no dearth of donors within our country.'*

These are familiar lines. These are lines that we hear from the mouths of authoritarian leaders across the world when they justify clamping down on civil society and, in particular, on NGOs. None of these words have anything to do with the law, legal reasoning, the Constitution or the practice of constitutional adjudication. Yet here they are, serving as the articulated major premise of a constitutional court judgment that is *supposedly* about whether restrictions upon the freedom of association—achieved by choking off funds to NGOs—are reasonable or not. But as we have seen, that is not *really* what this judgment is about. What this judgment is really about is giving formal judicial imprimatur to some of the more extreme and prejudicial rhetoric of the political executive, giving a dressing down to citizens who have the temerity to want to raise funds for NGO work and telling them to be 'resolute and firm' if they want to have rights. This is the language not just of the executive court, but of the executive('s) court.

Teesta Setalvad and Himanshu Kumar: Taking a Dagger to Article 32

The language of the executive's court is present most starkly in Justice Khanwilkar's notorious opinion in the *Zakia Jafri* case.[134] Once again, it is not my task here to examine the correctness of the judgment in

---

134 *Zakia Jafri vs State of Gujarat*, Diary No. 34207/2018 (24 June 2022).

refusing to set aside the SIT report that had found that there was no controversy at high governmental levels during the horrendous 2002 Gujarat riots (interested readers may refer to Nizam Pasha's analysis of the judgment here[135]; see also the discussion in Episode 2 of the ConCast with Abhinav Sekhri on the criminal legal standards applied—or not applied—by the court[136]). For the purpose of argument, let us say that the court found, as was its prerogative to find, that the petitioners had failed to provide adequate evidence to dislodge the SIT's findings of no political conspiracy, and that, therefore, the writ petition had to be dismissed.

But that is not the only thing that Justice Khanwilkar did. First, he spent some time in the judgment lavishing fulsome praise on the executive authorities ('indefatigable work')—something particularly embarrassing, coming from a constitutional court, in a case involving large-scale riots. Most seriously, however, he then went on to note that this case was the result of a 'coalesced effort by disgruntled officials', that those who had brought the present proceedings 'had the audacity to question the integrity of every functionary … to keep the pot boiling', and 'all those involved in such abuse of process, need to be in the dock and proceeded with in accordance with law'.

There are a few things we need to note about these lines. The first is that in a functioning legal system, lines such as these would invite immediate action for defamation, with heavy damages to follow. None of that, however, applies here. Following the example set by Khanwilkar J, it seems that the Supreme Court justices, *in the course of their official duties*, are free to engage in character assassination, insinuations and

---

135 Nizam Pasha, 'Supreme Court Judgment in Zakia Jafri Missed Both the Woods and the Trees', The Wire, 13 July 2022, https://thewire.in/law/supreme-court-judgment-in-zakia-jafri-case-missed-both-the-woods-and-the-trees

136 Abhinav Sekhri and Gautam Bhatia, 'The ConCast: Episode 2', Indian Constitutional Law and Philosophy, 27 June 2022, https://indconlawphil.wordpress.com/2022/06/27/the-concast-episode-2-27-june-2022/

personal attacks without being called upon to provide a shred of evidence for the same. Forget evidence, the Supreme Court did not even accord the petitioners the courtesy of a hearing on this point before damning them through its judgment. Needless to say, at the next available opportunity—judicial or extra-judicial—the same Supreme Court is likely to issue moral lectures on the principles of natural justice.

But what followed is even more alarming. The day after these 'observations', Teesta Setalvad—petitioner no. 2 in this case—was arrested by the Gujarat police. The paragraph of the Supreme Court judgment that I have extracted above was the *literal basis* of this arrest. It was cited in the FIR. In other words, the Supreme Court—through Khanwilkar J—by making statements such as 'all those involved in such abuse of process need to be in the dock' laid the groundwork for an arrest that State authorities followed up on within hours. And this arrest—it is important to note—was on the basis of a judgment in a case filed under Article 32 of the Constitution, which guarantees the right to move the Supreme Court for the enforcement of rights; in other words, the petitioner, in a case filed *against* alleged State impunity, *before* the Supreme Court, was arrested *by* the State, based on the judgment *of* the Supreme Court.

At the time of writing, Teesta Setalvad remains in jail.[137]

Perhaps you may say this is a one-off, an aberration. Except that, a few days later, the same thing happened all over again, and once again it was Justice Khanwilkar who was the senior judge on the bench (although the actual judgment was written by a future Chief Justice of India, Justice J.B. Pardiwala). *Himanshu Kumar vs State of Chhattisgarh* involved a 2009 petition regarding extra-judicial encounter killings in the state of Chhattisgarh.[138] As in the *Zakia Jafri* case, this was an Article 32 petition against State impunity,

---

137 She was eventually released in September 2022, after a Supreme Court bench headed by the new Chief Justice, U.U. Lalit, intervened.
138 *Himanshu Kumar vs State of Chhattisgarh*, WP (Crl) No. 103/2009 (14 July 2022).

seeking police accountability for a massacre of adivasis. As in the *Zakia Jafri* case, the Supreme Court dismissed the petition, and then took it upon itself to do more. First, it imposed a fine of Rs 5 lakh on the petitioner, Himanshu Kumar. And then, as in the *Zakia Jafri* case, it laid the groundwork for legal action against the petitioner. It noted:

> We leave it to the State of Chhattisgarh/CBI [Central Bureau of Investigation] to take appropriate steps in accordance with law as discussed above in reference to the assertions made in the interim application. We clarify that it shall not be limited only to the offence under Section 211 of the IPC. A case of criminal conspiracy or any other offence under the IPC may also surface.

Notice, once again, the loose language used by a constitutional court in a case that involved the undisputed massacre of adivasis: that a 'case of criminal conspiracy *or any other offence*' under the IPC '*may also surface*'. Without evidence. Without a hearing. Once again, this is exactly the kind of stuff that gets you cleaned out for defamation in functioning legal systems; maybe it would even in India, unless you were the Supreme Court. If you're the Supreme Court—and especially if Justice Khanwilkar is on the bench—it's open season, especially on citizens who take Ambedkar seriously when he said that Article 32 was the 'heart and soul of the Constitution'.

It is also important to note that during the pronouncement, the court only referred to the State of Chhattisgarh. The reference to the CBI was added subsequently to the judgment, *on the oral request of the solicitor-general*, after the pronouncement. Once again, you can see the attitude of the constitutional court in cases such as this—just add a reference to a central investigative agency in the judgment, on the request of the union government's lawyer, as if it were the correction of a typographical error. What else can we call this, other than the executive('s) court?

These two judgments—driven by Justice Khanwilkar—mark a profoundly dangerous shift in the history of the Supreme Court. It is one thing for the court to dismiss Article 32 petitions against State impunity. However, it is quite another—and truly unprecedented—for the Supreme Court to turn upon the petitioners themselves and pass prejudicial remarks against them that then become the basis of FIRs and jail time. In every way, this is an inversion of the rule of law, of the Constitution and of the Supreme Court itself—from the protector and guarantor of fundamental rights to persecutor-in-chief. Idi Amin is famously reputed to have said, 'I can guarantee freedom of speech, but I cannot guarantee freedom after speech.' Likewise, through these judgments, Justice Khanwilkar has said, 'I can guarantee freedom to come to court, but I cannot guarantee freedom once you've come to court.'

Sabarimala: The Unreasoned Volte-Face

The final case that I want to (briefly) analyse is not strictly in the same line of cases as the others but does bear a family resemblance in terms of significant judicial action not backed up by any reasons whatsoever.

In November 2018, a five-judge bench of the Supreme Court held that the Sabarimala temple's ban upon the entry of women between the ages of ten to fifty was unconstitutional. The verdict was 4-1. Chief Justice Dipak Misra and Justices Khanwilkar, Chandrachud and Nariman held against the exclusion. Justice Indu Malhotra dissented. All judges except for Justice Khanwilkar wrote separate opinions; Khanwilkar J joined the opinion of the Chief Justice.

I do not, in this post, intend to re-litigate the correctness of the *Sabarimala* judgment. The point, however, is this: An application for review was filed. Recall that for the Supreme Court to *review* its own judgment, it is not enough to just show that the judgment under review was mistaken on law, but to show that there was an inescapable error on the very face of the record (that phrase, *prima facie*, again!), and that this has to be demonstrated before the same bench that passed the original judgment.

The *Sabarimala* review was heard in open court. At the time, Chief Justice Dipak Misra had retired and been replaced by Chief Justice Gogoi. The rest of the bench was the same. By a 3-2 verdict, the Supreme Court decided to 'refer' certain 'questions' about the correctness of the *Sabarimala* judgment for interpretation to a larger bench (this, effectively, stayed the implementation of the judgment). Two of the judges who voted to refer were CJI Gogoi (new to the case) and Malhotra J (a dissenter in the original judgment). Two of the judges who dissented were Chandrachud and Nariman JJ (both in the majority in the original judgment). The tie-breaking vote was that of Khanwilkar J, who had been in the majority one year before, but now seemingly believed not only that the judgment that he had signed on to was arguably wrong, but *so* wrong—so *prima facie* wrong—that the threshold for review was activated.

Can a judge change their mind about the correctness of a judgment they have signed on to? Yes, of course. We are all changeable creatures. Can a judge change their mind about the correctness of a judgment they have signed on to *so much* that they not only believe they were wrong, but blatantly, egregiously wrong—within a year? Perhaps. Perhaps Justice Khanwilkar had a Damascene moment about the rights of women to enter temples. But if that is the case, is there not a minimum—a *bare* minimum—requirement for a judge to explain themselves? To provide reasons for the 180-degree turn? What is notable is that in *neither* of the two cases—*Sabarimala* or *Sabarimala* 'review'— did Justice Khanwilkar do us the courtesy of a reasoned opinion. We do not know the reasons he agreed with his brother, the Chief Justice, in 2018; and we do not know the reasons he came to believe that his brother, the Chief Justice, was egregiously wrong in 2019. Walt Whitman could well ask the rhetorical question, 'Do I contradict myself?', and expect his readers to nod knowingly when he answered, 'Very well then, I contradict myself'. But that is not open to a Supreme

Court justice who, with a stroke of the pen, can extend or withdraw rights from millions of people.

Conclusion: The Executive('s) Court

These examples could be multiplied. One could talk about Khanwilkar J's majority opinion in *Romila Thapar vs Union of India*—another UAPA case—where the Supreme Court turned a blind eye to obvious police misconduct in the prosecution of a case (see Abhinav Sekhri's analysis here[139]), and at the time of writing, the accused are still in jail without trial (can you see a trend here?); one could talk about the *Central Vista* judgment, where Khanwilkar J's majority opinion laid down a standard of public participation, and then refused to apply it to the facts at hand. One could talk about all these, but there is little benefit in belabouring the point.

And the point is this: The cases that we have discussed involve some of the most basic and crucial civil rights in our Constitution. *Watali* and *PMLA* involved the right to personal liberty; *FCRA* involved the right to freedom of speech and freedom of association; *Zakia Jafri* and *Himanshu Kumar* involved the right to enforce fundamental rights and the right to seek judicial remedies against State impunity. Enforcement of these rights is at the heart of the rule of law, at the heart of what it means to be a constitutional democracy *governed* by the rule of law rather than by State arbitrariness. Each of these rights is a crucial bulwark between the individual and the State, and it is the task of the court to preserve and maintain that bulwark.

However, when we look at the judgments in these cases (four out of five were authored by Khanwilkar J, and he was a party to the fifth), a

---

139 Abhinav Sekhri, 'The Supreme Court and Criminal Investigations – Romila Thapar vs Union of India', Proof of Guilt, 29 September 2018, https://theproofofguilt.blogspot.com/2018/09/the-supreme-court-and-criminal.html

disturbing picture emerges. It is not simply that the State always wins and the individual always loses. Regrettably, that is a familiar story in the history of our constitutional jurisprudence, with only a few exceptions scattered on the sands of time. Rather, it is the manner in which the State wins. When it comes to the State's claims, the State's interests, the State's (presented) facts, the State's vision of the world, the court treats all this with a feather-light touch, takes everything as true and occasionally takes the time out to praise the State and its authorities for the great job they are doing. On the other hand, when it comes to the individual, the court turns into the proverbial 'lion under the throne', baring its fangs and unsheathing its claws. Under this judicial philosophy, rights are nuisances, individuals are dispensable and to approach the court for justice is like playing a game of Russian roulette—it's you who might end up in jail after the dust has cleared. And as Justice Khanwilkar's conduct in *Sabarimala* shows, none of this needs justification—it is not the exercise of reason that drives this judicial philosophy, but the exercise of raw power. The court does, because it *can*. And that's about it.

This phenomenon of judicial rule by decree, of orders without reason—the language of the executive, in other words—is why, in a previous post, I referred to the court led by the previous Chief Justice as an 'executive court'—'an institution that speaks the language of the executive, and has become indistinguishable from the executive'. Judgments in cases such as *Watali*, for example, are classic examples of the workings of an executive court. But at the same time, the observations in the *FCRA* case, and in *Zakia Jafri* and *Himanshu Kumar*, are more than just that. It is not simply that the court is speaking the language of the executive, but has become an institution where executive ideology can be laundered and shown to the world as sparkling, *judicially declared* truth. This is what happens when, in *FCRA*, Khanwilkar J speaks about citizens needing to 'be firm and resolute' so that they don't need foreign remittances; and this is what happens in *Zakia Jafri*, where Khanwilkar J's character assassination of Teesta Setalvad and the suggestion that she be 'put in the dock' is immediately followed up by an FIR (which quotes his very words), arrest and jail.

Khanwilkar J is now gone. His individual legacy can be measured in the months, years and decades that people have spent and will spend in jail, without trial (indeed, the State's lawyers have already begun arguing that under the PMLA, a court can only ever grant bail on health grounds, and never otherwise). It can be measured in ruined lives and broken futures. But it is the coming time that will reveal whether the normalizing of the Supreme Court as the executive('s) court will, at the end of the day, be his most significant contribution to Indian constitutional jurisprudence.

Chief Justices

Introduction

IN SOME WAYS, THE story of the Supreme Court is the story of the Chief Justice of India. The Chief Justice's absolute administrative control over the Supreme Court enables them to do the following:

(a) Decide which pending cases will be listed, and when, and
(b) Decide the composition of the benches that will hear them.

Consequently, constitutional cases are heard in the Supreme Court *as and when* the incumbent Chief Justice elects to list them, and heard by a bench of the Chief Justice's choosing.

The first two essays in this section set out the powers of the Chief Justice and the concerns that are raised by the concentration of such extensive powers in one individual. The succeeding essays profile the tenures of five Chief Justices: Dipak Misra (2017–18), Ranjan Gogoi (2018–19), S.A. Bobde (2019–21), N.V. Ramana (2021–22) and U.U. Lalit (2022). These profiles seek to critically analyse not just the legacies of these individual Chief Justices but of the nature, character and direction of the Supreme Court, *as an institution*, under them.

1

ICLP Turns Four: Some Thoughts on the Office of the Chief Justice and Other Supreme Court Miscellany

(2 August 2017)

THE INDIAN CONSTITUTIONAL LAW and Philosophy blog turns four years old today. The past four years have been fairly turbulent—there have been important two-judge-bench decisions on diverse facets of civil rights (freedom of speech and expression, equality and the right to vote, same-sex relations and many more); Constitution bench judgments on the judges' appointments and the basic structure doctrine, the freedom of trade and the death penalty; seven-judge-bench decisions that have upended the jurisprudence on ordinances and reaffirmed the jurisprudence on electoral speech; a nine-judge-bench decision on inter-state taxation (with another nine-judge-bench decision on privacy due by the end of the month[140]); a lot of Article 142; and some interesting contributions from the high courts. On this blog, the attempt has been—and always will be—

---

140 This refers, of course, to the *Puttaswamy* judgment, which came out soon after this post was written.

to analyse, discuss and criticize our courts' constitutional jurisprudence in a straightforward, forthright and *adversarial* manner, and with as little technical jargon as possible. The idea is to both hold our justices to account and to create a forum for open and public discussion about the Constitution.

I have used previous blog anniversaries to discuss issues at the interface of constitutional practice and scholarship in India (for example, the need for doctrinal engagement and problems of access). My concerns arise from my own position at this interface. For three out of four years of the blog's existence, I have been a practising lawyer in Delhi, in different forums. From November 2016, I have been at the Supreme Court and have had a degree of exposure to some of its inner workings.

It is from that perspective that I want to highlight two issues today, which need greater scholarly and public scrutiny than they otherwise get. The first is the office of the Chief Justice. Although it is rarely discussed, the position of the Chief Justice is one that has tremendous power, and that power flows from two things: The CJI's discretion in 'listing' cases and the CJI's discretion in constituting the roster of the Supreme Court.

Let's take the second issue first. For the most part, the Supreme Court sits in benches of two judges (at present, there are thirteen functioning courtrooms in the Supreme Court—thirteen benches). In most of these benches, the senior judge is rarely crossed by his junior colleague, so, effectively, these are one-judge benches. Judges have their individual proclivities when it comes to almost all areas of law. One judge might tend to be pro-labour, another might always vote to uphold the death penalty, a third might be sceptical about claims brought to court by big builders. It, therefore, matters tremendously how the roster is arranged. Readers will recall, for example, that period in the mid-2000s when Justices Sinha and Pasayat were virtually writing duelling judgments on the death penalty—Justice Sinha would commute, Justice Pasayat would affirm. A convict's fate, often, would depend upon whether his case went up before the former or the latter. Consequently, how the Chief Justice arranges the roster—and what kinds of matter go before which bench—needs to be scrutinized in detail. There needs to be far greater detail paid to judges' ideological predilections over the course of their judicial career and how that maps on to the kinds of cases they are assigned to here.

This issue acquires even greater significance in constitutional issues, where larger benches sit. It is the Chief Justice who decides the composition of five-judge, seven-judge and nine-judge benches; it is he who picks, out of the nearly thirty-odd judges in the court (at any given time), *which* five, or seven, or nine, will be sitting on a bench. Again, as an institutional issue, this gives whoever occupies the position of the Chief Justice tremendous power to influence the outcome of a decision simply through the act of picking a bench. I am not alleging bad faith, or even saying that this is a bad thing (although, in my view, the fairest outcome would be through a draw of lots); however, once again, it needs to be *scrutinized*. Who has the Chief Justice picked to hear an important constitutional case about civil liberties? What is the prior record of these judges on the point? Do they have any experience adjudicating such cases before? And so on.

The second power of the Chief Justice is the power to list cases. By now, everyone knows about the huge problems of backlog that are faced by the Supreme Court (and all other courts). This entails a massive queue for cases to be heard. If 'leave' is granted in a particular case (*see below*), it will likely come up for hearing five or six years later. The queue, however, can be broken through an oral 'mentioning' before the Chief Justice. At 10.30 in the morning, before hearings start, lawyers line up in Court No. 1 to 'mention' a matter before the CJI; in many cases, the 'mentioning' is a request for an 'early listing' because of some urgency. The CJI has absolute discretion to allow or deny a mentioning request for an early hearing, just as he has absolute discretion in deciding when larger benches are to assemble (along with their composition).

The issue, of course, is that certain cases are simply more urgent than others (it's also important to recall that when it was established, the Supreme Court was primarily expected to function as a *constitutional court*; constitutional cases now occupy a negligible part of its docket). Through the course of the past year, I've chronicled, in particular, the career of two cases where time has been of particular essence (*Aadhaar*, and the *Delhi Govt vs Union of India* case). There are cases that, if not heard in good time, effectively entail that one side wins and the other loses (the *Delhi Govt vs Union of India* case is a classic example of this). In such a situation, the CJI's decision to accept or reject a mentioning request for an early hearing is no longer innocuous: *inevitably*, it acquires a political dimension. Consequently, it is important to scrutinize what kinds of cases the CJI allows for an early hearing and what kinds he does not, because the ramifications of delay in our system effectively, at times, amount to deciding a case in favour of one side without ever having a hearing. 'Absolute discretion', therefore, is not good enough.

[Rest of the post omitted.]

2

No Man Shall Be a Judge in His Own Cause* (*Conditions Apply)

(13 November 2017)

BY NOW, THE RECENT events that have convulsed the Supreme Court in an unseemly controversy have been discussed threadbare.[141] In this post, I do not intend to talk about the broader issues of judicial politics or institutional credibility. I want to focus on something more specific, drawing from a post I wrote here a few months ago: The manner in which power has been concentrated in the office of the Chief Justice, coupled with the uniquely polyvocal character of the Indian Supreme Court, raises some serious challenges for constitutionalism and the rule of law. The events of the past few days have provided us with textbook examples of these challenges—and now is the time, if there ever was one, to think seriously about them.

In particular, I want to focus on the order passed by the Constitution bench on 10 November 2017. This bench was constituted on the basis

---

141 Raju Ramachandran, 'Fracas in Supreme Court: There's Deep Distrust at the Top', The Print, 12 November 2017, https://theprint.in/opinion/fracas-supreme-court-theres-deep-distrust-top/15803/

of a reference from a two-judge bench that same morning. In their order, Justices Sikri and Bhushan had noted that the petitioner's lawyer had brought to their attention an order passed the day before, in a similar writ petition, referring the matter to a Constitution bench. Consequently, they were placing the matter before the Chief Justice for 'appropriate orders'.

The background was this. Two separate petitions had been filed, asking for an impartial SIT investigation into allegations that a retired judge of the Odisha High Court (among others) had been taking bribes to 'fix' a matter that was being heard in the Supreme Court. One of those petitions had been 'listed' before the court of Justices Sikri and Bhushan. The second petition was 'mentioned' on Thursday, 9 November, in Courtroom No. 2, and listed for immediate hearing on the same day at 12.45 p.m. During the course of the hearing, Justice Chelameswar noted that the allegations were serious, and referred the matter to be heard by the five senior-most judges of the Supreme Court on Monday, 13 November. It was this referral that Justices Sikri and Bhushan took note of when the other (first) petition came up for hearing before them on 10 November.

For those unfamiliar with Supreme Court lingo, a 'mentioning' refers to an oral plea by lawyers, normally before the court sits for its regular hearings, usually requesting that an urgent case be listed for hearing at short notice. Cases that have not already been assigned to benches are mentioned before the Chief Justice; in the present case, the Chief Justice was sitting in a Constitution bench hearing the *Delhi vs Union of India* case, and, therefore, as per convention, mentionings took place in Courtroom No. 2. This was Justice Chelameswar's court, and this was the context in which the second petition came before him.

After Justices Sikri and Bhushan referred the matter to the Chief Justice on the morning of 10 November, the Chief Justice constituted a bench to hear it that same afternoon. The bench consisted of himself and four other judges. In a short order, that bench effectively annulled the order of reference passed by Justice Chelameswar the day before.

The justification given by the bench was as follows: Every court has two 'sides'—the judicial side (that is, hearing and deciding cases) and the administrative side (taking administrative decisions such as listing cases). On the judicial side, the Chief Justice is only the 'first among equals'. However, on the administrative side, he is the 'master of the roster'—that is, 'he alone has the prerogative to constitute benches of the court and allocate cases to the benches so constituted'. Consequently:

> [N]either a two-Judge Bench nor a three-Judge Bench can allocate the matter to themselves or direct the composition for constitution of a Bench. To elaborate, there cannot be any direction to the Chief Justice of India as to who shall be sitting on the Bench or who shall take up the matter as that touches the composition of the Bench. We reiterate such an order cannot be passed. It is not countenanced in law and not permissible.

The Constitution bench, therefore, held that 'any order contrary' to these principles (i.e., Justice Chelameswar's order) was not binding on the Chief Justice. Soon afterwards, the Chief Justice himself constituted a three-judge bench to hear the case on merits. The bench—which consisted of three judges who had sat in Friday's Constitution bench and signed on to the above order—heard the case today and have reserved it for judgment tomorrow.

So far, so straightforward. The problem, however, is this: The FIR in question, alleging bribery and conspiracy, on the basis of which the CBI enquiry was taking place, and which the petition sought to have replaced by an SIT—implicated the Chief Justice himself. The Chief Justice was not named in the FIR; however, the case that the accused—the retired judge of the Odisha High Court—was claiming to 'fix' was being heard by a bench presided over by the Chief Justice. In other words, the principal accused claimed that he could fix a Supreme Court bench on which the Chief Justice was sitting.

Everyone is familiar with the basic legal principle of nemo judex in causa sua, which translates to 'no person shall be a judge in his own cause'. It is clear, therefore, that the Chief Justice could not hear the petition on merits. However, unlike any other judge of the Supreme Court, the Chief Justice's involvement with a petition is not limited to hearing it on merits. As we have seen, the Chief Justice being the 'master of the roster' implies both that he decides *who* should hear it and *when* it should be heard. On 10 November, the Chief Justice exercised both those powers with respect to a petition on a subject matter that, at least, implicated him.

Contrary to what might appear at first blush, the Chief Justice's powers on the administrative side are not minor matters. The power to decide when a case will be heard implies a power to delay its hearing (which did not happen in this case). And the power to decide *who* shall hear a case implies a non-trivial level of control over the outcome. As we have discussed before, the Supreme Court is a polyvocal court: Twenty-six judges sit in thirteen courtrooms, speaking in different and sometimes contradictory voices. It's trite to say that outcomes of cases are inevitably influenced by judges' legal philosophies (I have earlier taken examples of death references being listed before abolitionist or pro-death penalty judges, and labour matters being listed before pro- or anti-labour judges). There is nothing wrong or even abnormal about this—every judge has, and should have, a legal philosophy that influences how they decide cases. It is unlikely that anyone still believes in the idea of mechanical jurisprudence, which treats law as a logical syllogism with mathematically correct answers.

But while there is nothing wrong with judges having legal philosophies, we can immediately see how, in the collegial atmosphere of the Supreme Court, where judges know each other well (and, indeed, the senior judges having appointed junior ones), the Chief Justice's power to decide who shall hear a case vests substantial power in that office. Specifically, take the case under discussion: The decision of whether or not to appoint an SIT would depend, to a large extent, upon the activist or conservative proclivities of a judge, their notion of the separation of powers, the sanctity they attach to the Code of Criminal Procedure and so on.

The above discussion should make it clear that in the present case, there was a clear and direct clash between two principles. The Chief Justice being the 'master of the roster' on the administrative side and 'no person shall be a judge in his own cause'. Which one should prevail? The answer, with respect, is obvious. As the Constitution bench itself acknowledges, the 'master of the roster' stems from Supreme Court rules and conventions. Nemo judex, on the other hand, is one of the most basic and fundamental principles of justice. The Chief Justice is the 'master of the roster' for instrumental reasons and administrative convenience. But without nemo judex, justice cannot exist.

What, then, is the outcome of a clash like this? The answer is: The rule of seniority. Succession to the office of the Chief Justice is by virtue of seniority, and the presiding judge in Courtroom No. 2 is the next in line after the Chief Justice. Consequently, when the Chief Justice is precluded from acting as the 'master of the roster', that responsibility must devolve on the presiding judge in Courtroom No. 2.

Looked at this way, Justice Chelameswar's order on 9 November was not procedurally irregular. The Chief Justice having been disqualified by the principle of nemo iudex, it was Courtroom No. 2 that, temporarily, became Courtroom No. 1, and the administrative powers of the Chief Justice vested in his successor. Had Justice Chelameswar's order been passed by the Chief Justice, it would have been entirely regular; because the Chief Justice was disqualified from dealing with the matter at all, the order in question would have to be treated as an order of an (acting) Chief Justice, and deemed to be regular.

This, I would suggest, is the only way to ensure that the 'master of the roster' principle does not turn into an impenetrable shield for whoever it is that occupies the office of the Chief Justice, while they occupy it. The 'master of the roster' principle assumes that the incumbent

Chief Justice will always be entirely honest and maintain the highest standards of integrity. Of course, that is a reasonable assumption to have. However, institutions are designed not on the basis that the occupants of high office will be honest, but with the objective of ensuring their survival on the rare occasion that an occupant is *not* honest.

The Constitution bench's interpretation of the 'master of the roster' principle is unfortunate, because it effectively raises the office of the Chief Justice above the institution of the Supreme Court. It is unfortunate because it places institutional integrity in the hands of one man or one woman. It is unfortunate because it fails to ring-fence a vitally important public institution against the possibility of an implosion. And, of course, it is unfortunate because it elevates an administrative rule above one of the most basic and fundamental principles of justice.

For that reason, the order merits swift reconsideration. But it is also an opportunity for all of us to reflect more deeply on the institutional structures that we have to—and continue to—accept without demur or dissent.

3

Ends without Means, Outcomes without Reasons: A Look Back at Dipak Misra and the Constitution

(1 October 2018)

DIPAK MISRA IS NO longer the Chief Justice of India. It would be fair to say, I think, that his Chief Justiceship has been controversial. From the famous judges' press-conference, to the 'master of the roster', to the impeachment effort, a significant part of the controversy has been political. On this blog, I have covered some of those events. I have written, for example, about how CJI Misra constituted a bench to hear a case that indirectly implicated himself in criminal conduct, thus violating the cardinal 'no person shall be a judge in her own cause' principle. He has also presided over benches that have pronounced judgments dealing with the powers of the Chief Justice while *he* was Chief Justice. There have been issues as well, with disposing of cases without issuing notice or pleadings (Judge Loya), granting restitution in bail petitions (Unitech) or quashing a charge sheet against M.S. Dhoni in Andhra Pradesh in a challenge against a complaint registered in Karnataka.

In this essay, however, I will not discuss any of that. The political legacy that CJI Misra leaves behind is being debated, and will be debated in the years to come. Nor shall I discuss his judgments in terms of their *outcomes*. There has been enough of that on this blog, and it will be for future scholars to place his judgment in *Navtej Johar* and his signing on to the majority in *Aadhaar* alongside each other, and ask themselves how they stack up.

What I will do in this essay is situate CJI Misra in the broader context of his role as a judge in a constitutional court. My argument will be this: CJI Misra's judicial tenure represents the high-water mark of a tradition in the Supreme Court that can be described as 'outcome-oriented'. This tradition, which (arguably) had its beginnings in the 1980s, calls upon judges to use their power to do (what they perceive to be) 'substantive justice', even where the legal system has itself put checks and constraints upon the exercise of that power. These checks—statutory texts, judicial precedent, the separation of powers, doctrines of jurisdiction and maintainability, and, above all, the giving of reasons for an outcome—are treated as inconveniences to be negotiated rather than principles to be respected. And all of this is justified by nice-sounding—but intellectually vapid—catchphrases such as 'procedure is the handmaiden of justice'.

CJI Misra's tenure represents, as I said, the high-water mark of this tradition. In his judgments, legal constraints are devalued to such an extent that we reach a near-vanishing point. If earlier we had ends at the cost of means and outcomes privileged over reasons, in CJI Misra's judgments, we find ends *without* means and outcomes *without* reasons.

I should clarify, once again, that this is not a dispute over outcomes. I find CJI Misra's judicial instinct on social and gender rights—as reflected by his judgments in 377, adultery and Sabarimala—to chime with my own. At the same time, I disagree strongly with his instinct on free speech. But that is not the point. The point is whether the manner in which CJI Misra reaches these outcomes—which we may agree or disagree with—is consistent with a democratic set-up that prizes the rule of law over the rule of judges. I believe that it is not, and I shall attempt to demonstrate that in the examples that follow.

Ignorance of Statutory Text: The Make-Up Artists Case

In November 2014, Misra J (as he then was) struck down a clause of the Cine Costume Make-Up Artists and Hair Dressers Association bye-laws that prohibited women from becoming members.[142] This was immediately hailed as a landmark judgment for gender rights. Importantly, however, the association was a private body, which had the right to frame its own regulations. To strike down the bye-laws, therefore, Misra J had to find a way of holding that the constitutional norms of Articles 14, 15(1) and 21 were applicable even between private parties.

How did Misra J do this? He noted that the Trade Unions Act, 1926—under which the association was registered—said that *'any person who has attained the age of fifteen years'* was entitled to be a member of a registered trade union. He then argued that as the Act did not make a distinction between men and women, the association could not, through its bye-laws, introduce such a distinction.

This is impeccable reasoning, except for one fact. Section 21 of the Trade Unions Act, which Misra J quoted and relied upon, is about the rights of minors to membership of trade unions, and the full text states:

> Any person who has attained the age of fifteen years may be a member of a registered Trade Union *subject to any rules of the Trade Union to the contrary,* and may, *subject as aforesaid,* enjoy all the rights of a member. *[Emphasis mine]*

As you can see, the underlined portion knocks the bottom out of the argument. It is not that 'any person who has attained the age of fifteen

---

142 *Charu Khurana vs Union of India,* (2015) 1 SCC 192.

years' is entitled to membership of any trade union—her entitlement is subject to the *rules of the trade union*, which, of course, were what the respondents were relying upon in the *Make-Up Artists* case.

There is a larger debate to be had about private discrimination, especially when that discrimination is carried out by associations that have near-monopoly power in an industry. Misra J could very well have reached his conclusion on constitutionally justifiable grounds. But he didn't do so. Instead, he took a statutory text, relied upon the part that suited him, snipped out the part that didn't and got his answer. That will not do.

Ignorance of Precedent: The Devidas Tuljapurkar Case

In *Devidas Tuljapurkar*, Misra J (as he then was) was considering a plea for quashing charges of obscenity with respect to a poem titled *Gandhi Mala Bhetala* (I Met Gandhi), published in 1994 and meant for private circulation among the employees of the All India Bank Association (the SLP was filed by the publisher). Misra J rejected the plea, and, in doing so, invented an entirely new standard for adjudicating obscenity claims. The threshold, he ruled, would be higher in the case of 'historically respectable personalities'.[143]

I use the word 'invented' with due care. Where did the phrase 'historically respectable personalities' pop up from? It is not there in Section 292 of the Indian Penal Code, which defines obscenity. It is not there in any Indian judgment interpreting the meaning of 'obscenity'. As I pointed out at the time, it does not flow from the logic of the section or from the restrictions on free speech in the Constitution—indeed, it is at stark odds with both. The 'historically respectable personalities' test had no source at all outside the imagination of Misra J.

This is not a light matter. Freedom of expression is a crucially important constitutional right. Its contours have been carefully

---

143 *Devidas Tuljapurkar vs State of Maharashtra*, (2015) 6 SCC 1.

delineated in the constitutional text and restrictions been imposed. Over the years, courts have been engaged in a process of interpreting the right and its restrictions. Court judgments on the point have a huge impact in terms of self-censorship and the chilling effect. But in inventing a new restriction altogether—and then omitting to define it with any degree of precision—Misra J seemed oblivious to all of this.

Ignorance of Legal Logic: The Criminal Defamation Judgment

In 2016, Misra J (as he then was) upheld the constitutional validity of Section 499 of the Indian Penal Code.[144] There are multiple things profoundly wrong with this judgment, as I have discussed at some length (not least the invention of a whole new ground—'constitutional fraternity' as a basis for restricting speech).[145] But in keeping with the theme of this post, I want to focus on one specific aspect.

It was pointed out to the court that in *R. Rajagopal vs State of Tamil Nadu*, the Supreme Court had held that strict-liability defamation in *civil law* was too stringent a restriction upon free speech. To put it in simpler language, the civil law offence of defamation kicked in if it was established that a defamatory statement had been made, and the only defences open to the defendant was to show that it was true, or a fair comment, or covered by legal privilege. What slipped through the cracks was, for example, an honest mistake: a statement that had been made after due care and reasonable checking of facts, but which

---

144 *Subramanian Swamy vs Union of India*, (2016) 7 SCC 221.
145 'The Supreme Court's Criminal Defamation Judgment: Glaringly Flawed', Indian Constitutional Law and Philosophy, 13 May 2016, https://indconlawphil.wordpress.com/2016/05/13/the-supreme-courts-criminal-defamation-judgment-glaringly-flawed/; 'Why the Supreme Court's Criminal Defamation Judgment Is Per Incuriam', Indian Constitutional Law and Philosophy, 18 May 2016, https://indconlawphil.wordpress.com/2016/05/18/why-the-supreme-courts-criminal-defamation-judgment-is-per-incuriam/

nonetheless turned out to be false. In *Rajagopal*, the Supreme Court found that this was inconsistent with the Constitution and 'read in' the *NYT vs Sullivan* standard of actual malice—that is, as far as public figures were concerned, a statement would have to be false *and* made with actual malice (i.e., knowing that it was false or having a reckless disregard for its truth or falsity) for civil defamation to apply.

Now, as it was pointed out to the court, this set up an irreconcilable contradiction with Section 499 of the IPC, which not only retained the strict liability form of defamation in the criminal context, but also had *fewer* defences (an accused had to show not only that the statement was true, but true *and* in the public interest). In other words, the same legal standard that the Supreme Court had ruled unconstitutional in the context of *civil* defamation continued to hold for criminal defamation, and then some. As a matter of simple legal logic, therefore, the court had to *at least* bring the two on a par.

Misra J's response to this was ... to ignore it altogether. It is a 268-page judgment that ranges across wide swathes of law and life, but on the one point that is not even a question of legal argument, but just one of logic (and therefore unanswerable), it chooses to remain silent.

Ignorance of Maintainability: National Anthem

In late 2016, Misra J (as he then was) passed an 'interim order' in a PIL, directing that all cinema halls play the national anthem before every movie.[146] Once again, there are many things that were wrong with this order, and which I pointed out at the time—from the fact that Misra J had adjudicated a very similar claim (brought by the same petitioner), while he was a judge of the Madhya Pradesh High Court, to the fact that the order grossly violated both Article 19(1)(a) and

---

146 *Shyam Narayan Chouksey vs Union of India*, (2018) 2 SCC 574.

the separation of powers, and effectively involved the court in doing something it did not have the power to do: Censor speech *directly*.[147]

But all that apart, there was one very basic point that Misra J ignored entirely before passing this 'interim order' (which ended up lasting for more than a year). Article 32 of the Constitution states, in the relevant part:

> The right to move the Supreme Court by appropriate proceedings for the enforcement of the *rights conferred by this Part* is guaranteed. *[Emphasis mine]*

It is, therefore, beyond cavil that when you are moving an Article 32 petition (and PILs fall within that category), you *must* show that there is a violation of a fundamental right under Part III. In the PIL era, you are now entitled to move the court to enforce somebody else's rights on their behalf, but that does not exempt you from the burden of showing that there exists a right in the first place. And this straightforward point has been recognized in multiple Supreme Court judgments, which make it clear that for a PIL to be maintainable, there must be a right under Part III that is impacted.

What fundamental right under Part III was the PIL petitioner agitating in the *National Anthem* case? It is obvious that there is none. And Misra J's interim order did not even begin to address that rather basic point, focusing instead on 'fundamental duties', which, as a matter of *constitutional text*, are not part of the 'rights conferred by *this* Part' that Article 32 talks about.

Interestingly, midway through the hearings, while the interim order was already in force, this point was grasped by Rakesh Dwivedi, the senior counsel for the petitioner, the first time that *he* was engaged to

---

147 'The Illegality of the Supreme Court's National Anthem Order', Indian Constitutional Law and Philosophy, 30 November 2016, https://indconlawphil.wordpress.com/2016/11/30/the-illegality-of-the-supreme-courts-national-anthem-order/

appear in the case. Dwivedi promptly had the petitioner amend his pleadings, and at the next date, present a case that the Prevention of Insults to National Honour Act, 1971, violated Article 14, because it did not protect the national anthem as much as it protected the national flag. I think that that is a bizarre argument, but at least it is *an* argument for establishing maintainability in the first place. But even that threshold requirement was not deemed necessary by Misra J before passing his slew of orders that would have a direct impact on freedom of speech and expression.

Ignorance of Jurisdiction and the Separation of Powers: Meesha

Meesha was a case I wrote about recently,[148] and is perhaps most characteristic of CJI Misra's tenure—big words, grandstanding and empty reasoning. The facts of *Meesha* were that a novel serialized in Kerala generated some controversy. Certain groups approached the state government and attempted to have the book banned. The state government refused. A PIL was then filed to have the book banned. With dazzling alacrity, CJI Misra allowed a special mentioning, listed the case for hearing, reserved orders and then passed a judgment dismissing the PIL.[149]

The problem, however, is that he had *no* power to do most of this. Our constitutional scheme is a very carefully crafted one when it comes to free speech and other civil rights. It effectively sets up a three-step procedure. *First*, there must exist a law that sets out the circumstances under which speech can be restricted. *Secondly*, the executive implements that law. And *thirdly*, the court can

---

148 'The Meesha Judgment: Book Bans and the Supreme Court's Dangerous Grandstanding', Indian Constitutional Law and Philosophy, 5 September 2018, https://indconlawphil.wordpress.com/2018/09/05/the-meesha-judgment-book-bans-and-the-supreme-courts-dangerous-grandstanding/
149 *N. Radhakrishnan vs Union of India*, WP (Civ) No. 904/2018 (5 September 2018).

review either legislative or executive action for compliance with the Constitution. This is a multilayered set of safeguards, which ensures that before speech is censored finally, there are a number of checks and balances.

In the case of book bans, the system works like this. The relevant law is the Code of Criminal Procedure. The CrPC grants to state governments the power to ban books if certain specific laws have been violated. And this ban, in turn, can be reviewed by a three-judge bench of the high court on an application from an interested party (with a further appeal to the Supreme Court). What the Constitution *does not* permit is for the Supreme Court to unilaterally ban a book. And if the Supreme Court doesn't have the *power* to ban a book, it stands to reason that it cannot admit or hear a PIL for that purpose.

This careful constitutional scheme was torn to shreds by Misra CJI in *Meesha*, simultaneously creating an entirely new—and dangerous—jurisdiction for the court, where any interloper could show up at any high court or the Supreme Court with a PIL, asking for a book to be banned, and try his luck.

Ignorance of Procedure: Navtej Johar

It is trite to say that the Section 377 judgment was a welcome one. But a look at *how* it came about reveals, on more than one occasion, legally problematic conduct by Misra CJI, acting in his capacity as Chief Justice. *First*, technically, *Koushal vs Naz Foundation* was not yet over. The curative petitions in that case were still pending. But while the older proceedings were still in progress, Misra CJI admitted a lis (dispute) on an identical issue (the constitutional validity of Section 377) and had it referred to a Constitution bench. It will not do to say that the pending curatives were PILs while *Navtej Johar* was a writ petition. The point is that, effectively, the court admitted a petition asking for the *reconsideration* of *Koushal* before even the *Koushal* proceedings had attained finality! There was a correct way to do this, which was easily available—he could have listed the curatives, disposed of them and *then* admitted *Navtej Johar*. He did not do so.

Secondly, *Navtej Johar* was referred to a Constitution bench on the very same day and in the same hearing that it was admitted! Surely, referral to a Constitution bench is not something that ought to be done in such a cavalier fashion? Surely, the question of whether a matter involves a substantial question of law pertaining to the interpretation of the Constitution (the requirement of a referral) has to be separately contested?

And *thirdly*, the initial listing of cases had *Navtej Johar* as fourth on the list, to be heard after *Aadhaar*, the constitutional challenge to the adultery law and *Sabarimala*. *Aadhaar* took up the entire first half of the year and ended just before the vacations. On the Thursday after the court reopened, the list was juggled, and *Navtej Johar* was bumped up to the top of the list for the coming Tuesday. This effectively blindsided the State, whose counsel protested on Tuesday that four days was too short a time to prepare for a case of this magnitude. Expectedly, Misra CJI gave short shrift to this and went ahead with the hearing.

Koushal vs Naz was a horrendous decision, and deserved to be overturned at the earliest. But it is unclear to me why that needed to be done at the cost of inverting some very basic procedural requirements, especially when, at most, they would have caused nothing more than a few weeks' delay.

Ignorance of Intra-Court Discipline

On two distinct occasions, Misra CJI, using his powers as Chief Justice, has set himself up as the head of an intra-court appeals division. He did this first on the issue of the memorandum of procedure (MoP) for judicial appointments. After a different, two-judge bench had issued notice on the case, with respect to the government delaying the MoP, the case was transferred to Misra CJI's court, and promptly dismissed. As Bar and Bench wrote:

An intra-court appeal is unheard of in the Supreme Court and it is unclear on what ground the two cases were transferred to a 3-judge Bench when the 2-judge Bench had passed no order to that effect.[150]

Conclusion

There are other glaring examples of Misra CJI's ends-without-means constitutional jurisprudence. His attempts to introduce the doctrine of 'auto-block' on the internet (before better sense prevailed), his attempt to invent further restrictions to free speech on grounds of 'constitutional compassion' and so on. But the instances given above are sufficient, I feel, to make the point.

As I wrote at the beginning of this essay, this is not an assessment of CJI Misra's substantive jurisprudence. Over the past five years, I have written about almost all of his constitutional judgments, praising some and criticizing others. And at a moment when emotions are running high after the last week, it is probably too soon to engage in a dispassionate analysis of a judicial career that includes *377*, the adultery judgment and *Sabarimala* on the one hand, and *Aadhaar*, *Master-of-the-Roster* and all the free speech judgments on the other; takes into account other controversial cases such as *Judge Loya*, *Bhima-Koregaon*, the *Uttarakhand President's Rule* case and *Arunachal*; and, lastly, examines CJI Misra's administrative role in the allocation of cases.

But it is never too soon, I think, to make this simple point: In constitutional matters, CJI Misra has taken the trope of the crusading judge, who roams the field seeking out his own vision of truth, justice and beauty to its logical endpoint. I am not here saying

---

150 Murali Krishnan, 'Intra-Court Appeal? 3-Judge Bench of Supreme Court Recalls Two Orders Passed by Division Bench', Bar and Bench, 8 November 2017, https://www.barandbench.com/columns/intra-court-appeal-mop-case-supreme-court

that his judgments are motivated by extraneous considerations. No doubt that CJI Misra sincerely believes that he has been doing justice according to the Constitution. But in the course of doing that justice, every institutional check that has been put into place to ensure that we have a rule of law instead of a rule by judges, has been devalued to its vanishing point. In CJI Misra's judgments, text does not matter. Precedent does not matter. Legal consistency does not matter. Jurisdiction does not matter. Maintainability does not matter. Separation of powers does not matter. Judicial propriety does not matter. Reasons do not matter. All of this is subsumed within one overarching, totalizing vision of *his* sense of justice, topped off with language that is so opaque, turgid and impenetrable that all it does is remind you of those dark, slime-ridden ponds immediately after rainy season.

It would be unfair to blame CJI Misra for this entirely, since he is, after all, a product of a system that has systematically devalued these checks and balances, and where academics have contributed to that devaluing by castigating them as relics of 'Anglo-Saxon jurisprudence'. But ultimately, it is these relics of 'Anglo-Saxon jurisprudence' that stand between us and the tyranny of the unelected. The unchecked expansion of judicial power can only lead to a situation where judges feel less and less accountable to constitutional checks, and feel less and less inclined towards justifying their judgments on constitutional grounds.

CJI Misra's tenure reveals that truth in its starkest form.

4

'A Little Brief Authority': Chief Justice Ranjan Gogoi and the Rise of the Executive Court

(17 November 2019)

RANJAN GOGOI IS NO longer the Chief Justice of India. There is much to write about today. But this post will follow precedent (unlike some of the major judgments delivered during the former Chief Justice's tenure) and—like last year—focus on the law. I will not, therefore, discuss the sexual-harassment allegations of April/May 2019, although they constitute an important part of the former Chief Justice's legacy (discussed here,[151] here,[152] here,[153] here[154]

---

151 'A Question of Power', Indian Constitutional Law and Philosophy, 1 May 2019, https://indconlawphil.wordpress.com/2019/05/01/a-question-of-power/

152 Gautam Bhatia, 'Spectacle Fit for a Kangaroo Court', *The Mumbai Mirror*, 21 April 2019, https://mumbaimirror.indiatimes.com/mumbai/cover-story/spectacle-fit-for-a-kangaroo-court/articleshow/68972786.cms

153 'An Analysis of the Supreme Court's Order in "In Re: Matter of Great Public Importance Touching Upon the Independence of the Judiciary"', Indian Constitutional Law and Philosophy, *25 April 2019*, https://indconlawphil.wordpress.com/2019/04/25/an-analysis-of-the-supreme-courts-order-in-in-re-matter-of-great-public-importance-touching-upon-the-independence-of-the-judiciary/

154 Gautam Bhatia, 'Power Imbalances and Due Processes Don't Matter', *Hindustan Times*, 7 May 2019, https://www.hindustantimes.com/

and here[155]). I will not discuss the opacity of the collegium or what was done to Justice Akil Kureshi, where a judge seemingly not considered 'fit' to be Chief Justice of the Madhya Pradesh High Court was re-assigned to the Tripura High Court (see here[156]). I will not discuss the time that the former Chief Justice told the lawyers of a man who had been jailed for satirical speech that *'jail is the safest place for you'*. Or the time that he told the lawyers of a woman asking for her Article 19(1)(d) rights that *'Srinagar is a cold place, why do you want to move around?'* What these remarks say about the former Chief Justice's attitude towards constitutional rights can be left to individual judgment. I will not discuss the prioritization of cases—how, ostensibly, a 'land dispute' was somehow heard by a Constitution bench of five judges and fast-tracked, while civil rights claims connected to the lockdown in Kashmir went unheard because a court of thirty-three judges, according to the former Chief Justice, 'had no time'. And I will not discuss the problematic manner in which the former Chief Justice, while still the Chief Justice, defended his NRC orders in a public event, in the interests of 'development'.

Interested readers can consult this piece[157], which discusses some of these issues in detail, and what they mean both for the former Chief

---

analysis/power-imbalances-and-due-processes-don-t-matter/story-lNfq5jUQogriICnvIzIsqI.html

155 'Sexual Harassment at the Supreme Court: A Time for Institutional Accountability', Indian Constitutional Law and Philosophy, 30 October 2019, https://indconlawphil.wordpress.com/2019/10/30/sexual-harassment-at-the-supreme-court-a-time-for-institutional-accountability/

156 'Centre Has Its Way, Supreme Court Collegium Reassigns Justice Akil Kureshi', The Wire, 21 September 2019, https://thewire.in/law/supreme-court-now-recommends-justice-kureshi-to-tripura-high-court

157 Maneka Khanna and Surbhi Dhar, 'Did Chief Justice Ranjan Gogoi Discharge His "Debt to the Nation"?', Huffpost, 16 November 2019, https://www.huffpost.com/archive/in/entry/did-chief-justice-ranjan-gogoi-discharge-his-debt-to-the-nation_in_5dcfefeee4b0d2e79f8d5071?guccounter=1

Justice's legacy and for the institutional credibility of the Supreme Court. Here, I will consider some of the important judgments and orders delivered by the former Chief Justice during his tenure. My assessment will be simple: Former Chief Justice Gogoi oversaw a drift from a rights court to an executive court. That is, under his tenure, the Supreme Court has gone from an institution that, for all its patchy history, was at least *formally* committed to the protection of individual rights as its primary task, to an institution that speaks the language of the executive, and has become indistinguishable from the executive. The 'executive court' is visible in the former Chief Justice's substantive adjudication [e.g., the *NRC* case and the *Voice Samples* case], in his penchant for procedural opacity [e.g., sealed covers], in his contempt for the Indian Evidence Act, 1872 [e.g., Rafale], in his treatment of fundamental rights as charity rather than entitlements [habeas corpus petitions] and in his judicial rhetoric.

The NRC Case

The starting point of any discussion about the former Chief Justice has to be the urgent, almost messianic manner in which he drove the NRC process (even from before the time he became Chief Justice). Recall that the National Register of Citizens is a state-wide administrative process in Assam, aimed at creating a list of Indian citizens. The creation of the NRC flows from—and is linked to—the Assam Accord of 1985 and subsequent amendments to the Citizenship Act, 1955. As indicated above, the NRC was always meant to be an *administrative* process— implemented by the government and executed by the bureaucracy. In 2014, however, acting under expansive PIL powers, the former Chief Justice—sitting with Nariman J—effectively took over the entire process. Formally, it was Supreme Court 'oversight' over the preparation of the NRC; effectively, as soon became evident, there was little difference between 'oversight' and 'control'.

Why was this a problem? I have discussed some of the issues in detail (see here,[158] here,[159] here[160] and here[161]), and here I will summarize them. The NRC process wasn't just any ordinary administrative process. It affected citizenship—the underlying basis of all other rights, the right to have rights. While the NRC itself would not deprive an individual of citizenship, exclusion from that list would severely prejudice people's cases before the Foreigners Tribunals, which they would subsequently be hauled up before. Now with consequences as serious as this, one would expect the full panoply of constitutional safeguards to apply, with heightened rigour. And under our constitutional scheme, one of the most crucial safeguards is the separation of powers and judicial review. The executive implements policy, and if, in the process, it violates individual rights, the courts exist to test executive action on the touchstone of the Constitution.

The Supreme Court's takeover of the NRC process effectively amounted to taking a knife and slashing right through this constitutional fabric. In consultation with the state coordinator, it was the court that was determining how the process was to be conducted, what the deadlines were, what documents were admissible and so on. And because the court had taken over the executive's task, there was no place where aggrieved people could go if they felt their rights were being violated. After all, whom do you appeal to from an order of the court, apart from the court itself?

This is not an abstract, theoretical concern. To take just one example, the use of the 'family tree' method to determine citizenship was found to

---

158 'In the Court of Last Resort', *supra*.
159 Gautam Bhatia, 'Inhumane and Utterly Undemocratic', *The Hindu*, 10 June 2019, https://www.thehindu.com/opinion/lead/inhumane-and-utterly-undemocratic/article27705953.ece
160 'The NRC Case and the Parchment Barrier of Article 21', supra.
161 Gautam Bhatia, 'The Judicial Presumption of Non-Citizenship', *The Hindu*, 23 July 2019, https://www.thehindu.com/opinion/lead/the-judicial-presumption-of-non-citizenship/article28660624.ece

disproportionately disadvantage rural women, who had greater difficulty in accessing and producing the documents that it required. In an ordinary situation—that is, if this had been pure executive action—this could have been challenged before the courts on grounds of Articles 14 and 15, and struck down. But because the modalities of the NRC *themselves* arose from (often closed-door) consultations between the Supreme Court and the NRC coordinator, that entire set of remedies was blocked off. Examples of this kind abound; the situation, in effect, was like the poem from *Alice in Wonderland*: 'I'll be judge, I'll be jury'/said cunning old Fury:/'I'll try the whole cause,/and sentence you to death.'

'Death' is not a euphemism here. People died because of the NRC. People died when the court insisted on unachievable deadlines for publishing draft NRCs (to the extent that even the State—the *actual executive*—asked for more time and was denied). People died at the time of the publication of the final list, another accelerated process in which the government's requests for an extension were shot down. Things came to a stage where Genocide Watch issued a warning around the time of the final List—a rare time in history where *judicial* actions in a functioning democracy led to a genocide warning. In another world, this would be a moment where a constitutional court would be asked to step in and protect rights, but a world where the court had become the perpetrator was a world long turned upside-down.

The problems were not limited to the former Chief Justice's substantive role in the NRC process. The problems extended to process—they featured opaque proceedings where affected parties were not heard and decisions were taken on the basis of 'PowerPoint presentations' made by the state coordinator to the court. And they were taken on the basis of evidence in sealed covers—a point that brings us to our next issue.

Sealed Covers

Right from the beginning, the former Chief Justice's tenure was marked by secrecy, opacity and the ubiquitous use of 'sealed covers' (see here,[162] here[163] and here[164]). The NRC case was marked by sealed covers. The Rafale dispute was marked by sealed covers. The Alok Verma litigation was marked by sealed covers. Sealed covers popped up in the one hearing that happened on the issue of electoral bonds, and they popped up—bizarrely—in the litigation around the Prime Minister's biopic before the election.

I will, again, sum up an argument that I have made in detail in other posts. Sealed covers are the absolute antithesis of open justice, one of the fundamental principles underlying the judicial system. The reason for this is simple: Courts have to give *reasons* for their judgments. Citizens are entitled to assessing the strength of these reasons as part of the framework of democratic accountability over courts. If, however, the *evidence* on the basis of which judgments are delivered is kept hidden, any kind of scrutiny is nothing more than whistling in the dark. If I do not know why the court has come to the conclusion it has, I simply cannot make up my own mind about the merits of what it has done. In such a situation, the courts become little more than petty autocrats. Their judgments are upheld only by virtue of their institutional power and not by the strength of their reasoning. That is not how democracy works.

The former Chief Justice's penchant for sealed covers suggests another way in which the Supreme Court has transitioned to the executive court. Secrecy is the hallmark of the executive. We all

---

162 'A Petty Autocracy: The Supreme Court's Evolving Jurisprudence of the Sealed Cover', Indian Constitutional Law and Philosophy, 17 November 2018, https://indconlawphil.wordpress.com/2018/11/17/a-petty-autocracy-the-supreme-courts-evolving-jurisprudence-of-the-sealed-cover/

163 Gautam Bhatia, 'Justice Must Be Open, Not Opaque', *Hindustan Times*, 19 October 2018, https://www.hindustantimes.com/analysis/justice-must-be-open-not-opaque/story-uOIfNMAKfX0sijzmkAETnM.html

164 Vasudev Devadasan, 'Financing the General Elections: Electoral Bonds and Disclosure Requirements under the Constitution', Indian Constitutional Law and Philosophy, 19 April 2019, https://indconlawphil.wordpress.com/2019/04/19/financing-the-general-elections-electoral-bonds-and-disclosure-requirements-under-the-constitution/

acknowledge that there are certain kinds of executive action that cannot be disclosed, as that would defeat the entire purpose—war plans, for example, or complex trade negotiations. The crucial distinction, however, is that whereas executive legitimacy for these actions comes from *popular elections*, judicial legitimacy comes from open and public *reason-giving*. Apart from certain exceptional situations, therefore (such as two corporations litigating over commercially sensitive information, or where other rights are at stake, such as the privacy of sexual-assault survivors), the court simply cannot justify withholding information in sealed covers, and certainly not in public law cases involving fundamental rights, as that defeats the very purpose of having an independent judiciary in a democratic system. As I have argued earlier, if the court feels that certain information is sensitive because it pertains to national security, the answer is for it to decline to hear the case at all (insofar as it pertains to that information), on the basis that it is not institutionally legitimate to intervene. But the court cannot have it both ways (as it did in Rafale). It cannot both hear the case, but also hear it on the basis of secret material, and then pass judgment based on that secret material, so that nobody is in a position to understand or examine what it has done. That behaviour is more reminiscent of the Star Chamber.[165]

And it is important to note that what the Supreme Court does has ripple effects through the entire legal system. On more than one occasion in the past few months, for example, the Delhi High Court has upheld bans on organizations on the basis of evidence in sealed covers, which even the organization's *lawyers were not allowed to see*. In other words, people have been deprived of their fundamental rights to assembly and association on the basis of evidence that they could not see and could not contest. It is difficult to see how this kind

---

[165] The Star Chamber was a medieval English court, which, because of its conduct, has now become a byword for the denial of due process and arbitrariness in judicial proceedings.

of kangaroo-court behaviour could have gone on had not the sealed-cover practice received the direct behaviour of the former Chief Justice.

Contempt for the Evidence Act

If 'sealed covers' represented one significant departure from the judicial process and towards the executive process, the former Chief Justice's bizarre approach to evidence in the Rafale case represented another.[166] During the hearing of the PIL petitions challenging the Rafale deal, the former Chief Justice 'summoned' air force officials to court to 'interact' with them. It was then reported that the bench had an 'oral' interaction with the air force officials, questioning them and hearing their answers.

But this doesn't just take a knife to the Evidence Act, it takes a lighter and sets fire to it. One of the cornerstones of our legal system is the adversarial process—truth emerges out of a contest between rival views and competing evidence, and the foundation of that contest lies in procedures such as cross-examination. Ordinarily, it is only after the other side has had a chance to put testimony to the test, through cross-examination, that it can be given the status of 'evidence' and be relied upon by the courts. And the procedure through which this happens is set out in detail in the Evidence Act.

Once again, therefore, the former Chief Justice acted as if the obligations that apply to legal proceedings—to clearly follow the law and to provide legal explanations if one is departing from ordinary process—simply didn't exist for him. Laws and processes were for lesser mortals—and lesser judges, presumably. The former Chief Justice, however, could just call people to his court, 'interact' with them

---

166 Gautam Bhatia, 'Matters of Public Interest Must Follow Due Process', *Hindustan Times*, 22 November 2018, https://www.hindustantimes.com/analysis/matters-of-public-interest-must-follow-due-process/story-INSoFcK5CTDPUXiGS5Um0N.html

and *that* would become 'evidence'. We may call this 'Humpty Dumpty jurisprudence':

> 'When I use a word,' Humpty Dumpty said, in rather a scornful tone, 'it means just what I choose it to mean—neither more nor less.' 'The question is,' said Alice, 'whether you can make words mean so many different things.' 'The question is,' said Humpty Dumpty, 'which is to be master—that's all.'

Which, of course, is reminiscent of an imperial executive and not a constitutional court bound by the rule of law.

Habeas Corpus

After the events of 5 August in the State of Jammu and Kashmir (that have been discussed extensively on this blog), a clutch of petitions were filed in the Supreme Court. One set of petitions involved claims to habeas corpus: Relatives and friends of individuals in Kashmir claimed that they had been unlawfully detained and requested the court to intervene.

Habeas corpus is a simple thing. No, really, it is. It literally means 'produce the body'. All the court has to do is ask the government to bring the detained person and legally justify the detention. And habeas corpus, as just about everyone agrees, is one of the most foundational rights that individuals have against arbitrary State power.

What did the former Chief Justice do when these habeas corpus petitions came before him? Let us take the case of J&K MLA Yousuf Tarigami. His party chief, Sitaram Yechury, filed a habeas corpus for Tarigami to be produced and his detention explained. After hearing the petition, the former Chief Justice 'allowed' Yechury to 'travel' to J&K to 'meet' Tarigami and then 'report back' to the court—on the condition that he *could* only travel for this purpose and could not engage in any 'political activities' while there.

Where does one even begin with the extraordinary perversity of all of this? Article 19(1)(d) guarantees to all citizens the freedom of movement within the territory of India. J&K is part of India (is it not?). Yechury is an Indian citizen (is he not?). There was no Emergency declared in J&K, so Article 19(1)(d) had not been suspended (in fact, the government, to this day, insists that everything is 'normal'). If at all Yechury's movements could be restricted, it could only be on the basis of a 'law' that met the test of reasonableness under Article 19(4). So where on earth did the Supreme Court get the idea that it had any power or authority to 'allow' Yechury to travel to J&K and place 'conditions' on what he could or could not do when he was there? Where in the Constitution were these 'conditions' sourced from? Was the former Chief Justice the head of the Supreme Court or the head of the Supreme Internal Visa Issuing Authority of India? And what happened to the right to habeas corpus? Had it been erased from Article 21 by this newly minted Supreme Internal Visa Issuing Authority of India? As A.G. Noorani would point out a few weeks later, 'The Gogoi court has, at reckless speed, run a coach and four through the centuries-old established law on habeas corpus.'

Needless to say, the former Chief Justice refused to provide any reasons for any of this. No reasons for what was done to habeas corpus, no reason for the extraordinary order that made fundamental rights subservient to the whims and fancies of the court without even an effort to locate them in the Constitution, no reason for anything. This was a court—and a Chief Justice—that had liberated itself from that annoying little thing called the Constitution. *Aut Caesar, aut nihil.*

Judicial Evasion and Electoral Democracy

For someone who was willing to sit five days a week and after court hours to ensure that the Ayodhya case was decided, the former Chief Justice showed a surprising degree of reticence when it came to cases that went to the heart of our electoral democracy. At the head of the queue was the electoral bonds challenge. Recall that the electoral bonds law allows for *limitless, anonymous corporate donations to political parties*.[167] A challenge to the law has been pending from *before* the former Chief Justice became the Chief Justice, and has remained pending for the entire thirteen months of his tenure. During this time, multiple elections have taken place and multiple cycles of electoral bond-buying have happened (for the staggering figures—all anonymous—see here:[168] 6,128 crores, out of which a majority has gone to the ruling party, because of the structural asymmetry within the scheme that benefits the ruling incumbent, whoever that might be).

When the case came up for hearing before the Lok Sabha elections, the Chief Justice, after hearing it for a while, noted that the '*weighty issues ... would require an in-depth hearing which cannot be concluded and the issues answered within the limited time that is available before the process of funding through the Electoral Bonds comes to a closure*'. He then ordered that the details of the funding be given to the Election Commission of India in a sealed cover (again!), by 30 May.[169]

There is only one way to describe this order—judicial trolling. At this point, the case had been pending for over a year. To say that there was 'limited time' to hear and decide it somehow implied that the petitioners had been sleeping all this while and had only run to the court on the eve of the Lok Sabha elections. And besides, as the Brexit hearing recently showed us, if a constitutional court really needs to hear and decide a crucial case within a limited period

---

167 Gautam Bhatia, 'The Electoral Bonds Scheme Is a Threat to Democracy', *Hindustan Times*, 18 March 2019, https://www.hindustantimes.com/analysis/the-electoral-bonds-scheme-is-a-threat-to-democracy/story-PpSiDdUjIw5WNBUzDsSzxI.html

168 'Electoral Bonds: Rs 6,128 Crore Sold So Far, Highest in Mumbai', *The Indian Express*, 2 November 2019, https://indianexpress.com/article/explained/telling-numbers-electoral-bonds-rs-6128-crore-sold-so-far-highest-in-mumbai-6098700/

169 *Association for Democratic Reforms vs Union of India*, WP (Civ) No. 333/2015 (12 April 2019).

of time, it is perfectly capable of doing so—*and* writing a reasoned judgment to boot.

What, then, was the aftermath? 30 May came and went. Presumably, details were filed in a sealed cover. And the case has sunk without a trace. Another set of state elections has come and gone, in which electoral bonds were used—and the court is yet to hear it. This is, as I have pointed out before, classic 'judicial evasion'—the court effectively decides a case by not deciding it, because the status quo so obviously favours one party (most times, the government) (see here[170] and here[171]).

Slouching towards the Executive: The Voice Samples Case

This post would be incomplete before highlighting one final, extraordinary judgment of the former Chief Justice (no, not Ayodhya). In August, he headed a bench that found that the mandatory taking of voice samples during the interrogation of accused persons was not covered by any statute. Now, this should have been the end of the matter. If there's no statutory authority for taking voice samples—a process that undeniably infringes the right to privacy at the threshold (whether it is a justified infringement is another matter)—voice samples cannot be taken. Simple. The legislature has to amend the CrPC to allow it, and the amendment can be tested before the courts on constitutional grounds.

The former Chief Justice, however, invoked Article 142 of the Constitution to *judicially authorize* the mandatory taking of voice samples. As I pointed out at the time, this was utterly flawed and

---

170 'Judicial Evasion and the Electoral Bonds Case', Indian Constitutional Law and Philosophy, 13 April 2019, https://indconlawphil.wordpress.com/2019/04/13/judicial-evasion-and-the-electoral-bonds-case/

171 Gautam Bhatia, 'Supreme Court's Interim Order on Electoral Bonds Is Disappointing', *Hindustan Times*, 13 April 2019, https://www.hindustantimes.com/columns/sc-s-interim-order-on-electoral-bonds-is-disappointing/story-yIzsFRChHZMoMZwbezMk4N.html

profoundly dangerous.[172] Because, once again, the court was running roughshod over the most basic structural principles of the Constitution. Instead of the normal route, where laws are passed that prima facie infringe rights and are then tested before the courts, the court was *itself* legitimizing a rights-infringing procedure *before it had even been legislated, or even argued on merits before it!* And this, indeed, was the apotheosis of the executive court—judging a case, making law and implementing it all at once in service of an amorphous public interest that remains forever undefined.

Conclusion: At the Crossroads

I have not, in this post, examined the Constitution bench cases that have been delivered this week (although I have analysed them in separate blog posts). The *RTI* and the *Tribunals* judgments are regular judgments, analysed under regular legal frameworks. If this was all that the former Chief Justice's tenure consisted of, there would have been no need to write this post today.

Nor have I analysed the odd 'review' judgment in the *Sabarimala* case, judicial evasion and the strange final order in the *Alok Verma* case[173] or the 'balanced' order that never was in the Karnataka MLAs' defection case.[174] These are issues that will probably occupy political scientists in the years to come. This post, on the other hand, has attempted to

---

172 'The Supreme Court on Mandatory Voice Samples – II: The Rise of the Executive Court', Indian Constitutional Law and Philosophy, 4 August 2019, https://indconlawphil.wordpress.com/2019/08/04/the-supreme-court-on-mandatory-voice-samples-ii-the-rise-of-the-executive-court/

173 Gautam Bhatia, 'Judicial Evasion and the Status Quo', *The Hindu*, 10 January 2019, https://www.thehindu.com/opinion/lead/judicial-evasion-and-the-status-quo/article25953052.ece

174 'Postscript: The Supreme Court's Problematic Order in the Karnataka Case', The Indian Constitutional Law and Philosophy, 17 July 2019, https://indconlawphil.wordpress.com/2019/07/17/postscript-the-supreme-courts-problematic-order-in-the-karnataka-case/

show that the dominant tone of the former Chief Justice's tenure has been marked by a series of extraordinary judgments that fall within a coherent pattern—the rise and rise of the executive court.

I should be clear that this is not an issue pertaining solely to the former Chief Justice. It is not just Court No. 1 on Bhagwan Das Road that does this; the issue is a structural one, affecting courts across the board.[175] This has been accompanied by the courts resiling from core functions such as policing the bounds of electoral democracy. Electoral bonds is the most glaring example, but the rejection of totalizer machines (that guarantee voter anonymity and protect the secret ballot) and the VVPAT issue are others.[176]

But it is important to focus on the former Chief Justice and his court for two reasons. First, as I have indicated, there is a ripple effect that flows from what the Supreme Court does, especially in high-profile cases that invariably end up in Court No. 1, to other courts. And secondly, as the above analysis should demonstrate, in the former Chief Justice's tenure, the executive court has come to the fore in a particularly concentrated form. Taking over large-scale administrative exercises, sealed covers, undermining of evidentiary rules, disregard of constitutional rights, the abuse of Article 142—all of this, and more, has defined the past thirteen months.

This leads to two conclusions. The first concerns those who study, write and speak about the Supreme Court. For many years, there has been an established model to study constitutional courts in democratic republics (especially courts vested with the power of judicial review)—as counter-majoritarian institutions (that may sometimes succeed but often fail to check majoritarian impulses), as (imperfect but important)

---

175 Gautam Bhatia, 'The Fear of Executive Courts', *The Hindu*, 14 December 2018, https://www.thehindu.com/opinion/lead/the-fear-of-executive-courts/article25735185.ece
176 Gautam Bhatia, 'An Ineffectual Angel', *The Hindu*, 29 April 2019, https://www.thehindu.com/opinion/lead/an-ineffectual-angel/article26974278.ece

protectors of rights and as institutions that, at the end of the day, are built on a process of open and public reasoning and deliberations. Under the former Chief Justice, though, I would suggest that the court has departed so far from these fundamental principles that it is unrecognizable as a 'court' under the classical model. To continue to act *as if it was*, then, would be to make a category mistake. And this is why I have used the term 'executive court'—the trappings remain, but the substance is radically different.

The second, of course, concerns the court itself. We stand at a crossroads, and there is a clear choice that faces the court. It may keep walking down the road it has chosen in recent times (and there is a continuity between the tenure of the last-but-one Chief Justice and that of the former Chief Justice, but that is a discussion for another day). It may carry on with the disastrous management of the NRC, continue with sealed covers, keep acting as if habeas corpus is a weird Latin term with no relevance to India in 2019, keep evading crucial constitutional cases where the status quo benefits the government, and double down on Article 142. It may keep doing that, and soon there will be little left to call it a 'court' in the true sense.

Or, it may remember once again Patanjali Sastri J's words—back in the days when the government actually lost some constitutional cases when it mattered—that the role of the court is that of '*a sentinel on the qui vive*'. It may recall Justice Khanna's admonition, that '*the history of personal liberty is largely the history of insistence upon procedure*'. And it may recover its classic role as the counter-majoritarian institution that stands between the individual and unaccountable, arbitrary State power.

The choice has never been clearer. And the jury, as they say, is out.

5

Evasion, Hypocrisy and Duplicity: The Legacy of Chief Justice Bobde

(23 April 2021)

AT MIDNIGHT TODAY, SHARAD Bobde will no longer be the Chief Justice of India.

As on previous occasions, this post will assess the legacy of the outgoing Chief Justice. In the case of Chief Justice Bobde, this might seem a somewhat difficult task. What can one even say about a tenure that lasted seventeen months, through a particularly stormy time, and yielded precisely zero judgments of constitutional import, other than a late set of guidelines on the appointment of ad-hoc judges? But, as we shall see, the absence of constitutional judgments does not mean that CJI Bobde did not enjoy a hugely consequential tenure. Through a refusal to hear cases (judicial evasion), shoddily reasoned 'interim orders' (hypocrisy) and the arbitrary allocation of cases under the 'master of the roster' powers (duplicity), CJI Bobde's tenure saw the further acceleration of trends that begun under his predecessors—that of the Supreme Court, in effect, turning into an executive court. The difference between CJI Bobde and his predecessors was that under the latter, there were still occasions when the Supreme Court continued to act like a 'court' as we understand it. Under CJI Bobde, there was very little evidence of that.

I preface this post with three caveats. *First*, many of the interim orders that I will discuss were per curiam, i.e., authored and signed by all the judges on the bench. While CJI Bobde, by virtue of being the Chief Justice, headed those benches, in formal terms, he was not the sole author of those orders—the 'bench', as a whole, was. The reason these orders are discussed as CJI Bobde's legacy is that, as any observer knows, most puisne judges rarely disagree with the senior judge on the bench. Disagreement is even rarer when the senior judge is the Chief Justice. Thus, while this post is not meant to absolve puisne judges of their responsibility in being co-signatories to the orders that it will critique, its central thesis—that they constitute the legacy of CJI Bobde—remains intact.

Secondly, it may be argued that conducting constitutional hearings with multiple judges and a battery of lawyers was no longer feasible once the pandemic began and the lockdown was imposed. To this, two answers may be made. First, the Supreme Court was functioning normally during the first five months of CJI Bobde's tenure, but the only significant constitutional hearings were repeated attempts to send the *Sabarimala* case to a bench of nine judges and the referral hearing in Article 370. More importantly, however, during the pandemic, constitutional courts all over the world made arrangements to hear significant cases online. And a five-judge bench of the Supreme Court itself heard the *Maratha Reservation* case earlier this year. Consequently, the pandemic itself was no reason for the court to not schedule—and hear—matters of constitutional import.

Thirdly, in view of various remarks that fell from the Supreme Court today, it feels important to reiterate that critique is neither personal nor 'destructive' of the institution. Supreme Court judges wield tremendous power, and Chief Justices even more so. This blog has always taken the view that the function of words is to call power to account, and, when necessary, do so adversarially. This post continues in that spirit.

Two Days in Spring

CJI Bobde's tenure is perhaps best summed up by what transpired in Courtroom No. 1 of the Supreme Court on two days. On 26 March 2021, a three-judge bench comprising CJI Bobde and Justices Bopanna and Ramasubramanian passed an interim order refusing to stay the electoral bonds scheme, which allows for limitless, anonymous corporate donations to political parties.[177] The electoral bonds scheme had been notified at the beginning of 2018, and been immediately challenged thereafter. At the time, Dipak Misra J was Chief Justice. He did not list it for a substantive hearing. Then came Chief Justice Gogoi, who initially followed suit, then listed the matter on an urgent application just before the 2019 general election, and hypocritically claimed that there was not enough time to hear such an important case. This judicial hypocrisy was raised to the level of fine art during the tenure of CJI Bobde. He *also* did not hear the matter throughout his tenure, before listing an urgent interim application just before the (still-ongoing) state elections and granting it one day of hearing. Going further than CJI Gogoi, CJI Bobde wrote in his order that the fact that the 'bonds had been released without any impediment in 2018, 2019 and 2020' was one of the grounds why there was no urgent necessity for a stay. The Supreme Court's own evasion of the case, thus, became a ground for it to deny relief to the petitioners.

Not only that, however, CJI Bobde's order went on to grant a presumptive seal of approval to the electoral bonds scheme, based on a series of logical leaps and absurd presumptions (summed up here[178]). A starring role was played by the court's observation that electoral bonds were not, actually, anonymous. Anyone who wanted to know who was

---

177 *Association for Democratic Reforms vs Union of India*, supra (26 March 2021).
178 Manu Sebastian, 'Supreme Court's Refusal to Stay Electoral Bonds Undermines Transparency in Electoral Process', Live Law, 27 March 2021, https://www.livelaw.in/columns/supreme-courts-refusal-to-stay-electoral-bonds-undermines-transparency-in-electoral-process-171836

donating to a political party could simply look up companies' financial statements, political parties' statements of accounts and then engage in a 'match the following' exercise. However, as commentators pointed out, this was simply false, as a *matter of law and fact*. Thanks to various legal amendments that accompanied the enactment of the electoral bonds scheme, a *'match the following'* exercise was not possible. That apart, even if it was, this was an astounding argument coming from a court that has, in the past, piously commented on the 'right to know' in the context of elections, that citizens, to be able to find out who funds political parties, would have to access a political party's statement of account, look at the numbers, access (all?) companies' annual statements, look at the numbers and see if anything matched. That CJI Bobde believed this was a legitimate burden to foist upon the voting public was extremely revealing. Not only was the order shoddily reasoned, but *even if the arguments had been correct on their own terms*, all they revealed was contempt for citizens' rights and a bending over backwards to shield the government from scrutiny.[179]

Later that same day, CJI Bobde, sitting in a bench of three, heard a case involving the deportation of Rohingya refugees to Myanmar. The hearing stood out for a range of unverified statements made by government counsel, CJI Bobde's apparent bewilderment that Article 21 applied to non-citizens, and, in particular, his refusal to hear counsel for the UN Special Rapporteur. This last was another particularly hypocritical move, given that the Supreme Court has, over the previous four decades, built its reputation on the basis of how it has relaxed the rules of standing to protect fundamental rights. A few days later, however, the bench's order on the hearing surpassed even his order in

---

179 Note, however, that electoral bonds are asymmetrical, in that the government, via the SBI, is in a position to know who is donating money. This is why judicial evasion in this case has the effect of benefiting the central executive.

the electoral bonds case. As I wrote here,[180] the order ignored every contention that had actually been raised by the petitioners' counsel. It recorded 'serious allegations' by the Union of India (pertaining to national security and to 'touts') without any scrutiny. And on the issue of the political persecution in Myanmar, which was directly relevant to the principle of *non-refoulement*, it made the wholly illogical remark, '*We cannot comment on what is happening in another country.*' In short, CJI Bobde's bench condemned the refugees to be deported to a country that had engaged in a genocidal war of persecution against them, in an 'interim order' that could not muster up a single legal—or logical— argument in its defence.

The second day was 22 April, one day before CJI Bobde's retirement. As India reeled from the second wave of Covid-19, a number of high courts sprang into action to protect citizens' right to life: the Delhi High Court and the Bombay High Court passed crucial orders on the availability of oxygen supply. The Delhi High Court, indeed, sat until after 10 p.m. to ensure that oxygen reached hospitals so that patients' lives could be saved. The very next day, however, acting on an application filed by Vedanta Ltd asking that it be allowed to reopen its closed plant for the purposes of manufacturing oxygen, the court created a 'suo motu' petition with respect to Covid-19. It appointed Vedanta's counsel, Harish Salve, as an amicus (he withdrew the next day). It then passed an extraordinary order justifying what was effectively an attempt to interfere with high courts that were doing their job. CJI Bobde, joined by Justices Bhat and Rao, noted that '*the High Courts have passed certain orders which may have the effect of accelerating and prioritising the services to a certain set of people and slowing down the*

---

[180] 'Complicity in Genocide: The Supreme Court's Interim Order in the Rohingya Deportation Case', The Indian Constitutional Law and Philosophy, 8 April 2021, https://indconlawphil.wordpress.com/2021/04/08/complicity-in-genocide-the-supreme-courts-interim-order-in-the-rohingya-deportation-case/

availability of these resources to certain other groups whether the groups are local, regional or otherwise.[181]

Now this is a very serious accusation, and one would expect that when the Supreme Court effectively accuses high courts of acting to benefit their own jurisdictions, it would be accompanied by unimpeachable evidence. However, there was *zero*—yes, *zero*—evidence that accompanied the order. CJI Bobde and his brother judges did not produce a *single* high court order that, according to them, had 'slowed down the availability of resources' to any group. And it was on the basis of this unproven assertion—along with many other dubious claims (see this thread[182]) that the court issued notice and asked various petitioners to show cause why 'common orders' should not be passed on an extraordinarily broad range of issues, from the 'supply of oxygen' to the 'method and manner of vaccines'. Once again, the judicial hypocrisy was striking—throughout his tenure, CJI Bobde had repeatedly told petitioners to 'approach the high courts', that 'we are trying to discourage Article 32 petitions', and, in an extra-judicial interview during the first wave of Covid, publicly taken an 'executive knows best, the courts should refrain from interfering' line when it came to judicial scrutiny of State action during the pandemic.[183]

---

181 In Re: Distribution of Essential Supplied and Services During Pandemic, Suo Motu WP (C) No. 3/2021 (22 April 2021).

182 https://twitter.com/ideepakjoshi/status/1385235033078702082

183 The day after the hearing, the Supreme Court bench observed that people were misrepresenting its order, especially as it had not stayed the high court proceedings. This is disingenuous. The absence of a formal stay (which would have been truly indefensible) is not a ground for praise, and nor does it indicate an absence of interference. A record of oral arguments before the court shows that government counsel specifically stated that they would inform the various high courts that the Supreme Court had taken cognisance of the matter. Indeed, later the same day, government counsel did exactly that. It is a different matter that the various high courts elected to proceed with the cases before them, nonetheless. That apart, the Supreme Court's order, in asking petitioners before the various high courts to 'show cause' why common

There is a pattern to these three orders (which—taken together, and other than the Article 224 A guidelines—are probably the only significant orders on constitutional issues that CJI Bobde's benches passed during his tenure, other than the initial, wholly unprincipled expansion of the court's review jurisdiction of the *Sabarimala* issue, whose unprincipled character was revealed in how the court refused to apply it in the first significant review case before it after *Sabarimala*, i.e. the *Aadhaar Review*). *First,* they were all 'interim orders', passed while the underlying substantive petitions remained unheard. In the first two cases, the substantive petitions were pending for years, a classical form of judicial evasion where the court's failure to decide a case benefits the Central government; in the third case, the basis of Vedanta's application was a pending petition. *Secondly,* they were passed on the basis of factual and legal assertions that were either entirely speculative or blatantly untrue. *Thirdly,* arguments inconvenient to the conclusion were simply ignored. And *fourthly,* the outcome, in each of these cases, favoured the central executive. In sum, the effect of the Supreme Court's conduct was to turn it into an extended arm of the executive, either through silence or through unreasoned decrees.

Evasion

Previously on this blog, I have defined 'judicial evasion' in the following terms:

> [B]y keeping a case pending, and delaying adjudication, the Court effectively decides it in favour of one of the parties (most often, the party in a stronger position, i.e., the government), simply by allowing status quo to continue.

---

orders should not be passed on a range of issues is problematic on its own terms, for reasons discussed in the body of the blog post.

At the time that CJI Bobde's tenure began, in November 2019, the following important constitutional cases were pending adjudication:

- The constitutional challenge to the effective abrogation of Article 370, and the splitting of the erstwhile state of Jammu and Kashmir into two union territories (from 6 August 2019).
- The constitutional challenge to EWS reservations (from 10 January 2019).
- The constitutional challenge to the Aadhaar amendment ordinance (later the Act) (from July 2019).
- Judicial review over money bills (from 13 November 2019).

At the beginning of CJI Bobde's tenure, the constitutional challenge to the Citizenship (Amendment) Act (CAA), 2019 also came to court.

CJI Bobde's tenure, as mentioned above, lasted seventeen months. On the date of his retirement, *not one* of these cases had been substantively heard or decided. In each of these cases, with the possible exception of the CAA, judicial evasion directly favoured the central executive. In the 370/union territory cases, it allowed the continued consolidation of a status quo that has, by now, turned into a fait accompli (recall that although the case itself was not before the Chief Justice, the power of constituting Constitution benches remains within the sole prerogative of the Chief Justice). In the EWS reservations case, in the absence of a stay, the reservations in question continue. The Aadhaar amendment ordinance—which sought to revive provisions of the Aadhaar Act that were struck down by the Supreme Court in the *Puttaswamy* judgment—continues to be in force. So does the Aadhaar Act itself, which would fail if the court were to find that judicial review over speakers' certification of money bills was indeed permissible (although with Aadhaar, once again, fait accompli means it is difficult to see how ground realities will now be reversed, regardless of legal outcomes).

Seventeen months. Not a single judgment on any of these constitutional issues. There is little more to say, other than to point out that under CJI Bobde, the Supreme Court facilitated the creation of multiple fait accompli that directly benefited the central executive.

Hypocrisy

I have, in the first section of this post, dealt with three 'interim orders' passed by benches headed by CJI Bobde's benches that stand out for their lack of reasoning, reliance on incorrect or misleading facts and pro-executive outcomes. A fourth example is perhaps the most egregious of the lot. In February 2020, in a detailed and reasoned order, the Karnataka High Court granted bail to twenty-one CAA protesters. The matter was appealed to the Supreme Court, where CJI Bobde, alongside Justices Gavai and Surya Kant, *stayed* the bail order, ensuring that individuals who had been set at liberty by the high court would have to *stay in jail* pending trial. This order stayed in force for six months, until in September 2020, the Supreme Court quietly lifted it. At no point did CJI Bobde's bench provide any reasoning for why twenty men had to spend six months in jail, even after the high court had ordered their release. No reasoning was given for why the high court's order was insufficient or what had changed in six months to make it sufficient. This, in other words, is rule by interim order, where CJI Bobde's bench exempted itself from the obligation of providing reasons for its (hugely consequential) actions.

Duplicity

The Supreme Court of India has twenty-nine judges. As might be expected, these judges hold very different views on a range of issues, including the interpretation of fundamental rights. Some judges set a very high store by personal liberty and believe that the State ought to be held to strict account when it curtails the liberty of citizens. Other judges view personal liberty as something of a nuisance, and see nothing wrong with individuals spending months or years behind bars without trial.

This multiplicity of views does not mean, however, as some scholars have argued, that 'there is not one Supreme Court, but fourteen Supreme Courts of India'. This is not true for the simple reason that, after a series of judgments delivered during the tenure of CJI Dipak Misra (discussed on this blog), the Chief Justice, as master of the roster, has absolute, opaque and uncanalized power in assigning cases to specific benches: *Others abide our question, thou art free.* Let us, therefore, be clear that until the master-of-the-roster system is reformed, there is one Supreme Court, and that is the Supreme Court of the Chief Justice of India. It follows that when that court speaks with a forked tongue, the responsibility lies on precisely one set of shoulders—the Chief Justice.

As an example of this forked tongue under the tenure of CJI Bobde, compare the contrasting fortunes of two members of the media, Arnab Goswami and Siddique Kappan. Both were arrested and incarcerated at around the same time, in October/November 2020. The Maharashtra government booked Goswami for abetment to suicide, while Kappan was 'picked up' while on his way to cover the Hathras gang rape and later booked under the National Security Act, 1980 (for a detailed timeline, see here[184]). Petitions on behalf of both individuals landed before the Supreme Court—Goswami's through a special leave petition challenging an order of the Bombay High Court refusing him bail, and Kappan's (initially) through

---

184 Aishwarya S. Iyer, '188 Days and Counting: Kappan's Habeas Corpus Plea Pending in SC', The Quint, 13 April 2021, https://www.thequint.com/news/india/siddique-kappan-habeas-corpus-plea-supreme-court-delayed#read-more

a habeas corpus under Article 32 of the Constitution.[185] Goswami's case was listed overnight, heard, and bail was (correctly) granted; in a judgment delivered later in the month of November, Chandrachud J (correctly) stated that 'even a day' spent in jail was a day too many from the perspective of personal liberty.

None of that, however, had any bearing on Kappan's case, which the CJI kept for himself. First, the CJI asked why Kappan's lawyers couldn't approach the Allahabad High Court (a particular irony, given the CJI's strenuous efforts to stop the high courts from functioning on the penultimate day of his tenure). Then, on multiple days the case was adjourned while CJI Bobde was busy hearing the corporate dispute between the Tatas and Cyrus Mistry. On the date of writing this piece, more than *six months* have passed since Kappan's arrest. The Supreme Court—which ruled on the validity of Goswami's bail in a single day—hasn't seen it fit to pass a reasoned judgment yet. Kappan remains in jail, with the latest news being that he has been hospitalized with Covid. If, as A.G. Noorani wrote, that Chief Justice Gogoi had driven 'a coach and four' upon the writ of habeas corpus—the last bastion of the individual against State overreach—then CJI Bobde came back for the remains and drove a truck over them, just to make sure that the writ was truly dead.

As I have said above, this is not a case of polyvocality or the dissonance of jurisprudence, which comes with twenty-nine judges in a single institution. That excuse cannot fly when the Chief Justice retains absolute powers of case allocation. It is, then, not dissonance, but duplicity—duplicity in the exercise of the powers of the master of the roster, which, as this blog has pointed out before, in the context of the structure of the Supreme Court, have transformed

---

185 To forestall an inevitable—and flawed—objection, technically, the requirement for admission of a special leave petition is meant to be more stringent than that of an Article 32 petition, with the hint being in the word 'special'.

into *substantive* powers to direct the outcomes of cases. This is, of course, a single example. They could be multiplied.

Conclusion: The Mouse under the Throne

As with previous posts, I have limited this critique to CJI Bobde's judicial orders and to his conduct as the master of the roster. I have not, therefore, considered a range of problematic statements made in court, such as, 'we will hear the case when the violence stops', 'the RTI is being misused' and 'women should not be at protests'. These are on the record, and history will judge.

Some commentators have classified Chief Justice Bobde's tenure as that of a CJI who, effectively, did nothing in the face of multiple crises. This is a tempting—and not entirely incorrect—position to take. After all, it was under the stewardship of CJI Bobde that the Supreme Court, for all practical purposes, barring a few honourable exceptions, went missing during the first wave of Covid-19, its behaviour—and deference to the central executive—particularly egregious during the migrants' crisis; and it was under the stewardship of CJI Bobde that vital constitutional cases went into cold storage, if not buried altogether.

In my view, however, this would be a mistake. When summing up the tenure of CJI Gogoi, I wrote that he had overseen the rise of the executive court, a court that spoke the language of the executive and had become indistinguishable from it. Under CJI Bobde, this process was accelerated, but in a more insidious form. Because, while you can critique a judgment, it is much harder to critique a non-judgment, or a five-page interim order (although the shoddiness of the interim orders in question, as pointed out above, makes them fail even on their own terms). It is much more difficult to show how *inaction* has the effect of benefiting the central executive and unpack judicial evasion, rather than to show how a *judgment* is flawed in its understanding of fundamental rights and State power. But the entire tenure of CJI Bobde, as we have seen, was either evasion or judgment by interim order, where in either case, and invariably, the executive always prevailed.

Thus, perhaps the best image for understanding where CJI Bobde has brought the Supreme Court is this: In classical literature, the judiciary is sometimes called 'lions under the throne' (via Bacon). The implications, for present-day jurisprudence, are obvious. The task of the judiciary is to keep a check on the rulers without supplanting them. But now think of a mouse under the throne, who sometimes squeaks and sometimes ventures out to bite the toes of anyone coming before the ruler. One need not press the image too hard, but only say: A judiciary on its way to becoming a mouse under the throne is a sad sight indeed.

6

The Sound of Silence: The Legacy of Chief Justice N.V. Ramana

(26 August 2022)

SINCE 2018, THIS BLOG has assessed the legacies of Chief Justices of India upon their retirement. For the first two of these—Chief Justices Dipak Misra and Ranjan Gogoi—there was no shortage of material. These Chief Justices wielded their powers as 'masters of the roster' to hear (some) important constitutional cases, and cases involving high political stakes. The outcomes of these cases were critiqued, but at least there were cases, and there were outcomes.

With respect to Chief Justice Bobde—the last but one CJI—the situation was different. As I wrote upon his retirement, this was a seventeen-month-long tenure that yielded precisely zero judgments of constitutional import. Nonetheless, it was a consequential tenure, as the court's maintenance of the status quo directly benefited the political executive, and because, even though he didn't deliver judgments, Bobde CJI passed various interim orders that were also in favour of the political executive. CJI Bobde's tenure was also consequential because of the arbitrary allocation of cases to various benches that led to the

Supreme Court speaking with a 'forked tongue' when it came to crucial matters involving life and personal liberty.

CJI N.V. Ramana, who retires today, took over from CJI Bobde on 24 April 2021. When we look back at his sixteen-month tenure, the picture that emerges is similar to that of his predecessor, with one marked difference. Unlike CJI Bobde—and indeed, before him, CJI Gogoi—CJI Ramana did not indulge in the intemperate and partisan pro-State broadsides that had become something of a habit for his predecessors. To those who value appearances, this is no doubt important. However, once you strip away the rhetoric and focus on the record, it becomes easier to see the similarities between CJI Ramana and his immediate predecessor.

Judicial Evasion and the Sound of Silence

The most striking feature of CJI Ramana's sixteen-month tenure is the sound of silence. When he took over as Chief Justice in April 2021, the following crucial constitutional cases were pending:

- The constitutional challenge to electoral bonds (which allow unlimited, anonymous corporate funding of political parties) (from September 2017).
- The constitutional challenge to the effective abrogation of Article 370 and the splitting of the erstwhile state of Jammu and Kashmir into two union territories (from 6 August 2019).
- The constitutional challenge to EWS reservations (from 10 January 2019).
- The constitutional challenge to the Aadhaar amendment ordinance (later the Act) (from July 2019).
- Judicial review over money bills (from 13 November 2019).
- The constitutional challenges to the CAA (from December 2019).

During CJI Ramana's tenure, *not one* of these cases was decided. In effect, they have now been pending for sixteen months longer than they were when he took office. Indeed, the CJI's tenure—exactly like CJI Bobde's—did not see a single significant constitutional *judgment* (with the possible exception of the *Benami Act* judgment, delivered in his final week).

Why does this non-decision matter? It matters because in all these cases (other than the CAA case), the status quo directly benefits the political executive. This is what I call 'judicial evasion'. Judicial evasion is defined thus:

> [B]y keeping a case pending, and delaying adjudication, the Court effectively decides it in favour of one of the parties (most often, the party in a stronger position, i.e., the government), simply by allowing status quo to continue.

Judicial evasion is most starkly visible in the court consistently refusing to decide the electoral bonds case, even as election cycle after election cycle sees vast amounts of money being fuelled into the political system, with a disproportionate amount going to the ruling party (the reason for this is that, structurally, under the electoral bonds scheme, the government has access to donor data, while Opposition parties do not). This is a distortion of the electoral playing field—the ground rules of democracy—at its starkest, and exactly the kind of situation where the Supreme Court's role as constitutional umpire is most desperately needed. It is also the case where the political stakes are particularly high, and where the status quo benefits the political executive to a very high degree. Readers may, therefore, make up their own minds about what the continued refusal by the Supreme Court to hear and decide the case—a tradition in which CJI Ramana now follows his three predecessors—means. The consequences of judicial evasion are, in addition, clearly visible in the *Article 370* case and the *Aadhaar* case, where continued inaction by the court results in the creation of a fait accompli 'on the ground' that eventually becomes irreversible in fact, and makes a court judgment effectively infructuous.

For the sake of completeness, it is important here to briefly flag the *Maharashtra Political Crisis* case, where the Supreme Court changed speed and direction more quickly than a fencer. In June, when the political crisis was at its height, a vacation bench of the Supreme Court swiftly heard the case, effectively suspended the Tenth Schedule through an interim order and then compelled a floor test within twenty-four hours through a second interim order, having just immunized MLAs under threat of disqualification through the first order. Expectedly, the government fell. Once the new government came in, and court vacations ended, the matter came before the CJI. At this point, all the urgency the court had shown before vanished like a dream. The CJI showed no inclination to hear the case, suggested referring it to a Constitution bench (a guaranteed months-long delay), while the effects of the interim order—i.e., a wholesale change in government—continued, and continued to entrench themselves with each passing day. In effect, the interim orders, with all their huge consequences, for all practical purposes, seem to have become final.[186]

The One Case: Pegasus

The Pegasus spying scandal broke in July 2021. Shortly thereafter, the Supreme Court was approached. The *Pegasus* case is the only

---

[186] Almost one year after the fact, a Constitution bench decided the case, holding that the governor's calling of the floor test was illegal, but because the chief minister had resigned (as a consequence, it might be noted, of the Supreme Court's interim order), nothing could now be done about the situation. For a critique, see 'The Supreme Court's Maharashtra Political Crisis Judgment - I: To Be Hoisted on Someone Else's Petard', Indian Constitutional Law and Philosophy, 11 May 2023, https://indconlawphil.wordpress.com/2023/05/11/the-supreme-courts-maharashtra-political-crisis-judgment-i-to-be-hoisted-on-someone-elses-petard/

significant constitutional case that CJI Ramana handled himself, and its fate is instructive.

Let us begin with a caveat: The Supreme Court could have declined to hear this case. It could have said that the case belonged to the political thicket, or that the question of surveillance raised national-security issues that automatically took it outside the ken of the court's jurisdiction (indeed, this was strenuously argued by the solicitor-general). Had the court done that, the matter would have been fought out in the public sphere (such as it is), without judicial involvement.

The court did not do that. CJI Ramana was at great pains to stress that 'national security' was not a shibboleth that could be invoked to oust the jurisdiction of the Supreme Court. But here's the thing: Once the court agreed to take on the case, once it held that its jurisdiction had been properly invoked, a heavy burden lay upon it to do its job and vindicate citizens' rights against State impunity. This is because, now, the outcome of the case would have *judicial sanction*. Were the court to shield the State from accountability for mass surveillance, it would, in effect, amount to judicial validation, and stymie, if not bury, any other attempts at accountability.

Unfortunately, the bench, headed by CJI Ramana, completely failed to hold the State accountable. During multiple hearings in August and September 2021, the government categorically refused to state to the court, including in affidavit, whether Pegasus had been used by it or not. Note that this was not a question about specific details, which might raise questions around national security. As I wrote at the time, it was a straightforward 'yes' or 'no' question that the court was well within its rights to ask. Indeed, without this basic fact (which was also not forthcoming from the government in Parliament), nothing could proceed further. However, for two and a half months, the bench led by CJI Ramana refused to pass any consequential orders; indeed, not only did it refuse to pass consequential orders, but it also simultaneously *stopped* a committee (headed by a retired judge)—set up by the state of West Bengal—from examining the issues. What was the harm in a state government-appointed inquiry committee examining a potential case of mass surveillance? We do not know, but this is yet another example of a phenomenon that is growing increasingly common—when it comes to issues involving high political stakes (the FCRA matter is another recent example), the Supreme Court is loath to let any constituted authority other than itself have any say in the matter. This might still be justifiable if the court had a proud record of protecting citizens' rights. When, however, it has a proud record of protecting the State, it becomes a problem.

Instead, after a further delay of many months, the Supreme Court appointed its own 'committee' to look into the matter. This committee, in turn, took several more months before producing a report that was submitted to the court and taken up by CJI Ramana on his penultimate day in office (25 August 2022). What does the report say? We do not know, because the CJI refused to make it public. All we know is that there was 'no conclusive proof' to show that the malware that the committee found on five phones was Pegasus. But because the report is not public, it is impossible for cybersecurity experts to examine the methods used by the committee to arrive at its 'no conclusive proof' determination. We also know—because it was stated in court—that the government did not cooperate with the committee. What consequences follow from this? Presumably, none, because all that CJI Ramana ordered was that a set of recommendations—made by the judge heading the committee—about surveillance and privacy, be uploaded online. The value of these recommendations, as experience tells us, is not worth the digital space that they occupy.

CJI Ramana's handling of the *Pegasus* case inverts the relationship between the individual and the State, and the role of the court in protecting individual rights against State impunity. If fundamental rights mean anything at all, they mean that individuals who have reason to believe they have been subjected to State surveillance have the right to question that, to ask the basis upon which they have been surveilled, and to seek remedies. In the *Pegasus* case, the court's conduct ensured that at no point was the State made answerable for any of this—not before the court and not before the committee. To put a 'seal' on it (literally taking it in a sealed cover), the refusal to make the report public ensured that the citizen was not even in a position to question the basis on which the committee arrived at its 'no conclusive proof' determination.

In all but the name, this is what is called a 'whitewash'.

The Strange Controversy around 'Freebies'

Let no one think that his refusal to hear the electoral bonds case meant that CJI Ramana was uninterested in electoral issues. In the last month of his tenure, he suddenly, and inexplicably, took up a PIL asking the court to regulate and restrict political parties from offering 'freebies' during election campaigns. This 'freebies' case took up hours of court time (time that the court apparently never had to hear the electoral bonds case) and presented some truly astonishing spectacles, such as the counsel equating electoral promises to 'bribes' and the solicitor-general seeming to hint that it was impermissible for a political party to promise to eliminate a specific tax if they came to power.

As I have written elsewhere, the 'freebies' debate is not even a debate (as it suffers from definitional incoherence), and at the very least, not a debate that the court has jurisdiction to adjudicate. And, indeed, in his final week, CJI Ramana himself washed his hands off it—after repeatedly proposing to set up a 'committee' to look into the matter—by sending the matter off to another bench. However, the issue with the 'freebies' debate is not so much that finally, the court didn't 'do' anything—it is that for a number of days, the court's intervention set the public discourse (the issue was 'debated' on prime time by TV channels) *at the exact same time that the political executive was saying the exact same thing.*

To this, two other crucial things need to be added. The PIL that formed the basis of the 'freebies' debate in the Supreme Court was filed by a leader of the ruling party; and *in* court, the government's law officer, the solicitor-general, repeatedly egged the court on to find a way to prohibit 'freebies'.

Thus, if you were an external observer, you would see this:

- The head of the political executive criticizes 'freebies' in a public speech.
- Out of nowhere, the Supreme Court suddenly starts hearing a case on 'freebies', repeatedly calling it a 'very serious issue'.
- The 'freebies' case is itself filed by a leader of the ruling party.
- In the hearing, the solicitor-general and the court are completely at idem about how 'serious' the issue is, and the fact that 'freebies' need to be dealt with.

And if you were this same external observer, what would you conclude from this? Would you not conclude that the court and the executive were marching in lock-step, with the court providing *judicial* validation to what would otherwise have been a purely partisan piece of political propaganda? Would you not think that this appeared to be the behaviour of what I recently called 'the executive('s) court'?

Indeed, CJI Ramana's sudden obsession with regulating 'freebies' stands out all the more when you remember—and apologies for reiterating this yet again!—that there was a *genuine* issue concerning political-party funding that was pending before his court from the day he took office; and yet, instead of hearing and deciding the electoral bonds case, the CJI spent hours of judicial time on a case that, if we're being very charitable, was a non-issue—and if we're not, was yet another instance of the executive('s) court in action.

The Master of the Roster

In situations where a Chief Justice, during the course of his tenure, yields us with no significant constitutional decisions to analyse, some focus must then be cast on whether there were *judgments* during his tenure at all. This is important because the Chief Justice enjoys absolute power—as master of the roster—to assign (and re-assign) cases to various benches. That the Supreme Court, at any given time, has more than twenty-five judges is a fact. That judicial ideology exists is also a fact. What follows is that the Chief Justice's power of case allocation carries with it a *non-trivial* power to influence outcomes.

Let me be clear about two things. The first is that this is not a defence of the powers of the 'master of the roster'. This blog has repeatedly criticized the judgments that sanctified these powers. These judgments arose out of a specific crisis at the Supreme Court, where CJI Dipak Misra's authority was under threat and his response was to insulate himself from accountability for bench allocation. As I have maintained previously, in a polyvocal court such as the Supreme Court, the only fair system is either an arbitrary allocation or a permanent Constitution bench fixed according to seniority. But that said, this is the system we have right now. The Chief Justice *does* have absolute power to allocate cases among the judges of the Supreme Court. And this includes the absolute power to *re*-allocate cases (a power that has, indeed, been used before). For the reasons mentioned above, this does mean that the Chief Justice has power and influence over outcomes, and the choice to exercise this power—or not—therefore attracts scrutiny.

The second—related—point is this: The argument is *not* that there is some collusion between the Chief Justice and individual judges, where the Chief Justice simply escapes responsibility for pro-executive judgments by assigning them to reliably pro-executive judges instead of writing them himself. The point, rather, is that *given* the Chief Justice's powers as master of the roster, the CJI bears some degree of responsibility for the *overall record* of the court during his tenure, in a way that other judges of the court, who are responsible only for their own judgments, do not. And this becomes especially true when a Chief Justice has opted not to write constitutional judgments, and, instead, the heavy lifting in that regard has been done by others during his tenure (there is, of course, nothing wrong with the Chief Justice leaving certain cases to his colleagues—it is just that the nature of the scrutiny changes accordingly).

What, then, was the record of the Supreme Court on civil rights during CJI Ramana's tenure? It must be acknowledged, in fairness, that the strong bail order in Mohammad Zubair's case, handed down by a bench led by Chandrachud J, was a valuable order in the cause of civil liberties; so also was the refusal, by a bench led by Lalit J, to interfere with the default UAPA bail granted to Sudha Bharadwaj in the *Bhima Koregaon* case. One can very easily imagine different outcomes in both cases, had they gone to different benches of the Supreme Court. Thus, one must give credit to the CJI, as master of the roster, for assigning these civil rights cases to benches that have had a history of passing positive, pro-liberty orders in such cases before.

A Job Quarter-Done: The Sedition Case

Finally, one may point to the interim order passed by CJI Ramana's bench, which effectively put a stop to sedition prosecutions until further notice. There is little doubt that a halt on sedition prosecutions in the country is, in its own right, a good thing. But here again, context matters. The case in question was a challenge to the constitutional validity of sedition. The government attempted to buy time by stating that it would constitute a committee to look into whether sedition still served any purpose. To this, there is only one appropriate judicial response: to tell the government—politely, but firmly—that it was at perfect liberty to set up its committee, but that had no bearing on the constitutional case that the court was hearing.

CJI Ramana's bench, however, did not do so, and, instead, used the government's submission to pass its interim order. There are two problems with this. The first is that unlike a judgment, which has binding force, an interim order can be vacated at any time by whichever subsequent bench the case goes before. The second—as I have pointed out in some detail in this post[187]—is that given the vast range of criminal law provisions at the government's disposal to harass and jail its critics, not least the UAPA, any judicial order on sedition would, at best, be of merely symbolic value, unless it was accompanied by strong reasoning reiterating established constitutional principles on freedom of speech and limits to which the State could restrict rights—reasoning that could then be used to bring other, more draconian provisions in line with constitutional standards.

An interim order, by definition, fails to do any of that. And this is why it is a case of a job being quarter-done, at best. Yes, until further notice, people cannot be prosecuted for sedition, and that is a good thing. But, as we have seen repeatedly by now, if the State really wants to keep you in jail for years without trial, it does not need the sedition law to do that. When CJI Ramana took up the constitutional challenge to sedition, he had a chance to solve a few of those problems. Regrettably, however, the interim order that he finally passed did not do so.

Conclusion

It is not easy being a Supreme Court judge. It is specifically not easy being a Supreme Court judge in the time of an absolute majority government, whose approach to the Constitution is like Douglas Jardine's[188] approach to the Bodyline series—stretch the rules to their absolute breaking point and see what the umpire will let you get away with. It is reasonable for critics to temper their expectations of the court at times such as these, and to appreciate that—as a political actor with limited political capital—the court will have to negotiate a space for itself, and that negotiation will often require a degree of compromise.

---

187 'The Upcoming Sedition Case before the Supreme Court: Key Issues', Indian Constitutional Law and Philosophy, 2 May 2022, https://indconlawphil.wordpress.com/2022/05/02/the-upcoming-sedition-case-before-the-supreme-court-key-issues/

188 Douglas Jardine was a controversial English cricketer who was captain of England during the infamous 'Bodyline tour' of Australia.

But while one can sympathize with the difficult position that the court finds itself in, what is disappointing is when it appears that the court is not even trying. As with his predecessors, CJI Ramana's determination to avoid crucial constitutional cases with a ten-foot barge pole crosses the line from judicial caution to judicial pusillanimity—no matter how difficult the situation, there can be no excuse for the court refusing to do its basic job of at least attempting to hold the State to account. Why else do we have a Supreme Court in the first place?

But as the *Pegasus* case and the *Freebies* case show (in different contexts), what is worrying is not just the inability to protect rights, but the formation of the executive('s) court, which marches in lock-step with the executive, acting as both its shield and its sword. In *Pegasus*, the court acted as a shield, protecting the government from accountability—from the first day of the hearing, when it refused to ask the 'yes or no' question, to now, when it refused to publish the technical report of the committee. In the *Freebies* case, the court acted as the sword, amplifying, and providing judicial validation to, a debate that the political executive conjured up out of nowhere.

The executive('s) court did not begin with CJI Ramana. And we can perhaps be grateful that, at least, it did not become worse with him. We can also perhaps be grateful for the specks of light in his tenure, which were notably absent in the tenures of his predecessors—the *Benami Act* judgment, the last-day decision to reconsider Khanwilkar J's *PMLA* judgment (albeit on limited grounds), the interim order on sedition and the assignment of Mohammad Zubair's case to one of the more pro-liberty benches of the Supreme Court.

But at the end of the day, if we were to honestly ask ourselves, does he leave the court better than he found it, the answer would have to be 'no'. The Supreme Court's drift towards the executive court and the executive('s) court was neither reversed nor halted, but at best, perhaps temporarily kept in abeyance.

As CJI Ramana's tenure passes into history, we wait to see the direction in which his successors will now take the Supreme Court.

7

'The Freedom of One Single Human Spirit': On the Legacy of Chief Justice U.U. Lalit

(7 November 2022)

[**Update and Editorial Note:** Five days after the publication of the piece, former Chief Justice U.U. Lalit gave an interview to NDTV, where, among other things, he was asked about the Saturday-morning hearing that 'suspended' the Bombay High Court's judgment discharging G.N. Saibaba and five others in a UAPA case. As the Chief Justice sought to clarify the circumstances in which this special bench came to be constituted—something this blog post criticizes in some detail—in the interests of fairness, his response is provided up front. Readers may access it here.[189]

In my view, while the CJI's response goes some way towards clarifying the unusual composition of the bench, it does not satisfactorily explain the prior questions around the setting up of

---

189 NDTV, 'Ex Chief Justice UU Lalit: Nothing Unusual In Special Bench Hearing GN Saibaba Case', YouTube, https://www.youtube.com/watch?v=CP7OYCRcX6w

the 'special' Saturday-morning bench in the first place. That issue remains shrouded in ambiguity, and interested readers may also read this response to the Chief Justice's clarification.[190]]

THE FINAL CHAPTER OF Ursula K. Le Guin's legendary science fiction novel *The Dispossessed* features a conversation between the protagonist, Shevek, who is being hunted by his pursuers, and a representative of the Terran race, who can save his life. Shevek's discovery of the 'general temporal theory', which would make instant communication across space possible, places him in a strong bargaining position with respect to the Terrans, who desperately want it. Shevek, however, refuses to drive a hard bargain, and the following exchange takes place:

> 'I only ask your help, for which I have nothing to give in return.'
> 'Nothing? You call your theory nothing?'
> 'Weigh it in the balance with the freedom of one single human spirit,' he said, turning to her, 'and which will weigh heavier? Can you tell? I cannot.'

When we look back at the brief, four-month legacy of Chief Justice U.U. Lalit, the ending of *The Dispossessed* is perhaps an appropriate framework to think through what has happened.

It is true that four months is but a wrinkle in time. It is also true that these are four months in which a lot has happened. The live-streaming of Supreme Court proceedings, the setting up of Constitution benches, regular listings and mentionings, and the resurrection of cases long in cold storage are all things that people will point to when assessing the Chief Justice's legacy. Undoubtedly, when it comes to the administration of the Supreme Court as an institution, the brief,

---

190 https://twitter.com/OfficialSauravD/status/1591825371321995264

flickering tenure of CJI Lalit has accomplished significantly more than all of his immediate predecessors put together.

But in my mind, we must begin with the extraordinary events of 14–15 October 2022. On 14 October, the Bombay High Court handed down a judgment acquitting G.N. Saibaba and five others in a case under the UAPA.[191] The basis of the high court's judgment was that a vital procedural safeguard under the UAPA—the requirement of a sanction to prosecute, following an independent review of the evidence by the appropriate authority—had not been adhered to. Consequently, everything that came after, including the trial, was a nullity. In the result, Saibaba and five others, who had spent more than five years in jail at the time of writing, were to walk free.

The high court's judgment, however, carried a significance beyond simply the liberty of six individuals. By now, the weaponization of the UAPA for political repression has been well established. Its loose language and onerous bail provisions—facilitated by pro-executive judicial interpretation—have enabled the extended incarceration of individuals (including political opponents) for months and years, as well as the occasional conviction on flimsy grounds (Saibaba himself is an example). In this background context, the Bombay High Court's order sketched out a crucial line in the sand. If the State wanted to prosecute under the UAPA, it would have to go *by the book*—the statute's procedural safeguards would need to be complied with to the letter. Thus, the high court's order was, in essence, a judicial pushback against State impunity: Saibaba and his fellow prisoners were to be set free because the State had failed to meet the requirements needed to trigger the draconian, substantive provisions of the UAPA.

That freedom, however, turned out to be an illusion. That same evening, the case was 'mentioned' before the still-sitting bench of Chandrachud J. He correctly observed that there was no tearing hurry to list an appeal against a reasoned judgment of acquittal/discharge,

---

191 *Mahesh Kiriman Tirki vs State of Maharashtra*, Crl Appeal No. 136/2017 (14 October 2022).

and nor could such a judgment be stayed for the asking. But, of course, the State then had the liberty to approach Chief Justice Lalit for an urgent listing, which it did. The Chief Justice complied. The case was listed the next morning, which was a Saturday morning (a non-working day at the Supreme Court), before a 'special bench' of Justices M.R. Shah and Bela Trivedi (what is it with our Chief Justices and these Saturday-morning listings?). It is important to note that these two justices did not normally sit together and Justice M.R. Shah did not normally handle the criminal roster.

After a hearing, this bench of the Supreme Court 'suspended' the Bombay High Court's order on the basis that the offences were serious and that the high court had not considered the 'merits' of the case (instead proceeding on the technicality of sanction).[192] As a result, despite having a hundred-page reasoned order from a constitutional court sanctioning their liberty, the six prisoners (one of whom, G.N. Saibaba, is 90 per cent disabled) were condemned to stay in jail.

As many, many people have pointed out, the Supreme Court sitting on a Saturday morning to 'suspend' an order of discharge/acquittal and *keep* people in jail was historically unprecedented. Indeed, there is something profoundly disturbing about the Supreme Court holding special Saturday-morning sittings *against* individual liberty (as a certain senior counsel who often represents the State is fond of saying, 'would the heavens have fallen' if the Supreme Court had waited until the next working day?). But even more troubling is the manner in which this 'special' bench trashed the vital procedural safeguards under the UAPA as mere technicalities. While the high court had drawn a line in the sand against State impunity, the Saturday-morning 'suspension' reads like a paean *to* State impunity, not only in its reasoning, but also in the outcome. Pending consideration by the Supreme Court of the 'larger

---

192 *State of Maharashtra vs Mahesh Kariman Tirki and Ors*, SLP Crl. Diary No. 33164/2022 (15 October 2022).

issues' involved, despite having a high court judgment in their favour, G.N. Saibaba and others will stay in jail.[193]

Now, the question, of course, is what responsibility does CJI Lalit bear for this? Naturally, the *primary* responsibility lies with the authors of the order—Shah and Trivedi JJ. However, as I have written previously—in my assessment of the legacy of CJI Ramana—when we consider the record of a Chief Justice, we need to consider their actions as the 'master of the roster'—i.e., the position that gives them unlimited and arbitrary power to decide when a case will be heard and who will hear it. The opacity with which the office of the Chief Justice operates means that we will not know how, precisely, this decision was made and what the reasons for it were. However, what we do know is:

- The extraordinary decision to list the State's appeal against a reasoned order of acquittal/discharge on a Saturday morning—before the high court's order could be implemented—was CJI Lalit's decision, made in the exercise of his powers as master of the roster. I have questioned the urgency above; here, I will add that, for a variety of reasons, courts generally tend not to send released people *back* into jail. However, it is significantly easier for a court to suspend an acquittal/discharge that has not yet been implemented and when the individuals involved are *still* in jail. The Saturday-morning order accomplished precisely this.
- The decision to list it before a 'special' bench of two judges, who did not normally sit together, one of whom was not normally on the criminal roster and who, indeed, was previously on record making statements praising the sitting Prime Minister, which have raised serious concerns about the separation between the judiciary and the executive, was likewise a decision made by CJI Lalit. It is true that the roster is not always followed to the letter and is subject to

---

193 This was subsequently confirmed in a final judgment, a few months later.

the orders of the Chief Justice, but that only amplifies the point I am making here.

As I have written previously, in a polyvocal Supreme Court with more than twenty-five members, there will be some judges who will be reflexively pro-State in matters of individual liberty and there will be other judges who will be reflexively pro-individual. While there is nothing untoward about this—judicial ideology is inevitable and is distributed across the court—it is here that the powers of the Chief Justice as master of the roster, with the power to assign cases, turns into a power to significantly influence the *outcomes* of cases. This is specifically borne out by the fact that on Friday evening, Chandrachud J expressed severe reservations about the Supreme Court 'suspending' a reasoned high court order of acquittal/discharge, but the next morning, two other justices saw no compunctions in doing so. When you add to this the extraordinary Saturday-morning listing and the composition of a 'special' bench for just this case, the upshot of all this is that CJI Lalit's actions as the master of the roster on 14 October 2022 had a significant and non-trivial impact on the extraordinary judicial denial of liberty to G.N. Saibaba and five others. For that reason, notwithstanding the fact that he did not personally sit on the bench, the circumstances in which this order came about must play a significant role in the assessment of his legacy as he leaves the court.

For it is an order that characterizes the executive court at its worst, a court that speaks the language of the executive and that has, for all practical purposes, become indistinguishable from the executive. So if you were to ask yourself that basic question—did CJI Lalit leave the court better than he found it?—the events of 14 and 15 October must have their say. And what they say is that when it comes to the crunch, when the stakes are high, the Supreme Court is still an executive court, and, indeed, perhaps even more of an executive court than it was before. Because now not even reasoned high court judgments setting people free from jail are safe from being 'suspended' in under twenty-four hours.

But then you may ask: What of the balance sheet? What of the other things that CJI Lalit did as Chief Justice, which I flagged at the beginning of this post and which will, no doubt, feature heavily in the encomiums that accompany a judicial retirement? He granted bail to Teesta Setalvad and Siddique Kappan, two of the more egregious cases of State impunity in recent times. He listed many cases (although, like his predecessors, he steered clear of listing the Article 370 challenge and, regrettably, downgraded the electoral bonds challenge to a two-judge bench). He set up many Constitution benches (one of which even resulted in a judgment on the day of his retirement, albeit in favour of the State). He kick-started the live-streaming of court proceedings.

These are all good things, no doubt. But does organizational competence make up for the deprivation of freedom, as if the two things form part of the same currency, to be traded against one another? Or is freedom itself a tradable commodity, where bail to one individual justifies keeping six others in jail? Is not a live-streamed executive court, which sits on a Saturday morning to suspend an order of acquittal/discharge, still an executive court? And so, then, at the end of the day, when considering the 'good' that Lalit CJI did, we are left to ask ourselves the question that Shevek asked the Terran ambassador:

'Weigh it in the balance with the freedom of one single human spirit, and which will weigh heavier? Can you tell? I cannot.'

Epilogue
A Constitutionalism without a Court

(1 August 2020)

[**Editorial Note**: This is an excerpt from a post that was written on the seventh anniversary of the Indian Constitutional Law and Philosophy blog. The post summarized some of the more dispiriting developments of the year gone by and asked what, if anything, was the role of a legal writer at a time like the present. The following excerpt is by way of an answer, and an epilogue.]

IN LIGHT OF EVERYTHING that has happened, it is perhaps time to ask: Is the enterprise of legal writing worthwhile, or is it now an act of intellectual dishonesty? As Dahlia Lithwick asked a while ago in the context of the confirmation of Brett Kavanaugh:

> I've been waiting, chiefly in the hope that at some point I would get over it, as I am meant to do for the good of the courts, and the team, and the ineffable someday fifth vote which may occasionally come in exchange for enough bonhomie and good

grace. There isn't a lot of power in my failing to show up to do my job, *but there is a teaspoon of power in refusing to normalize that which was simply wrong, and which continues to be wrong.* I don't judge other reporters for continuing to go, and I understand the ways in which justices, judges, law professors, and clerks must operate in a world where this case is closed. Sometimes I tell myself that my new beat is justice, as opposed to the Supreme Court. *And my new beat now seems to make it impossible to cover the old one.*[194] *[Emphasis mine]*

But however impossible it feels at the moment, there are three reasons, I believe, that the process remains worthwhile, although it may need to be reshaped. In important and landmark works on the subject, such as *The Dual State* (dealing with the law in the Third Reich and discussing, among other things, 'ordinary courts' voluntary abdication of their powers of judicial review'[195]), *Legacies of Law, Politics by Other Means* (dealing with apartheid South Africa, including 'national security laws' and detentions), lawyers and legal scholars have deliberated upon the role that lawyering and legal writing can play before hostile courts. They correctly point out that whatever the court may do, and however it may act, it remains important at all times to articulate and defend *the rule of law* as an independent value, and to record and demonstrate how the actions of the court fall short in that respect. In other words, there must at all times be an active struggle to preserve the *idea* of the rule of law, despite, or even because of, what happens in the courts.

The second is that while the Supreme Court has come to occupy a disproportionate space in our mental landscape, the fact remains that it is not the only constitutional court in the country. Apart from

---

194 Dahlia Lithwick, 'Why I Haven't Gone Back to SCOTUS Since Kavanaugh', Slate, 30 October 2019, https://slate.com/news-and-politics/2019/10/year-after-kavanaugh-cant-go-back-to-scotus.html

195 Ernst Fraenkel, *The Dual State: A Contribution to the Theory of Dictatorship*, Lawbook Exchange, 2010, p. lxiv.

the fact that the court itself is a polyvocal institution with multiple judges (although the relevance of that fact is diminished because of the institutional issues discussed above), there exist numerous high courts, many of which have, on various occasions over the past year, stood up for the rule of law. See, for example, Karnataka and Allahabad on section 144 of the CrPC;[196] Bombay (on access to education);[197] Kerala, Calcutta, and Madras (on civil rights during Covid);[198] Madras (on free speech);[199] Gujarat (until an inexplicable change of bench) and Karnataka (on government accountability during covid);[200] Bombay (on medical access during covid);[201] and Andhra Pradesh (on electoral

---

196 'Civil Rights at the Bar of the High Courts: Section 144 in Karnataka, Privacy in UP', Indian Constitutional Law and Philosophy, 9 March 2020, https://indconlawphil.wordpress.com/2020/03/09/civil-rights-at-the-bar-of-the-high-courts-section-144-in-karnataka-privacy-in-up/
197 'To CAP or Not to CAP: The Bombay High Court on Equality and Access to Education', Indian Constitutional Law and Philosophy, 30 May 2020, https://indconlawphil.wordpress.com/2020/05/30/to-cap-or-not-to-cap-the-bombay-high-court-on-equality-and-access-to-education/
198 'CAA, Coronavirus, and Civil Rights at the Bar of the High Courts', Indian Constitutional Law and Philosophy, 22 March 2020, https://indconlawphil.wordpress.com/2020/03/22/caa-coronavirus-and-civil-rights-at-the-bar-of-the-high-courts/
199 'A Sullivan for the Times: The Madras High Court on the Freedom of Speech and Criminal Defamation', Indian Constitutional Law and Philosophy, 16 May 2020, https://indconlawphil.wordpress.com/2020/05/16/a-sullivan-for-the-times-the-madras-high-court-on-the-freedom-of-speech-and-criminal-defamation/
200 'Coronavirus and the Constitution – XXVIII: Dialogic Judicial Review in the Gujarat and Karnataka High Courts', Indian Constitutional Law and Philosophy, 24 May 2020, https://indconlawphil.wordpress.com/2020/05/24/coronavirus-and-the-constitution-xxviii-dialogic-judicial-review-in-the-gujarat-and-karnataka-high-courts/
201 Aakanksha Saxena, 'Coronavirus and the Constitution – XXXIII: N-95 Masks and the Bombay High Court's Dialogic Judicial Review', Indian Constitutional Law and Philosophy, 28 June 2020, https://indconlawphil.wordpress.com/2020/06/28/coronavirus-and-the-constitution-xxxiii-

independence).²⁰² Needless to say, some of these judgments were immediately stayed by the Supreme Court, sometimes ex parte and almost always without reasons, but it is important to engage with such decisions and avoid diminishing their importance.

And thirdly, whatever the court, or courts, may say or do, it is important to remember at all times that the Constitution is not reducible to the court. The Constitution remains a critical terrain where entrenched power relations can be challenged, undermined and democratized, and that process is crucial despite—and in some cases, because of—what happens in the court. In other words, today it is important to retrieve and build *a constitutionalism without the courts*, even as it remains equally important to continue to engage with and in the courts. After all, in the mid-nineteenth century, the American abolitionists argued that a true reading of the Constitution prohibited slavery, even though a pro-slavery Supreme Court had held to the contrary. A few decades later, labour republicans argued that the Constitution's forced labour clause was a promise of dignity and rights in the workplace—they knew well that a pro-business Supreme Court was never going to accept that interpretation. They made these arguments not because they hoped to 'win' in court, but because the Constitution *is so much more than* the court. The verdict of history tells us that they were right.

In recent times, Andras Jakub, a Hungarian constitutional law professor, makes a similar point in the context of another judicial system facing a similar crisis. Labelling this approach 'protect with dignity what you can', Jakub observes:

---

n-95-masks-and-the-bombay-high-courts-dialogic-judicial-review-guest-post/

202 Amlan Mishra, 'The Andhra Pradesh Ordinances Case – Towards Substantive Judicial Review', Indian Constitutional Law and Philosophy, 14 June 2020, https://indconlawphil.wordpress.com/2020/06/14/guest-post-the-andhra-pradesh-ordinances-case-towards-substantive-judicial-review/

You want to teach [ed.: in our case, write] something meaningful, but you are ashamed to teach [ed.: or write] the positive law because you would sound hypocritical and/or simply blind (remember: the rift between constitutional law and constitutional reality is growing every day). Therefore you begin to concentrate on theoretical questions, i.e. you talk more about 'the rule of law in general' as a theoretical abstract concept, and you can explain what the telos (abstract purpose) of a key concept is in the sense of a teleological (purposive) interpretation (e.g., in the case of the rule of law: *limitation of or fight against the arbitrary use of government power*). You can also only include cursory remarks (among them also a few critical ones in an emotionless lawyerly style) about the positive law of your country, but that should not be your main focus—you should rather concentrate on the fundamentals and the ideas behind them.[203]

Or, in the words of the great anti-apartheid lawyer Sir Sydney Kentridge (as quoted in *The Legacies of Law*), we must, at all times, 'tell the truth about law'.

This may require a slightly different framework of analysis—a frame that is more critical, that centres the Supreme Court less and that focuses more on the Constitution as a site of democracy and power relations (as opposed to something the Supreme Court purports to interpret from time to time). It is, of course, an evolving idea. What it will look like is something we will find out as we go along. But I believe that it is a task that must be begun urgently.

---

203 András Jakab, 'Moral Dilemmas of Teaching Constitutional Law in an Autocratizing Country', Verfassungsblog, 15 July 2020, https://verfassungsblog.de/moral-dilemmas-of-teaching-constitutional-law-in-an-autocratizing-country/

Acknowledgements

This is a collection of essays written over a decade for the Indian Constitutional Law and Philosophy blog. I am grateful to everyone whose work and contributions have kept the blog alive—guest-post writers (too many to name!), commentators, everyone who has submitted their work for consideration and, of course, the blog's readers: This book exists because you exist.

I am grateful to comrades and seniors at the bar with whom I've closely worked on many of the cases discussed in this book. It has been incredibly fun to work alongside people who share a mutual scepticism of power and authority, and take the profession seriously without taking themselves too seriously. I have learnt an immense amount from all of you—in court, in chambers and in briefings, and over cold coffee in the canteen.

My thanks to the HarperCollins India team responsible for this book. To Siddhesh Inamdar who commissioned it, to Swati Chopra who edited it, to Ujjaini Dasgupta for the thankless work of copy-editing, and to Saurav Das, for the cover.

Over the years, my parents have been concerned that some of the writings on my blog will land me in a pickle. As with most other things—from the time I was old enough to speak and immediately started getting myself into pickles—they have expressed their concern and then let me do my own thing. Thank you.

Index

Aadhaar
    amendment ordinance, 424, 431
    card, 304
    -esque mandatory-voluntary
        nature, 344
    number, 94
    ordinance, 273
    -PAN linkage, 103–4
    scheme, 49, 51
Aadhaar Act, 98, 305, 424
Aadhaar case, 305, 307–8, 432–33
Aadhaar judgment
    argument from inequality, 109–11
    data protection, 92–93
    demographic information, 90
    factual assumptions, 92
    individual, state, identity, 111–13
    legal standard for testing
        infringements of rights, 88–89
    overarching assumption, 89–91,
        103–4
    privacy, 93–99, 106–7
    provisions, 99–100
    Section 7 and proportionality,
        107–9
    special laws, 100–101
    surveillance, 91, 104–6
    uniqueness, 89–91
Aam Aadmi Party (AAP), 248
Aarogya Setu app, 344
accountability, 108, 188
active membership, 13, 25
acts and inflammatory speeches, 8
ADM Jabalpur vs Shivkant Shukla,
    221–23, 233, 235–36, 238–39, 241
AIADMK, 273
Aishat Shifa vs State of Karnataka,
    123. *See also* Hijab Case, Supreme
    Court in
A.K. Gopalan vs State of Madras, 53,
    220
al-Baghdadi, Abu Bakr, 20
All India Anna Dravidian Progressive
    Federation, 273
All India Bank Association, 393
All India Farmer Association, 315
Alok Verma case, 414–15
Ambedkar, B. R., 175
Amendments to Right to Information
    Act, 286–97

Article 19(1), 288
constitutional statute, 295
Court role, 291–92
incidental and ancillary aspects, 288–89
legislative framework, 292–93
negative and positive dimension, 289–91
NJAC judgment, 295
quasi-constitutional significance, 295–96
American Fourth Amendment, 52
Anand, Javed, 204–5
Anglo-Saxon jurisprudence, 401
anti-CAA protest, 14–15, 45
anticipatory referral, 338
Anti-Corruption Bureau (ACB), 258–59
anti-defection law, 265–66, 271
anti-discriminatory ethos, 72
anti-exclusion principle, 82
anti-homosexual legislation, 68
anti-labour judges, 387
anti-terrorist legislation, 3
anti-terror law, 27
Antony, Marc, 352–53, 356–57
Anuj Garg case, 67
Anuradha Bhasin case, 233, 233n72
Anwar, Tarique, 204n57
apex court, 318–19
Article 17, 82
Article 19(1), 55
Article 21, 55
and access to medicine, 181–86
-based arguments, 93
of Constitution, 53
NRC case and parchment barrier of, 213–14
protection, 225

refugee rights and non-refoulement, 224–29
Article 32, 272–73, 422
Article 141, 292
Article 142, 413–16
Article 224 A, 423
Article 239AA, 260
Article 370, 248–49, 448
amendments, 261–64
case, 432–33
C.O. 272, 262–65
artificial dichotomy, 70
artificial intelligence, 50
Arunachal Pradesh case, 271, 400
Arup Bhuyan case, 8, 8n3, 27
Asif Iqbal Tanha vs State of NCT of Delhi, 11n5, 13, 19, 22, 27, 32–33, 36, 44–46
Assam Accord of 1985, 404
Assam National Register of Citizens, 354
Assam Sanmilita Mahasangha vs Union of India, 354–55
Association for Democratic Reforms vs Union of India, 412n169, 419n177
Austin, Granville, 81
Authority/Union of India, 95
autonomy, 56–58
and human dignity, 54
physical and mental, 116

backwardness, 137, 139–40, 147–48, 153
bail
jurisprudence, 30
on merits, 11
and personal liberty, 18
Bains, Utsav, 324–25
balancing test, 97

Banerjee, Indira, 325
bank linking, 100–101
behavioural patterns of individuals, 105
Benami Act judgment, 432, 441
Bhambani, Anup Jairam, 44–45
Bharadwaj, Sudha, 439
Bharatiya Janata Party (BJP), 248
Bhat, S. Ravindra, 318
Bhatia, Gautam, 270n83, 370n136, 402n152, 407, 412n167
Bhima Koregaon case, 4, 439
Bhushan, Ashok, 258, 260, 385
Bhushan, Shanti, 148
Bijoe Emmanuel, 128
Bilchitz, David, 88
biological determinism, 62
biometric authentication, 90, 108
Birnhack, Michael, 185
B.K. Pavitra vs Union of India, 152–59
   creamy layer, 158
   efficiency concept, 156–57
   interrogating efficiency, 155–58
   principle of deference, 155
   Ratna Prabha Committee Report, 153–54
   standards of judicial review, 154–55
Bobde, Sharad Arvind, 50, 52–53, 55, 216, 325, 417–30
   Article 224 A, 423
   disagreement, 418
   duplicity, 425–28
   hypocrisy, 425
   judicial evasion, 423–25
   judicial hypocrisy, 422
   judicial orders, 428
   'lions under the throne,' 429
   Maratha Reservation case, 418
   personal nor destructive of institution, 418
   retirement, 421
   tenure, 428–29
Bombay High Court, 8, 22–23, 27, 33, 35, 332, 334, 348, 442, 444–45
   on Bail, 19–23
   in *Narasu*, 83–84
Bopanna, Ajjikuttira Somaiah, 216–17, 419
boundaries of religion, 76
brotherhood and fraternity, 125
brutality, 74

caste, 76
   -based temple-entry movements, 79–80
   -based untouchability, 80, 82
   groupings, 139
catchphrases, 391
celibacy and menstruation, 79
Central Bureau of Investigation, 324
Central List of Backward Classes, 135
Central Vista case, 359
chamber judges, 319–20
Chandrachud, D.Y., 29–30, 50–54, 56, 58, 60, 72–74, 75n24, 373
   B.K. Pavitra vs Union of India, 154–56
   disagreement, 106
   and indirect discrimination, 65–70
   National Capital Territory as national capital, 257–58
   and radical equality, 75–86
   Sabarimala judgment, 76, 374–76
   social reformers and revolutionaries, 81
Chelameswar, Jasti, 50, 52–55, 145–46
chief ministership, 258

Churchill, Winston, 354–55
Cine Costume Make-Up Artists, 392
Citizenship Act, 1955, 354, 404
Citizenship (Amendment) Act (CAA), 2019, 424
civil defamation, 395
civil liberties, 59, 382
civil rights, 11, 111, 380
'clash of rights,' 98
class backwardness, 139
classification test, 66
Code of Criminal Procedure, 332, 363, 388, 398
Colombian Constitutional Court's judgment, 190
Communist Party of India (Maoist), 25–26
conjugal expectation to sex, 115
consensual sex, 116
consent, 114
conspiracy, 7
Constituent Assembly of the State, 262
constitution(al)/constitutionalism, 122
   adjudication, 369
   balance, 274
   compassion, 400
   of convenience, 99
   convention, 267
   court, 10–11, 283
   democracy, 243
   entrenchment, 285
   fraternity, 125, 394
   freedoms, 85–86
   immunity, 84
   jurisprudence, 400
   morality, 71–73
   obligation of courts, 22
   rights of refugees, 225
   statesmanship, 258
Constitutional Drafting Committee, 79
constitutional evasion
   Aadhaar hearing, 303–6
   demonetization, 306–7
   judgment by evasion, 307–9
Constitution bench, 398
Constitution of India, 81
counter-majoritarian institutions, 415–16
Covid-19 pandemic, 187–91, 421
   civil rights and proportionality, 344
   and constitution, 342–49
   equality and non-discrimination, 344–46
   High Courts' vigilance, 347–48
   management by decree, 343
   migration on fake news, 346
   Supreme Court's deference, 346–47
'creamy layer' concept, 147–48
criminal conspiracy, 20, 35, 372
Criminal Defamation Judgment, 394n145
criminalization, 70
criminalized carnal intercourse, 60
criminal jurisprudence, 22
criminal law, 61
[Criminal Procedure] Code, 3

data minimization, 93
Datar, Arvind, 59
Dawoodi Bohra, 339
D.C. Wadhwa, 264
decisional autonomy, 121
decriminalization, 73
'defence of India,' 14

Index

defensiveness, 317–18
definitional incoherence, 436
degree of precision, 394
Delhi Govt vs Union of India case, 383
Delhi Gymkhana Club, 196
Delhi High Court, 72, 347–48, 408–9
    Article 21 and access to medicine, 181–86
    Bail Orders under UAPA, 10–18
    on forced evictions, 192–97
    judgment on taxation and the right to health, 187–91
Delhi riots cases, 4, 6–7, 11
    protests and *chakka jam*, 15
Delhi Urban Shelter Improvement Board Act, 2010, 193
Delhi vs Union of India case, 385
democracy, 55
democratic accountability, 407
democratization, 195–96
demonetization, 306–8
demonstration of choice, 63
depressed classes, 150
deprivation of freedom, 448
Desai, Mihir, 21
Devadasan case, 145, 156
Devadasan, Vasudev, 250–51, 251n77–251n79, 407n164
Devangana Kalita cases, 15
Devidas Tuljapurkar case, 393–94
devotion and fidelity, 71
Dhan Singh vs Union of India, 20
Dhoni, M.S., 390–91
Dhulia, Sudhanshu, 127–30
dignity, 55, 63–64
    and fraternity, 55–56
    and freedom, 57–58
    human right to non-discrimination and, 196

    and liberty, 56
    and privacy, 57
diktats of morality, 79
Dipak Sibal, 71
Disaster Management Act (DMA) of 2005, 343
discipline, 125–26
discrimination, 81–82, 158
    law, 78
    within religion, 80
Dispossessed, The, 443
Divan, Shyam, 92, 303, 318
diversity, expression, 131
duplicity, 427–28
Dwivedi, Rakesh, 396–97
Dworkin, Ronald, 175

Eagleton, Terry, 69
economically weaker sections (EWS), 134
economic marginalization, 150
educational backwardness, 138
egalitarianism, 72
Election Commission of India, 412
electoral democracy, 411–13
Emergency-era *ADM Jabalpur* judgment, 60
empowerment, 91
Enforcement Case Information Report (ECIR), 363–64
Enforcement Directorate (ED), 362–63
English-speaking apex courts, 318
Epidemic Diseases Act, 343, 349
equality, 73, 145, 190, 380
    concept, 175
    violations, 66
essential religious practices (ERP), 77–80, 84, 127–28

European Court of Human Rights (ECHR), 319–20
Evidence Act, 409–10
EWS reservations, 431
executive court, 376, 416
expression, 380

failure of authentication, 99
fake identity, 94
fake PAN cards, 104
'family tree' method, 405
federalism, 247–49
female genital mutilation (FGM), 337–38
forced evictions, Delhi High Court on, 192–97
   encroachers, 195
   levels of abstraction, 196
   meaningful engagement, 194
   privatization of space, 195–96
   rehabilitation, 194
   socio-economic rights adjudication, 197
forced sex outside marriage, 115
Foreign Contribution (Regulation) Act (FCRA) case, 359
Foreigners Act, 1946, 212–13, 226
Foreigners Order of 1948, 226
Foreigners Tribunals, 405
formal equality, 125
Fourth Amendment, 52
Fourth Branch Institution, 285
fourth-phase PIL, 332–34
fraternity, 55
Freebies case, 441
freedom
   under Article 19, 56
   of association, 369
   of conscience, 57
   and dignity, 129
   and expression, 7, 116
   of expression, 393
   of speech, 7, 54, 235, 380
fundamental rights, 232

Galanter, Marc, 150, 150n41
Gandhi, Maneka, 175
Gandhi Mala Bhetala, 393
Gaucher disease, 181–82
gay marriage, 62
gender equality judgments, 67
genocide
   complicity in, 216–23
   in Myanmar, 209–10
   watch, 354, 406
Gobind vs State of MP, 58, 303
Gogoi, Ranjan, 324–25, 374, 402–16, 419, 427, 430
   Alok Verma case, 414–15
   counter-majoritarian institutions, 415–16
   Evidence Act, 409–10
   executive court, 416
   Habeas corpus, 410–11
   judicial evasion and electoral democracy, 411–13
   NRC case, 404–6
   sealed covers, 406–9
   Voice Samples case, 404, 413–14
Goswami, Arnab, 426–27
grand chamber judges, 319–20
group
   affiliation, 157–58
   -based affirmative action, 157–58
   identity, 150
   rights, 127–28
Grover, Anand, 330
Guin, Ursula K. Le, 443

Gujarat Mazdoor Sabha case, 346, 349
Gujarat riots, 370
Gupta, Deepak, 330
Gurcharan Singh vs Ministry of Finance, 188, 188n51

Habeas Corpus case, 214–15, 410–11
Hair Dressers Association, 392
Harla vs State of Rajasthan, 233
Harper, Noel, 367–69
Harsh Mander vs Union of India, 211–12
Harvey, David, 195
Helfer, Laurence, 185
Hemant Gupta's judgment, 124–26
High Court of Delhi, 188
High Court of Karnataka, 123–24
Hijab Case
   Hemant Gupta's judgment, 124–26
   Sudhanshu Dhulia's judgment, 127–30
   Supreme Court in, 123–31
Himanshu Kumar vs State of Chhattisgarh, 371, 371n138, 375–76
historical discrimination, 86
history-sheeter, 52–53
home demolitions, 203–7
homogenous classes, socially and occupationally, 139
horse-trading, 272
human dignity, 96
human right to non-discrimination, 196
'Humpty Dumpty jurisprudence,' 365–66

ICLP turns four, 380–83

ignorance, 328–29
Illegal Home Demolitions, 198–202
illegal immigrants, 218–19
illegalities, 16, 302–3
immorality, 77
incitement of violence, 13
inclusiveness, 72–73
Indian Constitution, 49, 51–52, 193
   [Article 20(3)], 52
   jurisprudence, 57
Indian constitutional jurisprudence, 128–29, 377
Indian Contract Act of 1872, 65
Indian Council of Social Science Research (ICSSR), 136–37
Indian Evidence Act, 1872, 404
Indian jurisprudence, 10
Indian Penal Code, 60, 65, 114, 393–94
Indian Supreme Court, 384
Indian Young Lawyers Association and Ors. vs State of Kerala, 340
indirect discrimination concept, 67–68
individuality of person, 63
individual liberty, 36
individual rights, 97–98, 127–28
individual self-determination, 57
individual self-development, 55–56
Indore Development Authority vs Shailendra, 311, 311n96, 312–13, 318
Indra Sawhney vs Union of India, 134, 139, 144–45, 148, 154
Indu Malhotra J, 75n24
inflammatory speeches, 7–9, 15–16
informational self-determination, 57
inherent orientation, 63
inquilabi istikbal, 46
institution(al)

coherence, 319
incoherence, 319
racism, 328–29
Integrated Goods and Services Tax (IGST), 188–89
intellectual bias, 318
intellectual consistency, 45
Intelligence Bureau, 324
internal appellate mechanism, 319
International Conventions/Treaties, 218
International Covenant on Economic, Social and Cultural Rights (ICESCR), 183
intimate decision, 55
'intrinsic or core' traits, 72–73
inviolate personality, 56
IP address metadata, 104
Iqbal Ahmed Kabir Ahmed case, 19, 23, 27, 35–36
irrationality, 77
ISIS terrorist group, 20–21, 35
Iyer, Aishwarya S., 426n184
Iyer, Alladi Krishnaswamy, 79
Iyer, Krishna, 145, 149

Jahangirpuri demolitions, 199–200
Jamir, Lanusungkum, 224
Jammu and Kashmir High Court Bar Association, 240
Jammu and Kashmir Public Safety Act, 240
Jammu and Kashmir Transfer of Property Act, 1920, 356–57
Jarnail Singh vs Lacchmi Narain Gupta, 147, 147n40
Jat Reservations, 135–42
J&K Constituent Assembly, 262
Joseph Shine, 121, 126

judicial
evasion, 411–13, 432
hypocrisy, 419
ideology, 447
judicialization, 268–69
legitimacy, 408
lottery, 36
philosophy, 358–59
pushback, 36
pusillanimity, 441
sanction, 434
supremacy, 267–73
validation, 437
jurisprudence of liberty, 35
jurisprudential foundation, 54
Jyoti Jagtap cases, 35–46

Kabir Kala Manch cases, 8, 13, 23
Kafka's Law, 364
Kakkar, Shruti, 204n56
K.A. Najeeb case, 15, 21–22, 30, 33
kangaroo-court behaviour, 409
Kantaru Rajeevaru vs Indian Young Lawyers' Association, 336, 336n108
Kappan, Siddique, 426–27, 448
Karnataka High Court, 129–30, 273, 424
Kashmir
16 September order, 232–36
fundamental rights and sealed covers, 237–39
Kaul, Sanjay Kishan, 50, 56
Kerala High Court, 24
Khaitan, Tarunabh, 296
Khan, Shamus, 62
Khanwilkar, A.M., 61, 75n24, 351, 358–77
Kharak Singh vs State of UP, 52–54, 58, 232, 304

Khehar, Jagdish Singh, 50
Koushal vs Naz Foundation, 60, 63, 66, 74, 120, 398–99
Krishnan, Murali, 400n150
K.S. Puttaswamy vs Union of India, 12, 49–50, 57–60, 69, 87n28, 89, 233, 380n140, 424
Kumar, Sanjay, 224
Kureshi, Akil, 403

Lahiri, Karan, 163, 163n44
Lalit, U.U., 307n93, 442–48
Land Acquisition Act (2013), 310, 313, 316
Land Acquisition Bench, 310–15
land dispute, 403
Lawrence, Stephen, 328
lawyers collective order, 330–34
    High Court, 332–34
    maintainability, 331
    statutory scheme, 331–32
    threshold for an SIT Investigation, 331
Lefebvre, Henri, 195
legal
    formalism, 66
    philosophies, 387
    validity, 307–8
Legislative Assembly of the State, 262
legislative overruling, 153
legitimate expectation of sex, 118
legitimate State purpose, 71
LGBTQ+ community, 61, 68–69, 73
liberty, 56
    and dignity, 54
    and freedom, 5, 56
live-in relationships, 118
LiveLaw, 275
Lokur, Madan, 312–13

Lord Ayappa, 77–78
Loya case, 331
LPG Distribution Scheme, 95, 304

MacPherson Report, 328
Madhu Kishwar vs State of Bihar, 83
Madhya Pradesh government formation judgment, 277–83
Madhya Pradesh High Court, 395–96, 403
Maharashtra Political Crisis case, 433
Mahesh Kiriman Tirki vs State of Maharashtra, 444n191
maintainability, 397, 401
Make-Up Artists case, 392–93
Malhotra, Indu, 73–77, 79, 326, 373
    and truer vision of equality, 70–71
Maneka Gandhi vs Union India, 54, 220
Manipur High Court, 224–29
Maratha Reservation case, 166–77, 418
    50 per cent rule, 168–69
    Ambedkar's speech, 175–76
    backward community, 167
    Bhat's judgment, 173–74
    Bhushan's judgment, 169–72
    EWS reservation, 177
    Socially and Educationally Backward Classes (SEBC) Act, 2018, 166–67
marital rape exception (MRE), 113–22
    Hari Shankar J opinion, 116–21
    IPC, provisions in, 117–18
master of the roster principle, 388–90, 400, 446
Meesha case, 397–98
Mehta, Pratap Bhanu, 364n127

Mehta, Tushar, 237–38
memorandum of procedure (MoP), 399
menstruation, 78–79
Mental Healthcare Act, 2017, 64
MGNREGA scheme, 95, 305
Mian Abdul Qayoom vs State of J&K, WP, 240, 240n73
migrants, 228
minimal information/infringement, 97
minorities, discrete and insular, 141–42
Mishra, Arun, 310–11, 313, 318
Misra, Dipak, 75n24, 313, 373–74, 390–401, 419, 426, 430, 438
    criminal defamation judgment, 394–95
    Devidas Tuljapurkar case, 393–94
    intra-court discipline, ignorance of, 399–400
    Make-Up Artists case, 392–93
    Meesha case, 397–98
    National Anthem case, 395–97
    Navtej Johar case, 398–99
    substantive justice, 391
Mistry, Cyrus, 427
M. Nagaraj vs Union of India, 147
modern-day marriage, 116
mohalla clinics, 258
Mohammad Salimullah vs Union of India, 216n68
Mohammad Zubair case, 441
Mohd Ahmed vs Union of India, 181, 181n48
morality, 72–73
movement, 57
M.P. Sharma case, 51, 54, 304
M.R. Balaji vs State of Mysore, 139

Mridul, Siddharth, 44–46
Muralidhar, S., 194
Myanmarese refugees, 224–25, 228

Nagaraj/creamy layer judgment, 147–51
    creamy layer, 149–51
    quantifiable data, 148–49
Naishtika Brahmacharya, 77–78
NALSA vs Union of India, 73, 141
Namita Wahi, 306n92
Nandita Haksar vs State of Manipur, 224
Narasu Appa Mali judgment, 83–84
Nariman, R.F., 50, 52–53, 55, 351–57, 373
    judiciary independence, 355–56
    legacy, 353
    NRC, 354–55
    and presumption of constitutionality, 64–65
    in *Santosh Gupta* judgment, 356–57
Nariman J, 72, 75n24
Natasha Narwal's cases, 15–16, 45–46
National Anthem case, 395–97
national capital territory (NCT), 248
National Capital Territory of Delhi vs Union of India, 251, 259–60
National Commission for Backward Classes (NCBC), 135–37
National Honour Act, 1971, 397
national interest and internal security, 234–35
National Investigation Agency (NIA), 360
National Investigation Agency vs Zahoor Ahmad Shah Watali, 4, 359, 359n117

National Legal Services Authority vs Union of India, 140
National Register of Citizens (NRC), 210–11, 404–6
national security, 434
National Security Food Act, 2013, 97
natural orientation, 63
Navtej Johar vs Union of India, 60–74, 120–21, 126, 391, 398–99
Naz Foundation (2009), 61, 72
NCT of Delhi vs Union of India, 248, 250–60
    Article 239AA, 254–55
    Government of National Capital Territory of Delhi (GNCTD) Act, 1991, 255
    parliamentary democracy, 254
    representative democracy, 254
    services and ACB, 258–59
N.M. Thomas, 134, 139, 145, 155–56
Noel Harper vs Union of India, 367–69, 367n132
non-consensual sex, 114–17, 119–20
non-democratic colonial regime, 65
non-discrimination, 69, 190
non-refoulement principle, 217–19, 225–26, 421
non-trivial power, 438
Noorani, A.G., 427
NRC case, 211–15, 404–6
NYT vs Sullivan, 395

Objectives Resolution, 72
Odisha High Court, 344, 385
Odisha's vehicle ban, 344
Oka, J, 24, 26
Olga Tellis, 193, 197
orphan drugs, 182
Orwell, George, 203–7

oxygen concentrators for Covid relief, 188

parliamentary democracy, 268–70
parliamentary legislations, 99
Parmanand Katara vs Union of India, 183
Parsi fire temple case, 338
Parthasarathy, Suhrith, 217n69, 311, 311n94
Pasayat, Arijit, 381–82
Pasha, Nizam, 370, 370n135
Patents Act, 1970, 185
Patiala House, New Delhi, 6
Patnaik, A.K., 325
patriarchal order, 79
patriarchy, 76
PDS savings, 95
pecuniary bias, 318
Pegasus case, 441
Permanent Account Number (PAN) card, 90
personal
    autonomy, 71
    bias, 318
    liberty, 53–55, 57
Persons with Disability Act, 1995, 143
phone linking, 100–101
pluralism, 72–73
PM CARES fund, 346
PMLA judgment, 366–67, 375, 441
Poddar, Umang, 363n124
polar opposite approaches, 45
police surveillance, 53
political powerlessness, 210
political ramifications, 272
political repression, 444
political thicket, 268
polyvocal court, 316–20

POSH Act, 323, 326
power, 387
    anti-sexual-harassment laws, 322–23
    background, 323–26
    committee, 326–27
    sexual harassment, 322
    structures and institutions, 322–23
Prasar Bharati Corporation, 143
pre-constitutional law, 65
pre-constructed identities, 62
pre-existing inequalities, 111
presumption of constitutionality, 64–65
Prevention of Insults to National Honour Act, 1971, 397
Prevention of Money Laundering Act (PMLA), 362–65
pre-*Watali* Bombay High Court judgments, 13
prima facie case, 3, 6–7
    conspiracy, 8
    of terrorism, 17
    UAPA case, 9
Prithipal Singh vs State of Punjab, 289
privacy, 54–56
    aspects, 55
    equality and dignity, 47–48, 129
    judgement, 58–59
    reasonable expectation of, 96–97
pro-executive judges, 438
proportionality, 88, 125–26
propositions of law, 51–59
prosecution case, 7, 13
protected freedoms, 56
Protection of Human Rights Act, 1993, 193
protests and terrorism, 17
public employment, 148

public spaces, 76–77
    civil rights and, 79–80
Pune Municipal Corporation, 311–13
Puttaswamy vs Union of India, 12, 50, 57–59, 69, 89, 233, 380n140, 424

qua class, 139
qualified public spaces, 124

racial discrimination, prohibition against, 217
radical transformation, 112
Rafale case, 407, 409
Rajeev Kumar Gupta vs Union of India, 143n39
Ramachandran, Raju, 384n141
Ramana, N.V., 325, 430–41
    Freebies case, 436–37, 441
    judicial evasion and the sound of silence, 431–33
    master of the roster, 437–39
    Pegasus case, 433–36
    Sedition case, 439–40
    tenure, 441–42
Ramasubramanian, V., 216 17
Ram Singh vs Union of India, 135
Ranjitsing Brahmajeetsing Sharma vs State of Maharashtra, 20
Rao, Subba, 145, 155–56
Rastogi JJ, 25–26
ration card, 90
Ratna Prabha Committee Report, 154, 156
R.C. Cooper case, 54
real rape, 115
recovery of oath, 21
Reddy, Jeevan, 136
Refugee Convention, 217, 219
refugees, 228

asylum seekers, protection and
    rehabilitation to, 226
  -migrant distinction, 228
  and non-citizens, 209–10
  rights and non-refoulement,
    224–29
regular bail, 11–12
rehabilitation schemes, 105–6
religious dissent, 128
religious pluralism, 128
Reorganization Bill, 261
repose, 55
representative democracy, 251, 259–60
reservations in jobs, 133
reservations in promotions for
    disabled persons, 143–46
reservations (new) judgment and its
    discontents, 160–65
  NALSA vs Union of India, 164–65
Reserve Bank of India, 306–7
reserved-category posts, 143
review, 335–41
right
    to peaceful protest, 16–17
    to privacy, 53, 87n27
    to vote, 380
Right to Information (RTI) Act of
    2005, 286–97
Rohingya Deportation case, 216–23
Rohingya refugees, 209–10, 216, 225
Romila Thapar vs Union of India, 375
R. Rajagopal vs State of Tamil Nadu,
    394
Russian-style legislation, 367

Sabarimala case, 335n107, 336,
    373–75, 400, 414–15, 418
Sabarimala judgment, 75–86, 75n25,
    339, 339n109, 341, 373–74

Safoora Zargar Bail Order, The, 6–9
Saibaba, G.N., 442
Saint Oscar, 69
Sakal Papers vs Union of India, 233
Salimullah case, 224, 227
Salve, Harish, 421
same-sex relations, 72–73, 380
sanctuary, 55
Sapre, Abhay Manohar, 50, 56
Saran, Vineet, 317
Sarbananda Sonowal, 213
Sarkar, Sravani, 204n59
Scheduled Castes and Scheduled
    Tribes, 147–50
sealed covers, 406–9
Sebastian, Manu, 275, 275–85, 419–178
secrecy, 407–8
sectarianism, 125
Section 43(D)(5), 22, 35
Section 139AA of the Income Tax
    Act, 100–101
Securitization and Reconstruction of
    Financial Assets and Enforcement
    of Security Interest (SARFAESI)
    Act, 2002, 356–57
security threats, 227–28
Sekhri, Abhinav, 12, 30, 332–33,
    343–44, 361–62, 361n118,
    363n125–363n126, 366, 370,
    370n136, 375n139
self-censorship, 394
self-determination, 56, 63
self-incrimination, 52
self-righteousness, 317–18
Setalvad, Teesta, 371, 376–77, 448
sex/sexual
    -assault survivors, 408
    consent, 114, 116
    consent, violation, 119

discrimination, 67–68
harassment, 301, 316–18, 356
orientation, 61–64, 68
privacy, 69
sexuality, 62
shadow of criminality, 67–68
Shah, M.R., 445
Shakur Basti, 192
Shankar, Hari, 113–14
Shantanagoudar, Mohan Mallikarjunagouda, 312
Shirur Mutt, 339
Shreya Singhal v Union of India, 21–22, 30, 32–33
Sikri, Arjan Kumar, 88, 385
'silos' approach, 53–54
Singh, Chander Uday, 222
Singh, Jarnail, 158
Singh, Vijaita, 205n60
Slum Areas (Improvement and Clearances) Act, 1956, 193
smart cards, 96
social and gender rights, 391–92
social backwardness, 141–42
social compulsion, 82
social discrimination, 150
social emancipation, 80–81
social evil, 77
social groups, 139
social hierarchies, 81
social institutions, 76
social mobility, 151
social rights, 119
social subordination, 81
social welfare benefits, 110
society's reproduction, 62
socio-economic rights, 179–80
South African Constitutional Court, 194, 318

Special Leave Petitions, 33–34
speech-act and consequence, 9, 57
S. Rangarajan case, 8
Star Chamber, 408, 408n165
State Backward Classes Commissions, 137
State of Chhattisgarh, 372
State of Kerala vs N.M. Thomas, 133–34
State vs Safoora Zargar, 6n2
subjective satisfaction, 241
subordination, 150
Subramaniam, Gopal, 303
Subramanian Swamy vs Union of India, 394n144
Sudama Singh case, 193
Supreme Court, 400
    constitutional evasion, 302–9
    Criminal Defamation Judgment, 394–145
    in Hijab Case, 123–31
    Jat Reservations, 135–42
    judgments, 58
    jurisprudence, 25
    Madhya Pradesh government formation judgment, 277–83
    Maratha reservation judgment, 166–77
    Moment of Atonement, 60–74
    problematic order in Karnataka Case, 274–76
    reservations in promotions for disabled persons, 143–46
    (new)reservations judgment and its discontents, 160–65
    UAPA Bail Order in Iqbal Ahmed's Case, 29–34
    UAPA judgment, 24–28
Supreme Court Advocates-on-Record Association (SCAORA), 323–24

Supreme Court Bar Association
  (SCBA), 323
Supreme Court of India, 210
Supreme Deportation Authority, 211
*Suresh Kumar Koushal vs Naz
  Foundation*, 60
surveillance-based challenge, 91
Surya Kant JJ, 29–30
Susan, Nisha, 130
systemic discrimination, 71

TADA, 8
Taksin, Bismee, 205–61
Tarigami, Yousuf, 410
technological error, 110
Telecom Regulatory Authority of
  India (TRAI), 49–50
temple-entry movements, 79–80
Tenth Schedule, 275
terrorism, 13, 17, 45
third gender, recognition, 140
thoughtlessness, 329
Thwaha Fasal vs Union of India, 24,
  24n9, 27–28, 36
Trade Unions Act, 392
transformative constitutionalism, 71,
  73–74
transformative judgment, 86
transgender community, 140–41
*Treatment Action Campaign vs
  Minister for Health*, 186, 186–50
Tribunals judgments, 414
Tripura High Court, 403
Trivedi, Bela, 445

UK Supreme Court, 318–19
Umar Khalid cases
  bail orders in, 35–46
  and Delhi High Court, 40–44

  judgment, 45–46
unauthorized biographies or biopics,
  51
unconstitutional state of affairs, 200,
  206
unequal social order, 81
unfettered right to sex, 115–16
uniformity, 126
unintelligible differentia, 66, 70
*Union of India vs Sandur Manganese
  and Iron Ores Ltd*, 335–36
union territories, 259
unique demographics, 118
Unique Identification Authority of
  India (UIDAI), 49–50, 92, 108
Unique Identification Number, 90, 304
uniqueness, 94
  of biometrics, 103–4
United Nations High Commission for
  Refugees (UNHCR), 225, 227
Unlawful Activities (Prevention)
  Act (UAPA), 3, 6–7, 11, 24–28,
  359–60, 375, 444
  adjudication, 4–5, 36
  bail, 439
  bail hearing, 31
  Bail Order in Iqbal Ahmed's Case,
    29–34
  Bombay High Court on Bail, 19–23
  Delhi High Court's Bail Orders,
    10–18
  Section 43(D)(5), 20, 32, 34
  Sections 38 and 39, 25
Unny, Mukund, 268, 268–82
unprecedented scale, 7
unreasonable denial of sex counts,
  115–16
untouchability, 80–83
unwitting prejudice, 328–29

upper-caste women, 83
US Supreme Court, 318
Utsav Bains case, 331
Uttarakhand President's Rule case, 400

Vedanta Ltd, 421
Verma, Alok, 407
Victorian morality, 72
Vijay Madanlal Choudhary vs Union of India, 363n123
virtual impossibility, 33–34
Vishaka judgment, 218, 291–92, 322–23
Voice Samples case, 404, 413–14

Wahi, Namita, 306, 311
Watali case, 12–13, 19, 28, 360–61, 375
welfare delivery system, 107
Whitman, Walt, 45
willingness, 114
witness reports, 21
woman's consent to sex, 114

Yechury, Sitaram, 410–11

Zakia Jafri vs State of Gujarat, 369n134, 371–73, 375–76
Zargar, Safoora, 6–9

About the Author

Gautam Bhatia is a lawyer who has been involved in several important contemporary constitutional cases. He is the author of *Offend, Shock, or Disturb: Freedom of Speech under the Indian Constitution* (2015), *The Transformative Constitution: A Radical Biography in Nine Acts* (2019) and the science fiction books *The Wall* (2020) and *The Horizon* (2021).

30 Years *of*
HarperCollins *Publishers* India

At HarperCollins, we believe in telling the best stories and finding the widest possible readership for our books in every format possible. We started publishing 30 years ago; a great deal has changed since then, but what has remained constant is the passion with which our authors write their books, the love with which readers receive them, and the sheer joy and excitement that we as publishers feel in being a part of the publishing process.

Over the years, we've had the pleasure of publishing some of the finest writing from the subcontinent and around the world, and some of the biggest bestsellers in India's publishing history. Our books and authors have won a phenomenal range of awards, and we ourselves have been named Publisher of the Year the greatest number of times. But nothing has meant more to us than the fact that millions of people have read the books we published, and somewhere, a book of ours might have made a difference.

As we step into our fourth decade, we go back to that one word – a word which has been a driving force for us all these years.

Read.

 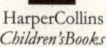